PACIFIC
WAR
DIARY

1942–1945

U.S.S. *Montpelier. U.S. Navy Photo*

PACIFIC
WAR
DIARY

1942–1945

JAMES J. FAHEY

SEAMAN FIRST CLASS,
U.S.S. *Montpelier*

HOUGHTON MIFFLIN COMPANY
Boston • New York

For information about permission to reproduce selections
from this book, write to Permissions, Houghton Mifflin Company,
215 Park Avenue South, New York, New York 10003.

Library of Congress Cataloging-in-Publication Data
Fahey, James J.
Pacific war diary, 1942–1945 / James J. Fahey ; illustrated with maps.
p.   cm.
Originally published : Boston : Houghton Mifflin, 1963.
ISBN 0-395-64022-9
1. Fahey, James J. — Diaries.   2. World War, 1939–1945 — Naval
operations, American.   3. World War, 1939–1945 — Personal
narratives, American.   4. World War, 1939–1945 — Campaigns —
Pacific Area.   5. Seamen — United States — Diaries.   6. United States.
Navy — Biography.   I. Title
D773.F24   1992   92-21716
940.54'5973 — dc20   CIP

Printed in the United States of America

AGM 10 9 8 7 6 5 4 3

FOREWORD

Personal narratives of wars by statesmen, generals and admirals are fairly numerous; but accounts by private soldiers and ordinary seamen are exceedingly rare, although of high value to historians and great interest to general readers. Hence I was delighted to read the following sailor's diary of World War II in the Pacific, one with a distinct flavor. The author, James Fahey, Seaman First Class on the U.S.S. *Montpelier,* was a shipmate of mine in the Marianas operation, and I can vouch for the authenticity of his diary, which he kept faithfully under conditions that were anything but conducive to literary effort.

The great merit of Mr. Fahey's diary is that it gives the American bluejacket's point of view about the naval war in the Pacific, with all its glory and horror, achievement and boredom; it tells how sailors felt going into battle, their opinions of their officers, their hunger off Okinawa when the long logistics line grew thin, and their fortitude in meeting the menace of the Kamikaze Corps.

Samuel Eliot Morison

CONTENTS

MAPS

AUTHOR'S NOTE

I WOULD LIKE to thank the following people for their part in the publication of this book. It was their confidence, encouragement, and hard work that made this possible and I will remember them always.

At the head of the list is Admiral Samuel Eliot Morison, who recommended my book to Houghton Mifflin Company, and I am only too happy to express my appreciation to this very thoughtful and generous man, and to Mr. Joseph Bryan 3rd, author of *Admiral Halsey's Story*, who was the first person to read my diary; Admiral Arleigh "31-knot" Burke, Admiral E. M. Eller, Professor Vernon D. Tate, and Mr. Ken Jones, who saw typewritten copies of this book and had them put in the Navy archives, the U.S. Naval Historical Foundation Museum, the library of the U.S. Naval Academy, and the Library of Congress; to my friends who typed the book, Mrs. Reidar Bomengen, Miss Helen Garrahan, Mrs. Leo Garneau, Mr. Paul R. Morrill, Mr. John Smith, and Mrs. John Sweeney, with my special thanks for their help; also to my many friends at Houghton Mifflin Company. I would like to mention every one of them but that is impossible.

I do not have to remind anyone that this is a once-in-a-lifetime event for someone like me because I am not a writer, but a truck driver for the City of Waltham, Mass. I cannot believe it myself because it seems like a dream. It could only happen in this great, wonderful country of ours.

JAMES J. FAHEY

PUBLISHER'S NOTE

JAMES FAHEY kept this diary from October 1942 to December 1945, on loose sheets of paper closely covered with writing on both sides. Sometimes entries were made several times during one day, sometimes not for weeks; sometimes several days were written up at one time. After the war he put it away until 1960, when he copied it in legible form, filling out his sketchy notes where necessary. Whatever errors it may contain, it reflects what he believed to be true at the time.

THE
SOLOMONS

October 1942–May 1944

October 3, 1942: I enlisted in the U.S. Navy today. It looks like the Navy got the makings of a very poor sailor when they got me. I still get carsick and cannot ride on a swing for any length of time.

I took my physical examination at the Post Office Building in Boston, Mass., a distance of about ten miles from Waltham, Mass. A fellow next to me was rejected because he was color blind. They told him the Sea Bees would take him. On the way home I relaxed in the old trolley car and felt like the Fleet Admiral himself.

October 7, 1942: I got up early this morning for my trip to Boston, on my way to Great Lakes Naval Training Station in Chicago, Illinois.

Before leaving I shook my father's hand and kissed him goodbye.

It was a clear cool morning as my sister Mary, brother John and I headed for the bus at the corner of Cedar Street. The bus and trolley car were crowded with people going to work. When we reached the Post Office Building in Boston I shook John's hand and kissed Mary goodbye.

After a long tiresome day of hanging around we were finally on our way to the train station. The group was very large and they came from the New England states. We were called the Lexington Volunteers in honor of the carrier *Lexington*. It was sunk by the Japanese Navy May 7, 1942, in the battle of the Coral Sea.

With a big band leading the way we marched through downtown Boston before thousands of people. It took about half an hour to reach the North Station and at 5:30 P.M. we were on our way.

When the train passed through my city it was beginning to get dark and I could picture the folks at home having supper. There would be an empty place at the table for some time. It would have been very easy for me to feel sad and lonely with these thoughts in my mind but we should not give in to our feelings. If we always gave in to our feelings instead of our judgment we would fall by the wayside when the going got rough.

It will be a long tiresome trip and our bed will be the seat we sit in, two to a seat.

October 8, 1942: The long troop train stopped in the middle of nowhere today. It looked like a scene from a western movie in the last century. All you could see was wide open spaces with plenty of fields and a small railroad station. It felt good to get some fresh air and stretch our legs for a change after the crowded conditions on the train. Some of the fellows like myself mailed letters and cards home. The postmark on the mail was STRATHROY, Ontario, Canada. It was a warm sunny day so we sat on the side of the tracks while waiting for the train to get started again.

At Great Lakes: On the evening of Oct. 9 we pulled into the stockyards at Chicago and stayed there for some time. It gave us another chance to get some fresh air and walk around on solid ground for a change. All the people in the big tenement buildings were at their windows looking at us.

At last the train was on its final leg of the journey. We were a tired dirty lot when the train finally pulled into Great Lakes Naval Training Station in the early morning darkness. The weather was on the chilly side.

They got us up bright and early after a few hours sleep on the floor of a large drill hall. We were far from being in condition for a physical examination but that was the way we started the day and it took a long time. We went from one doctor to another upstairs and downstairs and from one room to another. They checked us from head to toe and even asked us our religion. At last it was over and our first shower in some time. It sure felt good.

We spent four weeks of training and lived in barracks. Our

company number was 1291. A Chief Petty Officer was in charge of each company and our chief was liked by all.

Some of the Chiefs are hated because they go out of their way to make it as miserable as possible. They enjoy getting the fellows up at two in the morning and have them stand at attention in the cold for a long time with very little clothing.

The instructor who taught us judo enjoyed taking it out on the new recruits. He sent one of the boys from my company to the hospital in a stretcher. Our chief was boiling mad and if he could have gotten his hands on this punk he would have done a job on him.

You learned that your days of privacy were over while you were in the Navy and they would not return until you were back in civilian life again. When you ate, slept, took a shower, etc., you were always part of the crowd, you were never alone.

No one enjoyed sleeping in the hammocks because they were too tight. It was like sleeping on a tight clothesline. You felt like you were going to fall out if you turned over. You felt safe on your back but you can't sleep on your back all night.

We will never forget our first haircut. When the barber got through there was no hair to cut. It was shorter than short. It was funny to see a nice looking fellow with a beautiful crop of hair get into the barber's chair and leave with no hair at all.

Great Lakes is the largest naval training station in the world and they also have one of the best football teams in the country. I had the pleasure of talking to Bruce Smith the all-American back from Minnesota. He was the number one football player in the country in 1941. You could not help but like him. He slept in our barracks.

We always marched to the mess hall for our meals and kept in step by singing loud and strong.

I had to go to sick call one day because of a bad blow to the ribs I received in a boxing bout but they did not do anything for me even though the pain was killing me. They think everyone is a faker when he goes to sick call, that he just wants time off from work.

We were kept on the go at all times and at last our training was over. It was home sweet home for us. We were very proud of our uniform as we boarded the train for home. After a nine day leave we returned to Great Lakes and stayed here for two days before leaving for Norfolk, Virginia, our next stop.

November 23, 1942: Late Friday evening Nov. 21, a large group of us boarded a truck for the pier. It was a great feeling as I staggered up the gangway to the ship with my sea bag in one hand and the mattress cover loaded with blankets, mattress, etc., over my shoulder. The name of the ship is the U.S.S. *Montpelier.* It is a light cruiser. At last I have a home and a warship at that.

We slept in our hammocks in the mess hall at first but then we were assigned to divisions. I went to the 5th division. It is a deck division.

It will take some time before we know our way around this large ship. It is over 600 feet long and has many decks and compartments.

Today at eight in the morning we left Norfolk for the Philadelphia Navy Yard.

December 13, 1942: We left Philadelphia today, on our way at last. The weather is very cold and it is snowing. I hope wherever we go the weather is nice and warm. The *Montpelier* is a new cruiser commissioned in September. Most of the fellows are rebels from the South.

January 18, 1943: After 35 days and over 10,000 miles traveled, we finally reached our destination. It is the French-controlled island of New Caledonia. It is only about 700 miles from Australia, the continent they call the land down under because it is so close to the bottom of the world. Australia is the oldest continent on earth, and larger than the U.S.A. Now I will cover some of the things that happened during our many days since we left Philadelphia on Dec. 13, 1942.

When we left Norfolk, Virginia, we joined a big convoy of warships and transports, carrying thousands of troops plus supply ships. The weather was very cold and the seas were on the rampage. We thought the ship would turn over. Most of the crew was green and many of them were seasick. The mountainous waves tossed the 10,000-ton *Montpelier* around like a matchstick. Its 607 ft. in length did not have much of a chance in these wild waters.

Everything was lashed down. We ate our meals sitting on the steel deck of the mess halls because it was impossible to set the tables up. They would have been smashed against the side of the ship. Many of us were too seasick to eat much, and if we set our coffee cup on the deck it would shoot over to the other side of the ship into one of the other fellows sitting opposite us.

While we were on watch we wore a thick mask over our face. This protected us against the cold and icy winds. One of the troopships lost its rudder in the rough seas and it almost ran into us. It was in bad shape and out of control. Enemy subs were in the area but they did not attack. They said one of the battleships in the convoy is the old battleship *Texas*. The destination for most of the ships in the convoy was the European war. We got up one morning to learn that we had left the convoy.

The *Montpelier* and a few other warships were heading in a different direction and the weather was getting warmer and the seas calmer. We finally reached the warm Caribbean with its beautiful weather. After the cold, rough Atlantic, it was like going to Paradise when we reached the calm, sunny West Indies and Caribbean.

Philadelphia with its cold and snow was behind us. Now we could put the heavy winter clothes away and take in plenty of warm sunshine. The first day everyone tried to get too much sun and many of them came down with a bad case of sunburn. This warm weather put everyone in a happy frame of mind. I sleep topside every night in my shirtsleeves while the people back home are freezing in 15 below zero weather, such is life. I eat a lot of good food going around twice quite often and I put on 10 pounds so far.

On Thursday Dec. 24, 1942 we reached the entrance to the Panama Canal at Panama at twelve noon. It took eight hours for the ship to go through the locks. It was quite an experience going through the locks and the thick green jungle all around us was beautiful. They say every known animal in the world can be found here. If you go deep into the jungle you will come across savage tribes. If they leave the tribe and return they are killed because the rest of the tribe thinks he will be civilized. We could see some alligators on the beach in this beautiful spot.

They say the Pacific is 18 to 23 ft. higher than the Atlantic Ocean also the deepest. It was like going up a flight of stairs and then down again as we went through the locks. Big cable trains are used to pull the ships.

We spent Christmas Day here and also brought aboard supplies. We worked very hard but we enjoyed a good Christmas dinner. Church services were also held.

We left Balboa the Canal Zone December 26, 1942, at 10 A.M. and Dec. 27 we put the clock back one hour. I did not leave the ship at Panama as we were too busy carrying supplies. Most of us were green and many just got out of boot camp after four weeks training. The biggest gun they ever heard before coming aboard the *Montpelier* was a rifle. The *Montpelier* has 20 and 40 mm. machine guns and five and six inch guns. The ship is completely encircled with guns and the concussion from the big guns is very bad.

Our long voyage to New Caledonia was not wasted. We spent most of our time firing the guns. It was drill, drill and more drills. We shot down many targets that were towed by our planes and when we reached New Caledonia the crew was ready for action. I am in the 5th Division, it is a deck Div. and my battle station is a quad 40 mm. machine gun.

On Dec. 30, 1942 we crossed the equator and a big ceremony was held. This was the first time for most of us. The fellows who crossed before came around and cut our hair off and put us under the hose clothes and all and hit us with sticks. Some fun. It is quite an honor to cross the equator. We are now full fledged shellbacks and not polliwogs anymore. We will have our chance to take it out on some new men the next time we cross the equator. Even Capt. Wood had to walk the plank, but he took it like the great man he is. We think there is no one like him. He has been in the Navy for thirty-five years. They jokingly told him that he was going to die soon when he was brought before King Neptune.

On New Year's Day, Jan. 1, 1943, we lost one of our pilots. We called him Ensign Thompson, he was a Naval Reserve Officer. We carry two seaplanes and two pilots.

These planes are used for scouting enemy ships and planes, spot enemy targets and direct our fire on them, rescue those who are lost at sea, carry sleeves for gunnery practice etc. They are very valuable to have around.

On the morning of Jan. 1, 1943 Ensign Thompson and his radioman got in the plane that was on the catapult waiting to be shot into the sky by a charge of powder. Before they were shot off the ship was going about 30 miles per hour or around 30 knots. At last everything was ready and all hands were watching as the plane was shot into the air at the speed of fifty miles per hour. The men in the plane had to brace themselves from the shock of such a fast take-off. Instead of going down and then up as the planes usually do this plane just kept going down. It hit the water at full force and then the bombs that they were carrying exploded. They carried two 360 pound bombs that were to be used if they spotted any Jap subs. The radioman came out of it all right but the pilot was killed.

On the following day, Jan. 2, 1943, funeral services were held on the fantail. All hands assembled there and the Marines fired their rifles in salute. Prayers were also said and taps were blown. The American flag was over the box made by the carpenters that held Ensign Thompson. When the signal was given Ensign Thompson's body was dropped into the vast Pacific.

The ship kept moving all during the services and before you knew it we were on the other side of the horizon. The spot where Ensign T.'s body was dropped was many miles behind us and out of sight. We lost a great man.

I was talking to Ensign Thompson the day before he died. He looked like he would die of old age. He looked great, and was in the pink of condition. He was a very friendly person, everyone thought the world of him. He will be missed. A few days later we almost lost the radioman when he fell into the ocean while his plane was being hoisted aboard. They were just returning from a patrol. We thought he was gone for good because he was out of sight for some time. One of our whaleboats finally rescued him. This fellow must have a charmed life. The Good Lord does not want him yet.

RESTRICTED FOR		U.S.S. MONTPELIER
OFFICIAL USE ONLY	PLAN OF THE DAY	THURS., JAN. 7, 1943.

0450 Reveille.

0504 General Quarters. Necessary cooks to be excused.

0534 Set Condition "B."
Gunnery Drills. Secure Messmen and MAtts.

0554 Set Condition 2, Starboard Watch.

0604 Sunrise. Set Condition 3, Watch 3.

0620 Breakfast.

0730 Turn to. Continue paint removal.
All hands berthing forward of Frame No. 101 (A&B Compts.) air bedding.

0815 Quarters for muster and physical drill. Followed by emergency drill.

0845 Instruction of the following telephone talkers for all condition watches: JA Talkers in Crew's Lounge, Lt. (JG) Lee in charge. JB & JC Talkers in Main Battery Plot, Lt. Straker in charge. 1 JP & 2 JP Talkers in A.A. Plot, Lt. Thode in charge.
Training and loading drill for 20-mm. Condition 3 Watch 1 Gun Crews at Gun No. 8.

0915 Inspection of bedding and living spaces by Division Officers. Sick Call.

0915 Loading drill for 5" Mount Condition 3 Watch 1 loading crews. Drill for range finder operators on station.

0930 Drill for 40-mm. Condition 3 Watch 1 Mount crews and director personnel at Mount 44.

1000 Loading drill for 5" Mount Condition 3 Watch 2 loading crews. Drill for fire control radar operators on station.
Drill for 20-mm. Condition 3 Watch 2 Gun crews at Gun No. 7.

Main Battery spotting drill in Wardroom. Lt. Straker in charge.

—— Surprise firing by machine guns at burst.

1030 Secondary Battery spotting drill in Wardroom. Lt. Paton in charge.

1045 Drill for 40-mm. Condition 3 Watch 2 Mount crews and director personnel at Mount 43 and Director 43.

1055 Standby aired bedding.

1100 Pipe down aired bedding.

1115 Early dinner for Watchkeepers.

—— Dinner immediately after Watchkeepers have eaten.

1300 Lecture by First Lt. in Wardroom on "Fire Fighting Equipment" for all Officers who missed Wednesday's lecture. 20-mm. gun instruction for 10 men of R. Div. at Gun No. 5.

1330 Inspection of all food handlers in Sick Bay.

—— Surprise burst firing by Machine Guns, and/or 5″ Mount.

1630 Sick Call.

1700 Supper.

—— Sunset. Darken ship.

—— Movies.

–NOTES–

All hands must wear life preservers and keep clear of the life lines. All Officers will instruct men under their charge in the use of gas masks, protective clothing and decontamination procedure.

Condition 2 will be set from time to time after morning General Quarters. All hands must learn: (a) Their stations, (b) who they relieve, (c) who relieves them. All hands must wait until actually relieved unless their watch is blanked in the crew condition being set.

Water expenditure for January 5 was 15.7 gallons per man. This is considered a normal expenditure.

–LOST–

A small Navy wallet in Crew's Lounge with $115.00 contained therein. Finder please return to Aycock, Y3/c in Crews' Lounge.

P. B. KOONCE
Commander, U.S. Navy
Executive Officer

The weather is very good, it is warm and sunny. It is too hot to sleep below so we sleep under the stars at night. On our way to New Caledonia we always had something to do. We had to scrape all the paint off from one end of the ship to the other because it will burn if we are hit by enemy shells or torpedoes. The strong paint remover that we used on the paint would almost knock you out, it was like ether and was very sickening. You could not work in the compartment away down below the waterline very long at a time because of the terrific heat and smell from the paint remover.

Everyone was happy when all the paint was removed.

In the evening we had boxing on the fantail. I put on the gloves with Archie Stevenson; he comes from Detroit. Some evenings we had happy hours, and movies at night in the mess hall. Cigarettes cost sixty cents a carton. We have our own printing press and get the news every day. Alabama beat Boston College in one of the Bowl games, New Year's Day by the score of 37 to 21.

We carry a crew of about 1300 men and we get along like one big happy family. When we finally reached New Caledonia after a 35 day voyage we stayed there about one week. This is the Naval Headquarters. While we were in the harbor at New Caledonia we got our first chance to put our feet on land in 40 days. They sent us over to the village on a working party. After being on the ship for so long a time it felt good to put our feet on good solid ground again.

The weather was very warm. We bought some apples, coconuts and bananas from a Javanese girl. She carried everything in a little cart. It cost me about twenty cents for everything I bought. The natives are very small and their skin is yellow. When the men are on the lookout for some girl to marry they dye their hair red. The women blacken their teeth when they get married.

We took a walk into the city but there is not much to see. Three cans of sardines cost one dollar. They say savages can be found on parts of the Island. There is also a Leper Colony here.

The waters around here are full of fish, you do not need anything on the hook. On the way in I saw a shark and some big sea turtles.

We climbed one of the high hills while we were here and when we got to the top you could see for miles around. We came across native huts on the way up. The hills are almost like high mountains. They are very steep and bare. You have to hug close to the ground and take your time coming down or you will fall to the bottom, a long way down. It is almost straight up. I took my shoes and sox off because I did not want to slip on the way down but the heat was almost unbearable on my feet.

It was a funny sight to see the American sailors all over the high, bare hills. They looked like a swarm of little ants. If we knew what we were getting into we never would have tackled those mountainous hills. When we finally reached the bottom we went to the beach and dove into the water for a well deserved swim. The water was very warm. Back home in Massachusetts it is the middle of winter, the weather is near zero and there is plenty of snow on the ground. This was the first time I ever went swimming in January. It sure felt great. I'll take the warm climate anytime. They can have the frozen ponds and rivers.

When we finished our swim we went looking for some sea shells, the shells down here are pretty. We met some of the fellows who went into town and they told us not to buy any ice cream or soft drinks because many of the troops stationed here came down with cramps and the runs. We have thousands of Marines and Army troops in New Caledonia, plus the Navy. The troops train here before taking off for the coming campaigns. The big brains of all the Armed Forces can be found here.

While we are here, we will not have to get up at 4 A.M. as we did while at sea; now we can sleep until 5:30 A.M. Church services for all faiths were also held while we were here. A Priest who was in the North African campaign said Mass for us today, Sunday. On the morning of January 24, 1943 at six in the morning the U.S.S. *Montpelier* left New Caledonia.

January 25, 1943: After one day's run from New Caledonia we dropped anchor in Havannah Harbor, in the island of Efate, New Hebrides; we are now about five hundred miles south of the Solomon Islands. Guadalcanal is in the Solomons, our forces are locked in battle against the Japs there.

The first allied offensive against Japan in the Pacific War

started on August 7, 1942 at Guadalcanal when the first Marine
Division went ashore.

We do not know how long we will stay here, but we will have
to be on the alert at all times, because the Jap air force bombed
this place not too long ago. The harbor is sizable and is surrounded by high green jungles and the water is full of jellyfish
that cause a bad sting. It is very quiet and lonesome here. I
would not want to be here if the Jap planes attacked us. They
would be in on us and away before we knew what happened. The
high jungle would make it ideal for them.

The weather is very hot and humid, we do not get a breeze because of the high jungle. We do not care too much for this place,
the climate here takes the life right out of you.

There are many warships here and our ship is going to be the
flagship of a task force. That means we will carry the Admiral and
all the other ships will take their orders from the Admiral aboard
our ship. The Admiral's name is Aaron S. Merrill, he is a Rear
Admiral and they call him "Tip." He came aboard with his staff,
then inspected the ship, he had plenty of pep and vitality. I
would say he is in his forties, he is also very good-looking. Everyone took to him the first time they saw him, he looks like a good
scout.

We went over to the beach for recreation. There was little to
do but pick coconuts and lemons. There was a big stockade there
and the Marines and Sea Bees, stationed close by, carry knives
about 3 feet long. The natives in the interior still practice can-
nibalism. You also can pick up malaria here. The heat in the
jungle sucks the strength from you. It was just a waste of time
coming over here but it gave us a chance to get off the ship and
away from a working party. You sweat all the time here.

January 26, 1943: We are still at New Hebrides, but expect to
leave here tomorrow. We received fuel today. All hands went to
their battle stations because Jap planes were on their way here
to attack us. They must have been intercepted because nothing
happened.

Last night they said we were about 2½ hours from the Jap fleet, but let them come. I came out here to see action and I hope this is the biggest battle of all time and it is also an honor to be on the flagship so I think this baby will give a good account of itself. Most of the crew would rather keep on going and see action than go back to the States. As for me I would not trade my place with anyone back in the States. I do not know how I will feel when we run into action but right now I feel in the pink of condition and don't care how many Japs I run into.

January 27, 1943: We left New Hebrides today and it looks like we will get our first taste of action in a couple of days. It was quite a sight to see all the warships make their way out of the jungle-surrounded harbor and head for the open sea. It did not take long before all the ships were in formation. The sun was setting as we took our last look at the thick, green jungle of New Hebrides.

We cut through the calm blue water at a good speed, and the breeze was very refreshing to us after having been stuck in the hot humid harbor. I feel sorry for anyone who is stationed in that hellhole, even the natives don't want it. Everyone was topside to get their last look at the island. No one was sorry to leave. Even the natives won't live on the side of the island where we were anchored. It felt good to put on the dungarees again after having worn whites. Those white uniforms would make a good target, but what are you going to do if Washington tells us what to wear. This makes it hard on the men who are in command down here, it should be left up to them what to wear etc. From now on everything will be blue, hat, shirt and dungarees. My battle station is a quad 40 mm. machine gun, it is not far from the Bridge where the Admiral and Captain stay. We are not allowed to throw trash or garbage overboard because the Jap subs could trace and follow us. I got the midnight to 4 A.M. watch tonight.

Thursday, January 28, 1943: I got very little sleep because I got off watch at 4 A.M. and sunrise General Quarters sounded at 5:30 A.M. All the ships went through battle maneuvers today. My gun mount is very close to the twin five inch mounts and when the guns fire the concussion is terrific. It makes the inside of your throat and chest feel like it was being ripped out. Cotton in the ears does not help. Sometimes you can almost look down the gun barrels when they are fired, you can feel the hot blast when they go off.

We are getting closer to Guadalcanal by the second. The press news some time ago said the Japs are getting ready for something big. The ships in our force are zigzagging, and making numerous turns. We are ready for what may come.

January 29, 1943: It rained last night. I slept topside last night, it was too hot below. I used my hat for a pillow, put it on top of my shoes, we keep the rest of our clothes on. The steel deck is very hard. My sleep was interrupted by rain at 3 A.M. I changed my wet clothing and then it was almost time to go on watch. It is too hot to sleep below in the compartments so the men sleep topside under the stars. The ship is covered with sailors all sprawled out. In the darkness you will trip over someone who is sound asleep if you do not watch your step. When the rain comes, there is a big scramble to get under cover. The rain will not last long so they can go back to their spot again and continue their sleep. Some nights your sleep is interrupted several times and you hope that the next night you can get a night's rest, but something always comes up to prevent you from getting that sleep. We had field day today, everything was cleaned up and put in order. We will be ready for action in case we should run into the Japs. We are only twenty-five minutes from Jap air bases and we are getting closer to them every mile we travel. Today is Friday, Fish Day.

January 31, 1943: Today is Sunday and is the first chance I had to do any writing since Friday Jan. 29. I will try to cover what has happened in that time. First of all I would like to say that we returned to New Hebrides at 4:30 P.M. this evening. On the evening of Friday January 29 just before sunset General Quarters sounded our task force of warships were attacked by a big force of Jap planes. The Japs threw fighters, torpedoes and dive bombers at us.

I was standing my regular watch when our ships started firing, but I thought it was just another practice but it did not take me very long to see that it was the real thing. Before General Quarters sounded our ship was firing at the Jap planes, every ship in the force was under attack and Jap planes were coming at us from all directions and angles. Bombs were exploding very close to the ships and torpedoes were cutting through the water as the ships twisted and turned. We could see the Jap planes dive into our ships with their machine guns blazing away. Great fountains of water could be seen shooting high into the air as their bombs exploded close to our ships.

While all these things were happening our ships were filling the air with shells. The whole area was full of red tracers and exploding shells as they blasted the Jap planes. Before the battle ended some of our ships would be damaged and the heavy cruiser *Chicago* would be sunk by Jap torpedo planes. Our ship was much luckier than the *Chicago* because the torpedo that hit us did not explode.

The 40 mm. machine gun mount that I was on shot down the first Jap plane for our ship, a twin-engine torpedo plane. The water around us was full of Jap machine gun bullets, exploding bombs and torpedoes.

The Japs were out in full force, they were here for the kill. It was a hot, humid night and the whole encounter was a sight to see as the ships twisted and turned with their guns blazing away. Another torpedo plane dropped a torpedo, about 30 feet from us, the plane just missed our bridge as it passed overhead.

The heavy cruiser *Chicago* was hit by 2 Jap torpedoes and had to drop out of formation, some destroyers fell back to cover it. When our 40 mm. shells hit the water at low-flying planes some of them would bounce off the water. I would not want to get in their way. Our ship was firing 20 and 40 mm. machine guns and five-inch mounts.

When the Japs first attacked our ship, one of the crew was cut to ribbons by a Jap fighter that strafed the ship with machine gun fire. He got hit just as he was going down the open hatch. Some of the men on the other ships were showered with water from the exploding bombs that came too close for comfort. The Japs were not satisfied with one run against us, they kept coming back for more attacks against us. Some of the Jap planes exploded so close to our ships we thought they were hit, boy were we lucky!

When it became dark the Japs lit the place up with flares; they were doing everything to put us out of action. It was a long rugged night for the *Chicago,* the crew would be in for a long trying night. Water almost covered the deck. The engine room was flooded, there was no power or lights and the casualties were high. No one on any of the ships got any sleep because we were at battle stations all night.

During the night one of our cruisers had a rugged job of putting cables on the *Chicago* and towing it. It was extra tough in the darkness especially with Jap subs close by and Jap planes snooping overhead. The phosphorescence in the water lighted up as the ships cut through the water and tipped the Japs off as to where we are. Everyone had to be on the alert, because we did not know when Jap warships, subs or planes would attack.

This action took place south of Guadalcanal near Rennell Island. Our transports landed troops on Guadalcanal but the Japs took it out on us. Early in the morning on the following day, Jan. 30, a Jap sub tried to sink one of our ships but one of our destroyers sunk it. Everyone was glad to see the sun come up; now we could see what was going on. As we looked from our starboard side we could see the heavy cruiser *Chicago* not too far away. It was dead in the water, the main deck was almost under water. We left several destroyers behind to protect the *Chicago* and a tug from Guadalcanal that took over from the cruiser *Louisville.*

Later wave after wave attacked the crippled *Chicago,* and the small group of ships that were protecting her, but the Jap planes finally broke through and put 2 more torpedoes into the *Chicago.* This small force shot down many Jap planes, and the *Chicago* also took care of some before she went down with her guns firing up to the end. We spent the rest of the day at our battle station. The weather was very hot and sunny, everyone was dead tired from lack of sleep. We received word late Saturday evening that Jap planes had put two more torpedoes into the *Chicago* and sunk it.

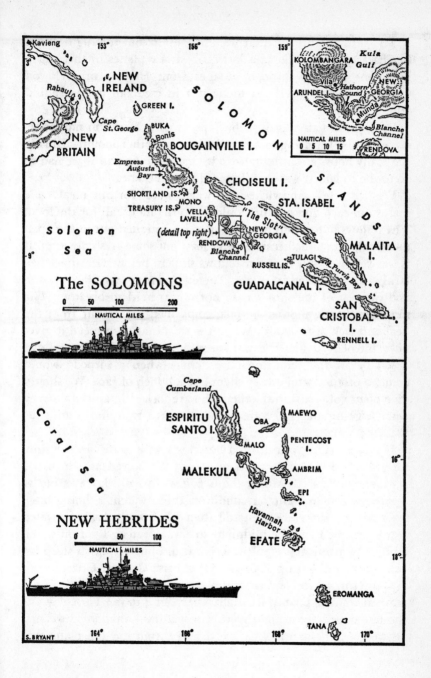

The Japs also hit the destroyer *La Vallette* but the tug brought her back to port. The Japs lost quite a few planes in this attack but some did get through. Planes from Henderson Field on Guadalcanal flew overhead today just in case Jap planes should attack us.

During the action against the Japs, our machine gun mount received praise for firing more shells than any other mount. During the many hours at battle stations we had to use a pail if we had to go to the toilet. It was then lowered over the side.

We had a few sandwiches and warm water for our meals, one man from each gun mount would go to the mess hall for the food. The fellows like myself were lucky to be stationed out in the open on the gun mounts, because we at least got some fresh air, even if it was very hot, but the poor fellows shut in below with the ventilating system off had it rough. The engine room was like an oven and the rest of the ship was so hot it was hard to breathe. The radio shack was another hotbox, some men passed out from the heat and lack of fresh air. When the ship is at high speed it gives off a lot of heat and the warm sea does not help. The fellows down below the waterline never knew when a torpedo would come in on them and drown them like a bunch of rats. We should give plenty of credit to the men who are locked in and cannot see what is going on. They are under a great strain and cannot defend themselves.

It's like locking you up in a hot closet with no air in the summertime and throwing the key away. We stayed at our battle stations from Friday night about 6 P.M. to Saturday evening at 8 P.M. We then went on condition three watch, 4 hours on 8 hours off. I had a few hours off then I had to go back on watch again because I had the midnight to 4 A.M. watch. I got off watch Sunday morning at 4 A.M. (watch) but did not get much sleep because all hands got up at 6 A.M. for sunrise General Quarters.

We returned to New Hebrides at 4:30 P.M. this evening and I am still waiting for my 1st night's sleep in 3 days. Thursday was the last time I got a night's sleep, just a few winks in-between is all we got. I took a look at the damage from the Jap plane that strafed us the night the *Chicago* got hit. Roy Melton was the fellow who was killed by the strafing plane as he entered the hatch to get to his battle station. He was a very nice fellow, I would say that he was about 20 years old. They said that he is the second one in his family to be killed in the war. He will be buried at New Hebrides. Another brother is also on our ship; it is very sad to see him sit by himself, his mind is a thousand miles away, he is heartbroken.

All the ships got fuel and ammunition today. Church services were also held. Capt. Wood spoke to the crew and congratulated all hands for their work against the Japs, he said that we were now seasoned veterans.

February 6, 1943: General Quarters sounded this evening. Jap planes were close by but they did not attack.

They must have hit Guadalcanal. I had my clothes off when General Quarters sounded, I was just going to take a shower. I put on my shorts and took off for my battle station with the rest of my clothes in my hands. When I got topside I almost ran into Commander Kounce, he got a kick out of me with no clothes on. Everyone likes him; he is also our Executive Officer. We could see the Solomon Islands in the distance today. It rains nearly every night, they are mostly showers. Last night I dreamed that I was back home playing hockey on one of the ponds. I got a kick out of that. The press news said that the air attack against us when the *Chicago* was hit was the first night-bombing attack of the war by Japanese planes against American warships. We had to laugh when we heard Radio Tokyo broadcast. It said that Jap planes on January 29 attacked a large force of American warships consisting of battleships, cruisers and destroyers east of Rennell Island on the southern tip of the Solomons group. Their planes sunk two battleships, three cruisers sunk, one battleship and one cruiser heavily damaged as well as three cruisers heavily damaged and three enemy warplanes shot down. They also said that some of their planes also crashed into our ships on suicide dives.

Our troops at Gaudalcanal are doing a job on the Japs. Most of the warships have left us. We are now operating with 8 destroyers and 3 light cruisers, a total of 12 ships. Our ship is the flagship and Admiral Merrill is in command of the task force. It looks like we will patrol the waters near Guadalcanal. If the Japs come down with their warships we will intercept them.

It gets dark at 7:45 P.M. in this area.

February 13, 1943: The press news said that our forces have complete control of Guadalcanal. Everyone was very happy to hear this. This is number one in the long climb up the Solomons that faces us. One of the fellows was electrocuted when he accidentally touched a live wire. We had church services for him, and his body was lowered over the side.

We have been patrolling for many days and nights now near Guadalcanal. I washed a lot of clothes today, they dry very quickly in the hot sun. Some of the fellows hang theirs on the blowers; these blowers are on the side of the ship and they throw off a lot of hot air. Our division officer Lt. Hutchins said we were to pull into Havannah Harbor, New Hebrides, soon and to put on whites. We expect to get mail, also send some. I hope this harbor is better than the other one we hit. I looked at the pay slip in the mess hall, I have $116 coming to me. You cannot spend any money here there is no place to go.

Thursday, February 18, 1943: I will cover what has happened in the past three days. We pulled into New Hebrides on the 15th at 2:30 P.M. The first thing we did was to put on our white uniforms, boy was that a joke! We got tons of supplies, that meant plenty of working parties, the heat in the holds of the ship was rugged. Monday got paid in afternoon, drew only $16, more coming. Got in ice cream line four times. We got mail last night but I did not get any yet.

This afternoon we left the ship in a small landing craft for recreation on the beach at New Hebrides; our ship is not too far from the beach. This side of the island is swampy and damp with plenty of insects, it is also very warm. You can pick lemons, oranges, limes and it is loaded with coconuts. Many of the natives speak fair English. They like our cigarettes and are friendly. We traded articles and money for their beads, knives etc. A lot of the

Sea Bees have been here many months and they work very hard. I had to laugh at the animals they had, one pet goat, a kitten and four dogs, the goat was very funny. Everyone brought back to the ship many kinds of fruit and other articles. The boat was supposed to pick us up at 6 P.M. but it did not get there until 8 P.M. We had a late supper when we got back to the ship, and I was one hour late for watch. When I got off watch at midnight I had to report to the Officer on Watch. I told him what happened and he told me not to let it happen again.

Boy, Freeman had his appendix out today. As I passed the operating room I could see the Dr. getting ready for the operation with his assistants.

February 19, 1943: We left New Hebrides at 1 P.M. today, it was very hot. Our task force is Task Force 39, Cruiser division 12. We are part of the Third Fleet under Admiral Wm. F. "Bull" Halsey. Chaplain Knudsen came aboard before we left. He had been gone for about ten days and he had a good coat of tan. I received my first mail in over two months. It takes a long time for the mail to catch up to us because we move around so much. Every day our task force has maneuvers, we operate like a bunch of pros now. The precision of the ships as they maneuver is quite a thing to see. Every ship moves at the right second in the same direction, as they twist and turn, they look like a first class drill team.

Sunday, February 21, 1943: Not much to say for Fri. and Sat. We came across some of our pilots who crashed into the water. We don't know how long they had been drifting on the raft. It was a good thing we came across them because they could have been picked up by Jap subs or maybe land on one of the Jap-held islands in the Solomons. If that happened it meant certain death and the Japs like to cut your head off with a sword. The waters are also full of sharks.

Saturday night while I was on the eight to midnight watch we sighted the Solomons. We were going to stop at Tulagi, it is across from Guadalcanal. As we approached the island we were told to be on the lookout for a blinking light. It should be easy to spot because it is a very dark night. This would be our signal telling us that it was safe to enter one of the harbors. The hours passed and about 4:15 A.M. the next morning, while all hands were at battle stations, the blinking light was spotted, our mount was the first one to see it, it was reported to the bridge at once. Now all hands could relax, some Jap subs are in these waters and you never know when you will come across one.

The weather is like a hot summer's night at home, it was very still and quiet. The air had a nice odor, it must have been the flowers in the jungle. We are not too far away from where the five Sullivan brothers lost their lives when their warship was sunk by Jap warships. There are still plenty of Japs hiding in the jungles here.

About 4:30 A.M. the earphones on our mount broke down, so I had to take them down to the repair shop. When I entered the shop the men were asleep, I felt foolish asking someone to repair a set of phones at 4:30 in the morning, but it had to be done because we never knew when the Japs might attack us, we are also in the Japs' back yard. I returned in fifteen minutes to pick up the phones.

When the sun came up we got a good look at Tulagi because we were very close to land. You could see where the Marines and Japs had fought some bloody battles.

The trees were blown to bits and huge holes from bombs and shells were all about. The hills had a lot of caves, some were sealed with dead Japs inside who would not come out to surrender. The jungle here is very thick and you can hear the monkeys squeaking and the crocodiles are not very far away. We will be in for a hot day in the Solomons because it was very warm early in the morning. This is a pretty good size harbor. We are ready to get under way in ten minutes, because you never know when the Jap planes from their bases just up the line will attack. We would be sitting ducks for their planes in here. In time this will be our regular base. This will be the pushing-off place for the coming invasion against the Japs in the Solomons.

Capt. Wood was in for a big surprise while we were here at

Tulagi. A PT boat came alongside and who should come aboard but Capt. Wood's son. He is in command of his PT. They had a great reunion, it was a very happy day for both of them. Some other PT boats also came alongside during the day and we gave them candy, cigarettes, ice cream etc.

The PT boats had Jap flags painted on them. The PT boats carry 4 torpedoes and some machine guns. There is no privacy, when it comes to the toilet it is just a toilet seat at the rear of the boat. It reaches out over the water. One of the crew from the PT boat told us that they picked up 5 nurses at Guadalcanal who had escaped from the Japs. Some of them were almost insane after what they had been through while being held by the Japs. He said the Japs also raped the nuns and then killed them, some had their heads cut off.

Some of the Jap prisoners are fellows who went to our colleges in California before going back to Japan. This is the hottest place we have hit so far, you could fry eggs on the steel deck, there is no air in here, you never stop sweating. It is impossible to sleep below in the compartments as the heat is suffocating. There is also plenty of fish here, the Dr. and some of the crew threw a line over the side of the ship and got themselves some fish. You can catch them on an empty hook.

March 3, 1943: We are now at Espiritu Santo. Our force consists of 3 light cruisers and 8 destroyers; we are Task Force 39, Cruiser division 12. Light cruisers, *Montpelier, Denver, Cleveland.* Destroyers, *Fletcher, Radford, O'Bannon, Nicholas Cony, Conway* and *Waller.* Our mission is to Hit the Japs in the Solomons.

Friday, March 5, 1943: The task force is on its way up the Solomons at high speed. Espiritu Santo is over 500 miles behind us. The Solomons cover over 500 miles and about 90% of it is in the Japs' hands. We are making good speed. We took it easy today because they want everyone to be rested for what lies ahead. It is a warm day and the breeze feels good.

The Dr. gave orders for all hands to take a shower and put on clean clothing just in case someone is wounded. Also eat plenty of salt tablets because of sweating and getting weak from the heat. We are to keep our sleeves down and collars up, this will help against flash burns.

Capt. Wood spoke to the crew and wished us the best of luck against the Japs. He said that we would hit the enemy tomorrow morning, Sat., about 1:30 A.M.

Our job is to go into Kula Gulf and bombard the Vila Stanmore plantation on Kolombangara in the Solomons. In peacetime it was a very busy place, but now it is a strong Jap base. It's about in the middle of the Solomons. The Japs have many troops here and we can expect to run into almost anything in the darkness. We will be very close to land. We did not know if the water was mined, besides at almost any time the ship might get grounded on the coral because most of the Solomons are not charted. They are using old maps and charts that are not complete. We could also run into PT boats, subs, warships not to mention Jap shore guns.

If you had to land on one of the islands the Japs would waste very little time cutting your head off, that is if the sharks did not get you first. This is going to be a very ticklish operation and it is going to take place right in the Japs' living room.

At 1:30 A.M. we will bombard the troops and knock out the radio stations and ammunition dumps. We will hit them while they are asleep. One of our planes will be overhead. It will be a Black Cat, for night work. The pilot from our ship will be up there. They will let us know if we are hitting the targets. His password will be "Dagwood" and ours will be "Baby Dumpling." Late this evening we received word from one of our night fighters that Jap planes and warships were seen coming down in our direction. We did not want them to spot us because that would put the Japs on the alert and they would be waiting for us. We are getting closer to zero hour.

Saturday, March 6, 1943: At 1 A.M. this morning we were on our way into Kula Gulf, it was very dark, land was on both sides of us, it seemed as if you could reach out and touch land. Everyone was at his battle station. Before our guns opened up on the

Japs our radar picked up something moving, without doubt Jap ships.* Our ship, being first in line behind a destroyer and nearest to the Jap ships, opened up at once with rapid fire, with her six-inch guns and we were the first to hit the Jap ships.

It was a Jap destroyer. It was a mass of flames and explosions, it disappeared in about 3 minutes. The other American ships did not waste any time after we opened up on the Jap ships. It looked like the 4th of July, all the ships' guns were blazing away. The second Jap warship was larger, it could have been a cruiser. It was also much harder to sink. The Japs did not waste any time firing back at us but we had too much fire power for it. We were smothering it with shells, the casualties on both Jap ships must be very high.

Our destroyers were also firing their torpedoes. It did not take long before the second ship was a mass of flames, it was a regular holocaust of red hot steel, flames were shooting into the sky. We must have hit the magazines on the first ship because it went down so fast. The second ship burnt for some time.

With the two Jap warships out of the way, Admiral Merrill gave orders for all ships to start firing at the shore installations and barracks. The Japs were alerted by now but this did not bother Tip Merrill. Another man would have been satisfied with what he did and then take off while the getting away was good but Merrill seemed to enjoy the challenge.

Some of the Jap shore guns opened up on us but we knocked them out in a hurry, our rapid fire was too much for them. There were many big explosions from the shore as our guns hit their targets. Our plane overhead said we were on target. We did an awful job on the Japs, we left the places in shambles, we hit troop barracks, ammunition dumps, radio towers, airfield planes, and broken bodies were everywhere. Our ship fired 1800 rounds of 5 and 6 inch shells in 15 minutes. We fired 700 rounds at the Jap ships; that will give you an idea what we did to the Jap ships. We

* What we did not know as we were about to start our bombardment was that late in the evening two Jap warships had pulled in here after sinking one of our submarines.

hit the Japs like a streak of lightning, it was all over before they knew what hit them. They will not sleep the rest of the night.

As we completed our circle in the Gulf and headed out to open water the Jap shore guns opened up on us but they did not hit us. While we were in the Gulf, we had Japs on three sides of us.*

We were a very happy group of warships as we made our way out of the Gulf with dead Japs and destruction behind us. St. Patrick's Day celebration came early this year and Admiral "Patrick" Stanton Merrill did the chasing, only it was Japs this time and not snakes.

Admiral Merrill, 31-knot Burke and Cap. Carney on the cruiser *Denver* must be doing a Jig, along with the officers and men on the rest of the ships in this little task force of Bull Halsey's 3rd Fleet. What we did was like having some enemy warship go up the Hudson River and bombard New York City and its shipping, then turn around and head for the open sea. We really rubbed it into the Japs, they will never get over this one. We left them talking to themselves.

About 6 A.M. in the morning as we headed south for our home base, Jap planes were picked up on our radar. We were very close to Jap airfields and could expect to be attacked at any time. It's a long trip down the Solomons and we would not be able to relax until we reached our base hundreds of miles away. The chances were that the Japs would be out looking for us with their planes and subs. It is Saturday, I suppose the Japs are now looking over the destruction we left them, early this morning. Our task force is cutting its way through the Solomons. At 6 P.M. this evening our radar picked up more Jap planes, but they did not attack us. Everyone could stand some sleep, we have not had a night's sleep in about 3 days.

Monday, March 8, 1943: I did not write yesterday, which was Sunday, so I will cover it today, although there is not much to write. We are still traveling towards our base in New Hebrides, the weather is hot and the seas are calm. Sunday Divine Services were held by the Protestant chaplain. On our regular news program at noon yesterday Mr. Francis McCarthey, the United Press

* I think this was also the first combat use of Mark 8 (FH) RADAR.

reporter, told us what he wrote for the papers back in the States. It reaches 1200 newspapers. He gave quite a story of our action in Kula Gulf. He also mentioned about the 22 Jap Convoy our planes sunk as they approached New Guinea. It rained a little Sunday. We also received a message from Commander of the South Pacific forces, Admiral Wm. F. Bull Halsey. He congratulated our force for its action.

This is what the press news had to say this Monday morning about our action against the Japs.

"A Navy Task Force bombarded Jap shore installations at Vila and Munda in the Solomon Islands Friday night. This was in the outer limits of the enemy defense zone. This was the first surface action to develop so far north in the Solomons Archipelago. Munda and Vila are close together and they are about 180 nautical miles northwest of Guadalcanal. There are several flying fields in the Munda area but darkness saved the American ships from air attacks."

I must not forget to mention that when Admiral Merrill gave his report of the action at Kula Gulf to one of the officers to be sent to Admiral Halsey's headquarters, this report also went by mistake to President Roosevelt, General MacArthur and who knows how many other big wheels. Admiral Halsey knew what he was doing when he put Admiral Merrill in command of Task Force 39, they don't come any better than Admiral Merrill.

The force that hit Kula Gulf consisted of 3 light cruisers and 3 destroyers. The other 5 destroyers in our force had their work cut out for them at Munda on New Georgia about 25 miles away. The light cruiser *Columbia* was suppose to be with us but she had to have some repair work done. Our trip from New Hebrides to Kula Gulf was over 700 miles one way. The chaplain said we would reach Havannah Harbor, New Hebrides, tomorrow Tuesday, March 9.

While I am writing this the ship is sailing along with the rest of the ships in the task force. The sun is shining and it is a beautiful day. I am on the starboard side not too far from where the Captain sits.

Tuesday, March 9, 1943: We returned to New Hebrides today

at 5 P.M. We traveled over 1500 miles since we left here Thursday March 4. We have not had a night's sleep in all that time. Before we entered the harbor we had gunnery.

Wednesday, March 10, 1943: I had my first good night's sleep in a week. I do not know how long we will stay here at New Hebrides. All hands will get up at 5:45 A.M. while we are here. It has been about one month since we were here last. What do you know, I was not picked for a working party. They must be saving me for something big. We got over 50 bags of mail, to put everyone in a good mood.

Lt. Boyle, the pilot from our ship, came aboard today with Jap helmets, guns etc. He was in the spotting bomber when we were at Kula Gulf. He spent 12 hours in the air during our raid. He spoke over the loudspeaker at noon during news time, and he said that after we sunk the 2 Jap warships he expected us to leave. He was surprised when he saw us stay and start bombarding the Japs on shore. If any of our ships were put out of action in Kula Gulf I hate to think what the Japs would have done to us the next day. They would have used us for target practice and then let the sharks finish us off. They say the Japs have a trick of shooting torpedoes from the beach at night. Lt. Boyle said our assignments had been carried out and that we left the place in flames and ruin.

He also said the Jap shore batteries did not fire very long at us because we knocked them out of action. He spotted the two Jap warships about 9 or 10 P.M. They were going in the direction of Kula Gulf, that was about 3 hours before we sunk them.

Wednesday, March 17, 1943: Today is St. Patrick's Day. I hope it is a great day for the Irish everywhere.

I will try to cover what has happened in the past several days. While at Efate, New Hebrides, we had recreation every day, but there is nothing over there but jungle. The heat is rugged, it is also very humid, and there are plenty of insects. The only reason we go ashore is to get off the ship for a change and miss a working party. We also get a chance to pick some fresh fruits, such as lemons, oranges, limes, etc.

We had church services topside, and during the services it rained, everyone got soaked. About 200 fellows from the other ships attended. One day I had my watch on the 40 mm. machine gun mount with some of the Marines; we carry about 50 as part of the crew, they man the 20 mm. machine guns. One of the Marines spent about 100 days on Guadalcanal fighting the Japs. He was wounded in action and they sent him to New Caledonia to the hospital. When he recovered they transferred him to our ship. He said many a rifle butt was broken over a Jap's head and many a bayonet thrust into Japs' stomachs. One Marine found a wallet on a Jap belonged to his brother. He killed the Jap with machine gun bullets. The bombardment which we gave the Japs at Kula Gulf was what the Japs gave him and his buddies on Guadalcanal. He said his buddies would have given anything to be with us the night we bombarded the Japs. It was in a bombardment like this that put him out of action. He said ship bombardment is the worst of them all. He enjoyed seeing the Japs get a dose of their own medicine.

We got our Christmas mail while we were here. I got a package and some letters from my sister Mary. She said they are having a very cold winter at home in Waltham, Mass. It dropped to 25 below zero, yet here I am in my shirtsleeves. We left port with some other ships for a few days of maneuvers. We were called Task Force 68, it could pack a good wallop against the Japs. My brother Joe's ship the carrier *Saratoga* was with us, it must be bigger than any carrier afloat, she looks so slick and graceful. We had war games and gunnery. Our shooting was 100%. We shot at targets towed by planes. The planes from our carriers came in to attack us, they would skim along the surface of the water and then go right up over our ships. It was quite a thing to see. This is how they will attack the Jap warships when they go into action against them. Our own subs as well attacked us. We also ran into a storm. Myers threw a bucket of water one deck below on two fellows, they almost had a fight over it. He just missed being put on report. The two fellows looked like drowned rats, we had to laugh, they did not know what hit them, it was better than a movie, this happened topside near the quarterdeck. We had plenty of working parties around the clock while we were in Efate, New Hebrides.

A lot of ammunition and stores came aboard. When we go on the beach now for recreation we get 2 bottles of beer; some of the fellows are willing to pay $5 for these two bottles. We spent about 4 days at Espiritu Santo, New Hebrides.

Saturday, March 27, 1943: While on watch at Espiritu Santo, I heard a very loud noise up in the clouds and not long after that I saw one of our planes spinning around like a top, nose first, like a bullet, with one wing off and smoke coming from its motor. Later I saw the wing follow the plane down.

The plane crashed into the jungle. I did not see any parachute. It happened so fast I don't think the pilot had time to bail out.

Our average fuel consumption is about 80 gallons per mile and almost 125 per mile while at high speed.

I got a letter from my sister Mary, she said the U.S.A. put out 5000 planes per month, Germany 2000, and the Japs 600 a month. A cook from the heavy cruiser *Chicago* told me that 3 cooks were killed near him when they were hit by Jap torpedoes.

March 31, 1943: We are patrolling on the Queen Sugar line. We have to keep the waters clear of Jap warships from attacking Guadalcanal. The weather is a little cooler. We do not get as much rain and the nights are not as dark as before. We had more war games. The heavy cruiser *San Francisco* has joined us. It was almost destroyed by Jap battleships during the battle of Guadalcanal, last November. Admiral Callahan was killed in this action. Sam Summerlin, a cox. in our division, was in that action on the *San Francisco*. Nearly everyone around him topside was blown to bits, he was one of the few lucky ones to come out of it O.K. They were so close to the Jap ships that the Japs could not lower their guns anymore, that is why the superstructure took such destruction, only for that the *Frisco* would have been sunk.

A report came in saying Guadalcanal was attacked by over 100 Jap planes, we could have run into something like that after our attack on Kula Gulf, but we were lucky. I would also like to mention that an Australian cruiser *Leander* and the carrier *Enterprise* are also with us on our maneuvers. While we were on watch we passed the time discussing our Civil War. The sides were almost even and no one got hurt. We have a lot of Southern boys on our ship. The crew comes from about every State in the Union.

I broke my glasses one night while the 5 inch guns were firing but I will be able to patch them up.

Robert Montgomery, the movie star, is a Lt. Comdr. on one of the light cruisers in our Task Force 39. The press news said that Malta has taken more bombing attacks than any other place in the world. Also Two-ton Tony Galento wants another shot at Joe Louis when the war ends.

May 1943: Fred Apostle, the former middle weight champ. of the world, came aboard for the boxing program put on by our ship. Apostle is also in our task force. He is on the light cruiser *Denver*, we call it the "Dirty D." It is just a nickname, she is as clean as the rest of the ships. Fred boxed with 3 different fellows from our ship.

I did not write for some time because it was about the same routine. We had plenty of gunnery, war games and practice bombardment on the islands, we were on the go, day and night. When the next action against the Japs comes off we can take it out on them.

Mr. McCarthey the news reporter is still on board, he is like one of the crew, everyone likes him. It looks like he will never go back to the States. After almost two months I finally put my feet on some good solid earth. There is not much over on the beach but jungle. I had to laugh at a story one of the Sea Bees told me while I was on the beach. He picked up a program on the radio from Japan and it was all about a Jap wrestler who beat up Pop Eye, one of America's favorite characters in the comic papers and movies. I told him that Pop Eye must have left his spinach back home in the United States. We have movies at night now on the ship. Some of the fellows went to a smoker on one of the carriers. They say you cannot buy potatoes in the States because the Govt.

bought them all. We get dehydrated potatoes and no one eats them, they are like soft cement, they stick to the trays like glue.

June 1943: I will start this report with sad news. On June 9, 1943 we lost our Capt., you could not ask for a better man than Capt. Wood, you could not help but like him. Everyone thought the world of him. He will be very hard to replace and we will never forget him as long as we live. The ship went to Vilner, New Hebrides, for Capt. Wood's funeral, that is where he is buried.

Our ship sent 4 men from each division to the funeral. When we crossed the equator about 6 months ago, Capt. Wood presented himself to King Neptune and the Capt. was told that he would die soon. It was only a joke and at the time no one thought he would be dead in about 6 months.

Our new Capt. came aboard. His name is Robert G. Tobin. He is a heavy set man and looks like a regular person. He has been in almost all the action down here against the Jap navy. He knows what it is to go out there and slug it out against larger warships. He has a stiff right leg, received injury in action against the Japs. He also had 2 destroyers sunk under him out here.

While I was walking through the jungle the other day in New Hebrides, I ran into a friend of mine from my own city. His name is Eddie Shaughnessy. He is the first person I have met so far from my home town, it was quite a surprise. He has been out here 13 months.

June 22, 1943: A very special visitor came aboard with Admiral Merrill this afternoon at 4 P.M. It was the number one man himself, Admiral Bull Halsey, Commander of South Pacific forces. He carried some bags with him. He must be here for some operation against the Japs. Things should start popping soon. Some of the crew have had all their hair cut off. A lot of troops and cargo ships have come and gone lately. A French destroyer came in yesterday. We asked one of the crew if he would swap his hat for one of ours but he refused because if they lose their hat they are put in the brig for 30 days. I would hate to think what would happen if the poor fellow ever lost his shoes. If we lose anything we just buy one in return.

Sunday, June 27, 1943: Protestant and Catholic services were held this morning. Capt. Tobin went to Mass and when the services were over the Priest said, "Good hunting on your next mission." We left New Hebrides at 11 A.M. this morning. Some say we go to Santo first and when we leave there we are going into the biggest battle they have had in the Pacific. I hope they are right, I do not want to miss this. I do not know what day the invasion comes off. It looks like more days and nights with very little sleep. We have had very little sleep in the past 6 months. They say that we are going to land Marine Raiders and Army troops this time, plus Sea Bees to build the airfield etc. It will be on Rendova and New Georgia in the middle of the Solomons. We are to take some minelayers with us. They will lay mines in the channels that are used by the Jap navy. The Japs will be in for a big surprise when they use these channels.

Tuesday, June 29, 1943: Nothing much happened yesterday, we put many miles behind us. Today is another day closer to the invasion. I got off watch at 4 A.M. this morning, it rained most of the time on watch, we were chilly because we got soaked. We were talking about everything in particular while on watch. The following message to all ships is from our task force Commander Tip Merrill. "We are faced with many days and nights of long tiring periods at General Quarters stations. In order that we may be fresh when the *trial comes* every officer and man off watch should be encouraged to get as much sleep as possible. Men on watch must be *correspondingly alert*. This looks like our big chance. LETS DON'T MUFF IT!"

About 9 A.M. this morning Capt. Tobin spoke to the crew. He said we should be on the alert at all times because we could expect trouble from air, surface and subs. We had a good dinner today, steak and lemon pie etc. Each man was told that he can buy 10 bars of candy at one time because we might not be able to get food for some time while at our battle stations. After I finished working at my cleaning station I got some rest topside. As I looked out across the water I could see the whitecaps in the distance, the water was not very rough.

At 12:15 this afternoon we joined a big force of warships and troopships, there were also some aircraft carriers with this force. Our radar picked up a force of Jap planes this afternoon but the planes from our carriers took care of them. We stayed at battle stations until 5 P.M. We went back to battle stations one hour before sunset. There was very little sleep tonight.

Wednesday, June 30, 1943: We are still at sea. I got up at 3:15 A.M. this morning for the 4 to 8 watch. About 5:15 this morning we could see land, it was the Solomons. The rest of the ships had left us. We made our way to Tulagi with the rest of Task Force 39, it is a very hot day.

While we were in Tulagi, a working party brought up a lot of food in cans from the hangar deck. We will eat this food at battle stations, the mess hall will not be used. It is up to the cooks to get this food ready. We will eat sandwiches during our many hours at battle stations. The fellows usually take clean clothing and soap with them also. Our gun mounts will be our home for some time. I got a few apples from Floyd when he was taking them up from the icebox. I took a shower this A.M. Smith & Floyd borrowed $1.00 each from me and Blankenship borrowed .50¢ this left me with the big sum of $2.25. Money is no good out here because there is no place to go or anything to spend it on. The only thing you see out here is jungle, and water. I saw our latest fighter plane, it is put out by Grumman. Late this afternoon everything was in readiness and at 6:30 P.M. Tulagi was behind us as we made our way up the Solomons. We are all by ourselves now, good old Task Force 39, Cruiser division 12. They should call us Merrill's Lone Wolves, because we operate as a small task force, without carriers, battleships or even heavy cruisers. We are always snooping in the Japs' back yard. We could not afford to send carriers or battleships up the Solomons, because they would be easy targets for the land-based planes, and also subs that would be hiding near the jungle. We don't mind losing light cruisers and destroyers but the larger ships would not be worth the gamble, when we can do the job anyway. The Solomons are over five hundred miles long and most of the islands are Jap-held fortresses. We call this going up the Slot. It is like going up an alley at night in the tough sections of any big city. You have to be on your guard at all times. You never know when a Jap sub will be up ahead of you dead in the water, just waiting to spring the trap. It is also a good hiding place for PT boats and warships. The Japs also have many airfields on these islands.

We did not eat supper in the mess hall tonight because we could not take the chance. We had 1 ham sandwich, 1 cookie, and 1 apple for supper at our battle stations. One of our pilots went to his battle station with a machine gun, he was very close to our mount which is one of the highest places on the ship. If Jap planes attack us, he wanted to get a shot at them. Capt. Tobin spoke to the crew at 7 P.M. and said we would bombard the Shortlands at 1:58 A.M. tomorrow morning, Thursday July 1, 1943.

The Japs have barracks there, a radar station, big fuel dumps, and plenty of troops plus ammunition dumps. We can expect to run into big 6 inch shore guns.

We also have to be on the alert for Jap warships, PT boats and subs. We will be away up in the Solomons; the Shortlands are south of Bougainville, the largest island in the Solomons. The Japs have thousands of troops there and plenty of airfields. We will be about 200 miles north of Tulagi. While we are hitting the Japs up here in the Shortlands, the Army and Marine Raiders will be landing, about 100 miles south of us on the island of Rendova and New Georgia. This kind of an operation will really put the Japs into confusion. Our job will be to bombard the Japs on shore and prevent Jap subs and warships from attacking our transports, minelayers and troops. Our bombardment will take place in darkness as usual right in the Japs' back yard. It will be a bad place to get hit because if you land in the water the sharks will get you, and if you land on one of the islands the Japs will get you, and of course that means torture and death.

July 1, 1943: The hours passed and we finally reached our destination. About 30 minutes before zero hour it began to rain but it did not bother us because we were going to have a ringside view of the whole show. They were not going to fire the machine guns so that would enable us to see what happened. We would have the night off, if we were needed we would begin to fire at once. The 5 and 6 inch guns will do the firing. When the word was passed for our ships to start firing on the Jap-held island we were soaking wet, and during most of the time we were here it rained. The Japs did not know what hit them as our ships sneaked in on them while they were sound asleep and ripped the place with 5 and 6 inch shells. Many a Jap died in his bunk. You could see big explosions as the ammunition dump went up. The visibility was very bad, because of the heavy rain and darkness. Our task force really poured it on the Japs as they knocked out the Jap targets and slaughtered the troops. Our battle station is only a few feet from the big guns and when they fired, the big flashes were blinding. We were so close to the guns that we could almost look down the barrels. The concussion was awful, it felt like our eardrums would be blown to bits, and the pain in our throat and chest was almost unbearable. The cotton and rubber plugs in our ears did not help, because we were too close to the guns. When these guns fire like this, they even snap the steel plates and ladders that go up to the mount. Jap shore guns opened up on us but no damage was done to our ships. While all this was going on, our ship was hit by a torpedo but lucky for us it must have been a dud. We did not know if it came from a sub or PT boat. This would have been a great place to get stranded. When we completed the bombardment Admiral Merrill ordered the task force back to its base, many hundreds of miles south of here. It rained until the sun came up on this cloudy Thursday morning of July 1, 1943. We had some peanut brittle candy for breakfast and for dinner we had two hard-boiled eggs, 1 orange, and 2 donuts. It was a cloudy day as we raced south. We were in the midst of Jap-held airfields and we never knew when they would attack us. We had 3 air raid warnings, but the Jap planes did not attack us. The cloudy weather must be interfering with their search for us. Everyone could stand some sleep but we will not get that, for sometime. They say we might be back in a day or so for more bombardments against the Japs.

It is late in the afternoon as we pass good old Guadalcanal. The sun is out now and we were lucky it did not come out this morning, we would have made good targets for the Jap planes. My glasses broke again, but I patched them up. It is the glass that is broken.

The sun and glare from the water does a job on your eyes, it is almost blinding and lack of sleep does not help.

July 4, 1943: Today is Independence Day, it is a great holiday in the United States. I will cover what has happened since July 1. On July 1 we were still heading for our home base at Espiritu Santo after our attack on the Shortlands. We stayed at Espiritu Santo one day, and during that time we had to work day and night taking on ammunition, we also got fuel from a tanker. The hospital ship *Relief* was also here. We are on our way to hit the Japs again, I guess there is no rest for the weary.

When Mr. McCarthey the war correspondent gave the news over the loudspeaker, it looked like world series time. Big crowds were gathered around all the loudspeakers as he reported. He said our bombardment of the Shortlands was a success, that we dropped 260 tons of shell, and we were only 20 miles from the big Jap base of Bougainville. The cloudy weather helped keep the Jap air force from attacking us. He said most of the work down here has been done by destroyers and cruisers and he also said that in a month we might be playing baseball on bases the Japs hold now. He said all our operations so far have been excellent and that the troops we landed were doing a good job on the Japs. He said that we were to meet 2 other cruisers and the battleship *North Carolina* tomorrow morning, and then to be on our way to hit the Japs again. While at sea this morning all the ships in the task force had gunnery.

Wednesday, July 7, 1943: Monday afternoon we left for Rendova in the Solomons where Japs had about 18 ships and about 12 were destroyers and cruisers. Another of our task forces got in contact first and sunk 3 cruisers and 4 or 5 destroyers that night. We lost one cruiser, *Helena*. Next day some more Jap ships were sunk. Tuesday we spent the afternoon next to Henderson Field

ready to go out when it got dark. All kinds of bombers and fighters here, quite a base now. We left just before dark. Admiral
Merrill spoke and said we were on our way to see if we could run
into a Jap force. We went to battle stations at 11 P.M. Tuesday,
that night, and came off at about 4 in morning. It rained very
hard that night and most of the early morning. The only thing
we ran into was a Jap sub that had surfaced to charge batteries
and one of our destroyers sunk it. Wed. morning we stopped at
Tulagi Harbor and oiled up. It is just 3:30 P.M. Wed. and we are
still here, do not know when we will go out. Just one month ago
today Japs sent 120 planes and bombers over here and Guadalcanal just on other side and had most of them shot down. This
harbor is very hot and it is surrounded by big thick green trees. I
do not know what kind of trees they are but they are very thick, at
this point we are only 100 yards from land and you cannot see into
the jungle. On the way down a lot of the jungle is cut away and
they are building the place up. There are quite a few little villages. The Marines at their guns on the hilltops are all brown
from the sun. It's a pretty quiet and desolate place down here.
A PT torpedo boat just pulled up alongside and it made sure it
was the shady side. Most of the fellows are laying topside in the
shade after being up all night and getting no sleep. They were up
all night on the prowl for Japs.* We sent whites to laundry today.
I bought some peppermint bars and ice cream this afternoon,
woke up at one in the afternoon and was too late for chow. The
place I was just talking about was Purvis Bay, a little further
down is Tulagi Harbor which we visited to fuel up.

July 11, 1943: We are now at Purvis Bay in the Solomons, it is
not too far from Tulagi. Mr. McCarthey, the news reporter, returned to our ship. He was on the troopship *McCauley* when it
was sunk by Jap torpedoes during the invasion of Rendova. He
covered that landing while we were bombarding the Shortlands,

---

* One of these PT boats could have been President Kennedy's PT 109. He was in
the fighting in the Solomons from March to November that year.
  We also had maneuvers with the PT boats and it was quite a sight to see them
attack us at high speed. When we were attacked by PT boats during the war I am
glad it was by the Japs and not our PT boats.

it was all part of one operation along with the landings on New Georgia. He said that he lost some of his belongings when the *McCauley* was sunk. He watched our troops shell the Japs and said that the fighting in the jungle is very rugged. The Jap troops are very tough and experienced. Mr. McCarthey said also that our Task Force 39 which consists of 4 light cruisers and 8 destroyers would go up the Slot and bombard the Japs at Munda on the island of New Georgia in the Solomons. He said we will bombard the Japs at 3 A.M. tomorrow morning Monday July 12th and that American lives depend on the attack and to do a good job. After our bombardment our troops are to advance from 3 sides and destroy the Jap troops not killed with our bombardment and in 24 hours Munda and its important airfield would be ours.

This bombardment will also take place in the dark. Every time we go up the Slot to take on the Japs it is dark, it is near midnight or early in the morning. We get very little sleep with this schedule but this is the only way we can do it. We are not strong enough yet to do this in the daytime, we would run out of warships and our air power is not strong enough either, there are too many Jap airfields in the Solomons. We only get about 10% of the war supplies down here while the European theatre of war gets about 90%. We are hanging on with a big prayer.

I think the rugged routine that we have had for the past 7 months has something to do with the way the men have been acting lately. The men have noticed it themselves doing it. Your mind goes blank and you find yourself walking around some part of the ship, some distance from where you want to go, and then it dawns on you that you are not supposed to be there. You forget what day it is, what you had for breakfast, what you did in the morning. You find yourself in the washroom with no soap or towel. When you turn the water on, then it dawns on you. You forget to take your toothbrush and paste with you, until you begin to brush your teeth. You go in to take a shower without towel or soap. Some of the fellows have a lighted cigarette in their mouths and ask for a match to light theirs. When you wake up, you think it is time to go on watch etc.

These things sneak up on you before you know it. You will find
yourself somewhere and ask yourself, "What am I doing here?"
Our routine for almost 7 months has not helped the situation.
We spend most of our time on the ship, which is 607 ft. long and
about 50 ft. at its widest point. Our recreation consists of a few
hours a month in the jungle. Some of the men have not left the
ship in 7 months because there is nothing to amount to on the recreation parties. We seldom get a night's sleep. The only thing we
see is, glaring ocean, thick green jungle and tropical rain storms.
The heat and the tropical storms and humidity are wicked and of
course the Japs always keep the pressure on us, you never know
what the outcome will be when you take on the Japs.

As our task force made its way up the Solomons tonight, I got
a good look at the photographer we have aboard with us. He will
cover our bombardment of Munda tomorrow. He is a photographer for the Life Magazine and will stay at battle stations from
now until this operation is completed, that means another night
of no sleep.

Monday, July 12, 1943: After many hours at our battle stations
our task force finally reached Munda and at 3 A.M. this morning
we started our bombardment on the Japs. They must have been
sound asleep this early hour of the morning but it didn't take us
long to wake them up, the others died in their sleep. The Japs
were in for a nightmare. It did not take long after we opened up
on the Japs, we could see great explosions. They looked like fuel
and ammunition dumps, they went sky high. It was a pretty clear
morning, not as dark as some of our other attacks.

The reporter for Life Magazine was up on the highest spot of
the ship taking pictures of the action, he was very close to the
searchlights and was in a perfect spot to take in everything. We
gave the Japs an awful plastering. I would not want to be in their
shoes. During the bombardment the sprinkler system on our
40 mm. machine gun mount broke due to the heavy bombardment and the water began to pour down on the ammunition. Not
long after that happened Red Longfellow, our Mount Captain,
received word for all hands on our mount to leave, because the

twin five inch mount not too far away from us had a 5 inch shell stuck in the barrel and it could go off at any time, they call this a hang fire. If it went off it might cripple the ship.

After about a half hour of very ticklish work the shell was taken out and dropped over the side. A big redhead was the big factor in freeing it and he was later commended for his bravery. When the shell was first fired instead of going through the barrel and into the Japs it got stuck. While we were waiting for the shell to be freed it felt like we were sitting on a time bomb.

Jap planes also appeared on the scene but they were driven off. This was also navigation at its best on our part because we had to go through the very narrow passage of Blanche Channel which separates the islands of New Georgia and Rendova.

When our bombardment was completed Admiral Merrill and his task force headed for our base at Espiritu Santo, we would reach it in 2 days. When the sun came up we had to be on the alert for Jap planes. Nothing happened during the day, but still we could not take any chances.

At night we could see the Southern Cross in the sky, it was a very clear night and the sky was full of stars.

I guess this is the only place you can see it. It looks like a group of stars in the shape of a cross, it is something to see. It looks like another night with no sleep. Another task force will take our place up the Solomons while we return to our base for ammunition and fuel.

Each task force takes turns relieving the other. We have to keep warships up in the Solomons at night because the Jap warships might come down from their base and bombard our troops or bring in reinforcements.

July 13, 1943: While we were still on our way to our base at Espiritu Santo, we received word that the task force that relieved us ran into a task force of Jap warships and 3 of our light cruisers had their bows blown off. They were the two American cruisers *St. Louis* and *Honolulu;* and the New Zealand cruiser *Leander,* we also lost the destroyer *Gwin,* plus some destroyers damaged. The Japs lost a cruiser and 5 destroyers. This action also took place in the early morning darkness, in Kula Gulf for the second time in about one week. This is the second straight time that we could have ended in the bottom of Kula Gulf. Our task force changed course and headed back to the Solomons and Kula Gulf for Jap warships.

Yesterday a big force of over 100 American bombers and fighters flew over head. They were on their way to Munda. A big air battle was under way. At first our pilots were told to get the Jap bombers first but when the sky became so thick with Jap planes, they were told to use their own judgment. We spent the night and early morning hours looking for Jap warships but there were none to be found. We then headed south for Purvis Bay near Tulagi.

July 14, 1943: We pulled into Purvis Bay today. We pulled alongside a tanker for fuel, it had 5 Jap flags painted on it to represent the Jap planes it had shot down. The *Denver* was on the other side of the tanker, getting fuel. We were told that our ship had used 4 million gallons of fuel and traveled over 42,000 miles since it was commissioned in September 9, 1942. Most of the miles have been in enemy waters. Just seven months ago yesterday we left Philadelphia to come down here, just about three weeks after I left boot camp. Time out here has gone very fast.

While we were in the open waters near Guadalcanal today, the cruisers *St. Louis, Honolulu* and *Leander* passed us. They were returning at about 15 knots from the battle of Kula Gulf. If the Japs' torpedoes had hit them in the right spot, they would have ended up on the bottom of Kula Gulf like the *Helena.* The Jap torpedoes are very destructive and the Japs are experts in the use of them. They like to fill the water with them, and in the darkness it is hard to dodge them all. The 3 cruisers looked funny with no bows, it looked like they were playing follow the leader. The huge holes in the bows were big enough to run a freight train through. They said the casualties on our 2 ships were not heavy. I suppose they will call this the second battle of Kula Gulf. In the first battle we lost the cruiser *Helena,* our destroyers rescued hundreds from the water. This took place under the Japs' noses. The Jap-held islands were not too far away. This was heroism at its best. The Japs lost 15 warships, sunk or damaged, in the two battles of Kula Gulf.

Two of our task forces have been knocked out of action in a short period of time, that leaves us as the only task force in the South Pacific. It will be up to us to hold the Solomons. If the Japs ever send some battleships against us we will not stand a chance. The big Jap base of Rabaul on the island of New Britain is north of the Solomons and you never know when a big Jap task force of warships will come down into the Solomons. Our task force consists of 4 light cruisers and 8 destroyers and we are called Task Force 39, Cruiser division 12.

We will go up the Slot of the Solomons again tonight, to see if any Jap warships are to be found. We will stay up there until the early hours of tomorrow morning.

July 15, 1943: We returned from our prowl up the Slot in search of Jap ships but nothing happened. I guess the Japs are licking their wounds. We are now at Purvis Bay and tonight we will not go up the Slot. This will be the first time in quite some time. Two of our cruisers left today, we don't know where they are bound. A big LST pulled alongside today, they can carry 200 trucks, hundreds of troops, tanks, etc. The proper name is Landing Ships Tanks about 300 ft. long. It was about 6 P.M. when it got here. I spent some time talking to the crew and this is what they had to say. They brought close to 300 wounded troops from Munda to Guadalcanal and then came alongside our ship. A lot of the wounded were cut very badly by Jap knives. Many had to be strapped down because they were insane, they were given something to put them to sleep.

They said our troops go for days with very little sleep. They live in foxholes and when they get wounded or hurt, cut their clothes off to bind their wounds. The wounded troops whom they brought back had hardly any clothes on so the sailors gave them theirs. Fighting the Japs is like fighting a wild animal. The troops said that the Japs are as tough and fierce as they come; the Jap is not afraid to die, it is an honor to die for the Emperor, he is their God.

A lot of the fighting is done at night and you can smell the Japs

25 yards away. The jungle is very hot and humid and drains the
strength quickly. The jungle is also very thick; you could be right
next to a Jap and yet you could not see him. The Japs also have
Jap women with them. The Japs watch from coconut trees in the
daytime and then when it becomes dark they sneak into your foxhole and cut your throat or throw in a hand grenade. A 200 lb.
soldier was pulled from his foxhole and killed in short time. You
also hear all sorts of noises made by the animals and you think it
is the Japs. This is too much for some men and they crack up.

They say the Japs also have some Imperial Marines who are
6 ft. 4″ tall. The Japs are experts at jungle fighting and they
know all the tricks. You would hardly believe the tricks they use.
In the darkness for instance, they like to throw dirt in your eyes
and then attack you. Many of our troops get killed learning their
tricks. The Japs take all kinds of chances, they love to die. Our
troops are advancing slowly, it is a very savage campaign. Very
few Japs surrender, they die fighting, even when the situation is
hopeless.

We also have some Fiji Islanders fighting here. The Japs are
afraid of them. They love to cut the Japs up. One Fiji had 40 Jap
dog tags which he had taken from the Japs he killed. They said
the Japs bury their dead at night so you will not know how many
Japs had been killed. When the Japs hear our wounded troops
moaning, they fire in the direction of the sound. When the Fiji
Islanders see a coconut tree with mud on it, they know a Jap is up
in the top hiding. Jap bombers fly very close together and this
formation makes it easy for the guns on the ground to hit them.

When I finished talking with the crew on the LST they showed
me Jap guns, swords, etc. that they picked up at Munda. They
said that they landed troops, supplies etc.

Sunday, July 25, 1943: I have not done any writing since July
15, because we had about the same routine. We went up the
Slot and landed more troops on Munda yesterday morning, Saturday, July 24 at one in the morning. The Japs are putting up a
stiffer fight for Munda than we expected. We have not taken

Munda yet, however, the Japs have only small arms to fight with now, but in jungle fighting, that is enough to make the fighting last for quite some time to come.

Today we are out on patrol, we will patrol the Able Fox line. This will put us in a position to intercept the Jap navy, if they try anything. One of the destroyers in our task force sunk a Jap sub that tried to set us up for the kill.

The other night while we were on our way up the Slot in search of Jap ships, they played the recordings of George M. Cohan. It was very colorful to hear these great songs as Old Glory waved in the breeze, and the sun setting in the distance. They finished the program with the Marine Hymn as the "Monty" cut her way through the calm Pacific.

Wednesday, August 11, 1943: We left Purvis Bay in the Solomons yesterday and expect to pull into Espiritu Santo, New Hebrides, tomorrow. We had a bad accident today. One of the men from the 7th division was crushed to death this morning. He was standing near the 6 inch director as it turned around. It crushed him against the steel bulkhead.

This is what has happened in the past 17 days. We spent 2 days on maneuvers with 30 warships. The force consisted of carriers, battleships, cruisers and destroyers, the carrier *Saratoga* was also with us. While I was on recreation, at Espiritu Santo I came across an Australian sailor. He was in the Java Sea battle in 1942 and other engagements against the Japs. He was from the cruiser *Hobart* and his ship was hit by a Jap torpedo the other night just before supper. All the lights on the ship went out, the huge turret was blown up in the air and fell back in the same place. They did not lose many men. The men are having a lot of trouble with skin rash from the heat. This has been going on for some time. Out here you sweat 24 hours a day, and that makes it impossible to cure the heat rash. Some of the fellows are in bad shape but the Dr. cannot help them. Some of the men's rash have turned into big sores. Many of the men also have trouble with their eyes, they are full of pus.

My eyelashes fall out and when I wake up in the morning I

have to put some saliva on my eyes to loosen them because they are stuck together. Some days I have a rugged time with my eyes owing to the pain. The climate and our diet plus very little sleep are to blame for our ailments. Some of the men have their whole body covered with a rash and sores. The rash gives you no rest, it itches and it is impossible to sleep below because of the heat. It is hard to breathe and you would wake up in a pool of sweat. Some of the men sweat so much in their bunks that they could not stand up, they were sick and dizzy from the heat and sweating. We had to take them to sick bay. The steel bulkhead is so hot during the day you cannot touch it in the compartments. When you go to the toilet the sweat just rolls off your whole body. It is just like standing under a shower. Sleep is also a hard thing to get, because you never know when a shower will come up and you have to run for cover. You stand there until it stops. It is too hot to sleep below in the compartments.

We have been eating bread that is full of little hard bugs for quite some time and this will not change because of the heat. When you put a slice of bread up in front of you, there seems to be as many bugs in it as there is bread. The flour is full of these small bugs, it would be impossible to separate the bugs from the flour. The bugs breed very fast in the heat down here. The bugs in our bread do not bother us, we are used to them. When you carry a bag of flour on your shoulder you get covered with these bugs.

On Sunday, August 1, I started my 3 months of mess cooking.

We traveled 10,000 miles in the month of July, most of it was up the Slot on the prowl for Jap warships.

On August 7, Munda fell to our troops, just one year after the Marines landed on Guadalcanal, the first allied invasion of the Pacific War. The fighting on Munda was rugged. We have taken about 3/4 of the Solomons, so far. If we try to take island by island it will take years to beat the Japs because they are like animals and you have to go into or blow them out of every foxhole, lime cave, or coconut tree and kill them all because they all fight while there is any life left in them. We received a message from Gen-

eral MacArthur congratulating us for our part in the capture of
Munda.

Saturday, September 3, 1943: We are now at Espiritu Santo.
For the 1st time in almost ten months we finally spent one day on
shore. This was quite a treat for us because we usually spend a
couple of hours on the beach when we have recreation, and that
wasn't too often. We left the ship in the morning on a landing
craft and did not return until around supper time. We had a
great time for ourselves. This would not be much of a treat for
the fellows with good duty in the States and other good places but
to us it was something great. We were very happy, and did not
have a worry or care in the world. We had hot dogs, cake, salad
and 4 small bottles of beer. We were able to buy ice cream and
Coca-Cola at the stand. We went swimming in the morning at
Paradise Beach. We had to walk through the jungle to get there.
The beach is shaped like a huge horseshoe. It is surrounded by
coconut trees and jungle and it is at the farthest end of the huge
bay. It is open sea, there is also plenty of sand on the shore. It is
beautiful here. The water was warm, we had a great time riding
the tide. You just had to lay in the water and it would ride you
into the shore, it seemed to hold you up. We also went looking
for cat eyes and other seashells. At the other end of the bay some
distance away near the open sea you could see something that
looked like a native village, but we are not allowed to go down
that far. You could see some natives in small boats on their way
to the village.

In the afternoon we took a stroll into the jungle to pick some
fruit, and we came across a big open spot with about 75 cows in it.
We were surprised when we saw them. We did not know if the
natives or the Gov't owns them. You can sell your beer checks for
2 for $3.

This is the best recreation spot we hit so far. You can play baseball, basketball, you can get the baseballs and gloves and boxing
gloves at one of the stands. All you have to do is give your dog tag
number. The ships have a baseball and softball league and play
each other when they are in port. When the softball league

opened, Admiral Merrill threw out the first ball and the *Mont-pelier* won its first game. We have a very good team. The pitcher is as good as they come. Capt. Tobin, Commander Koonce, and the Capts. from many of the other ships were at the game. The band from the repair ship *Dixie* played the National Anthem.

We also spent 6 days at sea on maneuvers and war games. We had about 30 warships in our force, carriers, battleships, cruisers and destroyers. The last few days we were up near Bougainville waiting for Japs to come out and attack our other task force who are doing a job on other Jap islands somewhere around the Gilbert Islands, I think, but the Japs did not do anything so we went back.

Some new men from the States have been assigned to our ship. I was talking to one of them, who was on the cruiser *San Francisco* when it was ripped to shambles by Jap battleships in the Solomons, and he said that after the battle you could walk around the ship and pick up arms, legs, etc. The dead were everywhere.

Joe Whittaker from our division made Coxswain, and Younce borrowed some money from me. I spent only $5 in the past month. When they put the pay slips in the mess hall, everyone likes to see how much money they have coming to them. The money increases a lot each month because there is no place to spend it here.

A big American task force of carrier planes and warships are giving the Gilbert Islands quite a pounding. The Gilberts are over 1000 miles north of here on the other side of the equator. Now that I am mess cooking I eat better and get more sleep. I take good care of my friends when I pass out the chow. When we are not at battle stations I have the early morning coffee watch 3 to 4 A.M. I do not have to stand the regular gun watches.

Monday, September 6, 1943: We are still at Espiritu Santo. The light cruiser *Columbia* left for Sydney, Australia, today. They expect to stay there for 10 days. It will take 3 days to get there and 3 to return. When they come back the cruiser *Cleveland* will go and then we will follow the *Cleveland* when it returns. We will leave for Australia in about 6 weeks. All the fellows are getting their blues pressed and fixed.

September 9, 1943: We received word of Italy's surrender to-night at 7:30 P.M. I was busy cleaning the mess hall.

September 18, 1943: Today was a very outstanding day for the men who went over to the beach in the afternoon. We saw our first woman in almost 10 months and it happened to be the First Lady of the United States. It was President Roosevelt's wife, Mrs. Franklin D. Roosevelt. She spoke to hundreds of sailors and marines who are stationed on the ships here. Her talk lasted about 10 minutes, then she walked around to see what the place looked like, she was with some officers and a woman from the Red Cross. The outfit she wore was very nice, she is much better looking in person. While she was here she also paid a visit on the other side of the island to see the wounded troops in the hospitals. Before coming here she visited New Zealand and Australia.

I watched them load a troopship yesterday. We can see the big transport planes going back and forth with supplies and the wounded, they are called C–46 and C–47 transports, they have 2 motors. They say that the harbor here at Espiritu Santo and Havannah Harbor also in the New Hebrides group are two of the best natural harbors in the world. You do not have to walk very far from shore in order to drop into a great depth of water.

Monday, September 20, 1943: The mess cooks had to get up at 3:15 A.M. this morning. We had to get mess hall ready for Special Sea Detail. Our task force left Espiritu Santo at 7 A.M. this morning. We are on our way to something important, no one knows what it is all about yet. On our way to our destination we had a lot of gunnery. Our guns shot down quite a few sleeves that were towed at the end of a plane. The mess cooks had to get a lot of food in the hangar, for what lies ahead of us. It looks like we will spend a lot of time at battle stations.

Tuesday, September 21, 1943: Today is the 1st day of Autumn. We went to general quarters at 5:04 A.M. this morning. Capt. Tobin spoke to the crew and said that he received word that the Japs were on their way down the Solomons, with a fleet of warships to reinforce or evacuate their troops at Vella Lavella or Kolombangara, and that we were on our way up to stop them. He said we would be at battle stations all night and that we might come in contact with them about 4 in the A.M. He said we could expect air attacks, and to keep our sleeves down at all times, in case of flash burns. We had cake for one of our meals so I put a lot of it in a cracker box. The boys on my gun mount will eat well. The fellows will be able to buy candy bars for their long hours at battle stations. As Chief Master at Arms Rath put it, it looks like we will beat the Japs again with candy bars. I will write later.

Sunday, September 26, 1943: We have been very busy for the past 5 days and nights looking for Jap warships in their own back yard but we could not find any. Our base of operations was Tulagi. Every day we would leave Tulagi at 4 P.M. for our trip up the Slot, and we would not return until the next day at noon. The few hours we stayed in Tulagi just flew, and then we were on our way back up the Slot again, we also got fuel before we left. The men were always on the go.

One night the Japs pulled one of their famous tricks on us from one of their islands and one of the cruisers fell for it. Our Captain, Captain Tobin, did not fall for it because he had seen the Japs do it before. The Japs on the beach would light a big fire, hoping that one of our ships would start firing at it. A Jap sub would be hiding close by. When our ships opened up, they would make a beautiful target for the sub to put a few torpedoes into it and sink it. We were very fortunate nothing happened that night.

One morning at daybreak we were very close to Munda and Vila. We had a good look at them but did not stay there long because it was too close to land and mainly too close to Jap airfields. If the Japs came over those high green hills with their planes, we would make easy targets for them. The jungle here is very green and also very thick, like a thick green wall. No wonder our troops had such a tough time fighting the Japs. The jungle must be very hot and humid. There are also some very high spots around here. The place is nothing but a green hellhole.

Tulagi is another hellhole similar to Munda and Vila, it is about the hottest place of them all. You never get a breeze, and the heat and humidity saps your strength away. If you do get a little sleep, you wake up feeling very sluggish. The heat from the big blowers that surround the ship, plus the heat that the steel throws from the hot sun pouring down on it from sunrise to sunset, does not help the situation to say the least. Tulagi is one place we will be glad to leave, they can give it back to the natives.

We left for Espiritu Santo because we were low on food. On our way to Espiritu Santo I brought the fellows on the midnight to 4 A.M. watch a big cherry pie. It was funny to see them eating pie at that time of morning but it really hit the spot. Mess cooking gives a fellow a chance to get plenty of fruit and sweets. Now that I'm mess cooking, the fellows are trying to bang ears with me, ha, ha. I almost forgot to mention that I saw a ship made of cement, it was one of ours, a tanker.

October 1943: We stayed at Espiritu Santo for two days and then headed back to Tulagi. On the way to Tulagi, you would find some of the men playing card games, writing letters, fooling with each other, or just sitting around talking. When we pulled into Tulagi, they told us that our destroyers went up the Slot the night before, and sunk 20 barges, Japs of course, loaded with troops. At 2 P.M. one afternoon, we received word that we were to leave at once for the Slot because the Tokyo Express was on its way down, and this time it had battleships with it. We traveled many miles up the Slot but we did not run into any Japs. They must have changed plans and returned to their base.

The Japs are evacuating their troops from Kolombangara with destroyers and barges at night and in the early morning hours. Our PT boats have been doing quite a job on the loaded barges up the Slot. One night we went up the Slot and ran into a group of barges loaded with Jap troops plus some destroyers. When it was all over the ships in our force sunk three destroyers and many barges. We lit the place up with star shells so that our destroyers could go in and slaughter the Japs. Our task force did not lose a ship. This took place about 250 miles from our base at Tulagi.

Just before we went to battle stations, it rained very hard for about 20 minutes, and after that we had a lot of heat lightning. The action against the Japs lasted about one hour and during that time it looked like the 4th of July. Jap float planes were overhead dropping flares. Warships were blazing away with shells and lighting up the place with star shells. Explosions could be seen all around us as our shells hit their targets. The Japs lost a great many troops and the sharks and fish ate good that night. The flares that the Jap planes dropped would go on and off in the water for a long time. They reminded me of a beacon. Someone said the reason for this was so the pilot could stay on course and also tip the Japs to where we were. It was a good thing for us that there were no Jap subs around because the place was really lit up. Our radar could not pick the subs up because we were so close to land. For many nights the Japs tried to evacuate their troops and every night the loaded barges would be destroyed by our ships. Thousands of Jap troops were slaughtered this way. The Japs never give up. They fight to the finish.

After our stay in the Solomons was over, we left for Espiritu Santo. While we were there, we received a new head doctor in place of Dr. Crosland, a Dr. Butler. Dr. Crosland must be going back to the States, everybody liked him. We did not stay very long at Espiritu Santo. We spent almost a week at sea with a task force of carriers, battleships, cruisers and destroyers. We had the battleships *Massachusetts, Washington, Alabama, South Dakota* and *North Carolina* with us. We spent many hours at battle stations during maneuvers and did everything in the books but fire live ammunition at each other. The smoke screens from our planes were so thick that you could not see the other ships for quite some time. We pulled into Espiritu Santo after our war games. While we were there the men were kept very busy painting the ship and getting it ready for our trip to good old Australia. We also spent a few hours of recreation on the beach, this was our first in about one month. The recreation is getting better. The movie stars, Ray Bolger and Jack Little, put on a good show while we were there. Everyone enjoyed it. This was something new for us. Our entertainment is usually plenty of fights. Some of the men get too much beer in them and all they want to do is fight, of course the ones who don't drink also go at it too.

The fellows come back to the ship with black eyes, etc. There is never a dull moment. One night while we were in port, Jap planes paid us a call at 11:30 P.M., but they did no damage.

Friday, October 15, 1943: Today was a very happy day for the men of the *Montpelier*. At 4:30 P.M. we left Espiritu Santo for Sydney, Australia; we took one destroyer with us.

Sunday, October 17, 1943: We pulled into Noumea, New Caledonia, about 6 A.M. and left the same day about noon. We picked up a lot of big brass such as English and Australian Generals and Captains and also a few Canadians. We also took on about 125 new men from the States. They have spent about a month here at Noumea. We got a kick out of them. They are real "boots." They do not know the navy lingo and are always getting lost on the ship. They do not know if they are coming or going. This is a new world for them. Most of them got out of boot camp about three months ago and have been tossed around ever since. Well now they have a permanent home for quite some time. They got a break being assigned to our ship just as we are on our way to Australia. We put on a gunnery show for our Australian, British and Canadian friends. We fired all guns. The weather on the way down was cool and we had to wear our heavy winter pea coats. We could use some of this weather in the Solomons.

Tuesday, October 19, 1943: About 6 A.M. we sighted Australia. We dropped anchor at 12:01 P.M., I should know the time because I won $250 in the anchor pool. The ship moved very slowly as it came alongside the pier but just slowly enough for me to win. You do not have to walk very far from the ship to the street outside of the pier. The houses and buildings are not too far away. Everyone was in dress blues and at quarters as we pulled into Sydney. I was on the port side, not too far from the quarterdeck. As we pulled into Sydney harbor we could see a long mass of solid stone. It looked like a cliff. It was very high, on the summit were many houses. As we drew closer we had a better view of Sydney. It looked like any large city in the States and appeared very clean. The bridge reminded one of the Golden Gate Bridge in California. The weather was beautiful, like a warm spring day at home.

A ferryboat passed close by as we were pulling in. It carried many people. They began to wave to us and we waved back. It was quite a sight and also quite a feeling to be back in civilization for the first time in almost a year. It was just as if we were coming home. A feeling came over us that we could not explain. It seemed like paradise. Summer begins December 21 in Australia, so it must be spring here now. Australia is larger than the United States but its population is only about six million. It is also the oldest continent in the world.

Later: Liberty started at 1 P.M. and we did not have to be back to the ship until the next morning at 11 A.M. There are three sections of us so that means we stay on the ship one day and have two days off. I am in the second section so we left the ship at one in the afternoon. The first thing I did was to go to an eye doctor and make an appointment. The secretary asked me if I was sure of keeping the appointment and I said I would, not knowing that I would be refused permission to go because it was one of the days I did not rate liberty. The doctor was the best in the region. He took care of the Australian Air Force. It did not take us long to find out that the Australian girls really went wild over the American sailors. The Australian people are very friendly and love the Americans. Some of the girls knew every state in the Union and its capital.

This was the first time in over 10 months for some of the men to leave the ship and put their feet on land. Donovan went 9 months.

Later: I will now try to cover some of the things we did while in Sydney: We had a big dance for the crew at the Grace Auditorium. The auditorium was full of girls. They also had a good floor show. You could have all the food, beer and Coca-Cola you wanted. The mess cooks had to serve. I waited on Admiral Merrill and Captain Tobin. Everyone had a great time.

When you leave the ship you go through a big beautiful park to get to the business section of Sydney. The name of the place is Hyde Park. The first thing that catches your eye are all the beautiful girls. The place is full of them. There are supposed to be five

(5) girls to every man but I think there are even more than that. Everyone is so friendly down here. I never saw such friendly people. The girls in the States could really learn something from the girls here. They treat you as if you were related and invite you to their homes to meet the family.

The little towns on the outskirts of Sydney were very pretty, most of the houses had a lot of flowers and a fence around it. You could smell lilacs as they were everywhere. Because of the war the taxis were run on coal and wood. Things are very cheap here and it does not cost much for a good time. We got fresh food for a change and our fortunes turned to the better as milk was acquired. It was our first milk in almost a year. All the beer parlors closed at 6 P.M. in this city of about two million. Nightclubs were open very late. The dance halls are always full. They are very nice and the orchestras are very good. Only two movies are open on Sunday and they are for servicemen and their girlfriends.

Sunday, October 24, 1943: We were told to be back to the ship at midnight instead of 11 A.M. Monday morning. That means we stay here only five days and get only three days of liberty. We were supposed to stay here ten days but will have to cut our stay short because we are going to invade Bougainville, the largest island in the Solomons, and also the last island in that group. If we take that, the Solomons will be ours. They say we might come back to Australia again sometime.

On my last day of liberty I bought a carton of cigarettes on ship for an Australian friend of mine as a gift. I left the ship with the cigarettes tied under my pant leg, and would have looked foolish if they had fallen down as I walked the gangway after saluting the flag and the officer of the deck. American cigarettes are like gold here. The last night we spent in Australia, everyone had to be back on the ship at midnight. Everyone had a great time and met many nice people. We did not like to leave. When you know it's your last night in civilization, you could walk on the soil all night, and just breathe the fresh air. It feels so good. You know it will be some time before you put your feet on anything like this again. It reminds you of when you go swimming and the water feels so good you hate to get out. As you walk back to the ship, it is very dark and quiet, everyone is asleep. The streets are deserted. Everything is so peaceful and quiet, you would not know that there was a war on. Then you think of the nice time you had and the friendly people you have met. They make you feel as if you had known them all your life. For many a day to come your mind will be miles away, thinking of the people you have met and the places you have visited. It is an experience you will never forget. You will put Australia down as the best liberty port in the world. You will also put the Australians in the same class as the Americans. The Australians think there is no one like the Americans and the Americans think there is no one like the Australians. When you go to Australia it is like coming home. It is too bad our country is so far away. Our best friends are Australians and we should never let them down, we should help them every chance we get.

Monday, October 25, 1943: We left Sydney, Australia, at 7 A.M. One of the Marines just made the ship before we pulled out. It was very hard to leave Sydney. Everyone hopes the ship will come back again soon.

Friday, October 29, 1943: We landed back in Tulagi in the Solomons. A lot of mail was waiting for us when we got here. I received gum from my sister Mary. Gum is hard to come by, in fact impossible. I wrote a few letters on our way from Australia. We had movies in the hangar. The cruiser *Nashville* pulled into the harbor with us today. The *Nashville* was one of the ships in the task force that Jimmy Doolittle used when he bombed Tokyo in 1942. I never saw so many ships in this harbor before. I remember the time when there were only three ships here and that included us. We never knew when the Jap Air Force would try to sneak in on us. It is much safer here now. We have pushed the Japs back hundreds of miles since those early days of the Solomons campaign. We have about five cruisers and about fifteen destroyers and many other kinds of ships.

One of the crew was talking about a story he heard from an American soldier who spent many months fighting the Japs in New Guinea. He said at one time our troops were fighting the

Japs with mud balls and knives, they were out of ammunition etc. Some of our whole outfits were wiped out by the Japs. Sometimes they were bombed by our own planes because the jungle was so thick. Our wounded would be lost in the jungle for a week before being found. Many of our troops went insane. The Japs had a great habit of surrendering and then when they got close to you, they would throw hand grenades. He said the Australians are great fighters, they would rather lay down their guns and fight the Japs with their knives.

Saturday, October 30, 1943: All hands up at 6 A.M. The plan of the day said that a destroyer would be named in honor of our late Captain Wood. We are supposed to leave here tomorrow for the invasion of Bougainville. The *Nashville* has just come back from the States. It spent three months there. They have almost 700 new "boots" out of a crew of about 1200 men. Two of our destroyers had their bows blown off. What a mess. It happened up the Slot of the Solomons while we were gone. They have portable fans in the mess hall. They are really needed down here but still they don't help much. We had church services at 3 P.M. on the forecastle today. Captain Tobin never misses church services. The priest who said the Mass was a prisoner of the Japs at one time.

Sunday, October 31, 1943: It is the last day of the month and also the last day for mess cooking. These three months sure went fast. Now I shall go hungry again. The only good meal we get is at noon. I shall start standing gun watches again. On the regular watch on our 40 mm. machine gun mount we have about six men on watch. When you step into the mount, it is like going into a hot oven. You say to yourself, "How can anyone stand that terrific heat for four hours with the hot sun beating down on you and the heat from the blowers pouring it on, not to mention the hot steel of the mount that almost surrounds you." You could not stand on the steel deck without shoes on. The temperature is way over 100 degrees. The sweat just rolls off you into your shoes and onto the steel deck. We have to keep wetting the canvas that covers the ammunition. The humidity just saps the strength from you and you do not get any breeze. You and another man stand

one hour on the lookout and then you sit in the hot pointer's or
trainer's seat for another hour, this is the toughest because you
cannot move around. You just sit there in the hot steel seat and
sweat. The glare from the sun and the water is very tough on the
eyes. The 12 noon to 4 P.M. watch is always the hottest. It is also
hard to stay awake when you are in the Japs' back yard at two or
three in the morning when you are standing lookout in front of
the gun mount. You have had very little sleep to start with and
while you are on the lookout for Jap subs or torpedoes your feet
just buckle under you. You are dead tired and actually fall asleep
standing up. You force yourself to stay awake but it is a losing
proposition. You continue to doze off for a split second, your
head droops, feet buckle under you and then you are awake again
to do the same thing all over again. While this is going on the
Mount Captain is walking back and forth pushing the fellows and
barking at them to stay awake. It is really the Agony in the Garden. This is what you call torture. If the guns are firing, we have
no trouble staying awake. When we stand watch in port at night
and one of the fellows should doze off in the pointer's or trainer's
seat, he gets two buckets of water in the face. Everyone goes up to
the fellow asleep and someone puts his hands in front of his eyes;
if he does not move, we know he is asleep. The bucket brigade
then goes into action. When he gets hit with the first bucket of
water, it almost knocks him out of his seat, and when he opens his
eyes, he gets the second bucket. It is better than a circus. The
rest of the crew break their sides laughing. The payoff comes
when he says that he was not sleeping, he was resting his eyes. It
does not take very long to dry your clothes because the water is
warm and the weather is very hot. This ceremony usually takes
place on the midnight to four in the morning watch.

After all this talk about what we do while on watch, it looks
like we are going to spend many days there, starting today. At
2:30 A.M., October 31, 1943, we left Tulagi in the Solomons. It's
very dark as usual. Every time we hit the Japs it is pitch black.
There is no moon. This way the Japs will not see us. We are going to travel about 500 or 600 miles up the Solomons to bombard

the Japs on Buka and Bonis. This will take place after midnight. When we finish we will turn around and pull off our first daylight bombardment of the war, on the Shortlands. It is also heavily defended. Bonis is a strong base on the furthest tip of Bougainville. The Japs will have plenty of planes on the airfields here. Above Bonis is the Jap-held island of Buka. Buka is between Bougainville and the Jap fortress of New Britain and New Ireland. It looks like we will have our work cut out for us. All hands were told to get as much rest in the afternoon as we could. The sun is shining and it is hot as usual. The sea is calm. As I look out on the starboard side, I can see many transports, supply ships, invasion barges, etc. Large barrage balloons fly above many of the ships. They will come in handy against Jap planes. This is the first time I have seen these in a convoy. We must have about 70 or 80 ships with us.

Bougainville is about 200 miles long. It is also the largest island in the Solomons. The jungle there is about the thickest in the Solomons. It also has high mountains. Most of the waters around Bougainville are uncharted and we have to go by photos taken from the air or old charts that are not complete. You never know when the ship will get stuck on a reef and stay there. The Japs would love to see that happen right in their own back yard. Our five and six inch guns will fire thousands of shells during these bombardments.

November 1, 1943: At 12:30 A.M. this morning Admiral Merrill's task force of four light cruisers and eight destroyers started bombarding the Japs on Buka and Bonis. They are very close to each other. We kept up constant bombardment for almost one hour. The pilots in the Black Cats overhead kept us informed about what was happening to the Jap targets. We got close to shore and you could see many explosions on the beach. Our gunnery was good. We were destroying ammunition dumps, fuel dumps, troops and the Jap airfields with their planes parked there. The Japs sent planes into the air and dropped flares so that the shore guns could go to town on us. This also made it easy for the PT boats that came out of their hiding places. We made it too hot for the PT boats. One of them was blown to bits. We also had to be on the watch for Jap subs. The big Jap shore guns were also firing at us, their shells were exploding all around us. They came too close for comfort. A piece of shrapnel came through the bridge hitting Admiral Merrill's typewriter. The way things were exploding, it looked like a shooting gallery. We left the place a mass of flames and explosions. Hours later we could still see the big fires burning about 60 miles away. We are surrounded by Jap-held islands. We are the first warships to travel this far to the north. Still further north is the powerful Jap-held base of Rabaul. We are about 600 miles from our base in Tulagi. When it gets light, the Jap Air Force will be out looking for us.

Later: After the bombardment of Buka and Bonis we headed south again. Our next target would be the Shortlands. They are south of Bougainville and are very formidable. On our way to bombard the Shortlands we spent our time carrying the empty powder cases, and fresh ammunition was carried up to be ready for our next bombardment. Many parts of the ship had sprung loose from the heavy bombardment and they were taken care of. One thing was sure we would not get any sleep. By bombarding Buka, the Japs would think that we were going to land there, and that would make our landing on Bougainville that much easier. While all this was going on, our troops were landing on Bougainville at Empress Augusta Bay. The crews on those transports and supply ships would work night and day getting them empty so they could be on their way south to the safety of their home base.

The hours passed as we sailed south in the direction of the Shortlands and about six in the morning we started bombarding the Japs on the Shortlands. This was something new for us, it was our first daylight bombardment.* For the past year all our work was done in the dark. Now we will be able to see the enemy if he tries to sneak up on us. When we bombarded the Shortlands, one ship was behind the other, just like follow the leader. It consisted of four light cruisers and eight destroyers. Every ship gave the Japs on the island quite a broadside. It was not long before the

---

* It turned out this was the first time in the war such a bombardment had been attempted against a functional Jap base.

Japs' big six inch shore guns opened up on us. We held our breath as the shells straddled us. They were falling all around us. Big geysers of water could be seen shooting into the air as the shells exploded close by. Just a little closer and we would have had it. The Japs' marksmanship is very good. We are like a bunch of ducks in a shooting gallery as we pass in view of the Japs, and their shore guns. One of our destroyers was hit by a six inch shell but the casualties were light. Smoke could be seen rising from the destroyer. The Japs also had some torpedo boats nearby. Our ships were twisting and turning to keep from being hit as our guns blazed away at the Jap seaplane hangars, shore batteries, repair shops, airfields, troops, etc. Many fires were started as our guns hit their targets. Our bombardment lasted about three quarters of an hour. When we had finished, we continued on our way south with the Jap shore guns still firing at us.

We stayed at our battle stations for many hours and then we set the regular watch. The decks were covered with empty powder cases. We spent sometime getting them out of the way. In the afternoon General Quarters sounded. A big force of Jap planes including bombers were on their way down from Rabaul. They were going to hit the beachhead of Empress Augusta Bay where our troops landed. Our task force was also an objective. Out of nowhere our planes came to the rescue. Both Air Forces were very large. It was a full scale air battle. Our pilots were coming out on top. All the ships were getting low on fuel, especially the destroyers. We had been going at high speed for some time and covered many miles. We could expect more trouble. The Japs would not give up in a hurry without putting up a fight. They did not want to lose the big island of Bougainville because we would be able to knock out their big bases on New Britain, New Ireland and New Guinea with our planes and bombers.

Tuesday, November 2, 1943: We got two hours' sleep as we continued south but 12:45 A.M. this morning General Quarters sounded. Everyone was very tired as he ran to his battle station in the early morning darkness, not knowing what we were in for. We did know that when we left our base at Tulagi, Sunday at 2:30 A.M., that most of the time would be spent at battle stations without sleep. Our food during that time was mostly sandwiches. The reason for battle stations was that a task force of Jap warships were on their way down from Rabaul to sink our transports and supply ships that were unloading at Empress Augusta Bay, Bougainville. Their objective also included bombarding our Marines and Army troops on the shore. The Japs' force packed a bigger wallop than ours. They had two heavy cruisers with them. Our biggest ships were our four light cruisers. The Japs had eight inch guns, our biggest were six inch guns. The Japs had two heavy cruisers, two light cruisers and eight destroyers. We had the light cruisers *Columbia, Cleveland, Denver,* and *Montpelier,* and the destroyers *Ausburne, Dyson, Claxton, Stanley, Spence, Converse, Thatcher,* and *Foote.* The action took place off the shores of Empress Augusta Bay. Our troops on shore had a ringside seat. Our job was to prevent the Jap warships from sneaking into the bay during the darkness and inflicting damage on our ships and troops there. The Japs knew these waters better than we. We never knew when our ships would get stuck on one of those uncharted reefs. Our charts were about fifty years old and were not complete. During this action only the five and six inch guns were to fire. That would give the machine guns a chance to take in the fireworks. We would be ready if they needed us.

You sense a funny feeling as both task forces race towards each other. We know the Japs are coming but do the Japs know that they will run into us in their own waters? Time passes as we stand there on the 40 mm. gun mount. The twin five inch mount is only a few feet away. The mount keeps moving around and you wonder if we will hit the Japs first or will they beat us to the punch. We keep getting reports on how close we are getting to the Japs. Finally . . . "Commence Firing."

It is about 2:45 A.M. Tuesday, November 2, 1943, and all hell breaks loose. The battle is on. Our guns are pouring it on as they maneuver. It is very dark and heat lightning can be seen during the battle along with a drizzle. Our ship did not waste any time in that it hit a Jap heavy cruiser. Flames and explosions were everywhere. When it was all over, the ship was dead in the water. It finally sunk. Jap shells were falling all around us and some of our ships were also getting hit. Both sides were firing away at each other. The water was full of American and Japanese torpedoes as destroyers from both sides attacked. The big eight inch salvos, throwing up great geysers of water, were hitting very close to us. The water sprayed the ship just in front of our mount. There are great explosions as some ships sink very fast. We received reports from the other ships that they had been hit. The cruiser *Denver* was hit and had another close call as a shell went through the smokestack. It would have been all over if it went down the stack. During all this action our ship was hit by two Jap torpedoes but they did not explode. There was also a near miss for one of our own destroyers as it came out of the darkness and came close to ramming our starboard side. It was going in the same direction in chase of a Jap warship. For a while we thought it would crash into our ship. Our force fired star shells in front of the Jap warships so that our destroyers could attack with torpedoes. It was like putting a bright light in front of your eyes in the dark. It is impossible to see. The noise from our guns was deafening. The guns on the port and starboard had plenty of firing as we kept cutting back and forth. They say the maneuvers Admiral Merrill pulled off in this sea battle would put German Admiral Sheer of World War I fame to shame. Sheer pulled his tactics in daylight off Jutland but Merrill had darkness to cope with and twice the speed. These maneuvers are very dangerous as collisions are the rule. It's a wonder the ships could work as a team in the darkness, each picking out his own target. During the action Jap float planes were overhead dropping flares. There are big explosions as some ships sink and others are dead in the water. The Jap warships lit the sea aglow with star shells. The destroyer *Foote* is now out of action, being hit by a Jap torpedo. The Jap Admiral* was the best the Japs had and he tried every trick in the book. Admiral Merrill was better. When things looked bad and

---

* The name of the Japanese Admiral who was in command of the Jap task force was Rear Admiral Sentaro Omori of the Eighth Fleet. It was a section of Admiral Kogas' combined fleet. At the time of our sea battle, the Jap Admiral thought we had twice as many ships than what we actually did have. Our fire power was terrific. We were part of Admiral William F. "Bull" Halsey's 3rd Fleet. Admiral Merrill was in command.

the sea was lit up by the Jap star shells, Admiral Merrill ordered a smoke screen. Thick black smoke engulfed the area. The Japs found it next to impossible to strike at us. We also were on the alert for Jap subs, and torpedo boats and to make sure none of the enemies' warships could sneak into the bay and fire on our transports and troops there. The battle raged hour after hour. No quarter was given by the Japs or us. It was a battle between two masters of naval warfare and the tide of battle could be turned at any time. During the battle one could see that the Jap star shells were brighter than ours. They really lit the place up. It's a funny sensation expecting to be hit by Jap or for that matter any shell or torpedo. I'll feel much better when it gets dark again. Sometimes we fired at Jap star shells and put them out. The sky was full of shells.

As the sea battle was coming to an end we passed a Jap ship under attack at close range. We did not fire on the Jap ship because we were very low on ammunition and our help was not needed. This action took place on our starboard side not too far away. It seemed like it was getting a little brighter as I watched the action. The Jap ship was dead in the water. I did not notice any other ships around but the three of us. The Jap ship was a mass of flames and red hot steel as the big guns covered it with exploding shells. It gave off a red glow that lit up the area around it. It must have been a nightmare in hell for the Japs as they were roasted and blown to bits. I don't see how anyone could escape. It was a horrible way to die, it was a slaughter. This type of warfare tops them all for horror. There is no safe place to hide and if you land in the water the huge sharks that are longer than a good-sized room are always close by. Our ships are now running low on ammunition and some of the destroyers have only star shells left, because of our earlier bombardments against the Japs. Our ship is also getting low on fuel. If this keeps up, we will only have machine guns and potatoes to fire at the Jap warships. After three hours of fighting, the Japs have had enough and head for their base at Rabaul. It's approximately 5:45 A.M. We started the engagement at 2:45 A.M. Losses for the Japs — at least One (1) heavy cruiser, and Four (4) destroyers sunk and Two (2) cruisers and Two (2) destroyers were severely damaged. Our ship accounted for one destroyer and one cruiser, the rest of the task force took care of the rest. Every ship in the force was in on the kill. At daylight nothing could be seen on deck except empty shell cases. The men on the five and six inch mounts and turrets looked like a bunch of ghosts. They were all worn out from lack of sleep, heat, very little food and the bombardments. Oh yes, I forgot to mention the sea battle. The men had spent the past three hours in a hot steaming steel mount or turret passing shells or powder cases. The six inch armor-piercing shells weigh 135 pounds and the heavy brass powder cases are approximately four feet long. They get very little air and the heat is unbearable. I imagine they believed that the firing would never stop. The steel decks were rivers of water from their perspiration. The weather from beginning to end was similar to a heat wave back home in August. Why they did not pass out from exhaustion was a miracle. They were all out on their feet. I would not want to be in their shoes for a million. When we go into action, the air blowers are shut off and the ones who are shut in really suffer. They actually gasp for fresh air. The ship keeps twisting and turning and they don't know what to expect from the enemy. The men who are many decks below in the handling rooms, have a tough job sending the ammunition up. They are surrounded by tons of ammunition. If a torpedo ever happens to explode close by, they drown like a bunch of rats. It's a long way up to topside.

It's still Tuesday morning, November 2, the same day of the sea battle. It is a beautiful warm sunny day as we make our way south to our base at Tulagi. We have still to be on the alert for Jap planes for they will be out looking for us.

Later: Approximately 8:30 A.M. we were attacked by 70 Jap planes. Our four cruisers and seven destroyers had plenty of target practice. The destroyer *Foote*, our eighth destroyer, is dead in the water as previously mentioned. All ships break loose as Jap planes come in on us from all directions. We fire every gun on the ship at the Japs, even our big six inch guns. The first plane we hit was blown to bits by a 6 inch shell. Jap planes can be seen falling all around us. The Japs are also doing some damage and one can see many bombs explode very close to our ships. At first you think they have scored a hit as the water shoots high into the air. Their machine guns are also cutting up the water.* Our ship is also hit by a bomb that destroys one of our catapults that we use for shooting planes off. It's a good size steel ramp. When the bomb exploded, the stern of the ship was covered with smoke. It looked very serious at first. If one of our planes had been on the ramp it would have been blown to bits. One of the machine gun mounts was also knocked out by the bomb. No one was killed. About fifteen men were wounded. We also received a hit up forward and more casualties, all wounded. One of the fellows almost had his head taken off.

A few Japs parachuted when they were hit but a few sailors and Marines on the 20 mm. opened up on the ones in the chutes and when they hit the water they were nothing but a piece of meat cut to ribbons. The men were blasted out for doing this. They were told not to waste ammunition in such a way. They were also told that it was good shooting. The Japs were the first to do things like this. They asked for it and we returned the favor.

During the air battle, our air cover did a mop-up job on what was left of the Jap force. They were a little late getting here but we were very happy to see them. We secured from General Quarters at noon and received some food for a change. We stayed in the waters near Bougainville all day. We are making sure nothing happens to our empty transports as they head for their base at Tulagi. If the Japs send down any more warships, we will have to use potatoes against them. We must have fired at least 5000 rounds of five and six inch ammunition during our sea battle. The concussion from the twin five inch mount knocked out Fuller and ripped Babe's sweater off. It also knocked him to the steel deck twice during the air attack. Babe is a rugged Jewish boy from New York who weighs around 200 pounds. Sometimes

* Before the attack was over, our ship got credit for five (5) Jap planes shot down. The remaining ships accounted for fifteen (15).

when these twin five inch mounts turn around, the men on the machine guns can look right into the barrels and almost touch them. The concussion from these, with all the steel around, is wicked on the eardrums. Many a man has had his eardrum broken with the guns. Our ship has close to a hundred guns on it: 20 mm., 40 mm. machine guns and five inch mounts, also six inch turrets. The turrets have three guns each, five inch mounts, two guns each. Admiral Merrill used the wisdom of Solomon when he let the men in his task force get some rest before going into action. At first we got very little sleep but after a while one can get along with what he can get. The little sleep we received went a long way. Old Bull Halsey knew what he was doing when he put Admiral Merrill in command of this task force. Old Bull knows how to pick them.

The new men we picked up before going to Australia were shaking like a leaf during the air battle, and we did not waste any time in kidding them about it.

We are still in the Solomons but expect to pull into port sometime tomorrow. It will take some time for the destroyer *Foote* to reach port. A tug is now towing it back. We secured from General Quarters at noon today Tuesday, November 3, 1943. During the sea battle the Japs must have had radar, their firing was so good. They have the best star shells. They light the place up as if it were daytime. Their torpedo tossing is handled by experts but quite a few are duds. If all torpedoes had been alive, I wouldn't be here to tell about it. Every one that had hit us, and there were a few, were duds. Their torpedoes pack an awful punch.

Wednesday, November 3, 1943: Today we pulled into Purvis Bay. It's not too far from Tulagi. It was about 5 P.M. We got quite a reception as our task force pulled into the bay. The empty transports were back from Bougainville. As we passed them, all hands were topside, and gave us a big cheer.

Several of our ships were damaged. Many things have happened since we left here four days ago. Everyone is dead tired as we had only a few hours sleep since we left port. The men on the transports said they would give us anything we wanted. They also said that we had saved their skins. If the Jap warships had ever got at them, they would have been slaughtered. This was the first time I saw Jap pilots use parachutes. Someone said that the Japs don't use parachutes. Purvis Bay is still the same old hotbox. All you do is sweat. I had a little sleep tonight but they got the deck division up at 11 P.M. to make the lines ready to take on fuel. We always get the dirty work.

Thursday, November 4, 1943: I did not get any sleep until 2 A.M. this morning. We were receiving fuel from one of the tankers. They told us to get some sleep while the ship was fueling. We fell asleep on the steel deck. They woke us up in one hour at 3 A.M. when we were refueled. I did not get to bed again until 4:15 A.M. We usually crawl under a near mount or turret and fall asleep. Reveille was 6 A.M. There was no resting for the weary today. All hands worked all day under a hot blazing sun, carrying tons of ammunition. The sun gave us quite a burn because we wore no shirts to beat the head-sapping sun. We continued into the night. Even some of the officers helped. It makes you forget the heavy work that you are doing when you see the officers pitch in and help. They did not have to do this. They could be catching up with the many hours of sleep they lost. It's no joke carrying a 135 pound ammo-piercing shell almost the length of a ship that is 607 ft. long. Two men are used to pick the shell up and put it on another man's shoulder which is bare. It's then carried or staggered on its way, always with the hope that it doesn't drop. Thousands of shells were carried plus the powder cases. Some of the smaller fellows could not carry the armor-piercing shells because of the extreme weight. Usually a piece of cloth on the shoulder was used in vain for the heavy shell still cuts into the bone. To see an officer work with the crew is great for morale. The men will respect him and naturally go out of their way to help same. A record machine is attached to one of the loudspeakers and music is played all day as we carry the ammunition. Some of the men who were wounded badly left the ship on stretchers in the afternoon. They will go to the States. That is the only way the fellows down here can get home.

A very special guest came aboard this morning. It was the brass himself, the number 1 man, Admiral "Bull" Halsey. The men would do anything for him. He rates with the greats of all time. A PT boat pulled alongside and he came aboard. He had a long handshake with Admiral Merrill on the starboard quarterdeck. Everyone wanted to get a look at the "Bull." Halsey is a tough-looking man and looks as if he could take care of one of his name-sakes. He had a pair of shorts on, tan in color and a short sleeve shirt of the same color, the shirt open at the collar. You would never believe that he was the number 1 man in the South Pacific. He wants his men to be comfortable. He doesn't go in for this regulation stuff. As they were putting a six inch 135 pound armor-piercing shell on my shoulder, who was standing in front of me but "Bull" Halsey and Admiral Merrill. He was on the starboard side, near the six inch turret, not too far from the fantail. As he stood there watching us carry ammunition, I tried to look right through him. I tried to study him and see what he was made of. I left him standing there, with the shell on my shoulder and the knowledge that he came from good stock. It did not take long to draw that conclusion because he had it written all over him. We got the best man in command down here in the "Bull." Admiral Merrill showed him the damage we received from the Jap bombs. Before he left the ship, he congratulated everyone for the great job they had done. I must not forget to mention that Governor Stassen of Minnesota was also on our ship during all of the action in the Solomons that we had just returned from. He is one of Halsey's staff officers.

Francis McCarthey, the news reporter for United Press, was also aboard our ship during all this action. He was the only corre-spondent with the task force. When we reached Purvis Bay, he had to share his scoop with other reporters. He was told that the Japs did not know the size of our force here, and that from the way we hit the Japs in so many places in such a short period of time they would think more than one task force did all the dam-age. The Japs do not know that our task force is the only one in the South Pacific and if they did know that, they would have hit

Bougainville with battleships and everything else that was available. Mr. McCarthey should get some kind of an award. It's tough when you get a scoop like this and then have to share it with several other syndicated reporters. Everyone thinks the world of Mr. McCarthey.

November 5, 1943: Our task force left Purvis Bay at 6 P.M. We stayed there just long enough to get ammunition and fuel. We also took on more ammunition and food this morning. Some of the men's skin is so bad from heat rash that they have to stay in sick bay. It looks very bad and they cannot move with it. Their whole body is covered with this ugly rash. Their skin is raw and gives them no peace. It's like a bad burn. There is no cure for it for they perspire twenty-four hours a day here. I got about five hours sleep while we were at Purvis Bay. This was my first night's sleep in over a week. I also bought two toothbrushes before we left. We are on our way back to Bougainville. For if the Japs come down with warships again, it will be up to us to stop them.

The cruiser *Denver* could not make the trip. The cruiser *Nashville* will take its place. We have a photographer from Life Magazine with us. He snapped some pictures of the men carrying the big 150 pound boxes of potatoes. He took their names and addresses. I got there just a little too late. All hands went to battle stations at 6:30 P.M. We always do this about one hour before sunset and sunrise while at sea. In that way we are ready for any sneak attack by the Jap planes. We were attacked by Jap planes at 8 P.M. tonight but they did not do any damage. We were up all night and of course, no sleep.

Saturday, November 6, 1943: Today is a beautiful sunny day. We are still in the Solomons near Bougainville. A big air battle took place over Bougainville today. One of our fast carrier task forces hit Rabaul with their planes today. They did quite a job on the Jap warships and planes. This raid against Rabaul saved us from being sent to the bottom of the Pacific. If the Japs ever sent those battleships and other heavy warships against our small task force, we would not have stood a chance. Our task force is the only one based in the South Pacific but the Japs don't know

it. We would like to thank the pilots from those carriers for coming to our rescue and also our troops at Bougainville. The Japs
could have set the war back many months if they came down here
with a big fleet of battleships. Jap planes attacked us tonight
while we were near Bougainville. We had one kill to our credit.
No Jap warships showed up. We stayed at battle stations all night.

Sunday, November 7, 1943: We did not get any sleep because
we were at battle stations all night and this morning. It is another
warm sunny day. As usual we did not have breakfast until noon.
We had sandwiches and coffee while we were at battle stations.
We spent almost all of our time here while in this neck of the
woods. Food is scarce, at least our stomachs tell us so. A few men
at a time from each station go below to the mess hall for something to eat. We cannot take a chance for we never know when
the Japs will strike. We had warm powdered milk, cold beans
and bread. Our diet up here will be sandwiches but we never get
enough of them. We are always hungry. We could eat the side
of a house. During the night some destroyers and the cruiser
Nashville went down to Munda to refuel. They rejoined us today. They picked up a Jap from the water.

We sailed south this afternoon and covered the landing of our
troops on Treasury Island. The landing came off at about 1 P.M.
The Treasury Islands are south of the Shortlands. They are both
south of Bougainville. Our carrier planes are still giving Rabaul
a good plastering. The carriers are the *Saratoga, Princeton, Essex,
Bunker Hill* and *Independence.* At 5 P.M. battle stations were
secured. We have been there since Friday night at 5 P.M., 2 days.
It felt good to get away from the close quarters of the mount. The
mount covers an area of about 15 ft. by 15 ft. with the big machine
gun in the center. The many men in the gun crew had very little
room to move around. It was like being in a small cell. We were
relieved by the cruisers *Santa Fe, Mobile* and *Birmingham.* Tonight while I was talking to Wallcott, he told me that during the
sea battle of November 1 our ship was hit by two torpedoes. One
of the torpedoes that hit us knocked the men who were in the compartment down. The other torpedo hit the stern. Wallcott's battle

station is below deck. If those torpedoes ever exploded, they would
have sent us to the bottom. Must have been the 3 ton torpedoes.

Our troops in the European War are 75 miles from Rome. It
felt good to get on the main deck after being cooped up at battle
stations. It feels good to be able to walk around. We were like
a bunch of caged animals. I could use some sleep but I go on
watch at midnight.

Monday, November 8, 1943: I knocked off watch at 4 A.M. It
rained all during my watch and I was soaked. All hands awoke at
4:45 A.M. I was lucky — thirty minutes' sleep. I'm so tired that I
could sleep for a week on a picket fence. We pulled into Tulagi
at 8 A.M. We had to man our fueling stations and ready the lines
as we pulled alongside of the tanker. We did a hard day's work
today. Tons of ammunition were carried, and stored until 7 P.M.
It rained in the afternoon and everyone was drenched for his
troubles. While I was walking past the pilot room, I heard the
radio playing a good song, "The Sun Never Sets on the A.E.F."
This was the first time I heard that particular song. I hit the sack
at 8 P.M. I slept under the stars on a steel ammunition box two
feet wide. I kept all my clothes on but my blue hat and shoes. I
used the shoes for a pillow and I covered them with my hat. I was
so tired that I felt like I was sleeping on a feather bed.

Tuesday, November 9, 1943: I arose at 3:15 to go on watch. It
was another busy day for us. Field day was held throughout the
ship. Everyone was busy cleaning the ship, and putting things in
order. Everything has to be in tiptop shape because we leave at
8 P.M. We spent the afternoon washing clothes. The laundry has
been closed for the past few days on account of the alert. It did
not take very long for the clothes to dry as the day was again hot
and sunny. We had church services topside today. The priest told
us to pray for the men who were killed in the sea battle, the
troops who landed on Bougainville and the pilots who hit Rabaul.

About five this evening two of the cruisers that relieved us
two days ago at Bougainville returned. They were the *Santa Fe*
and *Mobile*. They were in two air battles and the cruiser *Bir-*

mingham was hit by a torpedo and bombs. It will take a few days before it pulls in here. They say that it is only doing ten knots. The Jap planes also hit Treasury Island and Bougainville hard. This was the first time for these cruisers to go up the Slot to take on the Japs. It did not take very long for the Japs to rough them up. It's no disgrace to get knocked off. The odds are really stacked up against making it when you go up to those Jap infested islands. The Good Lord has really watched over us. We could have gotten it a long time ago. The Japs know we are going to be up there and they never stop attacking us. We left Purvis Bay this evening for Bougainville.

Wednesday, November 10, 1943: All hands arose at 5 A.M. It's another very hot day. We had our first good meal in quite some time, the apple pie really hit the spot. This afternoon, while we were south of Bougainville and just off Treasury Island, we came across a raft with four live Japs in it. Admiral Merrill send word to one of our destroyers to pick them up. As the destroyer *Spence* came close to the raft, the Japs opened up with a machine gun at the destroyer. The Jap officer then put the gun in each man's mouth and fired, blowing out the back of each man's skull. One of the Japs did not want to die for the Emperor and put up a struggle. The others held him down. The officer was the last to die. He also blew his brains out. The *Spence* went in to investigate. All the bodies had disappeared into the water. There was nothing left but blood and an empty raft. Swarms of sharks were everywhere. The sharks ate well today. The Japs must have taken the 7.7 machine gun from one of their planes before leaving the islands to escape advancing troops. We went to battle stations at 6:30 P.M. At 10 P.M. we were attacked by enemy planes. We emerged without damage. The night was as bright as day and rendered us clear targets for the Jap bombs and torpedoes. Later, darkness descended, and the rains came.

Thursday, November 11, 1943: We remained at battle stations the entire night until 7 this morning, another sleepless night. Word was received that another powerful carrier strike would hit Rabaul around 7:30 A.M. today. The land-based bombers from

General MacArthur's forces on New Guinea, under the command of General Kenney, would also join in the strike. This air strike will help keep the Jap ships and planes from attacking us.

In the past 13 months, the Japs have lost 50 warships and 800 planes.

Another hot day is in store for us as we are still in the Solomons, patrolling off Bougainville, in case the Japs should wander down to hit Bougainville with their force.

We received a message from General MacArthur congratulating the task force for the work it has done in the past ten days.

One of our destroyers picked up six of our airmen, who had bailed out of their crippled B–24 bomber. The bomber was badly damaged in its attack on Rabaul, and had to crash-land at sea.

It was another night of Jap air attacks. The stillness being broken by our blazing warships. The Japs came at us from all directions with their bombers and torpedo planes. We escaped some very close calls. One torpedo missed our starboard side by the minutest of fractions. The Japs have a tendency of dropping their torpedoes on the side that I'm stationed on. Give or take an inch and that one would have done it.

Friday, November 12, 1943: Another night at battle stations. We secured at 6:30 this morning. The men who are not detailed can get some shut-eye on deck. As one looks around, he can observe sailors spread around topside, getting well deserved sleep. The weather is boiling but they are too exhausted to notice it. Some of the men use their life jackets for a makeshift pillow.

We are constantly patrolling the waters off Treasury Island. We steamed south and picked up a convoy at 4 P.M. We will cover the landing. These reinforcements will land tonight or early morning.

I have three packages of gum left out of the carton of twenty-four. Surprisingly it was still fresh, even though it had taken the heat and humidity. The gum came in handy for it was the only thing I had to eat for long periods of time. I passed some of it to the fellows and rationed the rest for myself. Hunger is a torture.

When one spends 24 hours a day, every day, surrounded by salt water, you are bound to be hungry, even if food were plentiful. The little you receive is not enough. Yesterday was Armistice Day . . .

Saturday, November 13, 1943: We went to battle stations again last night and remained there until noon today. Jap planes tried another time. We have no intention of leaving until the Jap navy is unable to attack our newly won bases. Air attacks on Rabaul are making it very inhospitable for the Japs and actually stopping their warships from coming down to attack us. The night was very bright for quite some time. We ate some sandwiches around midnight. Being so hot around here, I could get along without any clothes, day or night.

Today, being the 13th, proved to be a very unlucky day for the light cruiser *Denver*. She is number 58. Adding the five and eight together, the answer — 13 . . . Early this morning Jap planes attacked the force. One of the Jap torpedo planes broke through and put a torpedo into the *Denver*. All the ships were twisting and turning during the action, but fate being what it is, the *Denver* was the unlucky one. As the torpedo exploded, a huge geyser of water rose hundreds of feet into the air. The *Denver* was behind us when she took the blow. The torpedo hit her amidships on the starboard side. The plane that scored on the *Denver* seemed as if it had come out of nowhere. The Japs have a frequent habit of striking at morning and then again at night. Later in the day, we were informed that the *Denver* was hit at the engine room. Twenty men were killed and a score wounded. This report was unofficial. The *Montpelier* was also hit by a torpedo . . . a dud. Unlike the *Denver*'s, our luck was still holding. Two destroyers were left with the *Denver* as escorts, as she crawled back to Purvis Bay, traveling at approximately five knots.

This afternoon I washed clothes and then a little shut-eye was enjoyed. I went on watch at 5:15 P.M. Another hot day was in the books.

Sunday, November 14, 1943: All hands to battle stations before sunset last night, remaining there until 6 A.M. Same as before

. . . no sleep . . . Breakfast at 7 . . . We then headed south to Purvis Bay.

Last night the Japs did not attack us. This was a first for them. They must be as tired as us.

I was detailed to the 8 to 12 noon watch. We passed the *Denver* at 7 A.M. She was being towed by a tug. Limping as she was, she would have made an excellent target for a Jap sub or plane. I still keep thinking that the torpedo that hit her was meant for us.

Anderson told me that we are using old maps, dating back to 1900. It goes without saying the validity of same wasn't to be relied upon. The Solomons are full of the dreaded reefs. These reefs are not indicated on the maps. Frequently a ship will become impaled or have its hull split open by one of these monsters. Last night, radar picked up something in the dark. It turned out to be more reefs, uncharted. These reefs were then located and charted on the map. It would seem that charting the reefs and fighting the Japs at the same time would call for time and a half. In the cover of the coves and the bays you never know what our friend the Jap has up his sleeve for us.

We have a reporter from Time and our own Navy Magazine aboard with us. During our many sleepless nights in the Solomons the past week, these reporters had a chance to sleep, but Dixon's foghorn voice had other ideas. They were just above us and wanted to know who he was. They felt like throwing something at him. We all got a big kick out of it. When Dixon opens his mouth, one can hear him for miles around. He makes a good mount captain, even the guns have competition from him.

We pulled into Purvis Bay today, November 14, 1943. One hundred bags of mail were waiting for joyful hands. Leaving here on November 5, it hardly seems to be the 14th already. We spent 10 days away and most of it was spent at battle stations.

Monday, November 15, 1943: I hit the sack at 8:30 P.M. under the stars and awoke at 5:45 A.M. This was my first good sleep in a month. The *Denver* came into port this morning with a gaping hole on her starboard side. Her mess hall is under water. Two Australian heavy cruisers and American cruisers left today.

As I sit next to the galley and write, I can see a native boat in the distance. Nearing the ship, it pulls alongside. The sailors buy produce from them. One of the natives has white hair. It must be bleached.

Waltham High is still undefeated. It looks like they will be the state champs this year.

I imagine the *Denver* will not stay here very long. We will miss her because she was very quick on the draw. If there were any Jap planes or ships up for grabs, you had to be on the ball, or she would beat you to the punch. I never saw such a ship that loved to fire its guns as the *Denver*. The "Dirty D" was a great ship, we hate to see it leave us.

Tuesday, November 16, 1943: I was relieved of watch at 4 A.M., all hands up at 6 A.M. We cleaned the ship today. Plenty of working parties were arranged for the unsuspecting hands. Tons of supplies were stored aboard. The cruisers *Honolulu* and *Nashville* arrived today. Another scorcher.

Wednesday, November 17, 1943: At quarters this morning our officer of the division, a Lieutenant Hutchins, told us that we were going to have a new Captain in a few days. Captain Tobin will be missed by all. He is a great man and everyone likes him. He deserves a good long rest after what he's been through. He was here when Guadalcanal was invaded, August 7, 1942. He's taken part in some rugged sea battles against the sons of Nippon.

The cruiser *Birmingham* left for the States yesterday. The *Birmingham* was hit three times by the Japs. A 1000 pound bomb glanced off the six inch turret, went through the deck and exploded, killing five and wounding fifty. All in all she was very lucky.

Ships are arriving every day now. I've never seen so many ships before. We held another field day aboard ship. The *Montpelier* has to be in tiptop shape.

Friday, November 19, 1943: Things are pretty quiet at Bougainville. I guess the Japs' back is broken. They can forget that island from now on.

They allowed a few men from each division to go on the beach this afternoon, for a few hours of recreation. There is nothing over there but jungle and swamp. There is a native village further inland but only officers are allowed there.

Some of the men who visited the *Denver* while she was in port said that twenty-five men were killed and many were wounded. The wounded consisted of men with broken backs, eyes blown out, bodies crushed, etc. The flooded compartments have sailors floating around in their waters. One of their dead, a chief, still had his pipe in his mouth. The odor from the bodies, still sealed aboard, is overwhelming. They cannot retrieve the bodies until dry dock is reached.

Sunday, November 21, 1943: We are still at Purvis Bay. A great many of the men are washing their blues. We have hopes of being in Australia by January of '44. We had movies on the forecastle for all hands as it was too hot below. Our regular movies were held in the hangar deck but because of the extreme heat, this was impossible.

Today I went to church services on Tulagi. This was the first time on the beach in over a month. We sang hymns. The same ones I used to sing in grammar school. It brought back memories. I could hear the birds singing in the jungle. It's much better here than at Purvis. This time last year, the Marines were fighting the Japs on the same spot. The fighting that took place here was a nightmare. Now peace and quiet has returned. The Japs are buried close by. Many are sealed in caves that are not too far away. They refused to surrender. It was much easier to seal them in their natural graveyard than risk huge losses. All of the huts are made of big leaves cut from the jungle. It doesn't take the natives long to build a hut. The little church is also made of the same substance. Bamboo is also used in these crude living quarters. The floors are generally dirt. As for the natives, they are intelligent in appearance. A large cage is teeming with birds. I never saw such striking colors before. The birds were captured by the natives from the jungle. Some were of enormous size while others had a resemblance to parrots.

I spent quite a bit of time talking to a fellow who was on one of the invasion barges in action at Bougainville. He said that the Japs mowed down over 300 Marines in nothing flat while they were attempting a charge on the beach. That we were only taking a small part of Bougainville, enough for our airfields. The Japs were to be pushed back into the jungle and there they would starve. If an attempt was ever made to clear the island of Japs, the process would take years to accomplish. There are thousands of Japs there and many of them are veterans of the China War. When the airfield is in operation, Rabaul will be rendered useless. The Japs will be forced back to their powerful island of Truk approximately 700 miles away. Truk is the Pearl Harbor of the Japanese Empire. No white man has set foot on this island in over twenty-five years. A formidable fortress, Truk can boast of its thousands of troops stationed there, ready and waiting to defend its shores.

I returned to the ship after church services on Tulagi. The *Denver* left for the States today.

Wednesday, November 24, 1943: Sitting at anchor in Purvis Bay, we took on fuel today. Espiritu Santo in a few days is the word. I hope so. Nothing fit to eat in over a month. A troopship arrived this morning. It left this afternoon for Bougainville. It steamed up from the Fiji Islands. This will be the last ride for many of those troops. Some will come back crippled for life. Going, they are young and in the best of health. Returning, they are old and beaten shells that once were men. Troops are transported there nearly every day. Crowded landing barges are usually their lot. The barges are very small and many of the troops are stricken with seasickness. On rainy days they are herded below where the heat is unbearable and no air reaches them.

Yesterday, the destroyer *Foote* left for the States, half of its bow was blown off. It happened at Bougainville in our sea battle. The patch job was a credit to the Navy. Jap torpedoes were the damaging agent and it was a sight to behold.

A number of the men were diving off the side of the ship having a grand old time until an officer happened by. Result . . . No diving . . .

Twenty new "boots" are on board today. They arrived by transport. No movies last night on account of rain. One of the movies that we have viewed while here was *Edison, The Boy.* Mickey Rooney was the star. It was enjoyable.

About a month from now, summer begins. It's hot enough as it is. I can imagine what we will be in for weather-wise. For now, darkness creeps in at about 7 P.M. Listening to the news report, I learned that the invasion of Tarawa in the Gilberts has begun. It's over 1000 miles to the north of us, north of the equator. It gave no date of the invasion.

Saturday, November 27, 1943: Only one thing to say, Purvis Bay. The other night a group of destroyers from our task force, led by "31-knot" Burke, sank four (4) Jap destroyers. They had quite a brawl. The sea battles down here, and there are plenty of them, remind me of the old days during the Revolutionary War. Then sailing vessels, like *Old Ironsides,* would venture out and slug it out toe to toe, regardless of odds, with the enemy. The only difference — theirs were generally during the daylight hours — ours during nighttime.

Some of us went to the beach for recreation. The only reason I went was to get out of a working party. There is nothing on the beach. Each of us was doled out one bottle of beer. I gave mine away.

The water is full of big black balls covered with long needles about 12 inches long. Some kind of a fish, I imagine. If your feet happen to bump them, they pierce the skin. As it looks, it's similar to a stinging needle. I have never seen anything like them before. Running into the water at night, not knowing that they were sitting on the bottom, would not be advisable.

Our recreation today consisted of walking and talking as the beach could not, in the general sense of the term, be called a beach.

Thursday was November 25. Back home in Massachusetts, it was Thanksgiving, one of the real big holidays. Everyone, or it seems just about everyone, goes to the high school football game in the morning. Then it's home for a big turkey dinner.

On board ship we celebrated Thanksgiving with a big turkey dinner and all of the trimmings. It really hit the spot.

Nickleson had a heat stroke from sleeping in the compartment last night. We carried him to sick bay as he was too weak and dizzy to go it alone. The flash-proof cover where he lay was covered with his sweat. He was kept in sick bay for a day. I can't understand how some of the fellows sleep in the compartment, especially ours, as it's above the waterline. The sun beats against the steel sides and the deck all day. The side of the ship is so hot that you cannot touch it. On top of that, there is very little air to breathe. Sleeping there is out of the question.

We had Captain's Inspection in whites this morning. What a joke. How stupid can intelligence get. We were told that these orders had come from the States . . . that figures.

I was talking to one of the crewmen today. It seems that the duty here is getting the best of him. He told me that he was going crazy. He appeared very nervous. We've been in continuous action for almost a year now. Some of the younger men in the 17-year-old group wish that they were back in the States and out of the Navy. One of them is here on watch with me now. He really does look homesick. He's sorry now that he was in such a hurry to enter the service. He's only 17 years old. I told him that after a few months he would recover and the Navy would seem like a second home to him and he'd never care if he saw home again. I also told him to forget about being homesick and think of something else. I never felt lonesome in all the time we have been here, in fact I never give it a thought.

Some of the new men cannot wait to get into action. They say, "I came down here to fight a war and that's what I want." It takes all kinds.

After being in so many campaigns, you're disappointed if one passes you by. There's always the next one. When you find yourself in it, there's always the realization of how crazy you were in thinking that way. When this one's completed, never again. When it's finally terminated, you're always ready for the next one. It gets to be a disease after a time.

Following chow, the fellows like to sit around and listen to the recordings piped over the loudspeaker. The songs are old but we enjoy them very much. It lasts for half an hour.

Thursday, December 2, 1943: Today at 1 P.M., we lost a great man — Captain Tobin. He left for the beach by PT boat. I imagine he will be flown to the States. The Captain has been down here for the good part of two years. In that time, he had partaken of some of the most furious sea battles ever fought. As he was going down the gangway, "Old Lang Syne," was played in his honor. One could tell by the look on his face, that he hated to leave. It was very touching. He has been Captain of this ship since July 1943. He never missed a church service and always went to communion. He was proud of his religion, his country and the Navy. They sent the right man when they sent Captain Tobin to command the *Montpelier*. The Captain was an easygoing person and made many friends. I still remember the day as I was sitting on the starboard side of the ship, next to the galley, reading. Captain Tobin and Commander Koonce happened by. I saw them walk towards me. It was my duty to stand at attention, but I pretended not to notice them. I expected Commander Koonce to bellow "Attention on Deck." They both passed by to my amazement as the Captain didn't want to disturb me. I shall never forget that as long as I live. Captain Tobin had much authority but he was not the kind to go around showing off. He was a very humble person. He had what it takes. How can you lose a war with men like that. I felt pretty low after he passed by. The next time I couldn't get up quick enough to stand at attention.

Our new captain, Captain Harry D. Hoffman, took command this morning. Purple hearts were distributed to the wounded in previous actions by the Captain.

A group of men were transferred from the ship today. Many Fiji Islanders were transported to Bougainville. They are all large and reported to be very good fighters.

I was talking to a Sea Bee and he told me that they work 9 hours a day, 7 days a week, frequently around the clock.

Saturday, December 4, 1943: I received shocking news today.

The Press News reported my brother John's aircraft carrier was sunk in the battle of Tarawa in the Gilberts. The communiqué stated that at approximately 25 November, 1943, the carrier went down. It was a converted job and the first of its kind to be sunk in the war. Last night at about 11 P.M., while sleeping under the stars, my friend Donovan came down from the radio shack to tell me what had happened. I must have answered him while I was asleep. I still don't remember talking to him. While on the 8 A.M. to 12 noon watch, he asked me if I saw the Press News and I said, "No, why do you ask?" Then he told me what had happened. I did not believe him until I picked up the press news and read it myself. It was the first item in the Press News. I wrote a letter to him the first chance I had. This wasn't the first close call for my brother John. My brother Joe and he were both at Pearl Harbor, December 7, 1941, when the Japs pulled their sneak attack. Both of them were transferred from two ships that were sunk by the Japs. They were transferred only a couple of weeks before. John was on the minelayer *Oglala* and Joe on the battleship *Oklahoma*. They had ringside seats on that day when the Japs attacked. Joe was on Ford Island, right in the center of the action, and not too far from Battleship Row. John was on the destroyer *Gamble*. Joe joined the Navy in 1936, John in 1938. The last letter I received from my sister Mary, reported that John had bumped into Joe out here somewhere. The carrier that was sunk is the U.S.S. *Liscomb Bay*.

Sunday, December 5, 1943: We experienced showers tonight, no movies. We have had showers nearly every night usually following chow. It reminds me of the spring weather back home with its April showers.

The doctor says that 4000 bags of mail are waiting for the task force, mostly Christmas packages.

While on the 12 noon to 4 P.M. watch, the men had a great time cutting each other's hair. We're not going anywhere for some time, so it makes little difference to us. Some of the men have let their beards grow. You would never know them. They look like a bunch of hermits with their long beards.

The men who missed the ship last October while we were at
Australia, came aboard last night. One of the men in this group
saw many of the wounded who were being shipped to the States.
There were about 800 of them. A sad sight as most of them had
lost arms, legs, etc. The Press News reported that we won't start a
big offensive in the Pacific War, until the European War is over.
We get the left-overs here, 90% of all war supplies go to the European Theater.

December 7, 1943: Two years ago today the Japs attacked Pearl
Harbor. Thinking back, it was a cold Sunday afternoon, and I
was at the Boston Garden, watching the Boston Olympics play
hockey. During the game, the loudspeaker announced that the
Japs had bombed Pearl Harbor. Interest was lost in the game.
Military personnel were told to report to their ships and bases.
Everyone rushed to buy newspapers. The next day the papers
carried the names of the ships that were sunk by the Japs. The
ships John and Joe were on had been sunk but we did not know
that they had been transferred a few weeks before the attack.
When we wrote to them, our letters were returned. We thought
that they went down in their ships. Before the month of December was over we received a letter and two money orders. They
were postmarked from Pearl Harbor. I will always keep mine as
a souvenir.

We left Purvis Bay in the Solomons at 6 A.M. We are on our
way to Bougainville to give the Japs something to remember us
by. We had a lot of rain at Purvis lately, but on our way up the
Slot, we did not receive any rain. The sea was choppy. Commander Koonce and Brown were promoted to Captain. They will
be transferred to the States in a few months. They will be given a
command of their own. Commander Brown is much younger
than Koonce. Both are well liked. Brown is a very smart cookie,
he should go places.

The invasion of Tarawa turned out to be a very bloody affair,
our casualties were high.

Last night we received a few handfuls of cookies from Cross.
They came in handy for we were starved. The only good meal we

get is at noon and then you have to wait twenty-four hours for another. Cross was on the *Nashville* when their task force with Jimmy Doolittle hit Tokyo.

I have not heard from John yet.

Thursday, December 9, 1943: We traveled all the way past Bougainville but came across no Jap warships. They were headed in our direction but have returned to their base. We were ordered to destroy everything we came across but nothing showed up. We then returned to Purvis Bay at 1 A.M.

On the way to the Solomons, you could smell flowers. On the eight to midnight watch, one would have thought the water was full of lilacs. All of the flowers in the jungle must be blooming now.

We had another lecture in the mess hall. We had to identify our ships, and planes, and also those of the enemy. We were shown movies and slides of both American and Japanese planes and their counterparts. We were given very little time to recognize them.

Friday, December 10, 1943: During the midnight to 4 A.M. watch, one of the fellows dozed off while he was in the trainer's seat. He received a big bucket of water in the face. It was around 2:30 A.M. when the bucket brigade let him have it. It broke up the monotony and of course the fellows broke their sides laughing. The unlucky one on the receiving end took it all in stride. His time would come. I suppose he had delusions of a sinking ship when the water descended. Whoever thought up this water idea should get it patented.

At quarters the Lieutenant informed us that Admiral Merrill would be presented with some medals tomorrow. All hands were to be in whites. He will receive these decorations for the great work he did in our sea battle at Bougainville.

A sailor on board said that the Marines ashore were jumping for joy the night we stopped the Japs from hitting the bay with their fleet in their quest of sinking the American transport and bombarding the troops on shore. They could see the gunfire from the beach. They knew that the Japs were on their way down to bombard them but that they did not know that we were on our way up to stop them.

Saturday, December 11, 1943: Today was a big day in the life of Admiral Merrill. After Captain's Inspection at quarters, all hands assembled topside on the fantail to witness the presentation of citations to our admiral. All the big brass were here, 31-knot Burke, who commands the "Little Beaver Squadron" of destroyers in our own task force also took part in the ceremonies. Admiral Halsey was scheduled to make the presentation but could not attend. Vice Admiral Fitch, 3 stars, took Halsey's place. He decorated Admiral Merrill with the Legion of Merit, one of our highest awards, for action March 5, 1943. Our task force at that time destroyed a Jap base in the Solomons as well as sinking the Jap warships, all in the same operation. Next was the Navy Cross, the second highest citation, the first being the Congressional Medal of Honor. This was awarded for the sea battle against the Japs, November 1, 1943, and other actions during the invasion of Bougainville. This sea battle was the longest of the war and one of the longest in Naval History. The weather was very hot for all the Captains and Admirals who attended. This was the biggest ceremony Purvis Bay ever staged and no doubt the last.

Monday, December 13, 1943: We toured every part of the ship. Our division officers, Lt. Hutchins and Graham, gave us a lecture on the different parts of the ship. We all laughed when Hutchins said that after a fellow stays down here for a certain length of time, his brain deteriorates and refuses to function as well. We call it "Jungle Happy" or "Asiatic."

On the midnight to four watch, we had quite a time for ourselves. A water fight was in progress and many a bucket of water and helmet of same was thrown. Everyone got a soaking for his troubles. It was better than a movie.

Most of the men are from the southern states but out here sectionalism is a thing of the past. About 80% of the division are southerners, the remaining men are pretty well distributed throughout the 48.

Wednesday, December 22, 1943: Nothing important has taken

place in the last nine days. We're still at Purvis Bay, leaving for Bougainville tonight. The Japanese are attempting to evacuate their troops from the island. It will be our assignment to stop them.

The food is still bad, i.e. for breakfast we were given hash, rice, half a pear and to top it off, bread and butter. Supper consisted of rice, baloney, a cookie and bread and jelly. The supply ships have failed to arrive, which means that we will go hungry for quite some time. We're hungry all of the time. Bedtime finds us starved. Waiting for morning and the next meal is agony.

Clothing is also running low. Towels have been exhausted at the small stores.

Having installed a dry dock at Espiritu Santo in New Hebrides, our repair work will be completed there, instead of the long voyage to the States. Five Liberty ships were used to haul it from the States, approximately 7000 miles away.

The new Captain has a lot of new regulations which we do not really need, he wants us to wear shirt and hat while topside and also white on watch. It would make a beautiful target if the Japs should ever sneak in. They should get on the ball, there is a war to be won, and this is no fashion show.

The Marines established a beachhead on New Britain, December 17, 1943. This section is near New Guinea. It would appear that we're not going to bother with the other end of the island, close to Rabaul, 200 miles away. Rabaul would be a tough nut to crack as there are reported to be between fifty to a hundred thousand of troops stationed there. Starving them out would seem to be the answer.

Mines were used extensively on Bougainville.

As we left Purvis Bay at 6:30 P.M., it was cloudy and dark. It looked as if a storm was in the making. There was much lightning. Not far away, we could observe the PBY bombers take off from the water. Pilots from our force manned them. The name of the pilot from the *Montpelier* was Lt. Boyle. He will do the spotting for the bombardment. As we were leaving the bay, ships pulled in from Bougainville, while other ships jammed with troops were preparing to leave for that island. Hospital ships were predominant.

At 8:30 P.M. Captain Hoffman issued the statement that we were going to drop some Christmas gifts in the laps of the Japs and for us to make every shell count. Rest was now in order for us.

Thursday, December 23, 1943: Today I have the 4 to 8 A.M. watch. It rained this morning and the sky is still cloudy. For breakfast we had pancakes and beans, 1 bun and a small piece of butter. We're traveling approximately at the speed of twenty knots. We have plenty of time to reach Bougainville. All hands on deck at 5 A.M.

The *Montpelier* fired its 20 mm. machine guns and the five inch guns today.

This afternoon, I had some shut-eye. The weather began to clear and the sun broke through. It's very quiet at sea as the task force cuts through the water.

All hands at battle stations at 7 P.M. Captain Hoffman informed us that we were going to bombard two bomber bases on the northern tip of Bougainville. Our ship should fire 3000 rounds of five and six inch shells. Also to be on the alert for torpedo boats for in this area, they were usually concealed very cleverly.

Our bombardment will start at 12:30 Friday morning, the day before Christmas. The Japs will never expect our attack so near Christmas. There are numerous troops and barracks on the island. Ammunition dumps and a radar station can also be found there. We expect quite a reception from their shore guns. Our force consists of three cruisers and about six destroyers. He said if there's any crap games in progress there, we hope to disturb the players. The Captain stated that he hoped the Japs receive all our Christmas presents. He also told the crew to be on their toes and not be a sucker for a slow ball. I get a kick out of Captain Hoffman, he informs us of everything. He would make a good radio announcer. He sounds like Bill Stern, the sports commentator.

Today around noon, the *Montpelier* picked up an army officer. He arrived from Munda.

Friday, December 24, 1943: We sneaked in on the Japs this morning while they were sleeping. At 12:30 A.M. we started our bombardment on the northern tip of Bougainville. Coming close to the shoreline, we proceeded to give the island a thunderous plastering. The guns of our ships never stopped firing, the sound was deafening. Enormous explosions occurred as the ammunition dumps were hit. It was quite a sight. Everything on the island seemed to be in flames, barracks, supply dumps, the radar station, fuel dumps and planes on the airstrips. As expected, the Jap shore guns opened up. They seemed like six or eight inch shells, nothing small. The night wasn't as dark as the ones we experienced during our other engagements, for instance, our own planes could spot us 15 miles away. Jap shells were near misses, we received no damage. As we were leaving, dead Japs were everywhere and the airfields were rendered useless. The island was in flames and could be seen at a distance of fifty miles. In the meantime Lt. Boyle was overhead in one of our planes, a Black Cat, receiving and relaying information. A great job of observance was done this night by the Lieutenant. Before Lt. Boyle departed, a few 500 pound bombs were presented to the Japs, as a going away present. We would like the Japs to know this Christmas that we had not forgotten them. Premier Tojo would remember this Christmas. The action lasted with a star studded sky for a half hour. We were on top of the island and out before they had time to organize. Battle station duty lasted for the remaining night up to 7 A.M.

I was on watch shortly after as I pulled the 8 to noon watch. The men who were not on watch were busy picking up the thousands of shell cases that covered the deck.

We were due to group at Bougainville again tonight, but that order has been countermanded. We will return to Purvis Bay. This is the seventeenth time that the task force has traveled up the Slot. It beats by a wide margin any other force. This has been our sixth bombardment.

The weather again was hot and sunny. This evening I pull the 8 P.M. to midnight watch, the same watch I had Christmas Eve 1942. On watch, we were fascinated by a star that kept changing colors. It would be red, then green, then yellow and then white. It would go through this process every second — another first for me.

Saturday, December 25, 1943: Christmas Day . . . This is my second away from home in a row. We returned to Purvis Bay at 7 A.M. All hands on deck at 5 A.M. We manned our fueling stations as we refueled from a nearby tanker. The remainder of the morning was spent in the hot sun removing shell cases.

Captain Hoffman spoke to the crew at noon for 10 minutes and wished everyone a Merry Christmas. He also said that he was thinking of his loved ones at home, just like the rest of the crew. Captain Hoffman also told us that 10 years ago when he was stationed in China, he used to observe the Japs on warships training for this war. They wore helmets and shoulder pads as they would strike each other with clubs. This was the kind of an enemy that we were fighting and should never allow ourselves to grow soft. When the Captain starts, one could listen to him all day.

We loaded ammunition the rest of the afternoon in a pouring rain. Supper was at 6:30 P.M. The dinner consisted of turkey as we celebrated Christmas. After chow we finished loading ammunition. The ammunition was loaded with a minimum of waste as we were on a two hour notice to be under way.

Christmas celebrations were held on the forecastle for all hands. We sang songs. Some of the officers came to the mike and sang, including Admiral Merrill, Captain Koonce, Captain Brown and the British Commander who boarded our ship at Munda.

The British Commander's name is Killen, and he told us that he has been in the war since 1939. He fought on Crete, Africa, Italy and other less known battle fronts. This was the best time he had in all the time spent in service excluding that which he has had with his family. That had been only once in all these years. Everyone liked him, we would like to keep him aboard. The celebrations were completed with an old movie. Everyone had a great time and they would remember this Christmas for a long time. After the movie I hit the sack and had some well deserved rest. I wonder where I'll be next Christmas.

Sunday, December 26, 1943: All hands up at 6 A.M. Ammunition was toted before breakfast and continued on after same. Church services at 9:30 A.M. up forward on the forecastle. The deck was oven hot as we knelt down, as it was another hot one. After church services, I went back to carrying ammunition. We finally completed the job at 2 P.M. That's the worst of a bombardment, you spend a couple of days taking off the empty shell cases and then replace them with hundreds of tons of live ammunition and thousands of shells. It fires fast enough but what a task afterwards. After the ammunition detail, I cleaned up, and then it was about time to go on watch.

The cruisers *Honolulu* and *St. Louis* pulled in today. The *Honolulu* is camouflaged. Their stay was short as they left this evening. A submarine also left today. Having been painted recently, it looked factory fresh. I hope that they have a successful patrol against the Jap Navy and sink quite a few ships.

The English Commander left here by plane this morning, I imagine he is returning to Munda. I hope he makes it back to England soon to be reunited with his family but I think he will be out here for sometime. He's 12,000 miles from home.

All hands to the fantail to view a show at 7:15 P.M. that was staged by the men from our ship and the cruisers *Cleveland* and *Columbia*. Our glee club sang and the orchestra played. Many good acts were shown. It lasted for an hour and fifteen minutes. The officer on our ship who trained our glee club played with the one and only Fred Waring. He made the glee club sound like one of the original glee clubs of his counterpart. One of the crew by the name of Wolf was at the piano, he played for the famous Harry James Orchestra. Mr. James is married to Betty Grable, the actress. The talent from the other ships were very good. A movie was shown after the show. The name of it was "Keeper of the Flame."

Condition Red was sounded at 9:30 P.M. All hands went to battle stations. The Japs did not attack. Our night fighters took care of them.

Wednesday, December 29, 1943: We're still at Purvis Bay.

Chow is still no good. We had corn bread and butter and a cookie for supper. No supply ships have arrived yet. This must be the lost outpost.

I went over to the beach yesterday on recreation. Everyone received four bottles of beer. I had one and gave the rest to Adkins and Tomlinson, two boys from West Virginia. As usual, nothing to do here. They're putting up a building, I guess it's for recreation. When they do erect it, I imagine we won't be here to enjoy it. We have recreation on the average of once a month from 1 to 4 P.M.

Today I left the ship with a working party. They took us to an ammunition barge, some distance from the ship. It was very close to the jungle. The jungle seemed to be a thick green rug. Someone could be peering at you at a few feet distance and it would be impossible to see him, for the jungle is so dense. We did not have to work very hard as we were put to work cleaning the five and six inch shells. Some of the fellows went in for a swim at noon. An officer, with little to do, took their names. How miserable can some people get? We returned to the ship for supper.

The cruisers *Honolulu* and *St. Louis* returned this afternoon, after being out for three days. They were up the Solomons, bombarding Bougainville.

Seventy men were transferred to the States this morning. No word from John. His ship was sunk over a month ago.

Friday, December 31, 1943: This is the last day of the year. It was the fastest year I can remember. It was because we were on the go most of the time. I arose at 3:15 to relieve the watch. It's a very busy day, as field day is conducted throughout the ship. We lugged benches from the mess hall to the forecastle. Because of rain, the movie was transferred from its original place to the hangar deck. It's New Year's Eve now, but to us, it's just another night. I found myself a place topside and commenced to fall asleep. It was only 7:30 P.M.

January 1, 1944: It's a good thing I fell asleep early last night, for Ski, the boatswain, woke Myers, Lovelace and myself at 1 A.M. for a working party. Tons of stores were stacked on the fantail. It looks like we're going to get some food for a change. What a great way to start the New Year. Such a thing makes a fellow talk to himself. The remainder of the crew looked so comfortable sleeping. It rained a good part of the time and we received a drenching. Finishing at 5:30 A.M., I took a shower and put on clean dry clothes. By that time it was time to work at my regular cleaning station. Afterwards, I had breakfast. I was as hungry after eating as before. For breakfast we had dry cereal, corn bread, butter and coffee. I don't drink coffee for I get cramps. Church services were held in the mess hall. The priest said that the European War should end this year, that the Pacific War would be over in 1945.

It rains nearly every night now, and is very hot during the daylight hours. The Press News informed us that the Germans had lost a battleship the *Scharnhorst*. It was sunk by the British Navy as it tried to attack a convoy on its way to Russia. The battleship *Duke of York* was credited for sinking same.

No one bothered me in taking a hand in the working party. I sat topside and did a little writing in my diary.

One of the fellows who left for the States today really has troubles. He is married and has three beautiful children, but his wife wants to marry someone else. After being away from the States for over a year, this is an awful thing to be going home for. Everyone feels sorry for him as he is a very nice fellow.

The most unpopular man on board ship is the one who selects the working party. Everyone stays clear of him in the hope that he won't select him for the duty. The early morning hours are a rule when this work is conducted.

Sunday, January 2, 1944: I awoke at 6 A.M. Still at Purvis Bay. I left ship early this morning on an all day, expense free working party. An ammunition barge was our objective. When a working party is called, all deck divisions send a certain number of men. Of course, I'm the good old stand-by. I always seem to be hooked into one of them. My record is unbroken by anyone. The ammunition barge is similar to a large boathouse, to me it seems to be of enormous size. The other ships in Bay also contribute men in the worthy cause of unloading.

A small boat, with natives aboard, stopped us on our way to our destination, and sold us some melons. The natives were very young, about eight or nine years old, they also spoke English. When one of the native men wants to marry, he has to donate to the girl of his choice 150 dollars before the father of the girl consents.

At noon we had sandwiches for dinner and relaxed a little before commencing work again. We returned to ship around supper time.

Tuesday, January 4, 1944: We left Purvis Bay yesterday morning, Jan. 3, at 8 A.M. and arrived at Espiritu Santo at 1:30 P.M. the same afternoon. All hands up at 4:15 as we had gunnery practice before coming into port. We fired the machine guns and five inch at a sleeve. The sleeve was towed by one of our planes. It came at the ship from all directions. As a sleeve was destroyed, a new one was put in its place. This is the first time in over three months that we have been back to these particular islands. It looks like we will be very busy on working parties during our stay here. Thousands of rounds of 40 mm. ammunition and 1300 rounds of six inch shells has been fired which means that more tons of ammunition are due on board. Hundreds of tons of additional supplies await us here. I hope the rain slackens a bit. I hit the sack at 9:30 P.M. but was quickly awakened at 11:15 P.M. for a working party on the fantail.

Wednesday, January 5, 1944: I began work on stores last night and did not stop until 7:30 this morning. I had breakfast, and then pulled the 8 to 12 noon watch. We're going to take on 300 tons of food plus ammunition. Little sleep is in store for us for quite some time. I ate a lot of fruit while on the working party, one compensation. The first fruit I had in over several months.

I went to the beach for recreation, the first enjoyable time we had yet. We played baseball and got our minds off work. We also received mail. I received a letter from my sister Mary. She had heard from our brother John whose ship had been sunk during the invasion of Tarawa in the Gilberts, November of 1943. She said that John was lucky to be alive. He is now in a hospital in California where he was operated on for a head wound. His back was also in bad shape. Before coming back to the States, he was taken to an island and who was there but my brother Joe. Joe received some new clothes for him. It was one for the books. Out of all of the thousands of islands in the Pacific, John should land on the same island as Joe. Joe is a chief petty officer in aviation. John is a store keeper, 1st class. Joe could hardly believe his eyes as he saw John.

The carrier *Liscomb Bay* was hit early in the morning. It went down very fast, 900 men were lost from a crew of 1100. I will receive the details later.

Thursday, January 6, 1944: Reveille at 6 A.M. We commenced carrying ammunition half an hour later. After breakfast, we left the ship for the island on an all day ammunition working party. We did not return to the ship until 6:30 that evening. We carried ammunition for about twelve hours. When we reached the beach, we had an excellent view of the island. It is an enormous base of buildings and barracks that seems to be everywhere. It's like a city in itself. We did not stay on the beach for long as an army truck loaded us aboard and we were transported about ten miles into the jungle. It rained very hard on our way into the jungle and everyone got soaked. I had worn only my pants, shoes and sox because of the heat. I had left my shirt and hat under the pier when I got off the landing craft. I will pick them up on the backward journey. We worked very hard loading ammunition. It finally stopped raining as the sun came out very hot. It did not take long to get a good burn since I had nothing to cover my back. For dinner, each man had one sandwich, one orange and an apple. It only increased our appetites, as we had a small breakfast as usual. Late in the afternoon we all trooped into the truck and headed back to the beach.

On our homeward journey, we saw a WAC in a car. This was a big thing for us because we never come across women where we are. We have seen women on two occasions in almost a year, this will make the third time. Before boarding the landing craft, I retrieved my clothes under the pier. It was 6:30 P.M. when we finally reached the ship. Supper was over with. We had to settle

for bread, butter, beans and one orange. We were so hungry that
we could have eaten for a week. Breakfast would be a long wait.
Everyone was tired and looked forward to a good night's sleep. I
was awoken for the midnight to 4 A.M. watch. I cannot depend on
sleep here, it seems.

Friday, January 7, 1944: I was relieved of watch at 4 A.M. and
boy was I tired. I had a couple of hours' sleep before arising at
6:30 A.M. After breakfast we went back to carrying ammunition.
We finished around 5 P.M.

The carriers *Bunker Hill* and *Monterey* arrived this afternoon.
The men on those ships are fortunate that they don't have to do
any bombarding. They miss a lot of extra work. Lt. Jg. Graham,
one of our division officers, lent a hand in carrying the ammunition. He's an easygoing person and everyone likes him. A newspaper I read today was dated December 2, 1943. The headlines
carried the sinking of the *Liscomb Bay*, the carrier my brother
was on before being hit by the Japs. The two carriers that arrived
today took part in the raids at Rabaul. Heavy damage was inflicted on the island.

Saturday, January 8, 1944: About twenty men were awoken at
5:30 A.M. and left the ship with Lt. Jg. Graham. Gunnery practice would be held many miles from here. Every day a different
group leaves the ship to partake in this practice. The island was
soon out of view as we were transported to our destination. Before we left the ship, we had chow at 6:30 A.M. A large box of
sandwiches were carried with us to serve for our dinner. The boat
that was used to carry us was squeezed to its capacity. Life jackets
were ordered to be worn. Fifty men had drowned on one of these
trips a short time ago. They had run into a storm and capsized, if
they wore life jackets, their lives may have been saved. Two
hours was taken to reach our destination. Fighter planes, Corsairs, would swoop down upon us. We could almost touch them
as they passed overhead. This was good practice for the pilots and
they were having great fun. We enjoyed it. A little rain fell but
did not last long. We reached the island and as one looked out to
sea, nothing was seen but water. No land was in sight anywhere.

The water beat against the coral on the beach and caused quite a noise. The coral reefs are as big as a house. After leaving the beach, we headed into the jungle. Coral could be seen everywhere in the jungle. It would make good bomb-proof shelters, it's hard as steel. It was a little cooler in the jungle but now the weather turned damp and moist. Once the heat penetrates through the jungle, it seems as if one is in a hot steam bath. No air could be found there also. The island was chock full of ants, flies and lizards, to mention a few of the countless hundreds of the crawling species that were found there.

The firing range was in a large clearing before us. It had been in operation for nine months. There was a mess hall and numerous men were stationed here. We spent the day firing the 20 and 40 mm. machine guns. The army was firing its 50 cal. guns. Compared to our guns, they looked undersized. Many targets were provided us, including planes carrying sleeves. Every man took his turn at all conceivable positions of the gun, i.e., pointer, trainer, loader and feeder. The reasoning behind this was if a man is knocked out of action, anyone can step up and take over for him. We had chow at the mess hall. We saved our sandwiches for later in the afternoon. Just before dinner it rained very hard. We were forced to wait outside the chow line in the pelting rain, and boy, did we get soaked. The sight of the fellows running in the rain with a tray in one hand and a hat in the other, as they tried to avoid the puddles, was something to see. Other sailors were running around corners, looking for a place to eat their meal in dry surroundings.

After the rain subsided, we resumed firing, until 3:30 in the afternoon. Everyone was hungry by now. We finished off the sandwiches and apples were also provided. The army group finally finished their practice here. They had been here for a good part of a week. We made our way back through the jungle and at last reached the beach. We had the appearance of pirates just returning from burying treasure. It was a well spent day and felt good to be on land for a change. Before leaving, Lt. Graham checked to see if anyone was missing. A storm was brewing as we left the island. All of the way back to the ship it rained very hard. The sea was rough and dark clouds hovered above. The salt water came gushing over the sides of our small boat. We had a mouth full of salt water as the boat hit each wave. It was during this kind of a storm that the fifty men, mentioned earlier, were lost.

Upon reaching Espiritu Santo, we were very chilly and wet, as the rain followed us our entire trip. We waited twenty minutes on the pier for a boat to return us to the *Montpelier*. While we were waiting, a WAVE passed by the pier. Everyone forgot his miseries as we scanned the surface of same. Things were picking up, this was the second girl we've seen in two days.

Upon reaching the ship we took a shower and put on dry clothes. I checked mail but none came. I went on watch but had not to stay there long because of the lateness of our arrival. I hit the sack at 8:30 P.M.

Sunday, January 9, 1944: All hands up at 6 A.M. Before breakfast the decks were washed down. For this duty, we break out the big fire hose and soak the deck with the ocean's water. Scrubbing comes next with big enormous brushes. We then use rubber squeegees and finish the process with swabs or mops. The men are shoeless and stockingless and pants rolled up to their knees as the work is being performed. When we finish, the swabs are lowered overside at the end of a line and receive a thorough cleaning. They are then put in racks upside down to dry. This routine is followed every day by us, if not at battle stations. Of course, we poor swabbies are last to get to chow and more times than not, miss out on some of the chow that has been depleted.

Our section spent the afternoon on the beach. It was scheduled this morning but rain delayed this. We like to go over on the beach for the recreation is very good now. Everyone had a great time. We had a regular picnic. Each sailor was given four small bottles of beer and as many hot dogs as we wanted. Coca-Cola and ice cream were also there but payment was required for them. We could also hear music over a loudspeaker. Before we left the ship, each man was allowed to buy two chits at ten cents apiece. On the beach we could purchase a bottle of beer with each chit. Chits were selling for a dollar apiece on the beach. Later in the afternoon when most of the chits were exhausted, some of the fellows would be willing to pay five dollars to acquire one of them. It was very expensive beer for some. Five dollars for a small bottle of beer is quite a price to pay. Recreation is so infrequent, the price matters little. The weather was hot but did not prevent us from playing a game of baseball. The men waiting their turn at bat would retreat to the jungle where in the shade it was a little cooler, and lizards were observed. One of the fellow's nose was broken by a baseball but it didn't seem to bother him much for he was playing again before the game finished. Fist fights were predominant as is usually the case when a sailor is mixed with beer. We arrived on board ship at 4 P.M. The food seems to be a little better now. At least it's eatable.

Today 128 men left for the firing range that we toured yesterday. They took their sacks with them and enough clothes to last a week. There are all new men who came aboard a few months ago. We received a bag of mail today. I hope for a letter. A movie was held topside tonight, it was "Sahara," and not too old.

Tuesday, January 11, 1944: We left Espiritu Santo this morning for gunnery practice. A sub also accompanied us. Its duty was to act as the enemy. We were ordered to be on the lookout for the sub and report it as soon as we spotted its wake or periscope. We were also attacked by F 4 U Corsairs, also acting as the enemy. We fired all our guns and shot down quite a few sleeves that were towed by the planes. I was at battle stations most of the day.

Thursday, January 13, 1944: For the past few days we took part in war maneuvers. We were very busy as most of the time was spent at battle stations. We remained there until late in the night. About 10 P.M. we exploded star shells, lighting the sea as if it were daytime. The Japs have better star shells. It may be because they fire 8 inch shells and we five or six.

Havannah Harbor is now our port. It's in the New Hebrides. We're about two hundred and fifty miles south of Espiritu Santo, and about eight hundred miles south of Guadalcanal.

There were five battleships anchored here. I think they were the *North Carolina, Indiana, South Dakota, Washington* and *Alabama.* Two were camouflaged. They're all new battleships, about two years old. They're very fast and pack a wallop to be proud of. I wish we had a few of them with us when we go up the Slot.

This place had not changed much since we were here about seven months ago. Everything here will be moved in time to Espiritu Santo. They had a party for Admiral Merrill and Task Force 39 on the beach.

Friday, January 14, 1944: I went to the beach today to find a friend of mine from my home town by the name of Edward Shaughnessy but he was transferred to the States about two months ago. The island is a very quiet and deserted place.

I received two shots in the arm today. Everyone gets these, about once a year.

We left Havannah Harbor for Espiritu Santo 5 P.M. today. The *Montpelier* is going to dry dock there. It's the floating dry dock mentioned earlier, the largest of its kind in the world. It's over 600 feet long. When the other section arrives, it will measure at least 1000 feet long. One section of it sank while here. Thirteen men were drowned. Some were abed when it happened. An officer went down to alert them and he also was among the victims.

The light cruiser *Cleveland* had the honor of being the first ship to use the dry dock. It was there for repairs last week. Our ship will be the second to use its facilities. When the dry dock is entirely completed, it will service four destroyers at one time.

Saturday, January 15, 1944: All hands up at 4:30 A.M. At 10 we pulled into dry dock. The weather was rainy. One of the men who was in charge of proceedings at the dry dock was named Hootman. Everyone on our ship was shouting Hoot Man, it sounded very funny at the time. He really knew his stuff though. The huge dry dock floats in the water with our ten thousand ton light cruiser snug inside. It's quite an experience. The ship looks as if it were sitting in the center of a huge ballfield. I was one of the first to be picked for the work detail. I was the first one from my division to reach the bottom of the dry dock. It's a long way from the ship, at least the height of a four or five story building. We used a rope ladder to reach our destination. Compartments are built into the dry dock, this is where the personnel stay. A large crew is employed here. The work is very hard and is referred to by the crew as a slave ship. The climate here is hot and humid.

The dry dock carries a large supply of scrapers and steel brushes. We don't have to look forward of running short of them. At 5 P.M. everything was in readiness as scraping the side of the ship was ordered. All the paint and barnacles will be removed. We have our work cut out for us. Our ship is 607 feet long and both sides will be worked on, which means around the clock, both day and night until completion. Some of the stagings are not too safe. It's a long way to the bottom. Some of the *Cleveland*'s crew fell off similar stagings and broke legs and arms.

I retired at 9 P.M. but Ski woke me at 11 P.M. to go over the side for scraping. A ham sandwich and one orange was provided us before work. It's still raining.

Sunday, January 16, 1944: I was relieved at 7 A.M. I looked like a coal miner. The stuff really sticks to you. It rained all night as we scraped paint. I took a shower and had breakfast. Recordings are played all the time and will continue until our stay here is terminated.

Each division has a section of the ship to scrape and paint. I slept until noon, had chow, and over the side again. The way the stagings move around, it's a wonder someone does not fall off. I knocked off at 5 P.M. for chow and then went on the six to eight watch. Still raining.

Monday, January 17, 1944: Had the 8 to noon watch. Ski awoke me at 10:30 P.M. to scrape paint. I will work there until seven tomorrow morning. One of the fellows had paint sprayed on his face. They took him to the hospital as he could not see. Still raining. It hasn't stopped raining since we arrived. A few miles away the sun is shining. We placed hot tar on the sides and three coats of paint. The ship is almost completed.

Tuesday, January 18, 1944: I was relieved at 7 this morning. I pulled the 12 noon to 4 P.M. watch. I will have the midnight watch tonight. A movie was held tonight topside in the rain.

Wednesday, January 19, 1944: I was relieved of watch at 4 A.M. this morning. Got up at 6:30 A.M., had breakfast and was ready for the working party that was sure to come. Everyone will be glad to leave its work and weather. Our clothes and shoes are ruined from the dirt, paint and tar.

We left dock at 2:30 P.M., heading back to Espiritu Santo. Arrival time was 5 P.M. On the way back we saw two nurses in bathing suits with two officers, they were in a small boat. The rain has stopped. The two carriers that were docked at Espiritu Santo had left. I wrote a letter to Mary and one to John. About 23 men were transferred today. A movie was held topside tonight. We received mail today. I hope to get some.

Friday, January 21, 1944: We left this morning for maneuvers and gunnery. We fired star shells at night. A large sled that was towed by another ship, was our target. I received a letter from my sister Mary. After three months from the time John's ship was sunk, I finally get to know what happened. John told Mary that he did not know what hit him on the head, knocking him unconscious and leaving him with a hole in his head. As his ship was sinking, a fellow sailor pushed him over the side. His life was saved by that action only. He was also cut over the eye. It later healed leaving a slight scar. His back and shoulders were also injured. A bad case of nerves later developed and he still wakes up with a cold sweat. I also received a letter from John. He was to have an operation performed on his head as it was still draining. His head was fractured and a plastic surgeon was to graft the opening and make it uniform. The doctor informed him that the only thing that saved his life was that his skull and bones are very hard. It would have killed an ordinary person. John is now located at a hospital in Corona, California. He wrote that it was a beautiful place, formerly being a country club. In the distance he can see the snowcapped mountains. He further wrote that his ship was sunk just before sunup. As another ship in the distance was viewing the rising of the sun, it seemed as though it were a flaming ball, then nothing. It was impossible for the sun to rise and then set all in the period of fifteen minutes, but for a ship to be hit and sunk in that time spread, yes. Nine hundred lost their lives including a three star admiral in those early morning hours. My sister Mary first learned of the tragedy upon returning from work by way of a newspaper that she had happened to buy. She was dumfounded. Finally receiving a telegram from John, she fell to her knees and thanked God for saving his life. Approximately 200 men were saved and of those numerous were wounded.

Saturday, January 22, 1944: We are still on sea maneuvers. All hands awoke at 4:15 A.M. Chow was served at 5:45 A.M. We destroyed some drones this morning. A drone is a plane guided by remote control. It dips and turns as a plane bearing a pilot. The *Montpelier* received an English officer on board today as a guest. We returned to Espiritu Santo at 4 P.M. Most of the fellows on board have colds. The first in over a year for anyone on board. Mary wrote that Ed Shaughnessy arrived home for Christmas after spending twenty-one months down here. He stayed undercover because it was too cold for him outside. He's not used to that kind of weather.

Tuesday, January 25, 1944: After four days of gunnery practice and maneuvers, we returned to Espiritu Santo. I had recreation today and spent some time talking to the troops ashore who had just returned from the States after being there twelve to sixteen months. Traveling time here involved some twenty-three days. They expect to be shipped to Bougainville in the near future. Most of them slept topside on the way down here, as it was too hot below decks. Space topside was like world series seats in the bleachers, hard to come by and still harder to hold onto.

Wednesday, January 26, 1944: We left Espiritu Santo this morning at 8. Our destination is Purvis Bay. Gunnery practice and maneuvers were conducted on the way.

Saturday, January 29, 1944: Purvis Bay. 500 miles of voyage are behind us as we again reach our destination. 50 bags of mail await us. I received a fruit cake from Mrs. Sweeney that had turned rancid. It traveled three months to reach me. The heat here destroys food swiftly.

Sunday, January 30, 1944: I'm writing in the 40 mm. magazine. The hatch is opened to air out the place. An exchange ship reached the States from Japan and the passengers related how cruel and barbarous the treatment the prisoners received from the Japs. They want Japan bombed at once.

Thursday, February 3, 1944: I left the ship at 6:30 A.M. for Tulagi. I went to see the eye doctor. My eyes are bothering me and I need eyeglasses. I did not get the glasses for they did not have any, in fact, the poor doctor didnt have much to work with at all. His quarters were housed in a small shack. An officer, sailors and a few Marines made the trip with me in a good sized craft. It took an hour of traveling time to reach Tulagi. It rained all day and the sea was very rough. We had no rain gear and were soaked. On numerous occasions I thought that we would capsize. We had a dog aboard and he was seasick before reaching land. I didn't feel any too good myself. On returning we came across a landing craft that was drifting out to sea. Its motor was dead. We threw a line to those aboard and towed them in. The waves were enormous and every now and then the craft would disappear. I was nearly thrown over the side as I lost my balance.

While on Tulagi, I looked the island over. The Marines had had some bloody fighting here. I approached a Marine cemetery. The hills and mountains are very high and one can see many openings in the sides. They looked like big coral caves. There must have been large chambers inside. Numerous caves are sealed with dead Japs inside. I arrived back at the ship at 2:30 P.M. I then had something to eat, the first food since last night at supper. The Press News reported the invasion of the Marshalls. The largest fleet of naval warships were assembled for that action. I will get a good night's sleep for a change.

Friday, February 4, 1944: Up at six with the sun to greet us. We had battle drills while all hands were at battle stations. We feigned that the enemy attacked us and that our ship was hit by shells from the Jap warships. Some gun mounts were knocked out in the imaginary action and men from other mounts were sent to relieve them. Stretchers were dispatched to carry the wounded. Those not badly hurt were ordered back to stations. Six men and myself were sent to another mount to keep the guns firing. We also received first aid instruction. Some of the fellows must be becoming "Asiatic," they have holes drilled into their ears and put a ring through it. It didn't last long as they put a stop to it.

Saturday, February 5, 1944: Went on watch this morning at four, had chow and then left the ship for an ammunition working party. Our destination, a barge, was well away from the rest of the other ships about twenty yards from the jungle in a corner of the island. We brought our dinner with us, consisting of a ham sandwich and an apple. The day like all days was hot. At noon we went swimming off the side of the barge. Native canoes would come by often, carrying bananas. A destroyer pulled alongside about three in the afternoon to receive ammunition. They had just returned from a bombardment. One of the destroyers in their group had been hit on the fantail by Jap shore guns. The crew from the destroyer carried its own ammunition aboard. With nothing for us to do, the officer in charge permitted swimming again. We arrived back at the ship at 4 P.M. Stew, bread and butter was served for supper.

Sunday, February 6, 1944: Up at 5:30 this morning. Church services were held topside. Received a letter from my sister Mary today, dated January 17. John is out of the hospital and on his way to visit her. He will stop at Chicago where he will visit a friend's mother. Her son was killed when the carrier went down. Went over to the beach, just sat around and talked. Stevenson received some pictures from his brother in the Air Force. He's stationed in Vermont. Steve comes from Detroit. He likes to sing the Michigan College song "Champions of the West." Movies topside tonight. We had a good supper tonight, apples and cup cakes. The troopship *President Johnson* arrived a few days ago followed today by another. Its troops cannot leave the ships.

Wednesday, February 9, 1944: No news today. I pulled the movie working detail and was kept awake until the movies were completed. After the movies were shown, we lugged benches back to the mess hall and swept the deck. The picture shown was "Stage Door Canteen."

Thursday, February 10, 1944: Awoke at 6 A.M. Had pictures taken of us on the forecastle this morning. Recreation was held today and everyone received three chits to acquire beer with. Steve rolled dice and lost his to one of the fellows. I gave him two of mine and he proceeded to lose them directly. We were then left with one bottle of small beer to share between ourselves. It rained a good part of the day forcing us back to the ship quite wet. I received another letter from Mary. John did not arrive home as yet. Tony Freitas dispatched $120 towards the building of a church in India. Each man donated $5. $500 was needed but the collections fell short. Only close friends and of the same denomination were asked to give.

Friday, February 11, 1944: Very hot today as usual. We had fish for dinner. We also took aboard six inch ammunition. Those armor-piercing shells are really heavy. They have a pointed steel cap on the head of the shell that penetrates the thickness of steel and then explodes. I was chosen for the trash working party. After collecting the trash, we were transported to a nearby island to burn it. We went through the submarine nets and traveled about five miles from the ship. Some of the boys took a swim on the way. While on the island, a man with only a "g" string as his wardrobe came around a corner of the jungle. He was upon us before anyone realized that he was there. He did not stay there long as he took off immediately. At the time it didn't dawn on us that he was a Jap. We believed that he was a Chinese. Maybe it was just as well for his friends might have been close by and us without any arms. It was the hand of the Lord watching over us. There are still plenty of Japs hiding in the jungles here.

There's about fifty ships stationed here now, around twenty-five destroyers. We received the pictures taken earlier. Today was the first time I noticed the number of my locker, 734.

Saturday, February 12, 1944: The destroyer *Renshaw* left this afternoon. We will pull out tomorrow afternoon at 4 P.M. Saw something in Life Magazine about the Bougainville Campaign, the November 27, 1943 issue, issue 43, page 36. The New Guinea Campaign is almost over and the fighting in Italy is a lot fiercer than they had expected.

Sunday, February 13, 1944: Arose at 3:15 A.M. for watch. Had church services topside. The priest wore sun glasses, it was that sunny. We had a good supper, turkey, pie and ice cream. Left Purvis Bay at 2 P.M. On our way to bombard Green Island and disembark troops. Green Island is approximately 700 miles north of here. It's between New Ireland and Bougainville, east of Rabaul, New Britain. We will patrol between Truk and Rabaul. We will prevent the Japs from reinforcing from Truk or evacuating Bougainville, Buka or Rabaul. We shall intercept and defeat them at any cost. Rather this than standing still at Purvis Bay. As the sun was setting, the *Montpelier* left Bougainville in the shadows of the approaching night.

Monday, February 14, 1944: All hands on deck at 5:15 A.M. I slept topside last night. The sky was full of stars, it was beautiful for sleep. All hands left battle stations at 6:30 A.M. We kept our sky radar off because that is how the Jap planes could find out where we were, they would follow the beam our radar sent out and follow it back to us. They also tipped their ships off that we were coming up to get them and the ships would go back to their base. Now they will not be able to tip the Jap Navy off and they might send a force of ships down and we can knock them off. We use the air coverage because the radar is off. The Japs cannot pick up beams from the Surface Radar because the planes do not go that low.

At 10 A.M., while off Bougainville, a Jap sub tried to attack but one of our planes, covering us well, sunk it. There are, according to information, eighteen enemy subs operating in nearby waters.

I got off watch at noon and ate chow and then went on fantail and started to do this writing but a little rain came and chased me down to the mess hall. The sea was very calm and the sun was out all morning. We were told to get plenty of rest because we would have G.Q. all night. The Japs' living room would be invaded by us again.

The planes that were sent from Munda, to relieve our air cover, were unable to find us for some time, as our radar was inoperative. The planes, F 6 F Hellcats and F 4 Us, Corsairs, were the best possible cover the force could ask for.

It was very hot in the compartments. The only relief is topside. At 7 P.M. all hands reported to battle stations.

This will be the furthest north we have ever traveled. We are close to Rabaul, on New Britain, and New Ireland. Task Force 38, with the cruisers *St. Louis* and *Honolulu* and a fleet of destroyers, are not too far away from the *Montpelier*. Task Force 38 has radar on, ours does not. In case of an attack on Task Force 38, our fleet will pull the old end run and come in on them. After five days we will change procedures with Task Force 38, i.e. radar and positions. Lookouts were posted because of the radar situation. Sky radar did most of our work before, we really miss it now.

Approximately 10 P.M., Task Force 38 was attacked by Jap torpedo planes and dive bombers. The *Honolulu* was hit by the oncoming planes, damage was considered light. If we, instead of they, had been using sky radar, we would have taken the brunt of the attack. The Good Lord is still with us.

Tuesday, February 15, 1944: At 4:30 A.M., the invasion of Green Island commenced. New Zealand troops were also in the contingent that was landed. Jap planes attacked the troops later in the day. No serious damage was reported.

Task Force 38 was again hit by Jap planes this morning. No damage to our ships was inflicted as countless enemy planes were destroyed.

Battle stations were sounded at 7 P.M. as we prepared for another sleepless night.

Task Force 38 was under fire for the third time. More troops were landed on Green Island with us on board hoping to meet an attacking enemy force at sea.

Sandwiches were served on deck about midnight. Apples and cookies were also added. Everyone is dead tired. We have had only a few hours sleep in three days.

Wednesday, February 16, 1944: Relieved from battle stations at 7 A.M. Lines were broken out at noon for fuel. We pulled alongside the tanker, just below Bougainville. A couple of hours' sleep was appreciated by me in the afternoon. Still too hot below, and mighty hot on deck in the sun. I chose the latter. We will be off again tonight. Our mission will be the same as in past nights. It will be another night without sleep.

Thursday, February 17, 1944: Heading back to Purvis Bay as the destroyers will take over. Our services are not required for the Japs refuse to dispatch ships from Truk. The sponge is being thrown in by the Japs, this time. They know it would be too costly to hold onto these islands. They have plenty more to fall back on. The Press News, this morning, said Green Island fell and it was ours now. The Solomons Campaign is over and this seals the doom of the Japs on Bougainville, about 25,000 of them. They cannot get supplies now and in time they will starve and die. Our troops are still fighting them on there.

The cruiser *St. Louis* suffered twenty-five killed and eighteen wounded from plane attacks.

Tonight on the way back we had no destroyers with us and we could see a Jap sub's periscope 1500 yards ahead of us. We made a complete turn and left the sub, we are too fast for a sub to catch us. We do not carry anything to fight a sub, unless it comes to the surface and then we can open up with our guns and sink it. There are a lot of subs here. The destroyers that left us this afternoon are on their way to Rabaul Harbor. They are going right through the nets and bombard the base in there. We cannot go now because we are too big to go in there yet. We may go up there next week. "I wish we were going with them" is what one of the fellows heard Admiral Merrill say, and I wish the same thing.

Friday, February 18, 1944: We pulled into Purvis Bay at 8 A.M. The *Honolulu* and *St. Louis* were here to greet us. The radioman informed us that Truk was being attacked by carrier planes. This assault is the first ever attempted on the island. A large fleet is taking part in the attack.

Received mail today. John is home. While at home, he will report to Chelsea Naval Hospital and have his injuries checked. His nerves are still bothersome to him.

Saturday, February 19, 1944: All hands on deck at 5:30 this morning. I took a shower and had chow. Ship inspection is scheduled for today. The Press News stated that hundreds of carrier planes had hit Truk.

Our destroyers returned at 3 P.M. They accomplished what never was thought possible. Barging into an enemy-held harbor and blazing away with all guns and torpedoes firing is quite an accomplishment. A strongly fortified island as New Ireland is doubly hard. The attack took place in the daytime as the ships broke through the nets before entering. A rousing ovation was rendered to the destroyers as they entered Purvis Bay. We sent them ice cream. 31-knot Burke was in command.

Wednesday, February 22, 1944: The Press News again reported that the Jap Fleet had pulled out of Truk before the carrier strike. Our planes were credited with sinking a few cruisers, destroyers and cargo ships. 200 Japanese planes were shot down. Tojo has taken the command of the Army and Navy in Japan because of the defeats suffered recently by its armed forces.

I received a letter from Mary. John still has recurring headaches due to his injuries. The Dr. says that they will leave soon. Mary says John may get shore duty in Boston.

Swimming is banned as many on board have the flu. There's a lot of scuttlebutt about us being in the States by June. That we will go to Australia presently.

I had the midnight to four watch. The procedure after supper is sitting around and talking. Around 6:30 we rush to the movies for a seat and discussions are further continued. If the Captain or Admiral attends the movies, a bugle is blown as they enter, everyone stands at ease until they are seated. After the movie, mail call is held, then sleep.

McElhone was relating to me that when the Japanese attacked us January 1943, and sunk the heavy cruiser *Chicago,* many of the dead were stuck to the deck after being roasted alive. A Jap suicide plane was the missile of death. McElhone was stationed on the *Chicago,* he was later transferred to the *Montpelier* a short time after the *Chicago* was sunk.

Thursday, February 24, 1944: Relieved of watch at 4 A.M. Thirty-one knot Burke, with his fleet of destroyers, returned after another raid on New Ireland. They have been back and forth for ten days now. They again entered the harbor in daylight and roughed up the Japs. They sank destroyers, blasted barges loaded with troops and bombarded troops and buildings on land. They chased one ship up on shore and used it for target practice. They exhausted their ammunition and ran low on fuel. Purvis Bay gladly replenished their needs. They will return as soon as this is accomplished. Little sleep is had by all on board, a rough routine. As our Captain put it, "they have the Japs punch drunk." Warships have never done what they are doing in any war. Hollywood couldn't write a better script. There's always the possibility of being hit by the Jap shore guns. That's right down 31-knot Burke's alley. He's quite a guy. We would like to be there with him, but cruisers haven't the maneuverability of the destroyers. Cruisers are irreplaceable right now, destroyers are not. Destroyers can accomplish what is needed.

About a hundred Japs were rescued from the water by the destroyers. They were left at Tulagi.

We have had little rain for the past week. I was detailed on the trash working party. We left the harbor and went outside the nets to another beach and dumped the trash there. It's burned not too far from the shore. There were about ten natives pawing the trash. They retrieved clothing and anything that they could make use of. A few children about seven years old were with them. They looked comical with their pipes in their mouths. The oldest of the group were the ones around thirty-five years old. They appeared intelligent. A little English was spoken by them. Crucifixes were worn around their necks. They helped us with the trash. As we left, they waved goodbye to us. We waved back. Their village was some distance from the shore.

Four cargo ships were outside the nets, waiting to enter. The *President Tyler* arrived a few days ago. Upon arriving back aboard ship, the time read 5 P.M. After chow I sat around topside near the galley and chewed the rag. Red Banilover was stationed on the ammunition barge when one of the destroyers returned from the raid on Rabaul for ammunition. One of the sailors told Red that they picked up 12 Japs from the water and left them off at Guadalcanal. One of the Japs committed suicide on the destroyer. A pearl handle knife was found imbedded in his stomach. A sailor retrieved it, with the blood still dried to its steel.

Fellows who like their beer will go without as the supply of it has been depleted.

Friday, February 25, 1944: Up at six this morning. Tracking and loading drills were ordered this morning. The big shots from the Pacific Forces came aboard. There were plenty of Admirals and Captains. A big conference was held aboard ship. I hope something big is in the making, like an invasion.

Saturday, February 26, 1944: Arose at 5:30 A.M. I took a shower, had breakfast, and then stood watch from eight to twelve. Oliver came out of sick bay today. He said that eighty men were in sick bay, stricken with the flu. The Marine Compartment was used for additional space by the medics. Steve and I had some Pepsi-Cola and played catch on the beach today. As I looked about me on the beach, while pursuing the baseball, I could see some of the men playing baseball, softball, basketball, horseshoes, or just sitting under the coconut trees chewing the fat. Over in the corner, away from such strenuous exercises, were the gamblers rolling dice. Everyone was busy at his own trade.

Some of our destroyers returned from Rabaul. Thirty-One Knot Burke had given the Japs another bad time.

Monday, February 28, 1944: Relieved of watch at 4 A.M. All hands up at 6 A.M. I had breakfast at 6:45 A.M. At 8 A.M. I left the ship for the ammunition barge, tucked in the corner of the harbor, near the jungle. I did not return to the ship until 5 P.M. We worked very hard in the hot barge carrying the 135 pound six inch shells. For dinner we had sandwiches and an orange. At 3:30 in the afternoon we received word that Jap planes were on their way down to attack us. As we looked out into the distance, we could see the men on all of the ships, running to their battle stations. An ammunition barge was no place to be when enemy planes were around. While waiting for the expected attack, some of us climbed to the top of the barge to see if we could spot the approaching planes on the horizon. Our fighter planes from Guadalcanal were airborne to meet the oncoming Japs. A battle was quickly over as the Japs headed home.

Supper was miserly proportioned as a bunch of hungry sailors were still hungry after mess. Luckily, a friend of mine, G. D. Wood from Carolina, who works in the soda fountain, sold me three Skybars. I ate two and gave the other away. The movie was held on the fantail tonight. A show was also staged by the crews of the other three cruisers and the repair ship *Whiting*. Bill Johnson at the piano was exceptionally good. The Admiral and Captain also attended.

Tuesday, February 29, 1944: I attended firefighting school which was held on the beach, commencing at 7:30 A.M. We had a series of lectures and then practiced putting out fires. If the ship should be hit, the practical knowledge that we learned there today, will come in handy. An enormous tank storing 80 octane gas was set afire. It was our job to extinguish it. It seemed as if a gasoline storage tank had burst into flame. The heat that it threw off was terrific. We poured a chemical compound on it. The chemicals put the fire under control in short order. Latest fire equipment was used. The officer in charge of our group hailed from Chicago. We had a rough idea of the working parts of the firefighting equipment before leaving. Dinner was brought with us. It consisted of sandwiches and an orange. We arrived on board ship at 4:15 P.M. The supper was as anticipated, rotten. The only meal fit for human consumption is at dinnertime and I have missed yesterday's and today's. A supply ship arrived today, that's a relief. More working parties will greet the weary for the next few days.

Anderson said that we would be operating with cruisers and battleships by March 15. I hope so because I would rather be doing anything than hanging around. Andy Callahan, the fighter, was killed in action in Europe.

Wednesday, March 1, 1944: A small boat entered the harbor. It was traveling at a high rate of speed. It carried three girls and one man. Someone said that they are part of a group of Hollywood stars that will stage a show for us in the afternoon. The whole section of our ship were excused, 13 men from our division attended. The show started at 2 P.M. and was completed in an hour. Everyone enjoyed the show very much. Ray Milland and three female stars of Republic Studios were the attractions. We have been promised that more shows will be forthcoming. The girls were the first white girls in these parts since the evacuation of the English in 1942. The European Theater has been playing host to star attractions for years. It's about time we got a break. Here one never knows when the Japanese will come out of the jungles and break things up. When Ray and his girls left the States, they had no idea where their final destination would be. They flew thirty-five hours in a plane before arriving at Noumea, New Caledonia, then to Purvis Bay. They will tour all the fighting fronts nearby.

Thursday, March 2, 1944: I awoke at 4:45 A.M. At 6 A.M. another working party aboard a supply ship, was arranged. I was one of the active participants. It felt good to be working in an icebox as we unloaded 100 pound boxes of potatoes. The cold air was refreshing for a change. In the morning we had the opportunity to buy a quart of ice cream and Coca-Cola. It really hit the spot. We will take on 84 tons of supplies all together. Our working party was relieved at noon. After chow I stood watch until 4 P.M. I went to sleep to be awoken for the midnight to four watch.

Friday, March 3, 1944: Press News reported the fighting in Italy was fierce.

Made the trash working party today. We stopped the barge that was transporting us and had a swim over the side. The mail we received was dated December 5. Rain now is at a minimum, the little we do receive is very appreciated.

Saturday, March 4, 1944: Towing drills were conducted today, to ready us for the possibility that our ship is knocked out of action. The six inch turrets had a good workout. Each man there was forced to pick up the 135 pound shell nearly 200 times.

The supply ship disembarked today. The destroyer *Farenholt* left for the States. It has been away for twenty-two months. Its record was impressive as many Jap flags denoting destroyed ships and planes could be seen. Island bombardments were also noted. The homecoming banner was flown from the mast to the fantail. It's a large cloth of red, white and blue. The original crew were few in numbers as death claimed many.

We'll leave Purvis Bay tomorrow with the *Cleveland, Columbia, St. Louis* and *Honolulu,* all cruisers.

I received my certificate for crossing the equator December 1942 today. It was signed by the Admiral and Captain. I bet Steve that the allies would land in France this spring.

Sunday, March 5, 1944: All hands up at 5 A.M. Chow was served at 6. We left Purvis Bay at 7 A.M. We had sleeve firing, also firing of the five and six inch guns. Dinner was exceptional. A news reporter is traveling with us. He came aboard the other day. We had sunset General Quarters. The Captain informed us that we would refuel from a tanker around seven o'clock tomorrow morning. It will be at Bougainville. About three in the afternoon tomorrow, we will cross the equator. We have been below the equator since December 1942. We will patrol approximately 150 miles south of Truk. It will be our lot to destroy any and all Jap ships that attempt to navigate from Truk to New Britain and New Ireland. This will be the first time allied ships have patrolled in these waters during the war. Sky radar will be turned off. We can expect air attacks from Truk and other Jap held islands. We'll be in the center of Jap-occupied territory. The nearest friendly base will be hundreds of miles distant. Enemy fortifications will surround us. I hope no Jap subs stumble upon us as to give away our position. We will be in these waters for at least five days. Our force consists of three light cruisers and five destroyers. The destroyers, "the little beavers" as they are called, are under the command of 31-knot Burke. On the 10th of March we refuel and await further orders. I was relieved of watch at midnight.

Monday, March 6, 1944: All hands on deck at 5:15. It was still dark and very windy. We pulled alongside a tanker and refueled at the same time as a destroyer on the other side was doing likewise. Our speed while refueling at sea was four knots. A chaplain's call for me was issued over the loudspeaker system this afternoon. Reporting to room 222, Chaplain Embry's cabin, I couldn't figure what he wanted me for. When I reached his office, he told me that he was very sorry to relay the news to me. It was a message from the radio shack from the Red Cross. It informed me that my father had died February 21, 1944, about two weeks ago. It came as a shock for I always looked forward to the day when I would walk in on him without letting him know that I was in the States. The last time I saw him was almost eighteen months ago. I never thought that it would be the last time. My sister Mary will be all alone now. The chaplain said that when we return to our base I can send her a wire.

We crossed the equator this evening at 6 P.M. Captain Hoffman said as we crossed, "I hope we kill a lot of those slant-eyed bastards who are polluting these waters." He also said that at 6 A.M. we would start our patrol, 300 miles below Truk, and go as near as 150 miles to the island. I can feel the difference in the weather on this side of the equator, it's a lot cooler.

Tuesday, March 7, 1944: From dawn to sunrise battle stations will be maintained for the next five days. Ham sandwiches were served at our places at 11:30 last night. At 4 A.M. oranges were added to the menu. Before leaving these waters, we will be approximately 2000 miles from Tokyo. The Marshall and Gilbert Islands are over 1000 miles west. Last night intermittent rain fell. The sunrise shone brilliantly all along the horizon. Battle stations were called for early this morning, lasting a short while. A bomber crashed into the sea nearby. We circled its debris. Men were dispatched from our destroyers to investigate in a whaleboat. The clock was hitting 9:30 A.M. at the time. Finding its Jap officers dead inside, valuable papers and maps of India and the Malay Peninsula were found. Lookouts from the *Montpelier* were first to spot the plane. The sea plane, supporting the force, also saw it come out of the clouds and crash. Engine trouble was the probable cause. Sky radar was off, detection of the plane was impossible by the force. If our patrol planes find any Jap convoys, information will be relayed to the task force and we will attack. Recordings were played one hour before stations were manned. Truk is now 118 miles away.

Wednesday, March 8, 1944: All night was spent at battle stations until 8:30 A.M. The clouds are so low, one can almost touch them. Rain fell also. We had bran flakes, bread, butter, one orange and coffee for breakfast. I worked at my cleaning station this morning. My buddy from the south, G. Wood, who works in the soda fountain, sold me twenty-four bars of candy. As food is scarce, candy supplements fine. The candy bar has been our number one stand-by. Irwin had a heat stroke today. He was dead tired from lack of sleep and fell asleep in the compartment. When he awoke, he found himself in a pool of his sweat. All the salt in his body was gone. He was unable to stand. Being weak and dizzy, everything looked to him as if it were spinning. We carried him to sick bay. The doctor instructed him to consume a quantity of salt tablets and drink plenty of water. We have not detected the enemy as of yet. It looks like we could go to Japan unopposed. It was chilly on watch tonight. Around 11:30 P.M. I warmed my hands on top of the coffeepot, it felt good. My clothing is damp from the rain.

Thursday, March 9, 1944: The sunrise seemed strange this morning. Red streaks or lines were around the sun as it rose through the clouds. Powerful Jap islands were not too far away, such as Ponape, Yap, etc. Still no action. We will be the first warships to hit these waters, since the war started. With the clouds so low and our sky radar off, Jap planes could come in on us before we knew what happened.

A B–24 Liberator Bomber, operating out of Munda, is overdue. As it was on duty patrolling these waters, we will search for it. A PBY–2 Catalina Bomber flew close to us this morning. Our patrol plane was one hour late before appearing. A large canvas bag was dropped on our deck by the plane. More than likely, orders from Headquarters. Rain squalls bothered us this morning after chow.

I was at G.Q. since 5 P.M. last night, was relieved for one hour and then pulled the eight to twelve noon watch. Three hours sleep was had by me this afternoon. We are picking up speed. Each ship is much further away from the other than before. We had spaghetti, peas, bread and jelly for supper. After supper I lay down on the communications deck, next to the 20 mm. guns, and listened to the recordings over the loudspeaker. The music was interrupted at 6 P.M. because Jap planes were spotted. General Quarters were sounded and everyone ran to his battle stations. The Jap planes did not come in.

The force had been spread out in hopes of finding the crew of the B–24 bomber downed recently. This area is a most precarious spot in which to crash land. In all directions Japanese fortify the surrounding islands. Capture by the Japs would mean their deaths at a whim from their tormentors. Torture first and then a slow and agonizing end. Covering many miles, the search proved fruitless.

Captain Hoffman said that it looks like the Japs will not come out and play ball with us. He also said that the next few months would be busy ones for us. I hope so.

Friday, March 10, 1944: We left for Purvis Bay today. It's about 1000 miles south of our present position. Battle stations were carried out all through the night. We are sailing south. Men who have nothing to do are sleeping topside. I cleaned my working station and went on watch this noon. We should receive some mail when docked. We crossed the equator a little after midnight, about 12:10 A.M. The weather is sunny and warm. The sea is calm. We are scheduled to enter the bay tomorrow morning. We had sunset General Quarters. It was too hot again to sleep in the compartment so a group of fellows slept in the crew's lounge, which is on the main deck, near the starboard side of the quarterdeck. The men are sleeping everywhere, under tables, on tables, etc. I slept on a bench about twelve inches wide. It was difficult for sleep to come for I never knew when I would fall off and land on deck. Everyone slept with their clothes on. We have not shed our clothes for six days. I had the midnight to four in the morning watch.

Saturday, March 11, 1944: I fell asleep topside for an hour, after being relieved of watch at 4 A.M. All hands went to sunrise battle stations at 5:15 A.M. We fired all guns at sleeves just before arriving at Purvis Bay. We pulled into the bay at noon. We had been away for almost a week. Mail call was held but I received none. My last letter was a month ago. Chaplain Embry sent my radiogram to Mary, telling her that I received word of Pa's death. It will take three days for it to reach her. I wrote a letter to my sister and told her that I received word of Pa's death. I knew that her spirits were very low and that she was all alone so I wrote her a few words of encouragement. I told her to keep her chin up and hold down the fort because I was looking forward to the day when I would walk up the steps of good old 94 Cedar Street.*

Sunday, March 12, 1944: Arose at 3:15 to stand 4 to 8 A.M. watch today. Church services were held topside. It was a very hot sunny day. I received a package from Mary today, containing two cartons of gum, soap, towels, comb, first aid kit, etc. They say we will leave soon and bombard some undisclosed Jap islands. We hope so.

Monday, March 13, 1944: I worked on stores in the hangar deck this morning. It was like working in a hot oven. I was down in the hold passing boxes of supplies to other men, who in turn walked up a very steep ladder to the other end of the ship. They had to go through the chief's quarters to get to where they were going. The hangar deck is where our two sea planes are stored. Below the deck are storage rooms for the tons of supplies kept there. Covered with dirt and sweat, no wonder no one is happy about these working parties. Sometimes I have to crawl into little tunnels to bring out the boxes. There is very little room to navi-

---

* Our parents died when I was three years old and Mary and I left New York City to live with our cousin Mr. and Mrs. John Bray in Waltham, Mass. Both of my brothers stayed in New York City with another cousin Mr. and Mrs. Patrick Fahey. I was the youngest, my sister was next, and two years separated each of us. These generous people treated us like their own. It was a great sacrifice for them because they had enough to do to take care of their own families. They saved us from being separated and lost in some State institution. The Brays had only one child but he died years before I was born. His name was also James and I took his place. We always called the Brays our father and mother. Mrs. Bray died when I was about 16 years old.

gate. My shoulders and head are the only parts of my body in view. When I stand up, I have to lift the goods up to my shoulders to place them on deck. We had three Pepsi-Colas and we really needed them. It was something to look forward to. No beer, who cares.

In the afternoon recreation was held. I read *Yank* Magazine while Stevenson slept on a table that was placed under a coconut tree until the rains came. It rained for about an hour. I talked to a fellow who had come down from the Marshall Islands. He informed me that hundreds of our warships are there now. The highest spot in the Marshalls is about fifteen feet above sea level. He said that two of our battleships collided and returned to Pearl Harbor for repairs. When the Navy finished bombarding the island, there was nothing left standing.

Bob Feller of the Cleveland Indians is on the battleship *New Jersey*. In his first ball game in the Pacific, he struck out fifteen. The second game, eighteen. Jim Britt, the radio sports announcer, returned to the States, after being in the Pacific nine months. He is a Lieutenant in the Navy, stationed on a bomber. He also landed on Tarawa in the Gilberts, after our troops landed there.

The Japs had on Tarawa enormous shore guns captured from the British Colony of Singapore.

We had movies topside. I had the eight to midnight watch.

Tuesday, March 14, 1944: All hands up at 6 A.M. Chow was served at six forty-five. All hands reported to quarters at 8:15 A.M. I had two of my white hats dyed blue today. Field day was observed today also.

The light cruiser *Birmingham* arrived from the States. It was earlier mentioned that it was hit during November 1943 by enemy bombs. It's camouflaged. Most of the ships now arriving from the States are camouflaged. A destroyer is tied up alongside of the *Montpelier*. Its crew says that warships are plentiful at Pearl Harbor, numbering twenty carriers among them. Many destroyers arrived today plus a troopship. There are six cruisers and twenty-five destroyers stationed here. Rain was again falling today. I will enjoy sleep tonight for a change as I have no watch.

Thursday, March 16, 1944: Arose at 3:15 A.M. Watch from four to eight. I left ship at 5:30 P.M. for recreation on the beach, this time a working party, carrying cartons of beer from a barge to a nearby building used for storage. Most of the 7000 cases of beer had been toted as we arrived. 3000 remained for us to carry. About 150 men were on this working party. Some of the cases were broken open and its contents quickly disappeared. At the conclusion of the working party, we were given one cold bottle of beer. We returned to the ship at 9 P.M. Payday was also observed today. I drew some money to send home to help pay the rent.

Friday, March 17, 1944: There was an article in the Press News today mentioning Admiral Merrill. It reported that Admiral Merrill told its reporter that the Japs are leaving their troops to live on their victory gardens.

We have been on three hour notice for the past two days.

Bill Dickey, catcher for the New York Yankees, joins the Navy.

We left Purvis Bay at 1 P.M. Someone said the Japs on Bougainville have recaptured the airfields there. That is why we are going up there. The Japanese troops have not received supplies of any kind for three or four months and are becoming desperate. Suicide squadrons are organized against our troops. The Japs have in the vicinity of 20,000 troops at Bougainville. The cruisers *Columbia, Cleveland* and a few destroyers left with the *Montpelier*.

Some of the crew were transferred today, States bound. Matter from Brockton, Mass., was one of them. J. W. Hall, Nelson, and Keenan, three southern boys, were also in the group. Hall was a very friendly person, one couldn't help but like him.

The *Montpelier* has been in the Pacific for sixteen months. A radio station on Guadalcanal has been established. It sends news and music, etc. to the islands close by. We receive news and music about four times a day. It's up to date. In the mess hall they have a radio secured to the bulkhead.

Captain Hoffman stated that we were on our way up to land troops on Emirau. On March 20 troops would land there from the Third Marines. Sea Bees would later arrive to construct a base and airfield. The Sea Bees would await the establishment of neutral grounds and be put ashore as soon as this was achieved. Emirau is approximately 900 miles north of Purvis Bay, and a little below the equator. It is above New Ireland and west of the Admiralty Islands. After acquiring control of this island, the South Pacific will be ours. Resistance is expected light for many Japs are not known to be there, unless landed in the past few days. We will patrol very close to shore just in case they need us to bombard the Japs for them. By taking the island, we will leave the Japs on New Britain and New Ireland to starve, rendering their supply lines useless, as they will be cut off from help of any kind.

In the meantime carrier planes and battleships will be close by. Battleships will bombard Kavieng, New Ireland, which is south of Emirau. Five battleships will hit Kavieng. I hit the sack at midnight.

Saturday, March 18, 1944: All hands at General Quarters at 5:15 A.M. After being relieved, we ate. We went to our cleaning stations as usual. I had the 12 to 4 P.M. watch. This afternoon the ships were picking up speed and heading north towards Emirau. It's a lot cooler and the sun had not made an appearance. It was like a fall day back home in Mass. Today, as we get closer to the equator, we have an old Marine Captain on board for the trip. He does a lot of painting. He's painted pictures of the ships in our group as we sail along. He has also painted different parts of the ship as the guns, mounts, turrets, etc.

Most of the men are laying around catching up on sleep because we will be at stations most of the night and early morning. The warships in our group are losing speed. The troopships and supply ships are behind us, below the horizon. Battle stations were called for at 7 P.M.

Sunday, March 19, 1944: We left General Quarters at 7 A.M. Our force consists of three light cruisers and six destroyers. Thirty-one knot Burke is in command of the destroyers. Admiral Merrill and Burke are fast becoming a legend, as their feats are told and retold throughout the world.

The destroyers refueled from the cruisers this morning. I

helped get the transfer gear from the sail locker. We sent food and ice cream to the destroyers. Stevenson and I received a big ham sandwich from Schmidt for aiding him in carrying boxes of meat from the shop. The bake shop supplied us with a pineapple. Our cleaning station is near the bakery and galley. When they want any work done, they ask us. We never refuse as it usually means food. I had some rest from 11 A.M. to 3:15, this afternoon. I missed noon chow. After awaking I washed and left for the 4 to 6 P.M. watch. Was relieved of watch, and had chow. I then went to the communications deck and lay on the 20 mm. ammunition box and listened to recordings over the loudspeaker. At 7 P.M. all hands went to General Quarters. We will be up all night again.

Captain Hoffman reiterated that we were leading the parade, the carriers, battleships, troopships were behind us. We could not see them. The carriers and battleships will strike New Ireland while we land troops at Emirau.

At night the stars looked very close, the sky was very clear. The Southern Cross could be viewed without bothersome clouds in the way. In a couple of days it will be the 21st of March and we will be close to the equator. Emirau is nearing and before long, the Marines will be establishing a beachhead.

Monday, March 20, 1944: Battle stations were observed all night. Tiredness left as the Marines from the Third Division started for the beach. It was not too bright and no rain fell. About 7 A.M. we had a wonderful view of the beach. There must be at least thirty-five ships here. From our vantage point very little opposition was met on the beach. A radio station will be one of the primary targets. The island is not as high as other islands that I've been to. B–24 Liberators, and Hellcat Fighters are also taking part in this invasion. No fire from the beach has been observed. It's 9:30 A.M. now. No Jap planes have appeared as yet. Every phase of this operation is proceeding smoothly. The Japs may be under the impression that we're going to land at New Ireland. They must be taking a terrific pounding from the battleships. The weather is cloudy as supplies are being put ashore. This will pull down the curtain on the war in the South Pacific.

We left General Quarters at 8:10 A.M. Around midnight last night we were served a sandwich, I supplemented it with a Skybar. Still at battle stations this morning, we received an apple.

Although there was no action, the landing was quite a thing to see. The taking of this island outsmarted the Japs as they anticipated our next move would be the invasion of the bigger and heavily fortified islands of New Ireland or New Britain. By landing on Emirau, we saved thousands of lives and shortened the war in the Pacific by months. It must be very discouraging for the Japs to see us pass their strongholds for more strategic islands without the awesome casualties that would have been incurred. The Japanese will begin to feel our breath down their backs pretty soon. When the airfield is in operation, bombing of the hostile islands will begin.

It's 10 A.M. Sleep is in order. We haven't had sleep for a few nights now, only a couple of hours in the daytime and that could only be considered as rest. I go on G.Q. at 5 P.M.

The Press News said that our planes and bombers struck 960 miles from Japan.

After sleeping from 11 A.M. to 3:15 in the afternoon, I missed lunch. I have not had a good meal in days, just sandwiches, apples and candy bars. We will be at battle stations again tonight.

While all hands were at General Quarters, Captain Hoffman spoke to the men at 7:15 P.M. He said that our troops landed with no opposition to greet them. The Sea Bees will start work on the airfields in the near future. That our battleships fired 1400 rounds of 14 inch shells at Kavieng, New Ireland, this morning, plus bombs and shells fired from our planes. Coupled with this, the place is a shambles.

It rained a little today. I almost forgot to mention that another island, not too far from Emirau, is fortified with Jap troops.

Tuesday, March 21, 1944: We were at General Quarters all night and were not relieved until 7:30 this morning. At home it's the first day of spring. I had chow then reported for watch. I had the eight to twelve watch. It's very sunny and warm today. We patrolled around Emirau for the rest of the day and night, in case the Japs should send ships down to hit the island. The carriers, battleships and other warships left last night for their bases. Our task force is the only group of warships here. This has been the easiest island to secure since being in the Pacific.

I had my noon meal, the first in three days as I've been asleep as noon chow was served previously. A few hours sleep seemed more important to me. I received three and a half hours sleep this afternoon. All hands reported to General Quarters at 7 P.M. The Captain said that we would leave here at 8 P.M. tonight. That seven destroyers would relieve the task force. That tomorrow morning the destroyers would refuel from us and we would head south for Purvis Bay. The Captain also said that we advanced many miles into Jap-held territory the past few months.

A few months ago no one thought that we would be here on an island in the back yard of the Japanese Empire. It's believed that our home base will be changed. We have traveled over 100,000 miles since leaving the States December of '42. Many miles of this total have been in Japanese waters.

It's been sixteen months since talking to a female outside of the three days I spent in Australia.

A few years ago if someone told me, I would have never believed that I would become efficient in landing troops and seeking battles against the Japs. It's becoming a habit like working in a factory. At first it was a frightening experience, now it's just another day's work. We still look forward to the next campaign. We left General Quarters at 11 P.M. and the regular watch was set. I hit the sack at midnight. It was too hot to sleep below. I fell asleep on an ammunition box under the stars. The ammunition box was made of steel and about two feet wide with a large space between my feet and head. It also had buckles that dug into me. It was uncomfortable but I was too tired to notice. After sixteen months of sleeping where one chanced to be, a little inconvenience like this was taken in stride.

Wednesday, March 22, 1944: All hands arose at 5:30 A.M. Sunrise General Quarters were ordered. Arising at one hour before sunrise was the rule to prevent the Japs from sneaking in on us unprepared. We left General Quarters at 7:15 to have breakfast. Rest was given to those who had no work to do. I finished cleaning my station and lay under the six inch turret at 9 A.M. At 11 A.M. I arose attired in sweat as it was another hot and sunny day. We are sailing south to Purvis Bay. The sea is calm. It's a long trip from Emirau to Purvis, approximately 900 miles. We met a camouflaged tanker as destroyers were refueling from it. I spent the afternoon on watch from noon to four.

At 2:20 P.M. sky radar picked up a Jap plane thirty miles distant. It was not long before we could see it heading towards us. When it was within range of our guns, it turned around and headed back in the direction from which it came. It was a Jap twin engine bomber. We call it a Betty. It was on patrol. We could have very easily have shot it out of the skies but we wanted it to return to Truk and report our position. General Quarters failed to sound as the situation was well in hand.

Thursday, March 23, 1944: I was relieved of watch at 4 A.M. It rained very hard commencing at 3:30 A.M. All hands appeared at General Quarters at 5 A.M. Gunnery was conducted in the morning and then again in the afternoon.

The Press News reported that U.S. submarines have sunk 642 Jap ships since December 7, 1941.

Before entering Purvis Bay, the Little Beaver Squadron led by 31-knot Burke came roaring past us on both sides at full speed. Everyone was present topside as they passed at close range. All of the destroyers' hands gave a big cheer. We returned the cheer. Admiral Merrill had no idea of what was happening. He ordered the flags hoisted saying, "What the hell's up." I could see the big grin on Burke's face and the rest of the men on the bridge as they flew by. We believed that he was in pursuit of Japs at first. We learned later that the Little Beaver Squadron was scheduled to leave us to operate in the Central Pacific. Burke thought that he would have a little fun before leaving. We will miss his squadron as we have operated as a team well over a year. You could always depend on them. We also learned that Admiral Merrill would leave for the States in a few days.

We sailed into Purvis Bay at 4:30 this evening. We pulled alongside a tanker to refuel, finishing at 8 P.M. I was on the refueling detail and while we were refueling, the rain came pelting down. Leaving here Friday March 17, and returning March 23, we will get our first night's uninterrupted sleep in a week.

Sunday, March 26, 1944: I arose at 5:30 A.M., took a shower, and then had breakfast. Chick Bartholow and I had the church working party. All there was to do was the passing of the hymn books before Protestant services started and return to collect them afterwards. Catholic services were held in the afternoon. It's another hot and sunny day. At 10:30 A.M. all hands assembled aft on the fantail to see Rear Admiral Aaron Stanton Merrill for the last time. Uniform of the day was whites. Everyone on board would rather hear him say that he was going to stay with us than to say goodbye. They don't come any better than "Tip." We all thought the world of him, and would do anything for him. He was a person one could not help but like. He was humble and was a very easy person to get along with. He will be very hard to replace. We will never forget him. He also has good looks to spare. In his spare time he use to like to hunt in the jungles. As he spoke to us on the fantail, he read his orders and then a little speech followed. He made it known that he did not want to talk about all the big things we accomplished since coming here, almost a year and a half ago. He thought that it would be bragging. He said that if we did not do anything else from now until the end of the war, what we have already done would be more than enough. When he neared the end of his talk, he told the different meanings of the Hawaiian word "Aloha" which means a quick return or return soon. He finished by saying, "Aloha to every goddam one of you." He walked to the quarterdeck as side boys stood at attention and he was piped over the side. He walked very slow down the gangway. He had to hold his lips tight and his eyes were moist. So were the crew's. He boarded a PT boat that was waiting for him and as it pulled away, he stood leaning against a long pole with one hand and waving to us with the other. All hands waved back. He kept staring at the ship until he was out of

sight. We will never see another one like Tip. May the Good
Lord always watch over him. No wonder our task force always got
the best of the Japs. With a man like Tip and an assist from the
Good Lord, we could not fail. Tip Merrill's task force fired more
ammunition and covered more miles against the Japs in the
South Pacific than any other outfit. Our ship alone has fired
20,000 rounds of six inch and 20,000 rounds of five inch ammunition, not to mention the 20 and 40 mm. machine guns. We have
the distinction of being in the Pacific longer than any allied force.
Tip Merrill is the only squadron commander, Japanese or American, who never lost a ship in the Slot. This task force has accomplished many things never before accomplished. This information
is not released for the purpose of patting ourselves on the back
but only to keep the record straight.

It looks like the end of the line for the *Montpelier* in the South
Pacific. The Navy's job is done as far as warships are concerned.
Our fighting will be conducted on the other side of the equator.
The weather there won't be as hot and humid. We attended
movies topside tonight.

Tuesday, March 28, 1944: I left the ship at 7:20 A.M. on a stores
working party. It was held at the corner of the harbor. Heat and
humidity were unbearable. We were wet from sweat. I looked as
though someone had drenched me with a pail of water. There
was hardly any air at all. Breathing was difficult. The Bay is still
a hell hole. It's so calm and yet a wind fails to blow. The high
jungle hereabouts keeps the wind from reaching the Bay. A good
name for it would be "Devil's Harbor." The climate stays the
same, the year round. The weather is always damp, hot and
sticky, every minute of the day, every day of the year. Food was
scarce all day. We finished work at 5 P.M. Supper was rated fair,
just fair. I took a shower and was asleep topside by 7:45 P.M.

Wednesday, March 29, 1944: All hands up at 5:30 A.M. I went
over on the beach in the afternoon and saw a U.S.O. show. It was
very good. Had two Coca-Colas there. We had chow. It was rated
excellent. Hit the sack at 8:15 P.M.

Sunday, April 2, 1944: Today is Palm Sunday. Had the eight to twelve noon watch and could see the church service from my mount on watch. Very hot as usual. There's talk about going to Sydney which has come up overnight. Rubinstein is taking bets that we leave for there soon.

Monday, April 3, 1944: It looks so good about going to Australia that I went down to the barbershop and had my hair cut. The word is now that we will leave April 6, nothing official yet. The fellows are washing their blues. I had the 12 to 4 P.M. watch so I'll wash mine tomorrow.

Thursday, April 4, 1944: Relieved of watch at 4 A.M. Got up at 6:30 A.M. At quarters this morning we were told that we would leave for Sydney, Australia, tomorrow. The cruiser *Cleveland* and about three destroyers will accompany us. The remaining cruiser in our force, the *Columbia,* will leave for the States today. It will travel to Espiritu, Pearl Harbor and then the West Coast of the good old U.S.A.

I washed and pressed my blues today. I also washed my white hats. At 4:15 P.M. the *Columbia,* No. 56, left for the States. Its homeward bound pennant was flying from its mast to its fantail. It toured the harbor, circling all the ships stationed there. Before it left all of its crew were topside waving. The *Columbia* left the States about 10 days before the *Montpelier.* It arrived here about 17 months ago. After all these months it deserves to go back to the States. It did quite a job on the Japs and saw plenty of action. It more than did its share against the Japs. We were lucky to have a cruiser such as she. The *Cleveland* is scheduled to leave for the States in July. The *Montpelier* in August or September is slated for stateside.

Wednesday, April 5, 1944: All hands on deck at 5 A.M. We left Purvis Bay probably for the last time, heading for Sydney, Australia. We have the light cruiser *Cleveland* and five destroyers with us. We expect to arrive at Sydney Easter Sunday, April 9. It was a 7 A.M. departure time. We conducted gunnery practice this morning. All the fellows are getting their clothes ready and are buying clothes at small stores. The barbershop has long lines of men waiting to get their hair cut. Everyone is talking about

Australia, and what they are going to do when we reach there.
Everyone is in a jovial mood, one would think that we were going back to the States. I hit the sack early.

Thursday, April 6, 1944: Awoke at 5:30 A.M., and had breakfast at 7 A.M. I was scheduled for the eight to noon watch. The
air is cooler here. It's just right. Lt. Jg. Graham went to small
stores to purchase clothing for us. Everything was all sold out.
An officer from each division has a paper with the names and
numbers of each article his men require. This elimates long lines
of men waiting for goods. On deck, I could see the waves spray
water over all the ship. It was cold on watch, we wore winter P
coats and jackets. The cool air peps up the appetite. Sleeping below in the compartments with blankets on is now the case. It felt
good to sleep in a sack instead of on a steel deck. What a drastic
change in the weather between here and Purvis Bay.

Friday, April 7, 1944: Relieved of watch at midnight and then
slept. Had chow at 7 A.M. Called to quarters at 8:15 A.M. We
were ordered not to send gifts home from Australia. Before,
everyone was planning to do so. Officer Hutchins received cigarettes for the division today. I washed my undress jumper this
morning, and hung it on the blower topside to dry. The blower is
a favorite spot for drying clothes. The hot air from the engine
room conducted through the blower dries clothing in an instant.
Blowers all over the entire ship have clothes hanging from them,
waving in the breeze. Lemon pie was secured from the bake shop
and disappeared soon afterwards. Firing from the mounts was
conducted this afternoon. Our speed is approximately seventeen
knots. Pay slips were posted. After supper I listened to Wolf playing recordings. I broke my glasses and they are in pieces. The
glasses I wear have a tint as the ones made of plain glass do not
help my eyes. The glare affects them. The glare from the sun and
water is terrific. Going to bed at 7, I arose at 11:15 for the midnight to 4 A.M. watch. Tomorrow we will be at Sydney, Australia.

Sunday, April 9, 1944: Today, as was expected, was a very
happy day for the crew of the *Montpelier*. Leaving Purvis Bay
Wednesday April 5, we arrived at Sydney, Australia, Sunday April

9, four days later. We docked at the pier on a beautiful sunny day. This will be one Easter Sunday that we will always remember. Liberty will start at 1 P.M. We do not have to be back until 11 A.M. the next morning, if no duty is called for, otherwise it's 9 A.M. reporting time. We will have six out of the eight days here on the beach. Three sections will be off at one time, the first section will remain aboard.

Monday, April 17, 1944: In eight days this is the first opportunity I've had to do any writing. I have been very busy in the meantime and have thoroughly enjoyed myself in the past week. I will try to cover in part what has happened during that time. All hands will be back on board ship at 9 A.M. for we leave for Purvis Bay at noon.

I had a great time while in Sydney. I visited many places and have met many Australians. The streets were full of sociable people. Easter Sunday was a holy day here in Australia. Hyde Park was crowded with girls, many strikingly so. They would rather date American sailors than anyone. When the girls here feel like working, they do so. When they feel like taking time off, they do that also. The population believes in celebrating many holidays while working can take care of itself.

I arranged a date for Stevenson. She was a very pretty girl, whose brother is an ace in the Air Force in England. He has to his credit thirty German planes shot down. It rained a couple of days during my stay there and P coats were generally worn as the nights turned cool. When the fleet arrives, the girls join in the festivities as work is stopped completely for them. A parade was in progress as I toured Sydney. The famed 7th and 9th Australian Divisions, who have been fighting since 1940, marched to the adoration of its inhabitants. General MacArthur has said that the 7th were the most accomplished jungle fighters in the world. A few hours of my time was spent talking to these illustrious heroes, in German and Japanese campaigns. Their respect for the New Zealanders was overwhelming, as they considered them the best fighting group in the entire world. These Australians were very friendly and reminded me of Americans.

The days passed like minutes. A group of men from my division entered a hotel and proceeded to demolish it. A little to drink went a long way that day.

I purchased a few goods at one of the stores and tried to order a pair of eyeglasses but failed.

One evening around 5 P.M. we saw a soldier, who was leaving for New Guinea the next morning, attempt to date a girl who was on her way from work. The soldier was getting nowhere until we convinced her that she should accept. When we left them, they were going down the subway stairs together. She invited the soldier home for supper and to introduce him to the family.

The last night I spent in Sydney, two Australians tried to relieve me of any money that I happened to have but changed their minds. As I walked through Hyde Park on my way back to the ship between 1 and 2 in the morning, two men came out of nowhere, and asked me for my money. I took them by surprise when I told them, with a big grin on my face, that I gave all my money to my girlfriend because I was leaving Australia in the morning. That Australian money would not be any good to me, where I was going. After hearing this, both stood facing me for quite some time and then disappeared into the darkness. The Good Lord must have changed their minds. I continued on my long walk through the park while the city slept. Everything was so still and quiet. Before reaching the ship I had to pass the gypsy section of the city. They must have been all asleep. I had heard earlier that servicemen were beaten and robbed here. When I finally reached the pier, I despised to board the ship. I wanted to walk all night, breathing the fresh air and walking on the soil of a place that I knew would be friendly. Tomorrow we will be tied down again for many more months to come with only a small area to move around in. I knew that confining space by heart.

We left Sydney Australia today at 12 noon, Monday April 17, 1944.

Tuesday, April 18, 1944: I was relieved of watch at 4 A.M. We are at sea and on our way back to the old grind once more. Arrival time at Purvis Bay, Friday, April 21. We exchanged our Australian money back to American today. I washed my blues while it was cool. The fellows wanted to know who was the pretty Australian girl they saw me with. One of the men in the division missed the ship. Only one is a pretty fair record.

Friday, April 21, 1944: We arrived at Purvis Bay at 1 P.M. We left Sydney, Monday, four days ago. We practiced gunnery every day since our departure. The sea was very rough for a couple of the days but here the sun is as hot and the water as calm as ever. The fellows are still talking about the good-looking girls in Australia.

Monday, April 24, 1944: Awoke at 6 A.M. We received much mail on board today. I received a letter from Mary. John is still at Chelsea Naval Hospital. We are commencing to paint the ship from top to bottom. The crew is all over the ship like flies. Admiral's inspection will be held Saturday. It's a nuisance.

The Press News reported our planes and bombers are giving Europe a ravaging bombing. 20,000 bombers hit the continent in one week alone.

Wednesday, April 26, 1944: Relieved of watch at 4 A.M. All hands on deck at 5 A.M. We departed Purvis Bay early this morning for gunnery. Our destroyers also fired torpedoes at us, traveling about 35 miles an hour. They leave a wake, bubbles, steam, or white smoke as they cut through the water.

We have around sixty new "boots" on board. Little training was afforded them in the States before shipping them out. The Marines assigned to the ship drill them every day. It's held topside.

Monday, May 1, 1944: In the last few days we had recreation on the beach. Another day was spent carrying ammunition. We had a sandwich, cookie and an apple for our dinner there. The sun gave us a bad burn.

Secretary of the Navy Knox died Saturday, April 29, 1944. All flags were at half mast Sunday.

While on a working party Sunday loading ammunition, two

motorboats crowded with nurses passed by. They had bathing suits on. They came from Tulagi and must be picnicking. They are the first nurses to be stationed here. They arrived two months ago.

The Press News reported Jim Tobin of the Boston Braves pitched a no hitter against Brooklyn, winning 2 to 0. The pitcher had also hit a home run in the game.

Monday we left Purvis Bay for good. Our new base will be at Munda. We will have gunnery for three days, starting today as a practice bombardment. Today being Monday. When the shells hit the target which was a nearby island, geysers of earth plummeted down, showing the overall extent of what damage can be achieved by this type of warfare. When the phosphorous shells landed a white flame spread for quite a distance. Phosphorous eats into the flesh like an acid. Water is ineffective to combat it as it can only be stopped by severing the limb that it has touched.

The cruisers *Honolulu, St. Louis* and *Birmingham* left Purvis Bay with us but expect to leave for the Central Pacific shortly. We will depart for those battlegrounds in the near future.

The following message is from the commander of the South Pacific, Admiral William F. "Bull" Halsey to our force. It appeared in today's Press News for all hands.

With the announcement of the virtual completion of the South Pacific Campaign, except for mopping-up and starving-out operations, I can tell you and tell the world that no greater fighting team has ever been up together.

From the desperate days of Guadalcanal to the smooth steamrollering of Bougainville and the easy seizure of Green and Emirau, all of us and allied services put aside every consideration but the one goal of wiping out Japs.

As you progressed, your techniques and teamwork improved until at last, ground, amphibious, sea, and air forces were working as one beautiful piece of precision machinery that crushed and baffled our hated enemy in every encounter.

Your resourcefulness, tireless ingenuity, cooperation and indomitable fighting spirit form a battle pattern that will everywhere be an inspiration, and a great measure of the credit for the sky blazing, seasweeping, jungle smashing of the combat forces goes to the construction gangs and service organizations that bull-dozed bases out of the jungle and brought up the beans and bullets and supplies.

You never stopped moving forward and the Japs never could get set to launch a sustained counterattack. You beat them wher-ever you found them and you never stopped looking for them and tearing into them.

Well Done.
HALSEY

Wednesday, May 3, 1944: Well we returned to Purvis Bay again after all, but the fellows do not feel bad as we will not re-main except for a couple of days. Our orders were changed at the last minute. We are to take aboard a quantity of ammunition. The ammunition being for the most part 6 inch and 5 inch. The six inch powder cases are about four feet long and about as round as a football. The five inch powder cases are about two feet long and not as wide as the six inch. The maneuvers and bombard-ments of the past few days are a dress rehearsal of the real thing to come. We arrived at Purvis Bay at 3:30 P.M. and before long, we were carrying ammunition. I received a letter from John, saying that the carrier which he was stationed on was nothing but a matchbox. It went down in eighteen minutes. One direct hit was all that was needed.

Thursday, May 4, 1944: Having the midnight to four in the morning watch, I hit the sack at 4 A.M. All hands were up at 6 A.M. We worked very hard today carrying ammunition. We loaded five and six inch shells plus powder cases that are provided for each shell. Thousands of rounds were stored aboard. Hun-dreds of powder cases were placed in the hangar deck, even the officers helped tote the ammunition. Storing of the powder cases in the hangar deck, the first time that this has ever been done, means a lot of firing in the near future for the *Montpelier*. The action is anticipated by all and we welcome it. We unloaded most of the armor-piercing shells and replaced them with bombarding shells. More ammunition was loaded than our previous operations. If hit in the right spot, we would be blown sky high. We're like an ammunition ship. Stores were also brought aboard. We will work all night carrying the mountains of ammunition and supplies. It would seem that wherever we are headed, ammunition will not be available. We will act as our own ammunition ship. Everyone on board is in a good mood because we know that we are getting ready for something big. This is what we have been waiting and hoping for.

I got my ears washed out this morning. I have been having trouble with them. The concussion from the guns have not helped my eardrums. The Press News reported carrier planes had hit Truk.

Friday, May 5, 1944: Arose at 6 A.M., had early breakfast and left the ship to work on the supply ship. It had plenty of good food there and we ate this day like kings. This is the kind of a working party that we appreciate. We had meat, cheese, crackers, juices, fruit, candy and other choice delicacies. Everything was fresh as it had just arrived from the States. These supply ships are refrigerated and carry all types of food imaginable. We ate until we could eat no more. Working hard for something like this, we didn't mind. Entering the hold of a supply ship is similar as entering a warehouse. Later in the day bags of sugar and flour were unloaded by us from a nearby barge. We toiled with only our pants on and at the end of the day had quite a burn. The sun was very hot. When finishing for the day we had a swim. I arrived back to the ship for the 6 to 8 P.M. watch.

THE
MARIANAS

May 1944–August 1944

S aturday, *May 6, 1944*: Arising at 5 A.M., we readied the ship to leave Purvis Bay at 7 A.M. Our destination is Hathorn Sound, next to Munda in the Solomons. We expect to pull in there at 5:30 tonight. It is 180 miles north of our present position.

We had gunnery in the afternoon and dropped anchor at Munda at 6 P.M. Everyone was topside and anxious to get a look at our new base. We manned our fueling stations and took aboard fuel from a tanker close by. The weather is a little cooler as the hills are not as high as at Purvis Bay, not hindering the breeze from floating down to us. It seems that all of the bases we are stationed at are dumps, nothing but jungles. One would think that the best part of the islands were kept inaccessible from us. Even the natives will not live in the places that these bases are located. Tonight I planned on getting a few hours sleep but an ammunition working party dispelled such ideas. There I was, ready to step into the shower, when chosen for the illustrious detail. This is what burns me up. It happens all of the time. I left the ship at 8 P.M. and did not return until midnight. Five and six inch ammunition was carried aboard. The men in the deck divisions are picked for all the working parties.

Sunday, May 7, 1944: I returned to the ship around 1 A.M. after an all night ammunition working party. I was covered with dirt and sweat so I took a shower. I am now sitting on the side of my bunk, writing in the diary. It's about 1:30 A.M. If anyone knew what I was doing at this time of the morning, after finishing an all night work detail, they would think that there was something wrong with me. I look forward to writing in the diary. It's like a tonic to me. I will now go topside and see if I can find a place to sleep. As I finish writing for now, the diary is on my knee. There is very little light and everyone is sleeping.

I went to church services, Mass was held topside. Before this war is over, we will have had church services in about every location in the Pacific. I spent the afternoon, 12 P.M. to 4 P.M., on watch on the 40 mm. mount. While on watch we spent some time talking about our sea battle against the Japs on November 1, 1943, off Empress Augusta Bay, Bougainville, and how our destroyers had only star shells left to fire at the Jap warships, having exhausted their torpedoes and having only machine gun ammunition left. The *Montpelier* had only five minutes of five and six inch shells left along with the other cruisers in the task force. It was the hand of the Lord that made the Jap Admiral gather what was left of his crippled warships together and head for home. I wonder if they ever found out that we were running low on ammunition. When we returned to our base at Purvis Bay to restock on ammunition, the ammunition ship had not arrived. It was very fortunate that the Japs did not send another task force down against us. Ammunition was not secured until the next day. The Japs could have demolished our troops and supplies at Bougainville if an attack was put in motion. The Japanese had no way of knowing how the situation stood.

We had a good supper tonight. At the other end of the harbor is a sprawling airfield. Entering harbor we passed Kula Gulf where the cruiser *Helena* was sunk. Two Jap destroyers which we sunk in the darkness March 6 and 7, 1943, also decorated our line of travel. The Jap island we bombarded shortly afterwards is not too far distant from where we're stationed. I hit the sack at 7 P.M. and was awoken for the midnight to four in the morning watch.

Monday, May 8, 1944: Had a little sleep around 4:15 A.M. to 6:30 A.M., then received breakfast. This morning we checked the life rafts, everything that they contained was checked and double checked, such as rations, dyes (that are mixed with the sea for easy spotting by planes), and refilling water kegs. The rafts are about 10 feet long and approximately 5 feet wide. Care and maintenance of these rafts falls on the deck division's shoulders. The amount of supplies carried by these rafts is surprising.

Today was payday but I did not draw any money. Blankenship from West Virginia returned the $5 he borrowed. I painted on the communications deck today. Later I left the ship on a trash working party. We visited the airstrip and looked at the planes, army P–38s and 39s, parked there. A numerous amount of coves and channels dot the island. The jungle is very thick. Recreation here is nothing to be desired. A small piece of clearing cut into the jungle next to the water serves as our playground. A group from the ship were permitted recreation today. They took one quick look at the section and returned to the landing craft and were ferried back to the *Montpelier* in a hurry. Looking at this piece of the Pacific chosen for our home, Devil's Island comes to mind. It also brings to mind that in wartime a little should go a long way. We expect anything and few things surprise us by now.

I arrived back at the ship at 5:30 P.M. We went to the galley for chow. They relinquished a ham sandwich and a piece of pie. It's 7:30 P.M. as I sit topside under cover and write further. Everything is still and peaceful. The jungle looks deserted from where I sit. One island is similar to another, jungle and then more jungle. The movies will be held topside at 7:45 P.M., rain or not.

While at the airstrip today, I had a chance to talk to the pilots. They said that after the P–38, the P–51 Mustang is the fastest plane. The Jap Zero is the best dog fighter in the world as they can maneuver like no one's business and can almost be made to stop on a dime. Our planes do not try to dog fight them. We sorta take runs at them at high speed and hit the Japs before they know what happened. If we dog fought them they would beat us. Our pilots are rated better than the Japanese. The Zero is light, has no armor, no self-sealing gas tanks and has not as many guns as ours. Our planes have too much of everything for them. At one time the Zero was the best fighter plane around. While we were there, the pilots received their mail. In my estimation I believe the best fighter plane we possess is the P–51 Mustang.

Wednesday, May 10, 1944: All hands up at 5:30 this morning.

We left for gunnery and returned at 12:30 P.M. The ships were about 4000 yards from their objective, a beach, and fired many rounds of ammunition at pillboxes deployed along the shore and inland. According to the pilots used as observers, we did a good job. Destroying pillboxes and bunkers will be our main aim on our next invasion. With this type of training completed, we will be able to knock them out with our eyes closed. Training will be conducted for the next nine days.

Yesterday we joined the 5th Fleet under Admiral Spruance. We spent seventeen months in the 3rd Fleet under "Bull" Halsey. When the anticipated invasion commences, it will be the biggest in the Pacific War to date. Marines were attached to the *Montpelier* yesterday. They were flown in from Pearl Harbor. They are fire control men who will practice with us, while we have training. When the real show begins, they will land with the invasion forces. They will direct our fire on the Jap pillboxes and gun positions. This must be a very important job that we are going to do and calls for a lot of practice and we cannot afford to near miss those pillboxes, we have to hit them or get hit by the shore batteries. All mounts have charts showing elevation and what the range will be at that elevation when we fire. More rumors have been spreading that we will leave for the States after this operation is over.

No one is sure where the operation will be. Some say Truk, others the Philippines. The Marines brought along all sorts of equipment with them, including a radio set to communicate from the beach to the *Montpelier*. Our ship is still the flagship, has the Admiral aboard. Orders will originate from here. The crew's lounge is being considered for a storage depot for the 40 mm. ammunition.

The band from the U.S.S. *Dixie* came aboard this evening at six and played for us before the movie started.

Thursday, May 11, 1944: All hands up at 6 A.M. The Press News reported that fighters and bombers are striking Germany in force. Thousands of tons of bombs are being dropped every day.

I painted today on the communications deck again this morning. I pulled the noon to four watch. Boxing bouts were on tap on the fantail tonight. Everyone enjoyed them.

After supper I sat around talking with the rest of the crew. I learned that our Marine spotters will land at night. When the invasion starts in the morning, the ones who were not captured by the Japs will inform us on our accuracy and will direct the firing from the beach. This will be different from Tarawa where the Marines were slaughtered by the Japs' gunfire.

Friday, May 12, 1944: We had quite a time for ourselves, on the midnight to four watch on the 40 mm. mount. Captain Harry "The Horse" Hoffman, if he had observed us dancing and laughing at three in the morning, would have thought that we all had gone "Asiatic." Some of the fellows were really cutting a rug. You would think that they were getting ready for a big dance on Saturday night.

Arose at 6:30 A.M., had chow and field day was held. I finished painting the communications deck today. The ship was inspected in the afternoon. Before the movie tonight, we had a singsong. Scuttlebutt being passed along is that we will not pull off the expected invasion for another month. Our objective will be Guam. No mail is dispatched here for no ships arrive other than the ones stationed here. Our sea plane flew to Tulagi and mail was flown back.

Saturday, May 13, 1944: We had ham for dinner today. We left in the afternoon for more gunnery exercises. We practiced hitting pillboxes on the island of Kolombangara. It's located north of New Georgia. I went to the dentist on board ship and had a tooth filled.

Sunday, May 14, 1944: Arising at 5:30 A.M., more gunnery this morning was held. Arrived at our starting point at 1 P.M. Today is Mother's Day. Went to Mass at 2:40 P.M. It was held in the mess hall. An officer was the altar boy.

The cruisers *St. Louis, Honolulu* and *Birmingham* arrived yesterday. A destroyer pulled alongside and I spent some time talking to the crew on board. They participated in the invasion of Hollandia on the northwest coast of New Guinea. Jap souvenirs were numerous aboard the destroyer. They had also retrieved English one pound notes that the Japs were intending to put into circulation when Australia was invaded. This destroyer took part in the Gilberts Campaign when the Marines landed on bloody Tarawa. Wounded were brought aboard as the fighting grew fierce. One of the Marines was holding his stomach in his hands and it was not long before he died. The leg of another Marine was held together by a single thread of flesh. It was later amputated. One had a bullet through his eye and was lodged in his neck. He was holding a pad over it to stop the flow of blood. He died shortly after. Another had his knee blown wide open. Part of the leg had to be cut off. Many boarded the destroyer blind. They were all doped to help combat the pain. The Marines were mowed down like grass. Blood covered the ship in all corners as Tarawa was considered one of the bloodiest in the history of the Corps. The Japanese thought that Tarawa was impregnable. The Marines, paying for every inch taken in dead and wounded, secured the bloody atoll. One by one the Japs were blasted from their fortifications until none remained. The destroyer, being used as an emergency hospital ship, was shelled and hit by shore batteries while offshore. The Marines who died aboard were awarded a watery grave, as they were buried at sea.

Went out tonight at 6 P.M. for more gunnery practice. We are having all this practice so there will not be another Tarawa. We are still at sea and do not know when we will return to base.

Monday, May 15, 1944: Gunnery practice was conducted as we are still at sea, heading up the Solomons. Battle stations were maintained during the whole day. Firing by all guns continued into the night as star shells were unloosed, lighting the beach aglow. While firing all guns at once, it seemed as if my head would be blown off my shoulders. The cotton plugs, placed in the ears, were useless. The pain from the concussion is unbearable. I could even sense it way down in my throat and tongue. My ears were set ringing. At 9 P.M. a halt was called in the bombardment. I slept for a couple of hours and then stood the midnight to four in the morning watch. The sky was brilliantly set afire with millions of stars. The night before I slept in a life raft, being too hot in the compartment below. Seeking a place to sleep topside is impossible unless early squatter rights are procured. Awaking on deck in the morning, one feels much better than in the compartments.

Tuesday, May 16, 1944: We pulled into Hathorn Sound, Munda, early this morning. A load of ammunition was stored aboard, replacing the spent rounds. Recreation will be held at 4 P.M. Eddie Peabody and his U.S.O. gang are putting on a show at that time. Eddie is famous for being the banjo king. I saw his troupe while in boot camp at Great Lakes in 1942. Only a few men from each division of the ship will leave the ship for the show. It does not rain here as often as it used to but the weather is still hot. Our division officer is in sick bay. Lt. Hutchins was boxing champ at Annapolis. The lieutenant will be in the hospital for three weeks. He has pneumonia. The fellows will miss "Hutch."

Saturday, May 20, 1944: Arose at 4:30 A.M. We left Munda at 5:50 A.M. We will travel to Bougainville for more gunnery exercises against pillboxes. On the way to our destination, Captain Hoffman spoke to the crew, saying that our targets will be live. There are still Japs on the end of the island that we will be shooting at. Shore batteries are reported there by a destroyer that was passing when the guns opened up on it. The Captain believed that the Japs there were being supplied by enemy submarines. This will be only classified as a practice run but return fire by the Japs is anticipated. We got quite a kick out of the Captain's phraseology. Having six inch shells being fired at us by the enemy, and they rate it practice. Planes will spot for us, informing us of our accuracy. We will have four destroyers and the cruisers *Cleveland* and *Birmingham* with us.

Arriving at 10 A.M., we commenced firing at 10:35 A.M. The Jap shore batteries on the beach returned the fire quickly after. Their guns were stationed on top of a hill. Their guns that were firing at us were the big 8 inch variety. Our largest caliber was the 6 inch. Our run on Bougainville was commencing as our starboard guns opened fire. On returning the port guns were brought into action. The first ship to be fired at by the enemy shore batteries, was the cruiser *Cleveland*. I was at my battle station on the 40 mm. machine gun mount and the Admiral and Captain were just above me on the bridge. As I looked to the rear, I saw big geysers of water, rising all around the cruiser *Cleveland*. It was a miracle that it was not hit. At first we took it as a joke, but then got very serious because we knew that our turn would come to be fired on by the big Jap guns. Cruisers make a very big target in the daytime, they are over six hundred feet long. While we were on our way in to hit the Japs, they opened up on us. They must have had us in their sights, because their big 8 inch shells began to explode all around us and fly through the mast, they could not have come any closer without hitting us. In the meantime our guns were blazing away but the Japs were in a very difficult spot for us to hit, behind a hill. We could not get any closer to the Japs, because it would be suicide. We could see the big flashes from their guns as they kept up a steady fire with their 8 inch guns against our six inch guns. The Jap shells sent big sprays of water up into the air just in front of my mount and one of the 20 mm. gun mounts up forward on the bow was knocked out by shrapnel, as it sprayed the ship with big chunks of red hot steel. Some of the wounded were carried to the crew's lounge, it is a battle dressing station. One Marine named Darling had a big piece of shrapnel go through his helmet and out the other side. When they picked up his helmet part of his scalp was still in it. One fellow almost went insane with the pain, and he was going to jump over the side. Blood and hair was splattered over the deck. Some had to have transfusions. One of the fellows will not be able to have the shrapnel removed until his wound is healed, then he will be operated on. They have to wait until the artery is healed. Another fellow's leg was a mess. Another received a notice today, saying that he would be transferred to the States, and he also got hit. It was a lucky break that one of the fellows had his life jacket on, because it was full of shrapnel. If our ship was going a little faster the Admiral and Captain would have got it and we are very

close to them. You hold your breath when you see the Jap guns
fire at you and then wait to see if they hit you. They could not
come any closer without hitting us. It does not feel very good to
see 8 inch shells falling all around you and you have no place to
hide. One of the fellows dove for the deck when he heard the
shells close by explode and an officer dove on top of him, we got a
kick out of it. A piece of shrapnel about six by six almost hit
Gallagher, and he had to pick it up with his hat because it was so
hot. When shrapnel hits thick steel it bounces around. The anchor chain which is about as thick as a football was almost cut in
half. Someone said the *Cleveland* also got hit. If the Japs ever hit
us with direct hits, they would have done an awful lot of damage
and you do not know what it might have led to, it could have
sunk us. The Japs didn't interfere with our "practice," because
we stayed here for two hours firing at them. The Japs did not
stop us from carrying out our plans. The Japs' firing was terrific
and they are supposed to be starving. I would hate to run into
them on full stomachs. The Japs also had anti-aircraft guns on
the shore and they opened up on our planes when they were
spotting for us. It was like a hornets' nest over there. I don't blame
our troops on shore for leaving them alone where they can do no
harm to anyone. Our ship knocked out the Jap radio tower and
some anti-aircraft guns, we also helped knock out some of the big
shore batteries. The cruiser *Cleveland* fired over a thousand
rounds of six inch shells not to mention what the rest of us fired.
The Japs must have thought they were at a shooting gallery firing
these big 8 inch guns at us and shell and shrapnel falling all
around us. Those Japs have plenty of guts, they are not afraid of
anything. This was a good old fashion slugfest, with no quarter
given by either side. No one was brokenhearted when we finally
left, and they call this practice. What will the new men who just
come from the States think. They will hate to face the real
McCoy. They said our troops pushed the Japs to this end of
Bougainville, where they cannot break out. I wonder if our
troops come down here and have practice against live Japs like we
are doing. It would be a good way to break in new recruits. It

was a very foolish idea having practice against something like
that. We had nothing to gain and everything to lose. They could
have sunk us. It was the most foolish thing I ever saw done while
in the Navy. They know 6 inch shells will not knock out those
pillboxes but still they had to have their practice against 8 inch
guns. If Halsey wanted them out of the way he could have sent
battleships or dropped blockbusters on it, but why waste stuff on
them? We did not return to Munda because of the wounded but
will go to Purvis Bay and transfer them to the hospital on the
beach.

Sunday, May 21, 1944: All hands got up at 6 A.M. and pulled
into Purvis Bay at 7 A.M. this morning. We have not been here
for almost three weeks. There was an awful lot of ships outside
the nets in Tulagi and in Purvis Bay I never saw so many ships
here before. The battleships *New Mexico, Idaho,* and *Penna.* are
here. We got a lot of mail, fifty bags. Mass was held in the mess
hall at 10:30 A.M. Some of the most serious wounded were transferred to the hospital at Tulagi. We got some supplies on today.

Monday, May 22, 1944: All hands got up at 5:15 this morning,
breakfast at 5:15 and all hands went to battle stations at 6:15 A.M.
We had a very busy day for ourselves, and quite a show was put on
if the Japs could only see us. We had a dress rehearsal for what
is to come. Our force consisted of over a hundred ships of all
types. The Marines were unloaded with all their equipment,
trucks, guns, etc., and they were hitting the beach at Guadalcanal
in a full-dress rehearsal. The warships fired over their heads and
the planes came in firing and dropping bombs as the Marines hit
the beach. It was like the real thing, it was quite a sight. It was a
regular bridge of ships across the ocean. The transports and supply ships were protected by the warships. The warships kept moving around them, giving them protection, our job is to keep
planes and ships away and bombard the beach. We were finished
at 2 P.M. The troops were left on the beach. We returned to
Purvis Bay at 4 P.M. in the evening.

Wednesday, May 24, 1944: Up at 6 A.M. and spent the day on
ammunition barge. We also carried a lot of depth bombs. The

sun was very hot, you could get a good tan. We brought our lunch, we had sandwiches and fruit for dinner. Some of the fellows went in for a swim at noon. Some natives came by in a canoe, they had a lot of bananas and pineapples with them. We offered to buy some from them, but they did not want money. They must have had some Irish in them, because they wanted Canned Corn Beef. We had to laugh when we heard this. They must have got the corn beef from one of the supply ships, or the troops. The young children about five years old can really handle a canoe. We got back to the ship at 5 P.M. The Captain on the *Cleveland* said that they would be home before Labor Day. We also got a lot of stores and ammunition today.

Sunday, May 28, 1944: All hands got up at 5:30 A.M. this morning. We had more gunnery, all guns were fired, we fired at a sleeve towed by plane, and also had target practice against a Jap destroyer that was beached. The place is full of sharks. There was a big school of them, you could see the fin just above the water. If you fell overboard here you would not last long. We have gunnery nearly every day. The ship is loaded with supplies. We will supply the small craft when the invasion comes off, because our nearest base will be too far away, and they run out of food in a short time. We even have food in the hangar tied down, so it won't move, we never did that before. We will be gone a long time. Yesterday we pulled into Hathorn Sound, Munda. They said we will go back to Purvis Bay June 3. We got sixty new men on today, 25 men left the ship for the States a few days ago. Some of the men who missed the ship at Sydney, came aboard today. I went to church services at 3:15 this afternoon, held topside.

Tuesday, May 31, 1944: I left the ship at 7:40 A.M. this morning for a working party on the beach. We picked up the beer bottles and broke them in a barrel, we also picked up all the papers and boxes and burned them. Red Banilover, from the East Side of New York City, and I had a game of horseshoes and then took a stroll down to the beach. Red is a hot ticket, very funny. As we strolled along we talked about the States and what we would be doing when we got back. We were going to walk in on our families and surprise them. The cruiser *Cleveland* had an army band on board and we could hear the music on the beach. Everything was so peaceful and quiet and all you could hear was the music. It was a hot sunny day, just like any summer day at home in Mass., the water was calm. There was only a few of us on the beach. We sat next to the water and watched the fish swimming around, I never saw so many beautiful fish in my life. They were not very big, but they were many different colors; blue, green, red, etc. There was also some funny looking fish, I never saw before. The fish stayed near the shore, so the big ones would not eat them, but once in a while the big ones would come in and chase the small ones away, they wanted something to eat. About 10 A.M. a party from the *Cleveland* came over on a picnic. Red and I sat on the float and watched them go swimming, they had quite a time for themselves. They also brought all kinds of food and drinks with them, and about 1 P.M. in the afternoon Harry and I were starved. After the *Cleveland* picnic party had finished we went over, and they gave us some apples that were left over, they really hit the spot. A lighter was supposed to pick us up at 11 A.M. but they forgot us. At 1:30 P.M. our recreation party came over, and we went back with the landing craft. We missed dinner so the galley had to give us some chow, we would miss the good meal. The noon meal is the only good meal of the day. Our laundry came back and for a wonder I got all my dungarees back. Some of the men went to Munda on a sightseeing trip, and they brought back Jap helmets, etc. The Japs had American spark plugs in their cars and trucks, and also American tires. A lot of the stuff they had was American. Maybe they got them when the Philippines fell. Only three men from each division went over there.

Saturday, June 3, 1944: We pulled into Purvis Bay this morning at 7:30 A.M. We worked all day and night carrying stores. The hangar is loaded with tons of food, never saw anything like this before. We got wet going over to the supply ship and were wet all day. We handled an awful lot of stores, like a bunch of longshoremen. About thirty-three bags of mail came over. I sent the rent to Mary and told her that I would be very busy. The men have been talking a lot about the coming campaign lately, and they hope everything works out all right. Some think it will be about 1000 miles from Japan, right in their back yard. It will be the closest invasion to Japan so far and also one of the turning points of the war against the Japs. It will be a big blow to them and they will put up quite a fight to prevent it. When it is over I think that we will go the States. Our Division Officer Lt. Hutchins was at quarters yesterday. He returned from the hospital a few days ago.

Sunday, June 4, 1944: All hands up at 5:30 A.M., chow at 6:15 A.M. and we left Purvis Bay at 7:30 A.M. The *Cleveland, St. Louis* and *Honolulu,* and some destroyers left with us.* About 8:30 this morning we picked up about twenty large troopships off Guadalcanal, they were loaded with Marines. We have a long voyage ahead of us, as we leave the old hunting grounds where the first allied offensive in the Pacific started Aug. 7, 1942. It will be good to leave here, and get away from the hot and humid climate, no air, it is a tough climate to live in, especially the spots we hit. At night and early in the morning you can see the damp steam come out of the jungle. This climate would rot anything, as we left today it was cloudy and it looked like rain. Down here you would pay anything for just a little breeze and a breath of fresh air. We got down here the first of 1943 and we sweat every day all day for almost eighteen months. This will be the first action for some of the new men. We got a lot of older men from the States in their forties and fifties, with big families, about three weeks ago. One of the new men by the name of Schaggs, from St. Louis, let me read a letter he got from his wife and kids, and he is very proud of them. It is a tough blow to send a man with children overseas.

---

* Admiral Samuel Eliot Morison came aboard our ship at Purvis Bay for the coming invasion and left Purvis Bay with us. I can still remember seeing him as I looked up from my 40 mm. gun mount. He was on the bridge with the Admiral and Captain, they were just above me. When I was writing in my diary at the time I never dreamed that we would meet almost 20 years later and he would recommend the publication of my diary.

The new men who just came aboard would give anything to be back with their families again. Now they appreciate them and see how lucky they were when they were at home with them. Some of the married men with children tell you how they ran around when they were back home as civilians and how wrong they were. If they ever get back home again they will live a good life and spend more time with wife and children. They will not take everything for granted and will appreciate things more. They want to make up for all the trouble they caused to their wife and children. It reminds you of a person on his last day, telling his confession. They are always thinking of their wife and children. The men who were good to their families cannot get home quick enough to put their arms around their family, pick them up and just hug and kiss them, they have so many nice things to do for them. They have not been down here very long, but they are ready to go back home. The first few months will be the toughest for them. It's a good thing they did not come down here with us about eighteen months ago. They will not stay out here as long as us because we should be heading for home in a few months and a year from now the war might be over.

The sick bay and Marine compartment is full. The men are coming down with some kind of a bug, they have the runs, cramps and a fever. More than a hundred have it, not to mention the ones who did not report to sick bay. About seven hundred had it on Guadalcanal. All the warships in our task force have it. They do not know what caused it, it could be the weather or a bug. One of the fellows on our ship went to the bathroom thirty-eight times in one day. They should give that fellow the Purple Heart. I had to laugh at one of the stories told by one of the men reporting to sick bay. There was a long line of men at sick bay with the runs, and when one of the fellows' turn came, to tell the Dr. what was ailing him, he told the Dr. that he was constipated. When the Dr. heard this he almost fell over, and after catching his breath, he said in a loud voice with a grin on his face, "What do you know, we have a man who is Constipated."

We fired at a sleeve towed by a plane this morning and afternoon. Some of the transports also fired at the sleeve. We are sailing up through the Solomons. Captain Hoffman spoke to the crew, and said that we will reach the Marshalls about Thursday, today is Sunday, we would stay there one day and then head for the Big Invasion. It will be the largest of the Pacific war, and we will have more ships in it than any other invasion. We will have hundreds of warships. We will meet a large force at the Marshalls and when we leave there he will tell us where we are going. While on watch I told Edgerton, Tojo, Bonnette and the rest of the crew that I might sound crazy for saying such a thing but if I had my choice of leaving now for the States, that I would turn it down rather than miss this big invasion. I would not want to miss this for anything, and they felt the same way. I might be scared stiff before it was over, but I want to be there. I think that is the way most of the crew feels. It gets into your blood, after you have been down here a long time, you want to get into all the campaigns, you do not want to miss any. I hit the sack at 9 P.M. and tried to sleep below in the compartment, but the heat woke me up. I was laying in a pool of sweat. I felt awful, it takes the life out of you, you find it hard to breath like someone had put a bag over your head. I woke up at 11 P.M. and had the midnight to 4 A.M. watch.

Monday, June 5, 1944: Got off watch at 4 A.M. got one hour sleep. All hands up at 5 A.M. Stayed at battle station until daylight. The Solomons must be behind us now, no land in sight. Early this morning four aircraft carriers joined us. They are not the big jobs. They had some destroyers with them. Our ship leads the convoy with destroyers ahead of us. The carriers are last behind the transports. We fired at some sleeves this morning and held drills in afternoon. We are supposed to be joined by other ships tomorrow. Yesterday they turned the five inch guns so close to Mount 42, when they were firing they ripped the big heavy canvas off and snapped the big heavy line that held it down. The concussion was very bad. Some day they will kill someone, firing the guns so close to the men. It's like standing next to the open barrel when they fire. It's a wonder all our eardrums are not broken. We should be near the equator by now. It is very hot, there is no air at all. It makes you very drowsy, you feel like sleeping. We got word over the radio tonight, that the American troops were marching through Rome with the Germans fleeing fast. I slept topside tonight.

Tuesday, June 6, 1944: Got up at 3:15 A.M. to go on watch. We crossed the equator at 8:30 A.M. this morning. We did not pick up any more ships yet. The Marshalls are about 1500 miles from Guadalcanal in the Solomons. I got some mince pie from Red Banilover, it was very good. At least a hundred more fellows came down with the runs. Most of the crew has it, the other warships in our task force also have it. The men are calling us "Halsey's Diarrhea Fleet." We do very little work, everyone is getting as much rest as possible before the action starts. I lay on the five inch mount from noon to 4:15 P.M. At 6:30 P.M. this evening the announcement came over the loudspeaker that the Allies landed in France. Everyone gave a big cheer when they heard this. I won $40 from the boys because some time ago, I bet the invasion would come off about the middle of June. The air is a lot fresher now. Since we crossed the equator it is not so hot and sultry. It makes you feel better. It wakes you up, not so much rain either. I fixed my glasses with some glue, they broke again. I have to look through the glue, they are a nuisance. Hit sack at 8 P.M. All night long.

Wednesday, June 7, 1944: All hands got up at 4:45 A.M., the poor fellows on the midnight to 4 A.M. watch got very little sleep. We secured from General Quarters at 6 A.M. and had breakfast at 6:45 A.M. We got a report from the radio shack about the invasion in France. Our troops had an air coverage of 11,000 planes, it was the largest in history, they gained about 25 miles and have airfields in France now. The Navy gave the coast of France quite a bombardment. We left the convoy this afternoon and expect to pull into the Marshalls tomorrow morning. While we were with the convoy our speed was about twelve knots. Our force now consists of the *Cleveland* and some destroyers. The fellows paid me off on the invasion today. At 7:30 P.M. we picked up more speed.

The nights are very bright, you can read a newspaper by moonlight. Most of the Marines sleep in folding cots topside. Their compartment is full of sick men, it is being used for a sick bay. The sick bay is also full, they have the runs and a very high temperature. Got eight to midnight watch. We had a great time for ourselves, we had a free-for-all. We were throwing wet rags and paper at each other, one fellow would stick his head around the gun mount and get a big wet rag right in the face, it was like one of the old time comedies in the movies. Another fellow would get set to hit someone and he would get one in the back of the neck. You would never know that we are on our way to the largest invasion of the Pacific War.

Thursday, June 8, 1944: All hands up at 4:20 this morning. The Dr. gave a first aid lecture from 4:45 to 5:30 A.M. this morning. The Press News said that the invasion in France is running on schedule. Some paratroopers were used. They were dummies loaded with explosives, they really fooled the Germans, they exploded on the ground. Some of our American Indians also had their hair shaven off their heads and war paint on their face. They said, let the Germans try to get these scalps. Last night they had a small model of Saipan on display, for all to see. This is the island we are going to invade. It has a couple of towns on it and some airfields, one of them is very large, it is for big bombers. The Japs have been building the place up for over twenty years. They say the Japs also got fourteen inch shore guns, and about 450 Jap planes here. We pulled into the Marshalls at noon today. They are about 50 miles long. It looks like the shape of a football. The center is water and surrounded by land and coconut trees, the land only rises a few feet, above the water the beach looks like sand. They are nothing but big reefs or atolls, quite a difference here and the thick hot sticky jungle of the Solomons. The atolls are about ten or fifteen miles long. You do not mind the sun because there is always a strong breeze blowing. The climate here is just great. It makes you feel good, everyone has more pep. This is a natural place for ships to stay, once you get in you are surrounded by solid coral. There are only two ways to enter and they are guarded. The Marshalls are nothing but little spots in the vast Pacific, some of the islands or atolls are only about three miles long with a few coconut trees and blinding sand with quite a glare, you need sun glasses. There are about fifty warships here, all kinds, we had modified watch Port side gun watch, that means I got all night in. They will have movies topside tonight. I collected some more invasion money today. No mail will go off here because it was not censored. We will not get any mail for a long time. My glasses broke again. I had to go without them while the glue dried. The glare did an awful job on my eyes. We are 3000 miles from the States, this is the closest we got to the States in eighteen months. The water is a little rougher here because it is open at both ends. The heavy cruiser *Louisville* is flagship here, and a conference was held there today and also one tomorrow, all the big brass are over there. I hit the sack at 8 P.M. The air is a lot dryer here, everyone sleeps like a log. This evening everyone brought his mattress up from below and slept under the stars. You could use a blanket. It was impossible to use a blanket in the Solomons. When you come up here to the Marshalls, you realize what a rugged climate we had in the Solomons and some of those other islands.

Friday, June 9, 1944: Davies, whose family is very good friends of President Roosevelt, was paid a surprise visit by his brother, who is on the carrier *Coral Sea.* He saw the *Liscomb Bay,* the ship my brother John was on, go down in the invasion of Tarawa in the Gilberts. He said they were fueling planes about 5 A.M. in the morning and it was very dark. The ships were told to be on the alert because a Jap sub was close by. The torpedo hit the magazine and half the ship was blown off, the 100 octane gas also helped. In no time it was a mass of flames and looked like the rising sun. It carried a crew of about a thousand and about eight hundred men were lost. It went down in twenty-four minutes, a mass of flames. The destroyers were left behind to pick up the ones that were not killed. They had catapulted most of the planes off, these small carriers had thirty or forty planes. They catapult one plane off every 40 seconds. The *Liscomb Bay* was flagship.

John would be here waiting to leave for the coming invasion, if his ship had not been sunk. John was one of the lucky ones to come out of it alive, although he was badly wounded. We went to battle stations at noon today. Jap planes were on their way but I guess our planes took care of them before they got here. There is a big hospital ship here and one of the men came over to see his brother. When he was leaving he shook his hand and told him to take good care of himself. He looked like he had tears in his eyes when he was leaving. The broken piece of glass fell off my glasses again. I have an awful lot of trouble with my glasses. We had Mass topside at 4 P.M. I hit the sack at 8 P.M. They said that we will leave tomorrow for the real thing.

Saturday, June 10, 1944: Slept under the stars, boy the air is great. I got up at 3:15 A.M. this morning for 4 to 8 A.M. watch. All hands got up at 5:30 A.M. this morning and we left the Marshalls at 7:30 A.M. Our task force consists of four battleships, two carriers, 14 destroyers, 3 minesweepers, 3 light cruisers and 1 heavy cruiser. Our task force was the first to leave, another force the same size will pull out after us. We will not see them but they will be close by. All our practice is over, we are now on our way to give Tojo and his boys a big headache. I got some rest this afternoon. The sun was out all day and the sea was calm, there is always a nice breeze. Captain Harry "the Horse" Hoffman spoke to the crew tonight, he said that there are ships all around us in big groups, even though we cannot see them. One task force a few miles ahead of us has seven battleships, many carriers, sixty-five destroyers, heavy and light cruisers, subs, etc. This will be the most powerful and largest fleet of warships ever put together and I have only mentioned some of our ships so far. We are going to hit Saipan, Guam and another island. It is about 1300 miles from the Marshalls to Saipan and Saipan is about 1200 miles from Tokyo and about 800 miles to nearest part of Japan. We will have traveled almost 3000 miles from our base in the Solomons to Saipan. We will be a long way from our nearest base, and right in the middle of Jap-held islands, we cannot expect any help from land based planes, they are too far away, our carrier planes will be the only ones but we will have plenty of them around. Our job is to hit those islands with everything and hit them hard, so it will be easier for our troops to land, then we have to hold on to them and prevent the Japs from turning us back with their Navy and air force. If some of our smaller craft run low on drinking water it will be our job to furnish them with some fresh water. All hands were told to go light on the water. This is a very big complex operation and nothing must be left out. Thousands of lives are at stake and it will help shorten the war. We also have pictures taken by subs and planes, showing every part of the island. It shows where the big guns are, barracks, towns, railroads, airfields, etc. Charts in the mess hall show where we are to bombard and where the other ships will open up, where our planes will hit and also where the Marines will land. They did not miss a thing. Some great brains planned this operation and deserve plenty of praise. Our speed is 15 knots.

Sunday, June 11, 1944: All hands got up at 4:30 A.M. this morning to man our battle stations. We had first aid lectures and instructions again this morning on main deck at 5:30 A.M. as we sailed on our way to the big invasion. We had breakfast at 7 A.M. I took a shower at 6 A.M., got 8 to noon watch. It is a beautiful sunny day. I wore the baseball cap I got from Booker T. on watch. It is very good while on lookout, helps my eyes from the sun, takes off some of the strain. There are supposed to be a lot of Jap subs around here. We are in Jap territory now, every day we will get closer to Japan and further away from our base. There can be no turning back now. We had a good dinner, and a big meal for supper. They must be fattening us up for the kill. Once we go into action we will not eat very good, because we will be at battle stations for days, we will live by our guns. I slept topside all afternoon, I got a shady spot on communication deck. The Captain spoke to the crew at 5:50 P.M. and gave us some more information on the invasion. Our biggest task force will hit the west coast of Saipan. We will hit the east coast. We start bombarding Wed. the 14th and the troops will land there the 15th. It will be the Second and Fourth Marine Divisions. The night before our troops land our demolition crews will use rubber boats with motors, to take them near shore and they will look for mines and anything that will hinder our troops when they land, they will clear a path in the water for our landing craft. Each man will carry explosives on his back, to be used for explosive mines etc. This is a real tough job because you never know when the Japs will open up on them with machine guns, they do not know what is in store for them, they will have a rugged night ahead of them. Later in the daytime our minesweepers will have their job to do and we will fire over theirs heads onto the beach to protect them from Jap shore guns. The beaches will be hit by our ships and planes just before our troops land, and a couple of days before they land we will have 1200 carrier planes to hit the Japs. A ring of warships will be around the island. Saipan is twelve miles long and five miles wide. Saipan is a big military base, at one time it was a hopping off place for the Solomons campaign. The chief industry is sugar, and a railroad runs all around the island. The population is about 50,000. There are also 6000 buildings. There are thousands of Jap troops on this island. This is supposed to be Japan's strongest base, it will be a very big loss. Our troops will land Thursday morning at 8:30. It will be called "Dog Day." This afternoon while on our way to Saipan we sent a lot of pills over to the cruiser *Birmingham,* they said that five hundred of the crew has the runs, hundreds on our ship also have it. The crew of a light cruiser is about 1200 men. I did not come down with it yet, too bad we could not give it to the Japs. The fellows will be pretty weak for the invasion, that comes off in a few days. We picked this bug up in the Solomons, it was our going away present. Look out Japs, "Bull Halsey's Diarrhea Fleet" is on its way. I got the eight to midnight watch and I thought it would be a good idea to wash two blue working shirts under the moonlight, it was about 9:30 P.M. I sat on a box with my bucket of clothes and sang some songs with B-24 Liberator, he comes from Penna., I think. I got off watch at midnight and rinsed the shirts out in the head. I then hung them up to dry. While on watch we received word that the Japs had one battleship, two cruisers, and five destroyers in the harbor at Saipan.

Monday, June 12, 1944: At 4 A.M. this morning we changed the clock back one hour. All hands got up at 3:50 A.M. this morning. We watched the planes take off from the carriers this morning. It is always very interesting to watch. Today is a beautiful sunny day, the sea is calm and every minute we get closer to Saipan. Our planes hit Saipan this morning. The people in the States got the report as soon as it happened. They did not waste any time getting the big news back to the States. We are surrounded by Jap-held islands. Now that the Japs know we are close by, they will get their subs, warships, and planes ready to attack us, they must have alerted everything by now. The Jap warships in the harbor left before our planes got there, because we have no report about them yet. The days are very long and the nights are very short. We get up now at 4 A.M. in the morning. I had a game of checkers while on watch this afternoon. A lot of the fellows have just their shorts on, they want to get some sun. You can get a quick tan, but it does not last very long. They showed the maps, charts, and pictures of Saipan to the crew today. Our ship is also going to knock out railroads. The Gunnery Officer said that the guns from our ship and our other running mate, the *Cleveland*, have fired more rounds of ammunition than any other ship in the whole operation. Of course we got the jump on the other ships because we left the States in 1942, and have been very lucky that the damage we received was not very serious, many of the others had to go back to the States. The Good Lord has been very good to us, he watches over us all the time. Our ship expects to fire about seven thousand rounds of 5 & 6 inch ammunition, four thousand 5 inch shells and three thousand 6 inch shells. When you add all the shells that the other ships are going to fire it will give you an idea what the Japs are in for, and then our carrier planes will also drop their loads of bombs and machine gun bullets. Our planes will hit Saipan today, Monday the 12th. Tues. our planes, battleships and us, Wed. more planes and ships will hit them and Thurs. our troops will land. We should have the Japs punch drunk by the time the Marines land Thurs. morning. Admiral Tip Merrill would love to be here with us. He might be on another warship out here somewhere.

Tuesday, June 13, 1944: I got off watch at 4 A.M. this morning but could not get any sleep because all hands got up at 4:45 A.M. for General Quarters. The Captain spoke at 5:15 A.M. this morning, and said the Japs lost 132 planes yesterday. Our planes also hit Saipan, Guam and Tinian. They are all in the Marianas chain. Saipan and Tinian are next to each other, Guam is further away. Had breakfast at 7:15 A.M. All hands were told to take a shower and put clean clothes on. The Captain said that we start bombarding the east coast of Saipan at 3 A.M. tomorrow Wed. the 14th. I went up to communication deck at 8 A.M. and it did not take the breeze long to dry my hair. It is a beautiful sunny day and the sea is calm. I watched the planes land on the carrier, coming back from their strike or covering the ships in case Jap planes attack, others are out scouting for Jap planes. Our planes are always patrolling around on the look out for anything. It is nice to have them around, they are the eyes of the fleet. While I was laying on the communication deck this morning, it felt like we hit a big wave, the ship shook. When I got up and took a look I saw our destroyers dropping depth charges on a Jap sub. It was not far away on our starboard quarter. Our patrol planes saw the periscope above the water and tipped us off. A two engine Jap bomber, a Betty, was snooping around about forty miles behind us, but two of our Hellcat fighter planes shot it down. Our battleships started bombarding Saipan this morning and in control aft you could hear the pilots telling the warships how good their gunnery was, if they were hitting their targets or not. They are spotting for the warships. You could also hear the pilots say, "Anti-aircraft fire is very heavy" when they got over Jap targets. At this very moment our battleships are doing a lot of damage on the Japs. We are not very far from Saipan as I write in the diary, it is just 12:30 P.M. Tues. afternoon June 13, 1944. The noon meal was no good. The only thing worth eating was the 2 slices of bread and butter, boy and am I hungry. The noon meal is usually good but they have not got much time to fool around cooking up something good, we might have to go to General Quarters any time. Some of the men are laying in the sun, others are in the shade. The ones who were up all night like myself are sleeping topside. There was no time to get any sleep after the midnight to 4 A.M. watch because General Quarters sounded. Some of the other fellows are up forward playing with a big heavy medicine ball, it is about the size of a basketball. Yesterday the Dr. operated on one of the men, he had a ruptured appendix. You can see the carrier planes patrolling all around us. I will get some sleep this afternoon and then get up for the 4 to 6 P.M. watch. Red Banilover said the bake shop is baking a thousand loaves of bread. Our diet for several days will consist of sandwiches, because we will be at our battle stations at all times. I feel very good, I am right in the pink. I wonder how the boys with the runs feel. I have not got the runs yet. Someone said that the warships in this invasion consist of 165 destroyers, about forty aircraft carriers, fifteen battleships, plus all kinds of heavy and light cruisers and subs. Just got word that we are 150 miles from Saipan. They said one of our ships was hit, it is smoking. It makes you feel good to see so many warships and planes around you, what a difference when we had only a small task force to do all the fighting and most of it was done in the darkness in the early hours of the morning, we were weak then but not anymore. There is a big difference in the Solomons and here. In about 14 hours from now, we will start bombarding Saipan. We are only about 1200 miles from Tokyo and about 800 miles from the nearest part of Japan. I guess I will go down and buy some candy for General Quarters, the candy has been our old stand-by, when we have nothing to eat at battle stations, for long hours.

A big crowd is in the mess hall. The fellows are around the radio listening to our pilots talk to our warships and telling them how they are doing. It looked like the world series. You can hear the gunfire from our battleships, one pilot told the battleships that they did a hell of a job on that spot, it is a mass of flames.

All hands went to General Quarters tonight as usual. Captain Hoffman said that we are going to start bombarding Saipan at 3 A.M. tomorrow Wed. June 14 morning and stop at 7 A.M. same morning. We will also bombard all Wed. night, this will keep the

Japs awake and they will be tired when our troops land Thurs. morning. We are not going to give them a chance to get any sleep, we will not get any and neither will they. The destroyers were supposed to do the night firing but they changed it now and we will do both, morning and night.

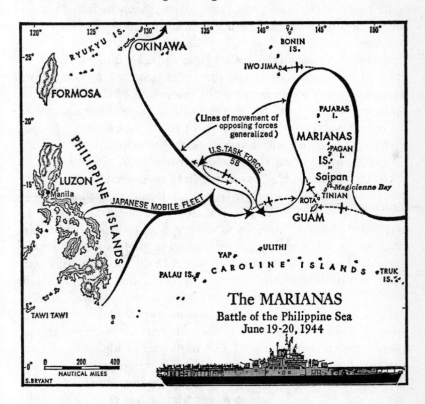

The MARIANAS
Battle of the Philippine Sea
June 19-20, 1944

Saturday, June 17, 1944: Well here I am back again with my pen in hand, last Tuesday June 13, 1944 was the last time I wrote in the diary, good old number thirteen is still my lucky number, a lot of things have happened since I last wrote. I am sitting on the communication deck, quite a bit of it has been blown away, the concussion from our guns did it. We fired the 5 & 6 inch guns from Wed. morning at 3 A.M. until Saturday morning at 7 A.M.

We did enough bombarding to last us a lifetime, I guess the *Cleveland* and us still hold the title of firing more shells than any other ship in this invasion and that includes the Japs and maybe any warship afloat anywhere in the world. There are an awful lot of sore ears, the cotton and ear plugs are no good. I will try to write down some of the many things that happened and what I saw. I do not know how to begin, I am no newspaper reporter, but here goes.

Wednesday morning at 2 A.M. June 14, 1944, all hands went to battle stations and stayed there until 7:30 A.M., Sat. morning June 17, 1944, you can just imagine the few winks of sleep we got in that time. We also had to get more ammunition in the meantime, now back to my story of what happened. About 3 A.M. Wed. morning a Jap sub surfaced and one of our destroyers sunk it. The ships firing made a good target in the dark, about 4:30 A.M. the same morning a big Jap cargo ship tried to sneak out of Saipan, but we sent one of our destroyers after it and they sunk it. We could see the high hills of Saipan, it was rather dark. Our guns continued to fire all day, we were very close to land. In the day-time we fired low and point blank, but at night we fired higher and further into the shore. Hollywood could get some great pictures, it was like a movie. Big alcohol plants were blown sky high, assembly plants, oil storage plants, ammunition dumps, miles of sugar cane, buildings, railroads, trains, trucks, etc., not to mention the military side of the picture, such as thousands of troops, planes, tanks, airfields etc. Thick smoke miles high was all over the island. I never saw anything like it before, it was like the great Chicago fire. Any large city would be in ruins if it took the shells and bombs Saipan took for almost a week. Our planes spotted for us, and we would knock the targets sky high, with direct hits. One time 25 Japs ran into a building and we got direct hits on it blowing it sky high. You could see freight cars and tracks blow up. A big ammunition dump was blown to bits. Our troops tried to take a hill with tanks, but the Japs artillery on top of it stopped them. We opened up on them and wiped them out. Another time the Japs tried to put radar and radio equipment into a truck, and we blew everything up, troops and equipment. We knocked out pillboxes etc. It was just like a movie. You could see big explosions everywhere. At night we fired a lot of star shells so our troops could see the Japs, if they tried to sneak into our lines. Our ship knocked out a twin 5 inch turret, on Magicienne Bay. Our five inch shell entered the Japanese five inch twin turret through a gun opening causing an explosion which put the Jap battery out of action, thus permitting our ships to enter Magicienne Bay without opposition. On another occasion Jap shore guns opened up on us and we were forced to put up a smoke screen. We then commenced firing on the Japs, and it was not long before we silenced their guns. The battleship *California* was hit by Jap shore batteries and thirty men were killed, not to mention the wounded. We fired at the Japs day and night, the idea was to have them punch drunk, but if you ask me I think some of us are also punchy. The men on the 5 & 6 inch guns had a rugged time. They were in those hot stuffy mounts and turrets all those days and nights with very little time off for rest, they spent most of the time passing the shells and powder cases into the guns and they had very little to eat. They were dirty from the dust and sweat. The deck of the mounts and turrets was covered with their perspiration, they looked like ghosts when it was over. If they did lay down to get some rest the concussion and noise from the guns shook them up and made sleep impossible. Some of the fellows passed out from exhaustion. They took quite a licking, you cannot go day and night. We had a candy bar for breakfast, two cookies and an apple for dinner, and at night we did not have very much either. The fellows on the machine guns, like myself, had it easier, not much to do. We could see everything that was going on. In the daytime it was quite a show. Our planes would go through a hail of machine gun fire, drop their bombs on the Japs and go like a bullet, straight up in the clouds and away. This island got the worst bombardment of them all. They said we landed 40,000 troops and the Japs have a good 30,000. Our Marines landed Thurs. June 15, 1944, at 8:30 A.M. They ran into murderous gunfire when on their way in to the beach, casualties were very high. Our warships were called in to open up on the Japs. Our troops will have their work cut out for them on Saipan. Saipan looks like the States, it has a lot of flat land and it is very pretty, everything is so green. The island of Tinian is not too far away, it looks like a stone's throw away, it also looks the same. Our troops will also land there later. Sat. morning we came alongside an ammunition ship, it also had a lot of Marines aboard who were waiting to get into landing craft, to hit the beach. It was not too far from the beach, you could see our tanks turned over where they had been knocked out by Jap gunfire or mines. Some of our tanks ran into coral on the way to the beach and tipped over. There are a lot of coral hills in the water that they did not see. This is the west coast of Saipan where the troops landed that I am speaking about, we had to leave the east coast to get more ammunition. This place is full of ships, what a sight. It is about 8 A.M. Sat. morning. You can see the guns on land firing and our tanks going up the hills after the Japs, you can also see our flamethrowers in action. The Marines have their heavy artillery guns ashore now. The battle is raging not too far away, there is a continuous noise from the exploding shells of the artillery, our planes are also doing their job as they come sweeping in for the kill. Smoke and dust covers the battlefield, it is quite a sight. I saw some landing craft blow up just before they hit the beach, they were full of Marines. Our troops are still landing all kinds of supplies.

There are still a lot of Marines on this ammunition ship waiting to hit the beach. I was talking to some of them, just before they went over the side of the ship to get into a landing craft for the beach and they said the hardest part is waiting. They would rather be over on the beach fighting. These Marines were also in the Marshall invasion. The craft that was to bring them to the beach brought back a Marine with a Jap flag in his hand. He killed some Japs getting it. The harbor has so many troop and supply ships here that I would not even attempt to count them, what a sight. The island also has a ring of warships around it, and another big task force of carriers, battleships, cruisers and destroyers are further away. You can see our warships firing on the Japs, boy this is a busy place, on land and in the water, everyone has a job to do. As we carry the ammunition we get a bird's eye view of what is going on at the same time, some of the fellows are down in the compartments, talking to the Marines before they hit the beach. Red Banilover told me he was talking to a Marine from my home town, but it was too late to look him up, it was time to leave. Some of our officers also helped carry the ammunition. While we were tied up to the ammunition ship, we had men standing by the lines with an axe in hand ready to cut the line if Jap planes should attack us. We would leave at once at full speed. Our carrier task force is making sure the Japs do not make an appearance. Someone said the Japs have underground hangers with planes in them.

At 11:30 A.M. Sat. June 17, 1944 we finished carrying ammunition and left this area. We are going to join another task force. A big Jap fleet is heading this way and our job is to intercept them. They have carriers, battleship, cruisers, destroyers and subs. They are not going to lose Saipan without putting up a fight. We are on our way to the open sea and we will not see any land for some time.

This afternoon Sat. June 17, 1944 at 4 P.M. we met a task force of warships, it consisted of five battleships, the *New Jersey* was one of them, two big carriers, two smaller ones, one heavy cruiser, thirty destroyers and also light cruisers, the *Cleveland* and *Birmingham* are two of them. We might meet more ships later. While I was writing this at 4:05 in the evening Jap planes were picked up and all hands went to battle stations, but nothing happened. I will try to continue writing, it is up to the Japs to stop me.

Friday while we were bombarding we received word that Japan was bombed by the Big B–29 Super Flying Fortresses. They are the largest in the world and have the longest range. They came from our base in China, a big cheer went up when the announcement came over the loudspeaker. This is the first time Japan has been hit since Jimmy Doolittle did it in 1942.

Then they flew their B–25 twin engine bombers off carriers.

Later this evening we met another big task force. It looks like it is in four groups. It must consist of hundreds of warships, as far as the eye can see, this is a fleet now, this is the Fifth Fleet, it is in one piece, what a sight. Before we met on the other side of the horizon, there was nothing, but later on you could see little specks appear and then they got larger and before long, you could see the complete outline and then more would appear and before you knew it, the ocean was covered with all sorts of warships, as far as the eye could see. They are all very fast ships. This is the most powerful fleet of warships the world has ever seen. We have carriers, battleships, heavy and light cruisers, destroyers and submarines. This is the 5th Fleet, Admiral Spruance is in command. We are part of Task Force 58, with Admiral Marc Mitscher in command. It was a beautiful evening, as we had sunset General Quarters. We are now in no man's sea a long way from the U.S.A. but close to Japan. I hit the sack at 8 P.M., it looks like I will get some sleep, it will be the first night's sleep in about a week, it will be under the stars.

Sunday, June 18, 1944: I got up at 3:15 A.M. this morning. I got the 4 to 8 A.M. watch. All hands got up at 4:45 A.M. I had a swell sleep topside last night even if it was only for about six hours. I will get some today if the Japs do not come. The air is very healthy here, it is dry, not like the South Pacific. At 9 A.M. this morning we were 250 miles closer to Japan. We must be only about 600 miles from Japan now. They said we are going in the direction of the coast of China, our direction is west southwest, we are going pretty fast. I started my 19th month out here. Yesterday was Bunker Hill Day. It is a holiday in Boston and Charlestown, Mass. It looked like Bunker Hill on Saipan with our troops advancing after the Japs. The first time in almost a week the fellows have a chance to lay down topside and get some well needed rest. Some of the men are washing their clothes. We had church service topside this morning, even though we are so close to Japan, and the Jap fleet might be close by. Someone said that four of our fastest subs, 18 knots, have been following the Jap fleet and they will let us know where to find it.

Monday, June 19, 1944: Slept topside last night. All hands up at 4:45 this morning. The closest we got to Japan so far is about 600 miles. At 10:45 A.M. this morning all hands went to General Quarters. Our carrier planes hit Guam early this morning. Jap planes attacked our task force at 11 A.M. this morning, they attacked us from all directions. Jap planes were falling all around us and the sky was full of bursting shells, big puffs of smoke could be seen everywhere. Our ship was leading the rest of the ships, we were up front in the force, with some destroyers screening us. Bombs were falling very close to the ships, big sprays of water could be seen and Jap planes were splashing into the water. One Jap plane after dropping its load and with a charmed life flew through a hail of gunfire as it flew over many ships, but when it got to us we riddled it with shells, and sent it into the blue Pacific. Our machine gun mount and MT 43, another 40 mm., knocked it down. The Captain said it was very good shooting. Later Admiral Mitscher sent word to all ships, saying they did a good job. When we passed the spot where the Jap plane was sunk, the water was all green, the pilot's goggles were still floating in the water, it was a Tony we shot down. Some men on a destroyer were wounded. The battleship *South Dakota* also got hit with a bomb, we did not get full details of damage we received. In the meantime our carrier planes were doing a job on the Jap air force, at Guam, and vicinity. The score so far stands at 250 Jap planes destroyed in air and on ground, reports are still coming in. One of our Corsair pilots shot down five Jap planes. The sea was calm and blue in the morning but got a little rough in the afternoon. The two sea planes from our ship landed in the water near Guam and could not take off. They picked up three of our pilots who were shot down. They were about fifteen miles from Guam. While they waited for one of our destroyers to reach them, Jap planes came down on them with their machine guns blazing away. They fired all their ammunition at the Japs and asked for fighter protection until our destroyer came to their rescue. When our destroyers reached them they had to sink the two sea planes. The Japs had shot them up pretty bad. All this happened about 5 P.M. About 2 P.M. this afternoon one of our TBFs could not make the carrier, it hit the water and sunk, but everyone was saved. One of our destroyers picked them up, this was close to us. It was a very busy day and everyone enjoyed seeing the Jap planes hit the water. We stayed at battle stations all day and all night, our food consists of sandwiches.

Tuesday, June 20, 1944: Got a few winks of sleep last night, no Jap planes attacked us. I guess they lost too many yesterday. We secured from battle stations at 7 A.M. this morning. I have not heard much about the big Jap fleet that was coming this way. Someone said our force went further west than any other, if we kept going we would have reached Japan. It was good to get off battle stations and move around after being cooped up on the small mount since early yesterday morning. Most of the men are laying around getting some well needed rest. I had to clean up the Communication deck and did not get a chance to sleep, when I finished I wrote in the diary. I do not want to get behind with it. As I look around some of the men are out like a light, the sleep is better than food. Some of the fellows have a bucket full of clothes and are washing them, every man to his own taste. No doubt but I am the only sailor in the whole fleet who is writing in a Diary. I go on watch at noon, also got midnight to 4 A.M., so I will not get much sleep. The sun is hot but there is a good breeze, the sun is out nearly all the time and the blue Pacific is always calm around here. You can pick up the radio programs from Japan, they play American recordings most of the time.

At 4 P.M. this afternoon we got the good news we have been waiting for, they finally know where the Jap fleet is, they said it is heading for the Philippines. Our carrier planes picked them up this afternoon, everyone was glad to hear this. The Jap fleet is running away from us and heading for their base. We picked up speed and are after them. This news has put new life into the men. It is getting late and our only hope of doing any damage to them is to send our planes after them. Some of the men on this mission will not return, the Japs will give them a hot reception. It was 4:30 P.M. when our planes took off, someone said about three hundred planes took off. Time would be a big factor, could our planes catch up with the Japs before it got dark and would they get back to their carriers on time. The time dragged as we waited to hear from our pilots, everyone kept his fingers crossed, hoping for the best. It was like waiting in the death house for a pardon, and then it happened. About 6:50 P.M. word came in that our pilots caught up with the Jap navy and it said three carriers were damaged, one sunk, one battleship listing, we will get more dope later. The Captain said some of our pilots will not come back, and we wished them the best of luck. The Japs are in three groups and have a lot of ships with them. He hopes we can catch up with them. It was still bright at 7:45 P.M. and at about 9 P.M. tonight our planes were returning. It was dark and they would have a tough job landing on the carriers, they were low on fuel and some were damaged, many had to make forced landings in the water. Then something never done before in war time happened, all the ships in this huge fleet put their lights on, and flares were dropped into the water. This all happened right in the Japs' back yard maybe 700 or 800 miles from the coast of Japan. We would be easy targets for Jap subs that might be around. It was a great decision to make and everyone thought the world of Admiral Marc Mitscher for doing this. This would make it easier for our pilots to land, and if they did hit the water they could be saved. The big carriers were all lighted up so the pilots could see where to land, a lot of our destroyers were left behind to pick the men out of the water, some men were picked up right away. It was a shame to see our planes hitting the water. I saw one pilot on the wing of his plane waving his shirt. There were so many lights it must have been hard to land on the carriers. A Jap plane also tried to land on one of our carriers. Our planes continued to land as we continued on our way after the Jap fleet. It was quite a sight to see all the ships lit up, flares and rafts in the water and some planes crashing into the water, and pilots and crews also in the water. You could see the planes circle and then land on the carriers. A great job was done by everyone to save our pilots' lives. The Japs would never do anything like this. I went on watch at midnight.

Wednesday, June 21, 1944: Got off watch at 4 A.M., got one hour sleep, all hands up at 5 A.M. The Captain spoke and gave us some dope. He said three Jap carriers were damaged, one sunk, one battleship missing. The Jap fleet is too far away for us to catch them. Our carrier planes will hit them again today. The Press News said that our carrier planes and warships destroyed 300 Jap planes Monday, but the official score was over 400. Our navy pilots accounted for most of them. No other country ever lost that many planes in one day. It was a black Monday for the Jap air force. I got some rest today, also took a shower. They said we were only seven hundred miles north of Manila. That puts us very close to Japan and China about 700 or 800 miles away. This must be the closest any warship got since the war started. Some of our destroyers fueled from the other ships. That's something, fueling in the Jap's back yard, and we are getting closer all the time, we are still heading west. A lot of our pilots must have been picked up today. We might catch up with the Jap fleet again. The Captain will tell us tonight how our planes made out this morning against the Jap fleet.

Thursday, June 22, 1944: Got up at 3:15 A.M. to go on watch, got 4 to 8 A.M. Had breakfast at 7 A.M., worked at cleaning station. It looks like we are going back to get some fuel, we are very low. They said the Japs lost 600 planes in eight days, that is since the campaign started eight days ago. It looks like the Jap fleet came from the Philippines and then headed for Saipan to knock our invasion force out, but it backfired on them, and now they are heading for their base again. The Japs never thought that we would be so powerful. They expected to hit our troop and supply ships at Saipan, but what a surprise they got when they ran into the 5th Fleet. If we found the Jap fleet sooner we could have knocked them off, but they had too much of a lead for us to catch up to them. The radio and Press News said everyone is waiting for the biggest naval battle in History, and the Jap leaders said they were coming out to beat us and retake Saipan. This was another big setback for Japan.

Yesterday we picked up one of the pilots who were shot down

when they attacked the Jap fleet, we came to the spot where the action took place. The pilot said he saw two Jap carriers go down and one battleship was heavily damaged. Everyone is disappointed we did not run into the Jap fleet. Monday while we were under attack from Jap planes, our planes were landing and taking off from the carriers, that was the day the Japs lost over four hundred planes. Our planes would fuel, get ammunition, and then take off again while the guns of the carriers were still firing at Jap planes. Admiral Nimitz said in the Press News that the 5th Fleet has enough muscle in it to take care of the Jap fleet. It is about 10 A.M. as I write this. I will write later if I get any news.

At about 1:30 P.M. this afternoon we met about six tankers. We fueled from one side and the big carrier *Enterprise* was on the other side of the tanker. A tanker holds about seven million gallons of fuel. The *Enterprise* holds about 4½ million gallons of fuel. Our ship holds 750,000 gallons. We only had a couple of days' fuel left. All the ships were low on fuel. Nearly all the planes on the carrier had Jap planes painted on them, one plane had 10 Jap planes shot down to credit. Admiral Marc Mitscher is on the *Enterprise* and he is in command of Task Force 58, the carrier task force in the 5th Fleet, he is a great man. The *Enterprise* is a great ship and has quite a war record. We are between the Philippines and Saipan as we fuel. It is a beautiful day as usual. Most of the men are laying topside, some are on the gun mounts, some in the shade and others getting a tan. We played checkers on watch. I had the 6 to 8 P.M. watch. It is still bright at 8 P.M. in the evening. Some more pilots were picked out of the water today, they have been in the water for some time. I slept topside as usual.

Friday, June 23, 1944: All hands up at 5 A.M., we left battle stations at 6 A.M. The tankers stayed with us all night and continued fueling the rest of ships today. The Captain said that we will join Admiral Raymond Spruance's Amphibious 5th Fleet tomorrow. The tankers left us at 2:30 P.M. this afternoon, they said we are on way back to Saipan. Our planes shot down a Jap bomber about 1 P.M. this afternoon. A lot of smoke came from it when it hit the water. It is a two engine job. It tried to attack our carriers.

Saturday, June 24, 1944: All hands up at 5 A.M. We are on our way back to Saipan. We just have some carriers, light cruisers and destroyers with us. The rest of the fleet is going somewhere else. At 7:45 P.M., just before it got dark, we left the carriers and joined up with four heavy cruisers, *Frisco* is also with them, plus some destroyers. Got up at 11:15 P.M. for watch, got midnight to 4 A.M.

Sunday, June 25, 1944: Hit the sack at a little after 4 A.M., all hands got up for General Quarters at 5 A.M., got few winks of sleep, very tired. We pulled into Saipan this morning at 7 A.M. after being away from here since Sat. June 17, 1944, those eight days sure went fast. It felt good to be part of the 5th Fleet with Task Force 58. We chased the Jap fleet back to the Philippines and into the China Sea. They said the Japs lost fifteen warships, in the Battle of the Eastern Philippines. The 5th Fleet is broken up into small groups again. We got very close to Saipan today, some of our ships are still bombarding the Japs and our planes are also doing a job on the troops. Most of the Japs are crowded up north on Saipan. It was funny to see some of the fellows fishing from the side of the ship, others laying in the sun getting a tan, and up forward on the bow some of the officers are boxing, while on the beach men are killing each other, some are in agony from wounds. Our planes are strafing and bombing and our ships are bombarding the Japs. The two scenes are so close to each other and yet it is from one extreme to another or two different worlds. We might bombard Saipan tonight. Our troops captured more stores and supplies on Saipan than in any other campaign in the Pacific War. We also captured a lot of Jap planes and parts. A lot of Jap ships were sunk off shore. We also have a lot of troops on the other side of Saipan on the east coast where we started our first bombardment. The Japs are still putting up a fierce fight for Saipan.

Monday, June 26, 1944: We returned to Saipan this morning, we were out all night patrolling. We came alongside an ammunition ship and got 5 & 6 inch ammunition. We are very close to shore. I was talking to one of the men from the ammunition ship who was on the beach, and he said some of the Japs are up in caves with big steel doors. They open a slide and fire at our troops and then close them. Our troops sneaked up on the Japs and when they opened the steel door they put a flamethrower in and wiped out the Japs. The bodies smelled when the flamethrowers hit them and the smell of burnt flesh is very strong. He said 1500 of our troops were killed the day before yesterday. There are a lot of civilians here and our troops have to guard them. They come down to the beach twice a day, I guess to wash up. They have very few clothes on. We can see them through the spyglasses. Most of the sunken ships offshore are above the water, they look in pretty good shape. They said the bulldozers push Japs in big holes and then bury them. One of the men from an LST told one of the crew that he was close to the shore and he saw our Marines cut about 500 Japs to pieces as they came down from the hills. He also saw some hand to hand fighting, both sides were cut up pretty bad, but our side had the edge, cutting the Japs to ribbons. The men from the LST that pulled next to us that morning had a lot of Jap stuff, they got it on the beach. I would give a month's pay to go on shore and look around. We pulled out at 6 P.M. tonight. It would be foolish for us to stay in this harbor at night because Jap planes might come in. We can move around better in the open sea and if the Japs should try to send any warship this way we will be in a position to stop them before they hit our transports and troops. We might bombard Saipan tomorrow at 5:30 A.M.

Tuesday, June 27, 1944: We are at it again. At 5:30 A.M. this morning we opened up on the Japs, it is also bright. If our troops come across Japs who are hard to get at, it will be our job to destroy them. Our Marine spotters on land will tell us what to fire at. All day we fired on the Japs and we also bombarded the island of Tinian, it is just across from Saipan. The Japs have airfields and hangars there. They also are supposed to have a lot of pillboxes with big guns. We will land troops there in a few days. We get very close to shore when we bombard the Japs. One of our destroyers got hit by shore guns yesterday, many were killed and wounded. We gave the place an awful pasting today. Saipan and Tinian are very pretty islands, there are not many trees but everything is so green. The pastures are so big and green, plenty of room. There are big cliffs on Saipan, they are very high, below is the ocean. The sun is very hot but there is always a good breeze. While we are bombarding, a few men at a time go below to get the food. We will stay at battle stations all day and night, we will also fire star shells at night and early in the morning darkness, so the Japs cannot sneak into our lines. We will keep them awake all night. If the Japs were not like animals they would have given up a long time ago because their cause is hopeless. But they seldom surrender, they would rather die for the Emperor. The Japs have been on the receiving end of bombarding ships and planes for about two weeks, they can really take it.

Wednesday, June 28, 1944: We fired at the Japs all day yesterday and all night and all today until about 2:30 P.M. this afternoon. We knocked out machine gun nests in the hills that were holding up the Marines. We also knocked out pillboxes and fuel dumps. The Press News said that the official count of Jap planes lost in the Big Air Battle was 403, in one day. That is a record in any war, anywhere. Our ship also holds a record for rapid fire against the enemy. While we were bombarding Saipan at close range some big Jap shore guns opened up on us and before they knew what happened our big 6 inch guns were firing back like a machine gun. We fired 99 6-inch shells from turret No. 3 in 2½ minutes. I never saw anything like it before. They just smothered the Jap guns and knocked them out in a hurry. When our guns stopped firing it was all over for the Japs. Talk about quick reflexes. The Japs were on a high cliff. Tonight we do not bombard Saipan, we go out and patrol between here and Japan, we do this just in case the Japs try to sneak anything in. Jap planes attack almost every night, but they do very little damage. Jap subs also try to sneak in.

Thursday, June 29, 1944: We pulled back into Saipan early this morning and left at 8 A.M. to do some more bombarding of Saipan and Tinian. We bombarded all day until 4:30 P.M. We knocked out many targets, including a radio station. At night we pulled out for our usual patrol. Some other ships will bombard the Japs all night. We never stop bombarding the Japs, all day, every day, around the clock, it never stops. This has been going on for over two weeks. Our planes also hit them in the daytime. In the European war the enemy will surrender when they know the situation is hopeless, but not the Japs, they die fighting. In the next war I hope the Japs are on our side, you have to admire their bravery, they are no pushovers.

Friday, June 30, 1944: Up at 3:15 A.M. for watch, all hands up at 4:45 A.M. We returned to Saipan at 7 A.M. We pulled alongside an LST and transferred all our empty powder cases. I got two Jap records from the crew. They have all kinds of Jap things they picked up on Saipan, some had Jap bicycles. They told us that the girls thought nothing of washing on the beach with no clothes on, some of them were good looking. He said that they looked like a mixture of Spanish and Jap, most of them are Japs. Some of the girls were only 13 years old and they were going to have children soon. Some of the civilians are fighting against the Japs. They want to surrender, but the Jap troops kill them. We keep the Jap civilians in a stockade and many of them are diseased. Some of the Jap troops are in caves up in the hills and they are very hard to get at, because they push these big guns out of the openings in the caves to fire at our troops, and then pull them back in again out of sight.

An amphibious tractor with four Marines in it also came alongside. The Marines came aboard. These tractors can go in the water and on land. It carries twenty-one men, one driver, one sub driver, a machine gunner and 18 troops. It is well protected with armor. A lot of our landing craft turned over when the waves pushed them against the coral, but the tractors stood up much better. The Marines who came aboard went up to Captain Hoffman. They gave him a Jap rifle and the Captain in return gave his .45 with his name on it to the Marines. They wanted to show their appreciation for the help we gave them. If the people back home only knew what our troops are going through. One of the

Marines put his bayonet through a Jap, but he could not pull it out, so he had to empty his gun into the Jap. Blood was going in all directions. He finally pulled the gun and bayonet free. We got fuel today, patrolled off Saipan at night, I slept on the steel deck under the stars as usual. As Banis the Marine would say, I hit the steel.

Saturday, July 1, 1944: I got off watch at midnight. All hands up at 4:45 A.M., breakfast at 6:30 A.M. Out patrolling all night, returned to Saipan at 6:30 A.M. Last night one of our night fighters shot down a 2 motor Jap bomber, it circled around in a mass of flames and then crashed into the water. The other night about 600 Jap soldiers got drunk or doped up and pulled off a Banzai or suicide charge against the Marines, they came in like crazy people and a vicious hand to hand battle took place. The Japs tried to brawl their way through our lines, but they were stopped. They had plenty of casualties on both sides, but the Japs got the worst of it. Someone said Jap civilians were sent to bury their dead but only 85 returned out of 285, they got out of order. We fired at Saipan and Tinian all day, we stopped at 5:00 P.M. One fuel dump has been burning for days and it is still burning. We knocked a lot of Jap guns out today, also some buildings, etc. The Press News said that our casualties at Saipan from June 15 to 28, are 9754, 1445 killed and 880 missing. Close to 5000 Japs were killed. We pulled out at 5:45 P.M. to patrol all night again, after being at battle stations all day bombarding. Everyone was hungry after supper because it was no good. My old stand-by Red Banilover came to the rescue, he got some cookies at the bakery from one of his friends. We ate them before going on watch, they really hit the spot. We have the 8 to midnight watch.

Sunday, July 2, 1944: Hit the sack after midnight, all hands up at 4:45 A.M. Breakfast at 6:30 A.M. At General Quarters all day until 5 P.M. We spent the day bombarding Tinian. We got very close to the shore. Knocked a lot of stuff out today. You could see the Japs running around, we would fire at them and blow them to bits. The P-47 Thunderbolts put on quite a show, strafing the Japs, they carry about eight 50 cal. machine guns. They would dive at Japs spitting hot lead at the Japs and then up they would go up into the sky like a bullet. Another hospital ship came into Saipan harbor today, that makes two big ones in here now. The Japs are all dug in and they have a tough job blowing them out of their holes. A Big B–24 Liberator Bomber, a four engine job, landed on Saipan the other day. Our troops advanced about a mile today. The Marines like the .45 pistols with them when they are in foxholes because they are easy to handle, you haven't got much room in a foxhole, the rifles are too long and clumsy to use if a Jap should sneak up on you. Every day you can see the supply ships unloading. Today we blew half of the big hangar to bits. I looked through the field glasses and got a good look at what was going on, on Saipan. You could see our troops but the Japs were all dug in. There is still house to house fighting going on in one of the towns. They said the hospital ship can carry a thousand patients. The hospital ships do not roll like other ships do, because they are made like two ships, the outer part moves but the inside does not. They carry about forty-five nurses. I almost forgot to mention that while we were bombarding, some Japs ran from one building into another and while they were inside hiding we blew up the building and Japs, sky high. Some of the new men who have been out here a few months told us fellows who have been out here 19 months that they could not stay out here that long, they would go insane, they can hardly wait to go home. They were married and had children. They are in their upper forties.

Monday, July 3, 1944: Last night I got about a half hour sleep. I could not find a place topside to keep dry. I took a shower at 10 P.M. and it stopped raining about 11 P.M. I went on watch from midnight to 4 A.M. I hit the sack after 4 A.M. and all hands went to General Quarters at 4:45 A.M. There is one thing you do not have to worry about getting out here and that is a good night's sleep. There is no such thing as that. Most of our time is spent at battle stations. In all the time that I have been out here I only slept below in my bunk a few times, because it is too hot. You sleep on the steel deck with your clothes on and use your shoes for a pillow, and your hat on top of the shoes. The hat takes the

place of a pillowcase. When it rains you stand back under cover
and hope it does not last very long. During the rainy season you
spend most of the night standing under cover talking to yourself,
because it will not stop raining and you have to go on watch at
midnight, dead tired. Then other times it stops raining and you
are just going to sleep and it starts raining again, some nights this
goes on all night. Then you top it off with Reveille, at 4 or 5 in
the morning. It will be quite a treat for us when we return home
and go to sleep in a bed and with nothing to spoil our sleep. It is
just the little things in life that you look forward to when you go
home. When you had them you thought nothing of them, you
took them for granted. Now you look forward to meeting your
family and friends, being able to go to the corner store and get the
morning paper, and read your favorite topics, or visit the drug-
store for a big ice cream soda, looking at the buildings and going
to the Parish Church, and the local theater. Eating plenty of good
food. You want to be free again and do what you want to do and
go where you want to go, without someone always ordering you
around, you want freedom. When you do get home you will be
able to carry yourself much better whenever a tough situation
comes up, it will not bother you, you will have more wisdom and
be more humble. Everyone is talking about us going back to the
States. Some of the officers said that we will leave soon for the
States. Someone said that Carlson, the officer in charge of Carlson's Marine Raiders, was killed at Saipan. They made a movie
about him and his Marine Raiders. We got some sad news today,
about the Marine officer who did the spotting for our bombardments on Saipan. They said that he is missing. Before he left our
ship he said that his job was to get on the big hill, even if he got
killed. Our country lost a great man when they lost him. Last
night the Japs got one of their planes from the underground
hangar, and were going to try to use it, but they were stopped by
our troops. Our two hospital ships left this morning. Someone
said that the convoy for Tinian comes in tomorrow, and that we
will invade July 5.

We did not do any firing this morning, for a change. I caught
up with some of my sleep. I slept on the five inch mount, it's a

nuisance when they turn the mount around while you are sleeping, you think that you might fall off, or be crushed against something. Red Banilover, my Jewish friend, gave me a piece of pie last night, and Irwin gave me four apples this morning after chow. They are both mess cooking. We have been bombarding so much that nearly everything that is close to the 5 & 6 inch guns is either broken loose or blown off, it looks like someone dropped a bomb on us. Tomorrow night is the night before the 4th of July. Last year this time we were in the Solomons taking part in the Munda Campaign. We have advanced a long way since then. We were almost 4000 miles from Japan then, but now we are about 800 miles away. We did not do any bombarding today, so I spent a lot of time watching the action on Saipan. You could see our troops firing on the Japs and advancing behind tanks. The Japs up in the hills were firing back at our troops. Tonight our ship will fire star shells at the Japs, we will continue until daylight tomorrow morning. This way our troops can watch the Japs, just in case they try to pull some of their tricks or counterattack. I sat on the mount and got some tan this afternoon, also looked through glasses and watched Marines and Japs go at it. A lot of Jap planes were headed this way, but our carrier planes took care of them. I don't know what we would do without our carrier planes. The weather was not so hot today.

Well about 5:30 P.M. this evening we had our night before the 4th fireworks. Jap troops were on a cargo ship that was put out of action at the beginning of the campaign. It was close to shore and the Japs were firing on our troops with 50 cal. & 20 mm. machine guns. It would be very costly to go in after them, so our planes went to work on them. Our planes would peel off, one after another, and dive at the Japs with their machine guns blazing away. Our TBFs were also dropping bombs, a near miss would send the water hundreds of feet into the air. The place was a mass of smoke and when the planes finished there was no more trouble from the Japs, they were wiped out. These sunken ships make good forts for the Japs to fire on our troops. The Army is also fighting on Saipan, but there are more Marines.

Tuesday, July 4, 1944: We fired star shells all last night and all

morning until daylight today. It rained for a while this morning.
The Press News said that in the first couple of weeks, over 6500
Japs were killed. There is a very strong odor from the beach, it
smells like burnt flesh. Yesterday and today our artillery on the
beach gave the Japs an awful pounding. Today is the 4th of July
and a good way to celebrate it is by killing Japs. Our troops have
the situation pretty well in hand on Saipan now. I was back in
the States for a while last night. I dreamt that I met Johnson on
Main St. He runs the pool room on Elm St., I ran over and shook
his hand. We will fire all day again. You can hear the continuous
noise of our land artillery, this afternoon we got very close to
shore and our ship opened up on the Japs, with our 20 & 40 mm.
machine guns. The Japs were running in all directions, but our
fire was too heavy for them. We also started several fires. We
fired thousands of rounds of machine gun ammunition at the Japs
and worked up quite a sweat doing it but was worth it. When we
finished the barrels were so hot you could not touch them, and the
grease on the mounts was boiling hot. It was hot and sunny and
we made it that much warmer. We were relieved by the light
cruiser *Birmingham* at 5 P.M. They will fire star shells at the Japs
all night while we go out and patrol all night. We will return to
Saipan in the morning. Whenever I hear some of the fellows complain how tough it is, I tell them that if they were on the beach
with our troops it would be a lot tougher, that usually shuts them
up. Cap. Harry "The Horse" Hoffman speaks every evening
about 7 P.M. and gives us the latest news about our troops on
the beach and about our firing. We have 10 inch or 250 mm. guns
on Saipan now, and they use them to bombard Tinian. We have
all the towns on Saipan now, our troops advanced a lot today. We
should have Saipan this week. That means it took about three
weeks for our troops to take Saipan, today is July 4th and the Marines landed June 15th. I got off watch at 8 P.M. and then hit the
steel. I had a blanket over me, the air is clear and fresh, good for
sinus. You need a blanket over you, because you get a breeze from
the ship moving. I don't know what it is like on the beach.

Wednesday, July 5, 1944: All hands up at 4:45 A.M. It did not rain last night, had good sleep. Pulled into Saipan at 6:30 this morning. We bombarded Tinian all day. The Japs have a lot of guns on it and they are well camouflaged. Our planes spotted for us. The Japs are pretty smart, they pull some tricks you would never think of doing and you would think that they could not get away with them, but they do. We stopped firing at 3:30 this afternoon and pulled alongside an LST and got some ammunition.

Thursday, July 6, 1944: All hands got up at 4:30 A.M. this morning, and at 5:30 we pulled alongside ammunition ship. We started carrying ammunition at 7 A.M. and finished at 3 P.M. in the afternoon. We got about 6000 rounds of 5 & 6 inch plus thousands of rounds of 20 & 40 mm. One of the new men who came on a few months ago said that was the hardest work he ever did. One of our officers has a brother on Saipan and he is going to get the Silver Star for bravery, he has not been hurt yet, he is alright. The Press News calls Saipan "Bloody Saipan." It said that our troops had to overcome tougher obstacles here than in any other campaign against the Japs. They played my Jap record this evening, it sounded funny, it was all Greek to us. I washed my clothes and took a shower. Got up at 11:15 for midnight to 4 A.M. watch.

Friday, July 7, 1944: Hit sack a little after 4 A.M. All hands got up at 4:45 A.M. very tired. They said we will not do much for a few days. Expect to invade Tinian July 10, 1944. We held field day, today, cleaned up ship and got it in order, too busy to do it before. I got some rest this afternoon. Four battleships came in this morning. One of them was the sharpshooter, the *New Jersey*. It stayed bright until 7:45 P.M. The supper was no good, had stew, bread, and butter. They called it stew, but it did not look or taste like it.

Saturday, July 8, 1944: We returned to Saipan this morning as usual and before the day was over we would have some bad misfortune. A lot of Jap planes were captured at Saipan and they were in good condition. You can see five of them on one of our small carriers not too far from us, about 25 are below deck. They also had some good underground hangars at Saipan. The Japs are almost at the end of the island, but when our Army troops tried to get behind them, the Japs drove them back into the water. Our destroyers had to come in and pick them up. Jap planes tried to attack Saipan, but our planes stopped them. The Japs sent some subs here to get the big shots off but our destroyers sunk them. The Japs only have a little section of Saipan left and they will be licked, but they are still putting up a fierce fight. This morning a working party was sent to the hangar deck to get stores, at almost the last hold. The hatch is airtight and the hold should have been open for twenty-four hours before anyone went into the hold. The men on the working party did not know this and the first fellow to go down into the hold was only there a short time when he passed out. When one of the fellows looked down to see why no stores were coming up, he saw his friend laid out. Another fellow went down to get him, but he also passed out. Another fellow rushed below and got there before it was too late. They called the repair party, who put on special masks. When the first fellow to be felled by the fumes was brought out of the hold, he was dead. His body was blue and slimy. They gave the other fellow artificial respiration etc., he may pull through. He was a very lucky fellow to be alive. One of the fellows from my division was on the working party and he said that the fumes had a sweet taste, he also felt a little sick. The fellow who died also has a brother on our ship, and he was heartbroken, he could not believe it. We left Saipan at sunset this evening, on our night patrol, and when we got out to sea, our friend's body was dropped over the side. The burial ceremonies were held on the starboard side of the catapult on the stern. All hands assembled with life jackets on. The American flag was over the casket, prayers were said by the Chaplain, taps were sounded by the Marines and the Marines also fired a 21 gun salute. The casket slid down a chute and dropped into the deep blue Pacific. Our country lost another good young man, may his soul rest in peace. In the distance you could see the guns flashing on Saipan and our destroyers were also bombarding Tinian. We then secured. We had hot dogs and bread for supper, after supper everyone was just as hungry. Some of us lay down on the deck and talked about the good big meals we could put away, that only made us more hungry, boy were we starved, our stomachs were barking. When we got home we were going to eat the best of everything. I said that I could eat a big chicken dinner and top it off with a big blueberry pie, covered with all kinds of Ice Cream. The sky was full of stars, it was a beautiful night to sleep topside under the stars.

Sunday, July 9, 1944: The Press News this morning said that our B–29 Flying Fortressess hit Japan again. Our troops have about one mile to go on Saipan. A lot of Japs are in caves and will not come out, there's also a lot of civilians hiding in caves. They were told to come out and we would give them water and food and they would not be harmed. If they refuse to come out, we will be forced to kill them. Someone said that we will have all of Saipan today. After chow I took a shower and sat in the sun and got some tan. There is not much doing so they let us get some rest. A body floated by on a stretcher, it was all blown up and some kind of a cloth was over its head. You could see blond hair sticking out. It was one of our Marines that was killed on Saipan. The Doctor got in a whaleboat and took a look at it. The battleships pulled out, they did not stay at Saipan very long. It is about 3 P.M. in the afternoon as I sit in the sun with just my pants on, getting some tan. Some of the officers are doing the same. I can see smoke coming from the northern tip of Saipan. You can see the Japs jumping off the high cliffs to their death. Our troops are trying to drive the Japs into the sea. The ships in the harbor are unloading supplies, etc., our destroyers are out about five miles patrolling back and forth, on the lookout for subs, just in case they try to sneak into the harbor, and do some damage. Some of the fellows are washing clothes. A big PBY flying boat is just taking off, they are very big, they have two motors. A big hospital ship painted white with a big red cross on each side is just leaving with a load of wounded. There is always a nice breeze, not like the South Pacific where you would pay ten dollars for a breath of fresh air. I got the 8 to midnight watch tonight. The Chaplain has a heat rash all over him, he can hardly walk, he looks like he lost some weight. We will leave Saipan again tonight, at 5:45 P.M.

for all night patrol. I guess I have covered all for now and will knock off.

Monday, July 10, 1944: Last night the Captain spoke, he said the whole island of Saipan fell to our troops yesterday afternoon. Commander Smithberg from our ship visited Saipan yesterday and this is what he had to say. The Japs had pillboxes eight ft. thick and we could hit them from now until next summer and not hurt them. The shells from our ship hit the gun opening on one of those eight ft. thick pillboxes and knocked the gun crew out. Something like that does not happen very often, that was one for the books. He said that it was a good thing for us that we did not land on the east coast because the Japs had between 35 and 45 pillboxes with 5 inch guns, and they were set up in such a way that they would have wiped us all out. We crossed the Japs up and landed on the other side of the island. Our ship did its bombarding on the east coast, boy were we lucky especially with all those big Jap guns trained at us. General Smith of the Marines said that with a hundred Marines he could hold off 5000 troops indefinitely, because the place was so strongly fortified. This gives you an idea what our troops were up against. The Japs were building more big pillboxes, and he said that if we waited four or five months more we might never be able to take Saipan. The Japs had all kinds of ammunition stored underground. General Smith had his headquarters in a house and three Japs were hiding under it without his knowledge. One of the Japs came out and threw a hand grenade in at the General, but it hit the roof and came back and killed the other two Japs. This must be Gen. Holland "Howling Mad" Smith, boy is he rugged. They captured a Jap doctor who spoke good English, he said that a naval bombardment is the worst thing a person can go through. It is so terrifying that only a person who has been through it really knows, and he was under all kinds of attacks. When the Jap General in command killed himself, the Japs were disorganized and did not know what to do. A lot of them left their guns when it was almost over, the Japs were jumping off the high cliffs committing suicide, rather than be captured, hundreds of them landed in the water.

Our destroyers tried to pick them up but they refused. Our ships then opened up on them, and they were dying like rats. There are still some snipers left in some of the caves. The Jap civilians were in a stockade and looked contented. Our troops live in small tents on Saipan, it is very dusty. They keep the troops busy un-loading supplies on the beach. A lot of Koreans were in another section by themselves. The Japs also had some three feet thick pillboxes, that was all Commander Smithberg had to say. Our troops landed June 15 and Saipan fell July 9, 1944. It was the toughest blow the Japs have received so far. This will be a great base for us. The harbor at Saipan is very good. The Japs on Tinian fired at Saipan, but our destroyers silenced them. Captain Hoffman said that he has not received any orders yet as to what we are going to do. A news reporter came aboard. Today it rained quite a bit this morning, but turned out to be a nice day. Left tonight for patrol.

Thursday, July 13, 1944: Not much has happened lately. We returned to Saipan this morning. The reporter who came aboard the other day landed with the troops on Saipan and had a rugged time, he has been over there all this time. A lot of people do not realize the dangers a reporter goes through to get his story during wartime, he is also another front line troop and should receive the glory due him. Tonight the reporter told us about some of the things he saw on Saipan. He said one of the caves on Saipan had a thousand tons of supplies in it. You could enter two ways and it is at least a hundred feet high. Hundreds of Japs were in there mostly civilians. They were told to come out and nothing would happen to them, they would be treated good, if they re-fused, we would drop phosphorus shells in and kill them. They all came out but a few Jap soldiers, who killed themselves. The women came out with very little clothes on, mostly from the hips down and the children had no clothes at all. Carlson of the famed Carlson's Marine Raiders was wounded while helping one of his wounded men. In one small section, thousands of dead Japs lay, along with dead and wounded Americans, after the Japs tried their last suicide charge. It was a bloody affair, many of the Japs killed themselves. Yesterday two Marines from Saipan came aboard, they took a shower and had their hair cut. They put their dirty sox back on after the shower, the only pair they had. They also found plenty of boxes of stuff to prevent V.D. disease. The Japs were not as careless as we thought they were concerning their troops. Yesterday I watched them put Jap planes on our small carriers, they were in very good shape, most of them were Zeroes. It was funny to look over at the carrier with us last night while we were patrolling, and know that it was loaded with Jap planes. Today the water was full of dead Jap bodies, you could see them floating by, men, women, and children. The north section was loaded with floating bodies. One of our destroyers picked up a signal man from Guam the other day. He was on there since 1939, he hid out in the caves and jungles, the natives helped him. His signals were seen from the beach and a boat was sent in to pick him up. They did not know if it was a trap at first. He will be able to give us a lot of information about Guam and the Japs. His name is George Tweed. He might have been signaling the other day when we were near Guam, but no one saw him. We went out on patrol again tonight as usual, and almost ran over a lot of Japs. One Jap was floating face up and he had a goatee, an arm also floated by. I never saw anything like it for bodies floating around. The water is full of them, the fish will eat good.

Friday, July 14, 1944: Same routine. Stay at Saipan during the day, patrol all night. The battleships left last night. The *Iowa* and *New Jersey* were there, they make quite a picture cutting through the water, they are so long and streamlined. Field day was held throughout the ship. After supper while we were out patrolling Saipan the fellows passed the time running from one side of the ship to the other, watching the Jap bodies float by. You could get a good look at them as they passed, because they were very close to the ship. Some were on their stomachs, others on their backs, they floated along like rubber balls. Some had army uniforms on, and others had no clothes on at all. They were bloated and their skin looked white. One looked like his back was all burnt. We counted 20 bodies just around our ship in no time at all and then stopped counting. If this was in the South Pacific those bodies would not be floating around very long, maybe the sharks are full. I got the midnight to 4 A.M. watch.

Saturday, July 15, 1944: Hit sack at 4 A.M., this morning all hands up at 4:45 A.M. It rained all the time we were on watch, we got soaked. We pulled into Saipan at 6:30 A.M. this morning, also got paid this morning. Worked at cleaning station, and got hair cut in the afternoon. The Press News said that the Japs lost 15,500 on Saipan, that's how many our troops had to bury, but they figure the Japs must have lost close to 18,000. How about all the ones in the water floating around, and the ones who went down with the ships we sunk? We lost 2500, 2000 missing and 13,000 wounded. Every campaign our casualties get higher. This campaign lasted about three weeks. We left again tonight on patrol. There is a lot of talk about the States.

Sunday, July 16, 1944: It was a warm sunny day although it rained a little during church services. Mass was in the morning, and we got wet. It was the first time I ever went to church services and saw dead bodies floating by, the Japs are still floating around, there must be thousands of Japs in the waters near Saipan. The ships just run over them. You can't miss them all, the water is full of dead Japs. Church services were held topside and as you looked over the side of the ship you could see the Jap bodies in the water. The intelligence officers cannot find the big officials on Saipan, such as the Mayor, landowners, teachers, etc. They think they were on the transport ships that tried to sneak out in the dark, before our troops landed. We had to sink them. It is nothing to see men, women, and children floating in the water. One of our destroyers sank a Jap sub, not too far from Saipan. A lot of valuable things floated to the top, such as the log. I hit the sack at 8 P.M., but had to go below at 2 A.M. because it rained. I sweated it out until 4:45 A.M.

Monday, July 17, 1944: We got some mail today, first mail in a long time. It must be our first mail in over two months. Got a letter from Mary. They presented John with the Purple Heart and he had to give a little speech. Pictures were taken with him receiving the medal from an officer. Someone said a carrier came in with a hundred bags of mail for us. Tomorrow we start our 20th month out here in the Pacific. Very few warships have spent as many consecutive months in combat as we have. Newsweek magazine had a picture of Admiral Merrill in it. They also had an article about him, it was very good.

Tuesday, July 18, 1944: This afternoon some Marines of the 2nd division came aboard to take a shower, eat, get hair cut, etc. They brought some Jap swords with them and the fellows bought them up pretty fast. One of the Marines had a hari-kari knife with a gold plated handle. We were talking to one of the Marines, and he was in nearly all the campaigns in the Pacific. He has been away from the States 30 months. This is what he had to say. At Tarawa in the Gilbert campaign, one of the Marines got a hari-kari knife with diamonds on the handle, it was worth $1500. A Marine came across a dead Jap with $2000 in American money on him. The Jap got it from a dead Marine who won it in a card game. A Jap on Saipan who could speak English told the Marines that everyone was told that in order for an American to join the Marines he had to kill his father and mother first. By telling them this, they figured the Jap troops would not surrender, but die fighting. That's why our troops had such a tough job defeating the Japs. Surrender was out of the picture. The Japs had a lot of those big giant imperial Marines on Saipan, and they were very hard to kill. They had a great habit of making believe they were dead and when you turned your back on them they would attack you, they would also sneak back to their own lines at night. The Marine I was talking to was bent over a big Jap going through the Jap's pockets, he thought the Jap was dead, but noticed his stomach move a little. He reached for his gun and shot the Jap in the head, he was still moving around, so he finished the Jap off by shooting him in the heart. One Marine liked to pull the gold teeth from dead Japs, he had 17 of them. The last one he got on Saipan, the Jap was only wounded, while he was pulling the gold tooth the Jap was still moving his hands. One night Jap tanks attacked the Marines and if it was not for us knocking the Jap tanks out, they do not know what would have happened. He said the towns were a mess from the Navy bombardment. He also said the Japs thought we were going to land on Guam, but we landed on Saipan instead. The Japs had sent a lot of special troops from China to Guam. Now they can use them when we invade Guam. Yesterday the 13th day in a row that our planes and ships hit Guam. We will be up there for invasion. Five hundred ships were used in the Saipan Invasion.

Thursday, July 20, 1944: Today while in Saipan harbor we were attacked by thousands of big flies, they came from Saipan. I guess the Japs use them for something, they came aboard for some good chow. I never saw so many flies in my life. It got so bad that they announced over the loudspeaker for all hands to turn to killing flies. Everyone laughed when they heard that announcement. You will never hear that kind of an announcement again, and the Pacific is the place you come across the strangest things. Last night, just before we left Saipan Harbor for patrol duty, some Marines from the 2nd Marine Division came aboard, they went up to the Bridge where Captain Hoffman was and presented him with Gold Shoulder Braids. I was near the quarterdeck when they came aboard with them and they were really something. They belonged to the Admiral who planned the attack on Pearl Harbor. He was killed on Saipan. The Marines wanted to show their appreciation for the way our ship treated them. Tomorrow morning at 8:30 A.M. we invade Guam, we will be in on it. Guam has been hit by ships and planes for fifteen days in a row. We will return to Saipan Saturday.

Friday, July 21, 1944: At 8:30 A.M. this morning our troops landed on Guam, it was the 3rd Marine Division. We were very close to shore and bombarded before the troops landed and after they landed. Guam is supposed to be 34 miles long and 5 to 9 miles wide. The place was a mass of smoke. Our planes were strafing and bombing. The Japs took an awful pasting. I saw one of our planes shot down by Jap machine gun fire. Our ship fired a lot of ammunition at the Japs, and they fired back at us, but they did not hit us. It was a very busy day, things were really humming. It was a hot sunny day with a good breeze. They only wanted our services for the day, so at 5 P.M. we left. We were at our battle stations from 7:45 A.M. until 5 P.M. in the evening. The Japs took Guam Dec. 10, 1941.

Saturday, July 22, 1944: We entered Saipan at 6:30 A.M. this morning and fueled. In the afternoon we got ammunition. We get a lot of radio programs from Tokyo, Japan, they are in English. They give the news, play American music and then they interview American prisoners. One day I heard them interview a friend of mine. I played hockey against him before he joined the Army. His name was Laforet. The prisoners tell how well they are treated and a lot of other lies. We received some news about Guam today. The landings were made with light casualties. It was hit for 17 straight days by planes and ships. The Press News also said Admiral King visited Saipan. Some of the German officers are trying to get rid of Hitler. There is a lot of unrest in Germany, and the Russians are in Poland. The National League beat the American League 12 to 7 in the All Star Game. I got the midnight to 4 A.M. watch.

Sunday, July 23, 1944: Got off watch at 4 A.M. All hands up at 4:45 and at 6 A.M. this morning we started bombarding Tinian, we did not stop until 6:30 P.M. tonight. They expect to invade it tomorrow. We hit Tinian with battleships, cruisers, destroyers and planes, the island had a ring of warships around it and they pounded it all day. I don't know how the Japs can take it. They are really gluttons for punishment. Our planes were swarming over them all day like flies, strafing and bombing. Our troops on Saipan are also shelling them, they are about five miles away. They have about 200 guns. It was quite a show, there were plenty of fires and explosions. Some of our planes also fired rockets. Late in the afternoon we had a very close call. One of our battleships was on the other side of Tinian bombarding. They over shot their target and the big 16 inch shells that weigh about two tons started to fall close to us. It's a good thing that we were moving at the time, because it went over our head, you could hear it as it went through the air. It sounded just like a big wind storm.

We moved to another spot in a hurry and the next one landed just where we had left, it was quick thinking on Captain Hoffman's part. As I looked out over the water not too far away, there was a big explosion in the water, chunks of steel flew in all directions. If the guns on the battleship had been trained around a little more, we would have got it about midship, if we got it there, the Navy might have been minus a light cruiser. It is an awful feeling to have big shells like that coming at you and you do not know where they are going to land. If a plane is overhead dropping them you can at least see them but gunfire is too fast to see, you just hope you don't get hit, you are helpless to do anything. I can just imagine how the Japs on Tinian feel. Today some Jap troops tried to load up a truck, but we took care of them. We also knocked out ammunition dumps, buildings and gun emplacements. You never get tired of watching our planes strafing and bombing, it is something to see. Our planes climb almost as fast as they dive. The sun was hot but there was a good breeze. The sky was clear all day. After being at battle stations from midnight until 6:30 P.M. this evening, I was tired, so I hit the steel deck at 7:30 P.M. I had to get up a couple of times because it sprinkled rain. I went down to the compartment to finish my sleep, but I had to come up because it was too hot. Our compartment is about the hottest compartment. The sun hits the top and side all day. It stopped raining when I came up so I lay down again.

Monday, July 24, 1944: The rain moved me again at 3:15 A.M. this morning. I then went on watch. Yesterday was my birthday. My last birthday I spent down in the South Pacific in the Solomons. The way the Captain spoke the other night, we will be on our way to the good old U.S.A. soon. This morning at 5:30 A.M. we started bombarding Tinian again and at 7:30 A.M. the 2nd Marines landed on Tinian. We did not lose too many troops on the landing. The Japs are supposed to have 10,000 troops there, but they usually have much more. The Japs are very good at camouflaging. You can be looking at their big guns and you don't know it. The Japs opened up with their big 6 & 8 inch guns and hit one battleship sixteen times, it was the *Colorado,* about twenty-five were killed and seventy wounded. They also hit the destroyer *Scott* and killed fifteen plus its Captain, twenty-five were wounded. One of the cruisers opened up on the Jap guns and knocked them out. Wave after wave of planes hit the Japs as the warships poured on the shells, what a sight. There are a lot of caves for the Japs to hide in. One of our planes was shot down and the pilot parachuted into the Japs. I felt sorry for that fellow because when the Japs got him they would torture him before killing him. We stopped firing at 6:30 P.M. this evening. Some of the other ships will stay here all night and fire star shells at the Japs so they cannot reorganize or sneak into our lines. On the 8 to midnight watch tonight we saw quite a show. We watched the big guns on Saipan as they fired at the Japs on Tinian. The guns on Tinian were also firing, you can also see the red streaks of the tracers. With the warships also throwing star shells it made the picture complete. It looked like the 4th of July. The Japs will not get any sleep tonight. I would not want to be in their shoes for all the money in the world, and still they will not surrender.

Tuesday, July 25, 1944: We started our bombardment earlier this morning. Last night they killed 500 Japs who tried to sneak through our lines. Those star shells really helped. Today is another hot sunny day. Our big artillery guns on Tinian fired plenty of shells on the Japs. We fired all day and when a big Jap ammunition dump went up it was quite a sight, shells were exploding in all directions, it was a terrific explosion. We are also going to fire star shells all night until daylight tomorrow morning. We knocked out many targets today as usual. The Press News said over 20,000 Japs were buried on Saipan, plus the thousands more who were unaccounted for, 1700 were captured plus 15,000 civilians captured. We had 3000 killed, hundreds missing and over 15,000 wounded. It was the bloodiest campaign against the Japs so far, and it lasted only three weeks. Real estate is very expensive out here, Saipan is only 12 miles long and 5 miles wide with plenty of high cliffs. After the loss of Saipan Tojo, the Premier, was relieved of his job and another Army General took over command, but Tojo is still the big boss, there were other big changes. In Germany some officers tried to kill Hitler. Things look bad for the Germans and the Japs. In baseball, both St. Louis clubs are in first place. In Sweden, Hage and Anderson, two Swedes, ran the mile in 4:01 and 6/10 record, it is a new world record for the mile.

Wednesday, July 26, 1944: We stopped firing at 5:30 A.M. this morning after being up all night firing star shells at the Japs. We left and pulled alongside an ammuition ship, we took off our empty powder cases, and got ammunition. We have been firing almost every day since June 14 and we still have more to do, that is almost a month and a half. For the past 19 months we have spent the biggest part of our time at our battle stations.

Thursday, July 27, 1944: We held field day, everything had to be cleaned and shining. I spent the afternoon on a working party carrying 150-lb. bags of white flour. No news now.

Friday, July 28, 1944: I got up at 3:15 A.M. this morning for 4 to 8 watch. We started firing on Tinian at 5:30 A.M. One day the *Birmingham* fires and then the *Cleveland* and then it is our turn. This morning our troops are feeling out the Japs and at 1 P.M. this afternoon they are going to start a drive against them. We open up just before the drive starts, our planes will also hit the Japs.

We were close to shore and could see our troops advancing behind tanks and then all of a sudden, they would fall flat on their stomachs. The fellows on the bridge said they could see our troops looking for souvenirs. You could see some of our troops on a big building watching our ship rapid fire on the Japs. Their tanks were left near by under some trees as they watched our ships fire away. You could see the land mines explode as our shells hit them. Thousands of Japs have been killed on Tinian since the invasion started on July 24. They said a lot of Japs surrendered with the tickets our planes have been dropping on them. We guarantee them food, and will treat them all right, I guess they like our chow, and think it's a good idea to live instead of dying. When the drive started we laid down an awful barrage, we fired all our guns, 5 & 6 and machine guns. By nightfall our troops advanced a good distance. Just before dark our planes attacked the town of Tinian. They came down strafing and dropping bombs. One pilot hit an ammunition dump and what an explosion, another plane fired into a cave loaded with ammunition and the shells kept exploding for some time. Our planes left the town in a mass of flames and smoke, they say a lot of Japs were hiding in the town and that was the way to get at them. This was not the first time the town was hit. It was quite a show while it lasted. Today was a warm sunny day, we must have about ⅔ of Tinian by now. When it gets dark we will fire star shells all night until daylight tomorrow morning. Our troops like to see the star shells because it lights up the place and if the Japs try to attack, they can see them and knock them off. This is better than the jungle fighting in the Solomons, when the Japs would sneak in on our troops in the dark and we would end up killing some of our own men. The Japs like to sneak into our lines at night, but the star shells make it tough for them to do this.

Saturday, July 29, 1944: We stopped firing at 5:30 A.M. this morning after being up all night firing star shells, also bombarding the Japs. We left battle stations at 7:30 A.M. this morning. The *Birmingham* relieved us at 8 A.M. I got the 8 to 12 noon watch, so that means I will not get any shut-eye until this afternoon.

We aired our bedding this morning. We put our mattress bedding on the life lines and aired them out for a few hours. We also got 8 bags of mail. It only took six days for air mail to get here. We are about 5500 miles from the West Coast of U.S.A. We never got mail this quick before. I did not get any mail this afternoon. I lay on the communication deck from 12:30 to 3:30 P.M. It started to rain about 5 P.M. I heard Radio Tokyo. The Jap announcer said that Japan was fighting for a better world and that the loss of Saipan was the hardest blow Japan has received, but the people would fight all the harder and would not be satisfied until victory was theirs. The Jap Government really feeds its people with a lot of lies. They tell them that it's an honor to die for the Emperor and that he is God. They finished the program with a Bing Crosby record, it was "Hawaii." I got off watch at midnight, it rained most of the time I was on watch. About 6 P.M. this evening the ship had to move because a big whirlpool came up and it might have sucked the ship under.

Sunday, July 30, 1944: Today will be our thirty-first bombardment against the Japs in the past 19 months, that must put us on the top. We will fire all day at Tinian. The *Cleveland* left for Guam last night. We got very close to Tinian this morning and opened up with our 40 mm. machine guns. A lot of Japs were in a big pocket between two big hills and we really gave them a bad time, our 5 inch shells also hit them. The Japs were cut to ribbons, what a slaughter. We also fired our 40 mm. machine guns into the caves, where the Japs were holding out. Our 40 mm. mount fired more rounds than any of the others. The orders for us to use machine guns on the caves came from our troops on the shore, there's a lot of caves on Tinian. We had Jello for chow at noon, this was the first time we had it in about a year. I asked for some more after chow and got it. It really hit the spot. It was the only good thing about the chow. We had spaghetti and ground meat also. It is another clear sunny day, it is also very hot on the side of the ship where there is not a breeze. Our troops are almost on the southern part of Tinian. We invaded on the northern end, it should be ours in a couple of days. This morning while we were firing the 40 mm. at the Japs, they also were firing back at us with their machine guns, our 6 inch guns did not waste any time firing back at the Japs. The Japs had a lot of dead to bury when we finished with them. You could see the Japs run for the caves as we fired our 40 mm. at them. Our 5 & 6 inch guns opened up on the caves and the Japs ran in all directions. It looked like follow the leader as the Japs were running in all directions. The Japs were really confused and did not know where to run, after a while, our machine guns knocked a lot of them off when they started to run. We will fire star shells tonight again and stay at our battle stations, no sleep as usual.

Monday, July 31, 1944: We were up all night firing star shells and also bombarding Japs. We also bombarded Tinian today.

We had to laugh at some of the reports from our lookouts as we were bombarding Tinian. The lookouts on our ship have to report everything they see, and here are some of the things they reported. A big cow is crossing the road, some Marines are chasing a Jap soldier, and all the Jap has on is his undershorts. You can see plenty of tanks moving around.

A big drive was started against the Japs this morning and this might be the end for the Japs on Tinian. Before our troops started their drive our battleships, cruisers and destroyers bombarded for about an hour. I thought they were trying to sink the island, it was a terrific bombardment. I do not know how anything could stand up under it. We were close to shore and just poured it on. Our planes also gave it a terrific going over. After that our troops advanced and nearly all the ships left that area. Our troops will now take over, I don't think we will do anymore bombarding. This was a farewell bombardment. As we left Tinian the Captain spoke and said he wished our troops the best of luck. After today it should be all over for the Japs on Tinian. We dropped anchor in Saipan harbor, along with the rest of the ships. We got a lot of mail. I got a letter from my sister Mary and she said that I was near Saipan, she hit it right on the nose. We left on patrol again tonight as usual. I tried to sleep topside, but it rained.

Tuesday, August 1, 1944: I got up at 3:15 A.M. this morning to go on watch, got 4 to 8 A.M. We got very little sleep in the past two months, we have been on the go all the time. I wrote a letter to Mary and told her that I would walk in on her one of these summer days. Everyone is talking about the States. The Press News said the Japs lost 50,000 men in the Marianas Campaign, this includes land, sea and in the air, so far. The Greatest Armada of tanks ever used in the Pacific war were used against the Japs on Tinian. We got some rain today. We started bombarding June 14, 1944, and finished yesterday July 31, 1944. We bombarded Saipan, Tinian and Guam during that time, this went on day and night almost all of that time during those 48 days, that must be some kind of a record. Our ship fired thousands of rounds of ammunition during that time, and most of our time was spent at our battle stations. We knocked off our share of Japs and did plenty of damage. The Good Lord watched over us again as usual. He likes someone on our ship, very special. We are thankful for His Blessings. When we come out here again after a stay in the States, we should hit Borneo, Java, Bali, Singapore, Philippines, China and of course Japan. If Japan gets hit hard, I would not be surprised to see Japan surrender. Right now it's U.S.A. here we come.

U.S.A.

August 1944–October 1944

Wednesday, August 2, 1944: All hands up at 4:45 A.M. as usual. Today was a great day, Tinian fell. Our troops landed July 24 and today it is Aug. 2. At 5 P.M. tonight we left Saipan for the good old U.S.A. Captain Hoffman spoke at 6:30 P.M. and said that we would go to the Marshalls, stay there for a few days and then to Pearl Harbor. Everyone was around the loudspeakers, and when they heard the goods news, they had a big grin on their faces. It was the best news we heard in the 20 months we have been out here. I got the 8 to midnight watch.*

Thursday, August 3, 1944: The past few days at Saipan were cloudy, but today out at sea it is a warm sunny day. The fellows are washing their blues and whites, and also buying new hats, shoes etc. They are also getting plenty of tan. Everyone is making plans for what they will do when they hit the States. It will be quite a treat to get back to civilization again. We have seen very little of it in almost two years. Our time out here consisted of jungle, ocean and Japs. We saw women on a few occasions during our stay out here and spoke to them on two occasions, the first time we visited Australia for three days and that was the first time, and again for about an 8 day stay on our second visit to Australia.

We left the States Dec. 1942 and here it is Aug. 3, 1944 already. The time went fast, because we were always on the move. It

* I would like to mention the names of every ship that took part in the Saipan, Guam, and Tinian campaigns but that is impossible so I will just mention a few. Carriers *Lexington, Wasp, Essex, Princeton, Enterprise, Cabot, Monterey, Bunker Hill.* Battleships *Tennessee, Idaho, New Mexico, Washington, South Dakota, Alabama.* Cruisers *Honolulu, Indianapolis, Houston, San Diego* and *Wichita.* Destroyers *Dyson, Thatcher, Ausburne, Patterson, Twining,* and *Monssen.* They are part of the 5th Fleet.

will be good to get back to the States again. It will be like coming back to another world. This is what everyone has been looking forward to. It is the happiest time in a person's life, when he returns to the U.S.A. The Greatest Country in the World, God's Country. It is worth fighting for. When you leave it, then you really appreciate it. If you want something you just go to the store and get it, they have it, no matter what you want. That's really something, we never give it a thought, we just take it for granted. After sleeping on a steel deck it will be quite a treat to sleep in a soft bed, inside with a roof over your head instead of the sky. You will not have to look for a dry spot to sleep on when it rains, and you can sleep as late as you want. You will not go to bed hungry. You will eat plenty of good fresh food, and your bread will not be full of bugs. You will not have to take orders for a while, and you will walk on good solid ground for a change. There is something I always wanted while I was down here and when I get home I will get it, and that is a big blueberry pie covered with all flavors of ice cream. The time we spent out here did us more good than harm, in the long run. Tonight I hit the steel at 7 P.M., got up at 11:15 P.M. for midnight to 4 A.M. watch.

Friday, August 4, 1944: Got off watch at 4 A.M. and all hands got up at 4:12 A.M. Only got ten minutes' sleep, it was not worth my while. We had breakfast at 6:45 A.M. It got bright very early. On our way to the Marshalls we passed Jap-held islands and had to be on the alert, the Japs like to sneak in on you at sunrise and sunset. We did not do much today, the fellows are still washing their clothes and buying clothes at small stores. No one knows how long we will be in the States. I sat in the sun and got some tan. It got dark about 7 P.M. tonight. I slept topside, but my sleep was spoiled twice because of rain. I had to stand under cover until it stopped and then back to sleep again. I will have to get up at 3:15 A.M. for the 4 to 8 A.M. watch tomorrow morning.

Saturday, August 5, 1944: Got wet on watch at 4 A.M. to 8 A.M. this morning. We had no General Quarters this morning. We did not have to get up until 6 A.M. this morning. This is the first time in over two months that the men slept this late. It was clear and sunny today. I washed my white uniform today, also bought new shoes, hats, shirts, etc. We pulled into the Marshalls tonight at 4 P.M. It took just three days to travel about 1300 miles. We got fuel. There are at least 200 ships here, I counted at least 50 oil tankers. The ships have movies topside now. We had our first movie in over two months, "Ali Baba and the Forty Thieves." It is supposed to be a new movie. A lot of the men are making ash trays out of the 40 mm. shells. I got all night in. I can sleep until 6 A.M. tomorrow morning, what a break, the hatches will be left open so the air can get into the ship. We must be getting into safe territory and they do not have to worry about the Japs attacking us. This is something new. About 4 men had their tonsils taken out the other day on the ship. There was nothing to it, just like going to the dentist. They do not put them to sleep, just a needle in both sides of your jaw and arm, also 6 pills. They freeze the tonsils and they are out before you know it.

Monday, August 7, 1944: We slept topside. I got up at 5 A.M. and had working shirt washed and dry before breakfast, chow was at 6:45 A.M. This morning we took nearly all the 5 inch ammunition off. Yesterday the cruiser *Denver* pulled alongside of us. They took a lot of ammunition and supplies from us. We are still at the Marshalls. There are over 200 ships here. They are mostly cargo and tankers. I counted 50 tankers all full, just around here. There are many other types of ships away down, I cannot see them very well. Eniwetok is the name of the place where we are anchored. The Marshall group of islands is about 50 miles long. There is a radio station here and it goes like this, "station WXY expedition station, En-i-we-tok (and we took) the road to Tokyo."

Tuesday, August 8, 1944: I put my name on the new clothes I bought. It is a warm, sunny day, I washed out my dress blues today. I can sleep until 6 A.M. tomorrow morning if we do not leave here tonight.

Wednesday, August 16, 1944: I have not done any writing for some time but I will try to cover what has happened in the past 8 days. On Wed. Aug. 9, 1944 at 2:30 P.M. in the afternoon we left our base in the Marshalls. As we passed the Marshalls you could see the beach, only a few stubs of trees were left from the invasion some months ago. It is very flat, all sand. We have quite a few troops on it. On our way to Pearl Harbor we changed the clocks. We went back a day, we got back the day we lost when we came out here. It took us 7 days to get to Pearl Harbor, we took our time getting there. It was Tuesday Aug. 15, 1944, 10:30 A.M. when we got there. It was a beautiful, warm, sunny day, not too hot, and there was a good breeze. The climate here is always nice. All hands were at quarters topside in whites. The old "Monty" looked good all dressed up for a change. Pearl Harbor is a big Navy Base and there are quite a lot of ships here. My section did not get liberty because the ship pulled in Tuesday morning and we left Wed. morning at 11 A.M.

We were disappointed because we did not have a chance to see Honolulu. I wanted to visit Ford Island to see my brother Joe, it is not too far away. Wed. morning at quarters I got permission to go to the dock and call Joe up. It took about a half hour to get him and he was surprised to hear my voice. He said that he would leave at once for the ship. I told him to hurry because the ship was leaving this morning. He came aboard at 10:30 A.M. all dressed up in his Chief's uniform and he did not know me until I put out my hand to greet him. This was on the quarterdeck and the 1st time we met in 15 years. Joe has been out here in the Pacific since the '30s. Our reunion only lasted about ten minutes because all guests had to leave the ship at 10:40 A.M. He said that he expected to go back to the States in a few months. He has been out here almost five years. We did our talking on the boat deck and I guess I did most of the talking. When I called Joe up the Hawaiian girl at the information desk had to call up quite a few places before she found Joe. She was very nice about it. They finally found him in the Censors Office, censoring mail. The men who had liberty yesterday brought back a lot of gifts to take home with them. They said the girls were very friendly and also good-looking. The Hawaiians call the States the Mainland and consider Hawaii one of the States. Wednesday morning before we left we brought aboard over 100 wounded soldiers, marines and sailors. They were in the Saipan, Guam and Tinian campaigns. Some were able to walk, but a lot of them were taken out of ambulances on the dock and carried aboard on stretchers. Some had legs off, some were paralyzed etc. and in bad shape. Not very long ago they were strong and healthy and full of life, now they were quiet and you could tell that they were thinking. Things happen very fast out here, you're O.K. one minute and the next minute it might be curtains for you. One of the wounded Marines who came aboard carried a Jap officer's sword. One of our passengers was Mr. Norman Soong, a war correspondent who has been in about every theater of war. He was also on the first American warship sunk by the Japanese, the gunboat *Panay*, in 1937.

We left Pearl Harbor, Aug. 16th Wed. at 11 A.M. 1944. We had the homeward bound pennant waving from midship to the stern. It was red, white and blue with stars on it for each officer. We also had balloons flying from it. All hands were at quarters in whites topside as we passed the other ships in the Harbor. The Capt. spoke to all hands at 6 P.M., he said it looks like all we can get in the States is 6 weeks. We do not know how long a leave we will get. It is a lot cooler, and from now on we can sleep below in our sacks. Last night was the first time I slept below in a very long time. We got all our old mail at Pearl Harbor, 171 bags, and I got the glasses Mary sent about six months ago.

I will now tell what happened while we were in the Good Old U.S.A. August 22, 1944, we docked at Mare Island which is in Vallejo, Calif. Our section had first leave. We left Vallejo, Calif., on a warm, sunny morning by bus for the Army air base at Sacramento, Calif., about 70 miles away. We got there in the afternoon and had to wait about 4 hours before our plane took off. If you had been overseas 1 year or more, you can take the Army bombers, they carry freight and passengers and it will not cost you a cent. The only drawback is that you don't know how long it will take you to get home, because sometimes you have to get off to make room for the big crates of cargo. You are allowed to take so much with you and no more. They weigh your things before you get on the plane. They are 2 engine transports and cargo planes. When you get tired of sitting in the plane you go up on the crates and fall asleep. The crates are in the center of the plane, you sit on the sides. Your ears feel funny and every now and then you hit air pockets when the plane drops. On long trips it gets very tiresome and about every 3 hrs. the plane would land and the freight would go off or some would come on. They also had to fuel the plane. It is something like a C-47, with two motors.

It is a good size, it carries about 30 passengers plus plenty of freight which was secured to the floor in the center of the plane. We sat shoulder to shoulder facing the crates of cargo, we sat on both sides of the plane facing each other also. Every place we stopped there was a Red Cross stand for the men to get free food and drinks. They come in very handy because everyone was hungry and the planes only stay about ½ hour. We got as far as Omaha, Nebraska, the next morning, Aug. 24th. We were over halfway home, to Mass. Tony Freitas and myself had to get off and make room for more freight, so we did not wait for another plane because we might have to wait a long time.

We went to the station but our train did not leave until the afternoon so we took a walk around Omaha, to see the sights. This is a very large city and a nice place but we did not see any servicemen. Just the ones waiting for trains. Everyone here must be overseas. We had a big meal and took the train that left in the afternoon. That same evening we changed trains at Chicago and the next day, Friday, Aug. 25th, at 9 o'clock in the evening we finally pulled into the South Station, Boston, Mass. We walked up Washington St. and I was impressed to see it so quiet, that was something new for Boston. Everyone must be overseas. We tried to buy some tailor-made blues, but the stores were closed so we took a taxi to the Y.M.C.A. We took a shower and hit the sack. I was very careful that nothing happened to my Diary.

When I got off the train in Boston I felt like I never felt before, it was great. We got up the next morning at 10 A.M. and took a taxi to a clothing store and had a suit of tailor-made blues made. It only took about ½ hr. to get them. A couple of shoeshine boys were outside and they gave our shoes a good polishing. It was a

nice, warm morning as we headed for the Boston Common. I left
Tony at the Common, because he had to get a bus for Fall River,
I went below and got the subway for Newton Corner and then
got on the bus for Waltham and home. I had 3 bags with me, my
clothing and some Jap souvenirs. I got off the bus at the corner
of my street, the place was deserted. I walked down the street and
up the front steps, the place was deserted. It was a feeling you
cannot explain. It was not only the idea of being away for almost
2 years so much but all the close calls we had and being able to
come through them all without any harm. It was about 1 P.M.
Saturday afternoon, Aug. 26, as I walked up the hall stairs and as
I got close to the kitchen I could hear the radio playing. As I
stepped into the kitchen my brother John saw me and you could
have knocked him over with a feather, boy was he surprised to see
me. No one knew I was in the States. I wanted to surprise them,
they thought I was still in the Pacific. John put on his uniform
and we went to Grant's store where my sister works. This was going to be a surprise for Mary. We locked the kitchen door and
left for the store. I was so overjoyed I felt like running. We
walked to the rear of the store where Mary worked and when she
saw me she was going to cry, she was so overjoyed. The Boss
gave Mary permission to take the day off and we headed for home.

On the way home I had to drop in and see one of my close
friends, Mrs. Sweeney. She was surprised to see me, she gave me
a big hug and kiss. She gave us some homemade pie and cake, it
really hit the spot. It was my first home cooked meal in almost 2
years. Mary lives with the Sweeneys and goes home on weekends,
because John usually has liberty. Mrs. Sweeney's son is also in the
Navy. He is a doctor. We left the Sweeneys' and headed for
home. That evening I had a meal that really hit the spot, you cannot beat home cooked meals. We expected a 30 day leave but had
to settle for 23 days. That gave me 14 days at home, because I
had to allow myself enough time to travel. The 14 days went very
fast and before I knew it I was on my way back to the ship in
Calif. I went everywhere and had a good time while I was home.
The city was dead, nearly everyone was in the service. When you
walked down the street there was no one to talk to, just women,

old men, and 4F's. You might just as well be in the service with
the rest of the fellows. We had almost 15 million in all branches
of the military and when you came home you could see that it
looked like everyone was in the service. The old gang was gone.
But it felt good to walk around the city.

Our troops were making such progress in Europe that they said
the war (over there) would be over in a couple of months. Well,
Sunday afternoon Sept. 10th I started on my way back to the ship.
It was about the 10th of Nov. 1942 that I left home for my 1st
stay in the Pacific, and here I was again doing the same thing all
over again almost 2 years later. I met Tony Freitas at the South
Station, and said goodbye to Mary, John, and Alice Sweeney.

The next time I come home the war should be over. I kissed
Mary goodbye and shook hands with John and Alice as I stepped
into the train. The train was crowded as usual, and it took us
some time before we found a seat. Everyone was in uniform. We
got off the train at New York at 6 P.M. and headed for the Newark
Airport. They told us that we could get a cargo plane about 2:30
A.M. Monday morning, for San Francisco, Calif. We told the man
in charge that we were going to take a look at the city and that we
would be back about 2 A.M. We walked around Newark and had
something to eat. We also brought back some food to the plane
for our trip. When we got back to the airport we took our dress
blues off and put on our dungarees, because your clothes get
wrinkled and dusty sleeping on the wooden crates. The waiting
room was very quiet, only the man at the desk was there. We lay
down on the bench and told the fellow at the desk to wake us up
when our plane was ready to take off. About 3:45 A.M. Monday
morning we got in the plane and took off for San Francisco, Calif.

We stopped about every 3 or 4 hours and it was the same routine, cargo coming and going off, new men coming on, some going
off. Some of the places we stopped were Arizona, Texas, Oklahoma.

We stopped at Tucson, Arizona, early in the morning and took
a stroll around the building. It looks like a good size house or
hotel. We were hungry but could not get anything to eat, everyone was asleep. The air was great here and the only sound you

could hear outside was the sound of insects. It was peaceful and quiet. We stopped in Texas early Tuesday morning about 2 A.M. and Tony left to see his brother who was at one of the Army camps.

He was about 40 miles from here. We made good plane connections so Tony could afford some time to see his brother. He went out on the highway and started to thumb a ride. A lady in the Red Cross trailer was the one who gave him the information about his brother. I waited here in Texas for the plane to get fuel. We could hear a radio playing Western songs. We had to wait 4 hours in Oklahoma City for a plane. This was a big Army Air Corps base. They had a few Big B–29 Super Flying Fortresses here, the kind that hit Tokyo. They are the largest in the world. We went inside and looked them over. They were very big, it was some plane. We also went to the mess hall and had something to eat. We reached Frisco about noon Tuesday. We stopped quite a few times and were held over for quite a while but still it only took us about 1 day and 9 hours. That was much better than a 4 or 5 day trip by train. I had a few days left for my leave so I took in Frisco and the other cities close by. My leave expired Sept. 15th/1944. The first few weeks we lived in barracks while the Navy yard crew worked on the ship and the chow was good. We also had 3 nights a week off. The last couple of weeks before we left the States we lived on the ship and things changed. We had to stand watches again, and we had one working party after another, as we took on hundreds of tons of supplies, such as food etc. We also unloaded about 15 freight cars of ammunition. The chow wasn't very good. It was a good thing that you could buy food in the Navy yard, the fellows were always eating. They might as well eat plenty now because once we leave the States it will stop.

We only got about one week end off while we were in the States. We usually handled ammunition on Sundays and had the evening off. If your section rated it. When a ship comes back to the States you get nothing but working parties. They want the ship ready for sea as soon as possible.

THE PHILIPPINES

MINDORO, LUZON, PALAWAN

October 1944–June 1945

Wednesday, October 25, 1944: We left Mare Island, Calif. at 9:30 A.M. this morning, for the Pacific war. We pulled in here Aug. 22, 1944, after being out there 20 months. The two months we spent in the States really flew, it seems like we just returned and here we are on our way back again to take on the Japs again. This will be our last look at the U.S.A. until the war is over. Many of the men's wives and girl friends were at the pier to kiss them goodbye. We passed Alcatraz prison and the Golden Gate before we got out to sea. Our first stop will be Pearl Harbor.

Tuesday, October 31, 1944: This afternoon at 4:30 P.M. we pulled into Pearl Harbor, it took us 6 days to get here from Mare Island, Calif. I will try to cover what happened on the way here from the States. The weather was very cold and the sea was very rough until we were about one day from Pearl Harbor. Quite a few men got seasick, I did not. We ate our meals on the deck because the sea was too rough to set the benches and tables; they would have crashed into the bulkheads. We had to wear plenty of clothing on watch to keep warm. The other ships with us would almost go out of sight in the heavy big seas because the waters were so rough. The light cruiser *Astoria* and the heavy cruiser *Baltimore* also had left with us along with the other warships.

The *Baltimore* was the ship that carried President Roosevelt to the Aleutians and Pearl Harbor. We fired all guns on the way to Pearl Harbor. Also, the same day we pulled into Pearl Harbor, B–26 Bombers towed sleeves for us to shoot at. Our ship knocked down 12 sleeves without a strain. Our shooting was very good even if I do say so. When we pulled into Pearl Harbor we tied up to a buoy. The weather was warm and it felt good to go around in your shirtsleeves. Our mail went off the ship and movies were held topside the first night we got there.

Tuesday, November 7, 1944: This is what happened during our stay at Pearl Harbor. I got a special pass to visit my brother Joe on Ford Island. He censors mail 6 days a week. He has 1 day off, and no watches to stand. His hours are 8 A.M. to 4 P.M. He also showed me where he was on Dec. 7, 1941, when the Japs attacked Pearl Harbor. He came very close to being hit by Jap machine guns and bombs. You could still see the spot where the Japs hit. He also showed me around Honolulu and we took in a pro football game, we had a nice time. The climate here is very good, you can't beat it. Joe will have 9 years in the Navy, March 1945. He is going to put in 20 years and then retire, he will be 42 then. The people here are very small, the girls are good-looking. The war news for the last week of October said that our Navy knocked the Jap Navy out and our troops landed in the Central Philippines on Leyte. The Jap fleet lost many warships, all kinds. They called it the greatest sea battle in history, the Japs lost 64 warships. We will be out there soon. Today is election day, I think Roosevelt will get elected again. Everyone here thinks he will get in by a big margin. We left Pearl Harbor this morning at 8 A.M. for a couple of days of gunnery.

Wednesday, November 8, 1944: Yesterday we fired all day at targets on the beach and sleeves towed by planes, we also fired all night until 10 P.M. We were at General Quarters all day and night. Capt. Hoffman said whenever a ship gets new guns they have to be tested to see that they pass all the tests. Our 5 and 6 inch guns proved to be very good. We fired at targets on the beach that we could not see, spotters on the beach directed our fire. We also opened up on the beach with our machine guns. The Capt. said we might leave here for good in a couple of days. The Press News this morning said that Pres. Roosevelt is ahead by 2 million votes. The radio said the Japs subs sank 2 cargo ships between the States and Hawaii, they were 2 days behind us without escorts. Someone said they were supposed to meet us. Jap subs could have hit us easy at night because we did not have any escort. From now on though all ships will have destroyers or destroyer escorts with them. It was a little cloudy and we got some rain, but it turned out to be a warm day.

We also fired at radio-controlled planes, called drones, we will fire all day and night again.

At night we fired all guns at a sled towed by another ship. We fired by radar. We also fired by searchlight, the lights are connected with the radar and it gets on the target right away. We may go in tomorrow.

Thursday, November 9, 1944: This morning we finished our gunnery and pulled into Pearl Harbor at 9 A.M. I could not leave the ship because we had to carry ammunition all day and night until 4 A.M. the next morning, Friday. We got a lot of armor-piercing shell on, boy, are they heavy, about 135 lbs. each.

Friday, November 10, 1944: We worked so hard on ammunition that they let us sleep until 8:30 A.M. this morning. They never let us do that before. We left Pearl Harbor this morning, and on the way out, a light cruiser and 2 destroyers came in. They were all banged up from the sea battle Oct. 23, 1944, it will take some time to repair them. It looked like they were hit by shells from warships and strafing planes, they were also hit by torpedoes. The Bridge on one of the ships was blown off. They must have had a lot of casualties. In this sea battle the Jap and American warships slugged it out with each other. It took place in the dark and what a slugfest. When a battleship opens up on you it does not take long to put you to the bottom of the sea. Just as we got outside the nets Capt. Hoffman spoke and told us where we are going. He said that we are going to an island we took over last Sept. called Ulithi, it is about 125 miles N.E. of Yap and about 1000 miles from Leyte in the Philippines where our troops invaded about 2 weeks ago. Yap is still held by the Japs. We expect to get there in 10 days. I suppose we will go to the Philippines from there. He said that we would have gunnery every day on the way to Ulithi. We also have the battleship *New Mexico* with us and 5 destroyers.

This morning we had drills against torpedo boats. A smoke

screen was put up and the boats came at us from all directions at high speed. It was quite a show, they can really maneuver in the water. At a distance they are very hard to see and if it was getting dark, they would be very hard to hit. They can really take care of themselves. We also fired at sleeves towed by a B–26 bomber. I think the war will be over in 1945. On this Dec. 7, they should have a big raid on Japan. I hope the fleet is on it.

Saturday, November 11, 1944: Got off watch at 4 A.M. this morning, all hands up for General Quarters at 5:45 A.M., breakfast at 7 A.M. We did not do much today. We got the results of the Army–Notre Dame game. Army won 59 to 0, Army has not lost a game all season, they have the best team in the country. Everyone at Notre Dame must be in the service. We fired at a sleeve this afternoon. It was towed by our own seaplane S.O.C.

Sunday, November 12, 1944: Today we had church services in the mess hall. It was a nice sunny day, the sea was calm. We had our big meal at night. We set the clock back 1 hour at 5 P.M. They played music over the loudspeaker at 5 P.M. I hit the sack at 8 P.M.

Monday, November 13, 1944: We went to General Quarters at 5:30 P.M. It was pretty warm in sack last night. I think I will sleep topside from now on. Today was the hottest day so far, like old times. The 5th div. that's us, got a lot of new cleaning stations. We are not going very fast, about 15 knots.

Ulithi is about 3400 miles from Pearl Harbor and 400 miles from Palau.

Tuesday, November 14, 1944: We passed the 180 meridan late tonight and we also gained a day this morning. It was Wed. instead of Tues. The new Executive Officer is not liked by the crew, he is too regulation for wartime. Before long everyone on board will be on report. You cannot put your hat on when topside, you have to do it below. He made a lot of new changes, if you lean on the life line you get extra duty. He thinks this is a peacetime Navy where you have liberty nearly every night. We are at war but he does not realize it. Men like him disorganize a ship and are responsible for the crew to go over the hill. In peacetime he would have an excuse but not now. When it comes to a little wisdom and everyday common sense, he is a complete failure. Pulling the stuff he pulls, no wonder so many men went over the hill and missed the ship. They call our ship "the floating jail," because nearly every day fellows have to go before him and he passes out the sentence. "The U.S.S. Concentration ship" is another name. Times have changed since the good old days in the Solomons. I don't think that we are running out of good officers. It is a good thing that we are not in the States because half the crew would go over the hill. I hope he gets on to himself but then again maybe he is a sick man, who knows?

Wednesday, November 15, 1944: No news, yesterday we fueled 2 destroyers, we also gave them food and ice cream. It was very hot today. It is too hot to sleep below.

Thursday, November 16, 1944: Hit the sack at 4 A.M. and got up at 5:30 A.M. We broke out the paravanes today and had practice clearing mines. They are put over the side of the ship and cut any mines we come in contact with. It looks like a big cigar, it has wings on it, it lays in the water. They also showed movies in the mess hall on 20 and 40 mm. machine guns today.

Friday, November 17, 1944: The Capt. spoke this evening and said we would pull into Ulithi early Tues. morning. He also said the Japs are sending suicide planes against our ships in larger numbers now, they crash their planes against our ships, the pilot stays in the plane also. The Japs did this before but on a small scale. A suicide plane with its bombs can do a lot of damage when it hits a ship, you have to destroy it before it reaches you. When we reach Ulithi we will receive more orders, telling us where to go. About 8 P.M. we were about 25 miles below the Marshalls, you could see a lot of lights coming from that direction. It must be from the movies topside. The Capt. said that Ulithi is just like the Marshalls. A big hole in the center full of water and coral and sand beaches all around it. There are some openings for ships to enter. It is a natural anchorage for ships. The land around it does not rise very high. At one time it was an island but a volcano came up through the center of it and now it is full of water.

It was dark on watch today. It also rained very hard and the wind was very strong. I stand my watch on a different mount now, everyone has been changed around. This mount is smaller. There are so many men on report that they have to use the O.D.'s shack on the quarterdeck for another brig, the regular brig is full. The regular brig is nothing but a dark hole down in the bottom of the ship, it is very hot down there and you have very little room to move, the men look all washed out when they come out, you get bread and water and one full meal. You would think the men killed someone. If the Executive Officer has his way the crew would spend most of their time in the brig for the least thing. I got paid today, sent the rent money home, when we hit Ulithi it will go off. I had a working party in hangar deck, it was like an oven down there, we were covered with dirt and sweat when we finished. Hit the sack at 8:15 P.M.

Saturday, November 18, 1944: I got up at 5:30 A.M. had breakfast at 7:15 A.M. and had 8 to 12 noon watch. We had ham for dinner today. It did not rain today for a change, also a little cooler. One of the men was put on report because they found his hat on the deck, what a joke. We started water hours again this week. The water is on for 1 hour and off 4 or 5 hours. It is a nuisance. We have drinking water at all times. We sleep topside, too hot below, also put the clock back one hour at 5 P.M.

Sunday, November 19, 1944: Church services were held in the mess hall today. I had the church working party. Our new Chaplain is a Catholic Priest. All the other Chaplains we had were Protestant ministers. They were very friendly and everyone liked them very much. The new Chaplain's name is Fr. Wilson. The sea was very calm today, just like a pond. We were about an hour's airplane drive from Truk this afternoon. It is the Gibraltar of the Pacific. No white man has been on it in over 30 years. That would have been a very hard place to invade and capture. It was a good thing we bypassed it, it would have been a long, bloody campaign. Today is the 8th day since we left Pearl Harbor, 2 more days to go and we reach Ulithi. It was very hot today, also very hot in the mess hall, our shirts were soaking wet. You do not enjoy your meals, you want to get topside as soon as possible. It is getting like old times again, and we are also supposed to eat salt pills every day. I take them every day. We get a lot of radio pragrams from Japan, they tell an awful lot of lies to their people. They said that they sunk 11 aircraft carriers, 8 battleships and many other warships, 55 in all. This was to have taken place in the Philippine campaign. The Japs are the ones who took the big losses not us. Our forces are doing a job on them in the Philippines. In the European war they expect to drop 100,000 tons of bombs on Germany. In the first 15 days they dropped 50,000 tons of bombs. I bet we hit Japan on Dec. 7, from Tinian with our Big B–29's. It is a beautiful evening, just like a summer night back home. Everyone is topside sitting all over the ship. I will sleep topside and then go on watch, got midnight to 4 A.M. Hank Lawrence had his tonsils taken out yesterday. Last year this time this stretch of water was known as "no man's sea." It was Jap territory and it was very dangerous to send any ships here. But today it belongs to us. It is getting dark now as I sit topside and write. The time is 6:30 P.M. in the evening.

Monday, November 20, 1944: I hit the sack at 4 A.M. This morning all hands up at 5 A.M. for General Quarters. Today is our 9th day at sea. We should reach Ulithi tomorrow. There is a convoy behind us and it was attacked by Jap planes this afternoon. The planes must have come from Truk. This morning at 9 A.M. our destroyers picked up 3 Jap subs. The Japs sent word that 2 American battleships were on their way to the Jap-held island of Yap. The Japs thought we were battleships because we are very long, we are as long as the battleship *New Mexico*. The Japs are always watching us and we don't see them. The Japs must have thought that we were going to bombard their island of Yap, it is near Ulithi. I was told by a good friend of mine many months ago that we had broken the Jap code, but this was during the Solomons campaign. I did not pay much attention to him at the time. He knew what he was talking about after all. It is a warm, sunny day. Someone said Jap subs sank one of our ships the other day. They were quite a few miles ahead of us. There

are a lot of Jap subs in these waters, because they know we have
to use these waters to get to our destination. We turned the clock
back at 5 P.M. this evening. I slept on the boat deck tonight, it
was too hot to sleep below. Modock and I slept on some boxes of
potatoes, they have an awful lot of them stored on the boat deck
with a canvas over them. We lay down at 6:30 P.M. and chewed
the fat for about an hour and then we fell asleep. It was a beautiful night, the moon was out for a while. Most of the nights this
month have been very dark.

Tuesday, November 21, 1944: I got up at 3:15 A.M. to go on
watch. At 5 A.M. this morning one of our planes was dropping
flares. They said a Jap sub had surfaced. Today is the 10th day
since we left Pearl Harbor, it is a 3400 mile trip.

At 9 A.M. this morning we pulled into Ulithi. It is 125 miles
northeast of Yap, a Jap-held island. Ulithi looks like the Marshalls. When we pulled in we went alongside a tanker. It took
about 3 hours to get the fuel. There are many ships here, all
types, also numerous carriers. The big, powerful force of warships that we have here could do an awful lot of damage on the
Japs. I was talking to one of the men on the tanker and he told
me that a Jap sub sunk one of our tankers right in here in Ulithi.
He said 4 Jap subs have been sunk here so far. They do not know
how they got in here. Maybe followed our ships in. The Japs
held Ulithi for a long time, they could have been hiding in here
when we took over. Maybe they have a secret way of getting in.
A couple of the Jap subs were small, they were manned by 8 men
crews. Some of the Japs were picked up on the beach, the others
killed themselves.

Our destroyers went all over the place dropping depth charges
just in case more Jap subs were hiding here. They think that Jap
subs are still hiding out in here. This is a very large place and
covers quite a few miles. It is like one big circle surrounded by
coral and sand beaches with coconut trees. The land does not rise
very high. They think the reason the Jap sub sank the tanker instead of hitting a battleship or carrier was because they figured
that would throw us off guard long enough for the Jap subs to

sneak in and hit the battleships and carriers, but we were not distracted or fooled by their tricks. One sub tried to sneak out behind a net tender, but our destroyers sank it.

About 150 men were lost on the tanker the Japs sunk here, it was a mass of flames. He said quite a few of our damaged ships from the Philippine sea battle came in here. The light cruiser *Birmingham* had 190 men killed when it pulled alongside the carrier *Princeton* to take aboard the men, before it went down. The high octane gas and bombs went up and did quite a job on the *Birmingham*. The water is very calm here, there is also a good breeze. It is very hot in the ship. The Dr. inspected all living spaces today. We sent a working party to an LST for mail, and we got 3 bags of airmail. The LST is used as a post office. It was a beautiful evening to sleep topside, the air was dry. Many of the fellows did not want to sleep below because Jap subs might be hiding here. They said some of the Jap subs stay right under our ships. It gives you a funny feeling to be in a big lagoon surrounded by every kind of warship in the books and never knowing when one of them will be blown up by a Jap sub. The Jap subs are trapped in here, and in time they will be sunk like a bunch of drowned rats. I bet the men on the Jap subs must be talking to themselves when they see all these big, juicy targets and yet they cannot do anything about it. This is a situation submarine men always dream about, but never come across. I wonder what an American submarine would do in this sort of a situation.

Wednesday, November 22, 1944: The sun was shining at 5:30 A.M. this morning. We got ammunition and mail today. A Jap sub was sunk outside the net this morning. No news today, still at Ulithi.

Thursday, November 23, 1944: We left Ulithi at 1 P.M. this afternoon. Capt. Hoffman spoke to the crew. He said that we are on our way to Leyte, in the Philippines. Our troops invaded that big island Oct. 20, 1944. We expected to get there Sat. morning Nov. 25th. Our ship will be flagship of a task force of warships again, and we will join the Seventh Fleet. We still have Admiral

Robert W. Hayler aboard, he was with us when we were out here before. The Seventh Fleet is the same fleet that defeated the Jap Fleet last Oct. at Surigao Strait in the central Philippines. The Japs lost battleships and every kind of a warship in this engagement. This was the greatest sea battle of all time. Admiral Oldendorf crossed the T on the Japs during this action, this is something that happens once in a lifetime. The Japs lost many ships and plenty were damaged.

Friday, November 24, 1944: The sea was calm and the air a little cooler today. About 6 P.M. tonight we were about 270 miles from Leyte Gulf. We had sunset General Quarters. I wrote some Christmas cards today.

Saturday, November 25, 1944: We pulled into Leyte Gulf in the Philippines at noon, this is a very big place, they say it is 60 miles long and 30 miles wide. We also passed the spot where our Navy and the Jap navy slugged it out at 3 A.M. in the morning. We will now be under the Supreme Command of General MacArthur. Our job is to patrol near the spot of the sea battle and destroy any Jap warships that try to attack our merchant ships and our troops on Leyte. Leyte is about in the center of the Philippines.

They say that there are over 7000 islands in the Philippines. Capt. Hoffman said the Japs have a force of 400 PT boats in these waters, they also have many airfields and they hit this place every day. We had sunset General Quarters, as usual the Jap air force came out and attacked the beach at Leyte, also our merchant ships. None of them attacked us. We could see the gunfire from where we were. Our troops inland also were attacked. I slept topside tonight.

Sunday, November 26, 1944: We had early General Quarters as usual. All hands went to battle stations at 10 A.M. this morning because of Jap planes, but no damage was done. At sunset General Quarters about 25 Jap planes hit the beach and transports in Leyte Gulf. They did not attack us, the all clear signal sounded at 9:30 P.M. but we were back again in 15 minutes, more Jap planes attacked. We stayed at battle stations until 11:45 P.M. The

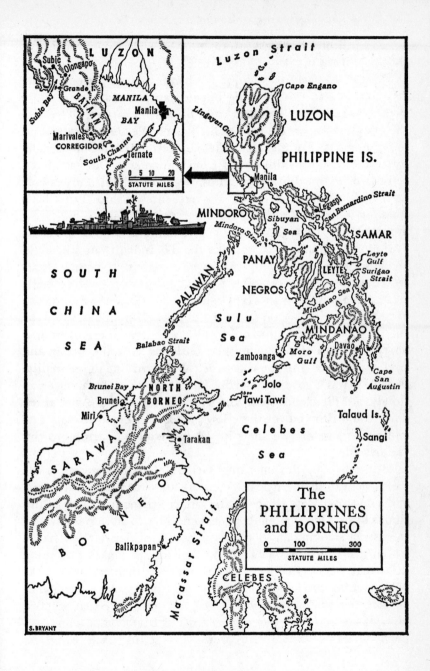

LUZON

Subic
Olongapo
Grande
Subic Bay
BATAN
MANILA
BAY
Manila
Marivales
CORREGIDOR
South Channel
Ternate

0 5 10   20
STATUTE MILES

Luzon Strait

Cape Engano

LUZON

PHILIPPINE IS.

Lingayen Gulf

Manila

MINDORO
Mindoro Strait
Sibuyan Sea
Legaspi
San Bernardino Strait

SAMAR

Leyte Gulf

PANAY
LEYTE
Surigao Strait

NEGROS

Mindanao Sea

SOUTH

CHINA

SEA

PALAWAN

Sulu Sea

Balabac Strait

MINDANAO
Davao

Zamboanga
Moro Gulf

Cape San Augustin

Brunei Bay
Brunei
NORTH BORNEO

Jolo

Tawi Tawi

Talaud Is.

Miri

Sangi

SARAWAK

Tarakan

Celebes

Sea

B O R N E O

Balikpapan

The
PHILIPPINES
and BORNEO

0   100   300
STATUTE MILES

Macassar Strait

CELEBES

S. BRYANT

sky was full of red tracers as our guns fired at the Jap planes. I slept topside as usual.

Monday, November 27, 1944: All hands went to General Quarters at 5:30 A.M. this morning but no Jap planes attacked. The Press News said our bombers from Saipan hit Tokyo. This was the first time Saipan was used to hit Japan. We are still patrolling near Leyte. We got fuel from a tanker today. It was quite a sight to see the way our ships fueled from the tanker. Our task force consists of 18 warships, battleships, heavy and light cruisers and destroyers. While the tanker was refueling 2 ships from both sides, at the same time, all the other ships formed a big circle around the 3 ships. The ships kept circling at a good speed all during the operation. It was like the old Indian wars when the Indians use to keep circling our covered wagons. If Jap planes attacked while we were refueling we would throw up a wall of shells around the tanker so the Japs could not break through. In the meantime a sailor would be near the lines with an axe, ready to cut the lines so the ship could pull away from the tanker in a hurry. When a ship was finished refueling it would get in the circle so another ship could get fuel. It looked like the merry-go-round. It was a good day for the Japs to attack us because it was cloudy and the clouds were low with a little rain now and then. They could drop out of these low clouds and be on us very fast and be gone before we knew it. We were almost surrounded by Jap airfields.

At 10:50 A.M. this morning General Quarters sounded, all hands went to their battle stations. At the same time a battleship and a destroyer were alongside the tanker getting fuel. Out of the clouds I saw a big Jap bomber come crashing down into the water. It was not smoking and looked in good condition. It felt like I was in it as it hit the water not too far from the tanker, and the 2 ships that were refueling. One of our P–38 fighters hit it. He must have got the pilot. At first I thought it was one of our bombers that had engine trouble. It was not long after that when a force of about 30 Jap planes attacked us. Dive bombers and torpedo planes. Our two ships were busy getting away from the tanker because one bomb-hit on the tanker and it would be all over for the 3 ships.

The 2 ships finally got away from the tanker and joined the circle. I think the destroyers were on the outside of the circle. It looked funny to see the tanker all by itself in the center of the ships as we circled it, with our guns blazing away as the planes tried to break through. It was quite a sight, better than the movies. I never saw it done before. It must be the first time it was ever done in any war. Jap planes were coming at us from all directions. Before the attack started we did not know that they were suicide planes, with no intention of returning to their base. They had one thing in mind and that was to crash into our ships, bombs and all. You have to blow them up, to damage them doesn't mean much. Right off the bat a Jap plane made a suicide dive at the cruiser *St. Louis,* there was a big explosion and flames were seen shortly from the stern. Another one tried to do the same thing but he was shot down. A Jap plane came in on a battleship with its guns blazing away. Other Jap planes came in strafing one ship, dropping their bombs on another and crashing into another ship. The Jap planes were falling all around us, the air was full of Jap machine gun bullets. Jap planes and bombs were hitting all around us. Some of our ships were being hit by suicide planes, bombs and machine gun fire. It was a fight to the finish. While all this was taking place our ship had its hands full with Jap planes. We knocked our share of planes down but we also got hit by 3 suicide planes, but lucky for us they dropped their bombs before they crashed into us. In the meantime exploding planes overhead were showering us with their parts. It looked like it was raining plane parts. They were falling all over the ship. Quite a few of the men were hit by big pieces of Jap planes. We were supposed to have air coverage but all we had was 4 P-38 fighters, and when we opened up on the Jap planes they got out of the range of our exploding shells. They must have had a ring side seat of the show. The men on my mount were also showered with parts of Jap planes. One suicide dive bomber was heading right for us while we were firing at other attacking planes and if the 40 mm. mount behind us on the port side did not blow the Jap wing off it would have killed all of us. When the wing was blown off it, the plane turned some and bounced off into the water and the bombs blew part of the plane onto our ship. Another suicide plane crashed into one of the 5 inch mounts, pushing the side of the mount in and injuring some of the men inside. A lot of 5 inch shells were damaged. It was a miracle they did not explode. If that happened the powder and shells would have blown up the ship. Our 40 mm. mount is not too far away. The men threw the 5 inch shells over the side. They expected them to go off at any time. A Jap dive bomber crashed into one of the 40 mm. mounts but lucky for them it dropped its bombs on another ship before crashing. Parts of the plane flew everywhere when it crashed into the mount. Part of the motor hit Tomlinson, he had chunks of it all over him, his stomach, back, legs etc. The rest of the crew were wounded, most of them were sprayed with gasoline from the plane. Tomlinson was thrown a great distance and at first they thought he was knocked over the side. They finally found him in a corner in bad shape. One of the mt. Captains had the wires cut on his phones and kept talking into the phone, because he did not know they were cut by shrapnel until one of the fellows told him. The explosions were terrific as the suicide planes exploded in the water not too far away from our ship. The water was covered with black smoke that rose high into the air. The water looked like it was on fire. It would have been curtains for us if they had crashed into us.

Another suicide plane just overshot us. It grazed the 6 inch turret. It crashed into Leyte Gulf. There was a terrific explosion as the bombs exploded, about 20 ft. away. If we were going a little faster we would have been hit. The Jap planes that were not destroyed with our shells crashed into the water close by or hit our ships. It is a tough job to hold back this tidal wave of suicide planes. They come at you from all directions and also straight down at us at a very fast pace but some of the men have time for a few fast jokes, "This would be a great time to run out of ammunition." "This is mass suicide at its best." Another suicide plane came down at us in a very steep dive. It was a near miss, it just missed the 5 inch mount. The starboard side of the ship was showered with water and fragments. How long will our luck hold out? The Good Lord is really watching over us. This was very close to my 40 mm. mount and we were showered with debris. If the suicide plane exploded on the 5 inch mount, the ammunition would have gone up, after that anything could happen.

Planes were falling all around us, bombs were coming too close for comfort. The Jap planes were cutting up the water with machine gun fire. All the guns on the ships were blazing away, talk about action, never a dull moment. The fellows were passing ammunition like lightning as the guns were turning in all directions spitting out hot steel. Parts of destroyed suicide planes were scattered all over the ship. During a little lull in the action the men would look around for Jap souvenirs and what souvenirs they were. I got part of the plane. The deck near my mount was covered with blood, guts, brains, tongues, scalps, hearts, arms etc. from the Jap pilots. One of the Marines cut the ring off the finger of one of the dead pilots. They had to put the hose on to wash the blood off the deck. The deck ran red with blood. The Japs were spattered all over the place. One of the fellows had a Jap scalp, it looked just like you skinned an animal. The hair was black, cut very short, and the color of the skin was yellow, real Japanese. I do not think he was very old. I picked up a tin pie plate with a tongue on it. The pilot's tooth mark was into it very deep. It was very big and long, it looked like part of his tonsils and throat were attached to it. It also looked like the tongue you buy in the meat store. This was the first time I ever saw a person's brains, what a mess. One of the men on our mount got a Jap rib and cleaned it up, he said his sister wants part of a Jap body. One fellow from Texas had a knee bone and he was going to preserve it in alcohol from the sick bay. The Jap bodies were blown into all sorts of pieces. I cannot think of everything that happened because too many things were happening at the same time.

These suicide or kamikaze pilots wanted to destroy us, our ships and themselves. This gives you an idea what kind of an enemy we are fighting. The air attacks in Europe are tame compared to what you run up against out here against the Japs. The Germans will come in so far, do their job and take off but not the Japs. I can see now how the Japs sank the two British battleships *Prince of Wales* and the *Repulse* at the beginning of the war at Singapore. You do not discourage the Japs, they never give up, you have to kill them. It is an honor to die for the Emperor. We do not know how many Jap planes were shot down or the total of planes that attacked us during all the action but they threw plenty of them at us. I have not heard how many planes our ship shot down but at one period of the attack our ship shot down 4 suicide planes within 2 minutes. I think most of the Jap planes that attacked us were destroyed. The attack lasted for 2 hours, we went to battle stations at 10:50 A.M. in the morning and secured at 2:10 P.M. in the afternoon. The action took place not too far from Leyte. Every ship had its hands full with the Jap planes during those 2 hours. The Japs started the attack with 30 planes but after that more planes kept joining them.

After we secured from General Quarters the men looked the ship over to see the damage. The ship was a mess, part of it was damaged, cables were down, steel life lines snapped and steel posts broken. Big pieces of Jap planes were scattered all over the ship, life rafts damaged. Our empty shell cases were everywhere. Some of the other ships were in worse condition than ours. The wounded were brought down to sick bay and some had to be operated on at once.

When it was all over the tanker was still in the middle of the circle and the Japs did not hit it.

Someone said a couple of rafts were in the water with some Japs in them and one of the Japs was in bad condition. We will get more information about this action later when all the reports are in. We had chow at 2:30 P.M. in the afternoon and at 6:30 P.M. we went to sunset General Quarters. The Japs did not come out tonight, guess they had enough action to hold them this afternoon for the day. We secured from General Quarters at 8 P.M. We got some rain this evening. I got the midnight to 4 A.M. watch. No sleep.

Tuesday, November 28, 1944: While I was on the midnight to 4 A.M. watch this morning Jap planes were picked up not too far away. All hands went to battle stations at 2 A.M. and we secured at 3:15 A.M. The Japs did not attack us, they hit someplace else. A fellow does not get much sleep with all these General Quarters. I was on watch anyway so it did not affect my sleep. The Jap planes pay this place a visit at least twice a day. We had sunrise General Quarters this morning at 5:15 A.M., chow at 7 A.M. A ship came alongside and we transferred the most seriously wounded. It will bring them to a hospital in Leyte. We have been at General Quarters so much lately that they let the men not on watch sleep until 11 A.M. Today we will try to continue where we left off yesterday when the Jap planes attacked us as we were refueling from the tanker. The weather today is just like yesterday, cloudy and overcast, looks like rain, the clouds are very low. Another good day for the Japs to attack us. Only a few ships got fuel because about every 3 or 4 hours Jap planes were picked up. Most of the day was spent at battle stations. We got some dope about what happened yesterday.

Close to 70 Jap planes attacked us yesterday. The Japs also attacked the troops and cargo ships at Leyte. They said our task force knocked down 30 Jap planes plus the ones that crashed into our ships. Some ships were attacked more than others. The Jap planes picked our ship out as one of the ships they wanted to sink. I guess they did not like the Jap flags we had painted on the Bridge. We also made a good big target with our new paint job. I bet they thought our ship was a battleship because we are just as long as the old ones, over 600 ft. It is a good thing that every bit of space on the warships out here have guns on them, not a foot of space is wasted. Against the Jap suicide planes you need all the guns you can get. Our warships out here have more guns and more fire power than any other ships in the world. The battleship *Colorado* had 19 men killed, plus many wounded. They had a hole 10 ft. wide from a bomb. I think it was also hit by a suicide plane. The light cruiser *St. Louis* lost 14 men plus many wounded. I think 2 suicide planes hit her. I did not hear anything about the damage to our other ships yet. This afternoon

Radio Tokyo said the attack their planes made on us Tuesday resulted in their favor, they sunk 1 battleship, 3 battleships heavily
damaged, 4 cruisers sunk or heavily damaged and all their pilots
returned but 2. What a laugh. The Jap. Govt. never tells its people the truth, they fill them up with lies. The Jap commentator
also said that the planes that attacked us were a special fighter air
squadron.

He should have called it a suicide squadron. Every one of them
tried to crash dive against our ships. Suicide planes are the toughest to fight against. When they come in at you hundreds of miles
an hour nothing will stop them unless you blow them up. The
ship that took our wounded also went around to the other ships in
our task force. We had General Quarters as usual, and about
10:30 P.M. our cargo ships were attacked by Jap planes. We could
see the fireworks. The sky was full of tracers and bursting shells.
I slept on some tanks of 40 mm. ammunition tonight.

Wednesday, November 29, 1944: At 2 A.M. this morning we
went to battle stations, because of Jap planes, but they did not
attack. We had regular General Quarters at 5:15 A.M. and chow
at 7 A.M. About every 3 or 4 hours, day and night, 24 hours a day,
General Quarters would sound and everyone runs to his battle
station. It looks like the Japs don't want us to get any sleep, so
they can wear us out. They want to get us punch drunk, I guess.
Sometimes the planes attack us, other times the transports at Leyte
Gulf and our troops get it also. I have to laugh at the men who
are caught taking a shower when General Quarters sounds, they
have to run to their battle stations naked carrying their clothes in
their hands.

Sometimes about 2 A.M. in the morning after being at battle
stations you lay down to get some sleep and General Quarters
sound, you have to jump up and run to your battle station again.
When you sit down or lay down at any time of the day or night
you never know what second General Quarters will sound for you
to take off.

General Quarters has an awful loud frightening sound, it has
trouble written all over it. It is enough to put the fear of the Lord

in you. About 4:30 P.M. this evening General Quarters sounded, and we did not have to wait very long for the Jap planes to attack us. Not too many attacked but it was quite a tussle while it lasted. We knocked 3 planes down. About ½ hour later they came back again and tried their suicide attacks as usual. There were a lot of close calls, planes and bombs were dropping all around. One Jap plane came in on the heavy cruiser *Portland,* but its bombs just missed its target. The same pilot then turned around and flew across our formation. I don't know how he got through the exploding shells alive. He then shot up into the sky, and put on quite a show for us. The pilot was an expert, he did every trick in the book, what an acrobat he was. When he finished he turned over and started a power dive right at the battleship *Maryland.* This was suicide at its best, he wanted to go out in a blaze of glory, he wanted to sink an American battleship. He came down so fast that if he dropped a bomb he would have beaten it to the ship. He crashed on one of the 16 inch turrets and froze it. There was a big explosion and it burned for sometime. I do not know how many casualties they had. It is a good thing he did not hit a little closer, because he would have gone down the smokestack and that would have put the finishing touches to the battleship. You will never see a stunt like that again. Something like that happens only once in a lifetime. One thing about these suicide pilots there is never a dull moment, they go all out to kill themselves.

About 1 hour after this we secured and had chow. We had a late supper and while I was in the mess hall eating, General Quarters sounded again. Everyone ran to his battle stations but before I left I got myself a big supply of cookies from the trays. The men in their haste left their cookies behind, that was the best part of the supper. I got to my battle station on time, and we had a little picnic for ourselves with the cookies the fellows were foolish enough to leave behind. Everyone was hungry and they really hit the spot. When General Quarters is sounded I have to laugh at some of the fellows. They are in such a hurry to get to their battle stations that they almost run up the back of the man in front of them on the ladder. The Jap planes did not attack us so we secured in about 1 hour. We also replaced the ammunition we used earlier. It was bright tonight and also dry. I slept topside but about 10:30 P.M. it rained, so I slept in the 40 mm. ammunition room on some tanks of 40 mm. ammunition. It was like sleeping on a sword, the edges of the cans are very sharp. The air was not too good in there either.

Thursday, November 30, 1944: I got a pretty good night's sleep. The Japs did not bother us for a change. All hands up at 5:15 A.M. this morning. The Capt. spoke just before we secured. He said today is Thanksgiving Day, we cannot have a turkey dinner, because it takes a longer time to cook one and it would be impossible to have one because we go to General Quarters so often. But we will have our turkey dinner when we have more time to cook it.

He said after what has happened in the last few days we have a lot to be thankful for. Everyone agrees with the Capt. on that statement. The weather has been cloudy, and it rained quite often, lately. Today is a warm, sunny day. One of our battleships and a cruiser left for Manus Island, it is below the equator between New Guinea and New Ireland. The ships have to get repaired. They have recreation there but I suppose it is like the rest of the places out here, no good. A hospital ship passed us today. We are still patrolling. Some of the ships got fuel today. There is talk about our troops invading Luzon. It is the main island on the Philippines, Manila the capitol is on Luzon. It is up north and also the largest island in the Philippines. The landing is supposed to take place Dec. 7. The Japs will remember Dec. 7, 1944. The Press News had something about our air battle against the Japs, Monday. It said the Jap planes consisted of fighter planes, dive bombers, torpedo planes, and that they attacked a fleet of American warships off Leyte, it also said the Jap Air Force was known as the hot core unit and that they made an all out attack to destroy the American fleet units off Leyte. This was the most determined enemy bid against our naval might since the Leyte Gulf battle against the Jap Fleet last month. Today was sunny for a change, no General Quarters today. I guess they plan to attack us when it is cloudy.

Friday, December 1, 1944: This morning an ammunition ship and tanker came out from Leyte. We got ammunition. We were supposed to get fuel but we received word that Jap planes were on the way so we had to call it off. We were almost ready to fuel when it happened.

We pulled away from the tanker in a hurry but the planes did not reach us. It was cloudy today, it rained hard all day. We got soaking wet. All machine guns were manned and ready to fire while we were alongside the ammunition ship. While we were eating supper General Quarters sounded. Some Jap subs got into our formation, they threw some torpedoes at our ships, there were some close calls but no damage was done. Our destroyers did not waste any time dropping depth charges. You could feel the explosions on the ship. I do not know if they sunk any of the subs. The explosions brought up some big monster sharks, the largest I ever saw. You could see them swimming in the water, only a few feet from the ship. The concussion down in the mess hall was terrific when the depth charges were dropped. It felt like the sides of the ship were going to fall in. The noise was very loud. The Japs in the subs must have sweat it out. We secured in about an hour and continued chow. It rained all night so I slept in the ammunition room. I got up at 11:15 P.M. for the midnight to 4 A.M. watch.

Saturday, December 2, 1944: Got off watch at 4 A.M. this morning, then got some sleep surrounded by ammunition. I came out of my hole at 5:15 A.M. for General Quarters. Breakfast was at 7 A.M. We now have 25 warships instead of 17 with us. It is a nice, warm, sunny day for a change. We are still patrolling near Leyte. At 7 P.M. tonight we left for the Island of Palau, it is between Ulithi and Leyte. The Marines captured this island from the Japs after a bloody campaign. It is about 550 miles from here. Our part in the Leyte campaign has ended. We left a few ships behind. They said we will reach Palau Monday morning. We will get stores and new orders for our coming campaign. The ships we left behind were attacked by Jap planes, not too long after we left them. We also were attacked late in the evening, torpedo planes dropped their fish at us in the dark, no damage was done. Later we came in contact with Jap subs, our destroyers dropped depth charges on them.

Sunday, December 3, 1944: I arose at 3:15 A.M., had the 4 to 8 A.M. watch. They had the Army-Navy football game on the radio at 4:15 A.M. this morning. It is Sat. afternoon back in the States. The game was played in Baltimore and the Army won 23 to 7. The Army is the No. 1 team in the country, they did not lose a game all year. Mass was held in the mess hall this evening. We got some dope about the Jap air raid. A big force of Jap planes attacked the ships that relieved us at Leyte, and they sunk one of our new large destroyers. They said all hands were lost. A destroyer carries quite a few hundred men. They also tried to sink the hospital ship with torpedoes but they missed. At night a hospital ship is all lighted up. The ship must have been in Leyte Gulf. We left those warships just at the right time, that could have been us instead of the destroyer. We had a pretty good dinner today. Most of the men lay down topside after the noon meal. They lay down under the 5 and 6 inch mounts and turrets and all the other shady places. I slept topside tonight until it started to rain at 1:03 P.M. The rest of the time I slept in the ammunition room. It is too hot to sleep below. Those ammunition cases are really hard and sharp pointed.

Monday, December 4, 1944: All hands up at 5 A.M. We came across a Jap tug but no one was on it.

We left one of our destroyers behind to tow it into Palau. It was very hot on watch, I had 8 to 12 A.M. We had the sun on our side all the time. Today was the 1st chance we had to have our Thanksgiving Dinner, almost a week late but it was worth waiting for. We really had quite a feed. Turkey, and all the trimmings. It was very good. At 3:30 P.M. this afternoon we pulled into Palau. Before we got to where we dropped the anchor we passed a long line of islands, they looked like jungle from here, they are not very big. At the end of our trip we came to a big lagoon, it looked like the Marshalls and Ulithi. Where we stopped it is one big circle of coral with water in the center. The coral could not be seen above the water. There are quite a few ships here, they have 6 small carriers here also. We had movies topside this evening. "They Fly by Night" was the name of the movie. The Marines are still fighting for some of the islands here. I saw our planes hitting the Japs this morning, they really gave this place a going over.

Sunday, December 10, 1944: Nothing has happened in the past few days so I did not write. We have not received any mail yet. An ammunition ship pulled alongside. We had a work out for ourselves. Movies are held topside every night. It rains a little every other day but not like it did at Leyte. It is the rainy season on that side of the Philippines, and it makes the fighting very tough. It is almost at a standstill. It is a break for the Jap planes though. In the past couple of months the Jap air force has gone all out for suicide attack. The Japs call them special Attack Corps units. We get radio programs from Japan every day and they give these units a lot of praise. They call the pilots who do not come back "Sacred." When these suicide pilots take off they have no intention of returning, they want to die for the Emperor. We had to laugh at the propaganda they pass out. They said since Oct. they sank 51 of our aircraft carriers and 26 battleships since the war started. The Press News said that Tokyo was hit by an earthquake, it was quite serious, the Japs also admitted it. They know we can pick up the earthquakes. We have not got any mail in 3 weeks and it looks like we won't get any for some time to come because we pull out today, at noon. Last night we had Mass in the crew's lounge at 5 P.M. The Priest heard confessions in his office at 7:15 P.M. He hears confessions almost every night, and we have Mass every day we can get the time. Yesterday afternoon they let the officers and crew swim over the side of the ship. It was funny to be swimming in the middle of the Pacific Ocean and 3 marines on the 5 inch mount with their guns ready to fire, just in case some sharks should attack the swimmers. It is 10 A.M. Sunday morning as I write, Frank Brathor is close by, making a pair of wooden shoes for when he takes a shower. We just got some apple turnovers from the baker. They really hit the spot. Most of the ships in our task force are getting low on food. We might get some today, before we leave. We aired our bedding today. It was a warm sunny day. The swimming we had yesterday from 3:30 to 4:30 P.M. was our first recreation in over a month. The last time we put our feet on land was about 6 weeks ago while in Hawaii, and it will be some time before we get a chance to do it again. This morning at 10 A.M. Protestant church services were held on bow and Catholic services were held on the stern. A minister from one of the other ships held the services. We left Palau at noon today. Our force consisted of 3 battleships, 5 small carriers, 3 heavy and 3 light cruisers, and about 20 destroyers.

Monday, December 11, 1944: I slept topside last night. Modock and I talked for quite a while before we fell asleep. The rain woke us up at 1:30 A.M. I got up at 3:15 A.M. to go on watch, got 4 to 8. Last night the Capt. spoke and said that we would be in on the Mindoro invasion. It is a big island in the Philippines.

We will land troops there on Uncle Day, December 15, 1944. It was supposed to take place Dec. 7th, for Pearl Harbor Day, but it had to be delayed for some reason. The Capt. said there are not supposed to be many troops on it, but the Japs could send thousands of troops on it, because it is very close to the main island of Luzon. Gen. MacArthur likes to land troops where the Japs least expect them, he can really fool them. Of course they don't come any better than the Gen, great men like him come but once in a lifetime. Now he will have something to fight with. In New Guinea he was lucky to get the right time, he received very few supplies and equipment. Mindoro will make a good air base to soften up Luzon and the other islands, and also support our troops when they invade Luzon. On Wed. Dec. the 13th we should be in Leyte Gulf, from there we go through the Mindanao Sea and then to the Sulu Sea to Mindoro. We will be surrounded by Jap-held islands. For a change we will not have to do any bombarding, some other ships will do that. Our job will be mostly to protect the carriers in case Jap warships show up and also give them fire support against Jap suicide planes. The Japs are supposed to have warships near Mindoro.

When this is over we are supposed to return to our base, and get food, supplies and mail, we should be back by Xmas. It was partly cloudy today. One of the planes from the carriers almost went over the side after landing. We are in Task Force 77 point 12. Last night the Capt. also said that he thought we would be home for Xmas next year. I also think the war will be over in 1945. I hope the rainy season is over when we reach the Philippines. It rained most of the time the last time we were there.

Tuesday, December 12, 1944: I slept topside, not much news. The planes from our carriers are always in the sky. The Capt. spoke tonight and said we would be going through Leyte Gulf tonight about 11 P.M. and tomorrow morning at 5 A.M. we would be on the other side of Leyte, leaving it behind us. If we kept going straight we would run right into the coast of China. I had the 8 to midnight watch tonight. Land was on both sides of us. The ships in this force will be the first to go through Philippines since the Japs took over at the beginning of the war. We can expect anything in there.

Wednesday, December 13, 1944: Got off watch at midnight. I slept in ammunition room because of the rain, it is warm there but not as bad as below. All hands got up at 5 A.M. When you come to a new place everyone is topside, they are very anxious to get a look at it. We are right in the middle of the Philippines and land is on both sides of us and all around us as our ships make their way to Mindoro. It is a beautiful, sunny day and some of the islands are very large and reach high into the clouds. They are so green with jungle. The water is calm and blue. We are very close to land. It is very interesting as we sail along.

We are just like explorers, we do not want to miss a thing. Many of the islands are the size of some of our states, others are larger. Another task force of cruisers and destroyers came out from behind some islands. I think they will bombard when we get there. Someone said we will pass 700 islands on our way to Mindoro, there are over 7000 islands in the Philippines. Our planes are in the air ready for anything. One of our planes sank a barge with Jap troops on it this morning, on our port side. A lot of smoke came from it, it was a good size. Our job is to cover the landing in case any Jap ships or planes should attack. The Japs have 3 battleships, some cruisers, and destroyers in Borneo. Borneo will be south of us at Mindoro. Mindoro faces the China Sea.

We started Condition 2 watches this morning. You stay on watch 4 hours and you are off 4 hours. This does not give you much time off. All guns are manned and ready to fire, because there are so many Jap-held islands and every hour we get deeper and deeper into them, it is like getting in the center of a big cobweb. We will be swallowed up in all these islands very soon. We will be surrounded by Jap bases and airfields. All the battleships are the old ones, the same ones that destroyed the Japs in October. All our new and fast ships are out in the open sea, where they can defend themselves better and are not close to land-based planes. We would rather lose these small carriers and older ships than the new ones, and the older ones can still do the same job. It would be foolish for us to bring our big carriers and other new ships in here where you are surrounded by land-based planes. We cleaned up the petty officers' quarters this morning. It also gave me a good chance to wash some clothes. We also got some cookies from the bake shop. I go on watch at noon. In dangerous waters like this no one sleeps below. You never know when Jap ships, subs or torpedo boats might be hiding behind an island in the thick jungle. It is 10:30 A.M. as I sit in the P.O. head and write. I will write later in the day if anything comes up. This afternoon the Capt. spoke and said we were in the Mindanao Sea, he also said a lot of the islands in this section have people on them that are still uncivilized. We passed the 2nd largest island in the Philippines when we passed Mindanao.

There are many Jap prison camps on it, they treat the prisoners very cruel and a lot of them are mostly American prisoners of war. A few escaped from there about a year ago and told how cruel the Japs treated them. I guess our subs picked them up. This is the first time in history of the Philippines that a force as large as this ever came through these waters. There will be over 200 ships of all kinds — this does not count the warships. We are surrounded by islands now, some of them are very pretty. Many old coconuts came floating by this afternoon and a little bird was sitting on one as it floated by. The birds around here are very smart. The weather is great, it is not too hot and the sun is out all the time. Our troop and cargo ships are just behind us on the other side of the horizon. Tonight about 4:45 P.M. Jap planes attacked us. One ship was damaged. This evening I saw something happen that is almost impossible to do and I never heard of it happening before. While the warships were cutting through the water at a good speed a Jap plane came out of a low cloud and dropped a bomb down the smokestack of one of our destroyers. It was not too far from our starboard quarter. A few degrees and we would have got it. I could hardly believe my eyes, that pilot should get cited for that kind of marksmanship. A moving destroyer is a very hard target to hit and when you put a bomb down the stack that tops them all. Everyone was talking to himself after that performance. The Japanese Govt. should preserve that Jap's body for all to see. When the bomb was dropped down the stack, white steam and smoke shot into the air where the stack was supposed to be. The destroyer looked funny with no smokestack. I do not know how many casualties they had. They say the steam from a warship is so powerful that it will cut your arm off. The destroyer was dead in the water. Another destroyer pulled alongside it. As we kept moving we left them behind.

The Jap planes attacked the transports, cargo ships and warships. The place was full of Jap planes. These Condition 2 watches are tough, you are back and forth from your battle station every 4 hours, you leave and it seems like you are right back again, one thing is for sure you don't get much sleep.

Thursday, December 14, 1944: Got off watch at 4 A.M. took a shower and all hands got up at 6 A.M. got 1 hr. sleep had breakfast and then went on watch again. This morning nothing happened, it is warm and sunny. You can see our carrier planes flying around, the warships and the convoy behind us. They give us good air coverage, the other carrier planes are miles away scouting for the enemy. Borneo was south of us today. From one end of the Philippines to the other it is over 1000 miles long and it is about 500 miles wide. At 12:30 this afternoon our convoy got closer to us, it came over the horizon, it is still behind us. We got a good look at it. The sea was black with ships as far as the eye could see. Transports, cargos, LSTs, LCDs etc. There are over 200 of them. The 3rd Fleet is operating up north in the Philippines up near Luzon. All our big carriers are there with a big, fast, hard-striking force. They will soften Luzon up for the invasion. The Japs have 20 airfields in the vicinity we are in. At 1:30 P.M. this afternoon we were between Borneo and Mindanao. We are in the Sulu Sea.

The last part of Oct. these waters were full of Jap warships of all kinds. They were on their way up to meet our Navy in the greatest sea battle in History. Jap planes attacked our transports today but no damage was done. Some Jap planes were shot down, about a half hour later we went to General Quarters again but our fighter planes shot the Jap planes down. Tomorrow morning at dawn on Uncle Day, our troops will land.

Friday, December 15, 1944: Today is Uncle Day, our troops landed on the island of Mindoro at dawn without opposition. They took the Japs completely by surprise. The carrier planes gave our troops plenty of support and we were kept busy all morning. It will not take long before we have an airstrip on Mindoro. Jap planes attacked us all morning, none of the ships in our task force were damaged, we shot down quite a few Jap planes. The Japs attacked us with fighters, dive bombers and torpedo planes. It was a rugged affair with plenty of close calls for everyone. Jap planes were coming from every direction dropping bombs, strafing and cutting the water with torpedoes. Our ships were twisting and turning as each ship fired away. Bursting shells covered the sky and Jap planes were falling all around us. Some Jap planes would just skim the water as they attacked, others dove right down on us and some more would fly about mast height looking for a big juicy target. Big splashes could be seen very close to the ships and sometimes it looked like a Jap plane crashed right into our ships but at the last moment it would just miss and crash into the water, then there would be a big explosion. Two dive bombers dove at one of our carriers one right behind the other but both just missed the carrier crashing into the sea. They did not miss by much. They were both on a suicide dive. A big torpedo plane was coming at us very close to the water but we blew it to bits. It made an awful explosion. When a Jap plane attacks low in the water he is surrounded by exploding shells and you can see the 40 mm. machine gun shells bouncing off the water. I would not want to get in the way of one. It is just like you take a stone and scale it across a pond. Sometimes you think they are going to bounce right on our ships. One destroyer had a torpedo plane come at it, but it turned away just in time, the plane exploded into the water. The Jap planes skim close to the water on their way to hit us as our guns fire away at them. The Jap gets close and closer and it looks like he will make it and then all of a sudden you hit him and he explodes. It is a race to see who gets to his target first. While this is going on Jap planes are attacking the ships from all angles and directions. One plane blew up in front of us and a parachute came down a few seconds later in the same spot, there was no one in the parachute.

It was a good, clear sunny day, the kind of a day we don't mind if the Japs attack. The Japs kept us busy all morning. While this was going on the big 3rd Fleet was a couple of hundred miles away on the east coast of Luzon, hitting the airfields at Manila and the area around there. Our carrier planes destroyed 77 Jap planes on the ground. Fifteen came up to intercept our planes but they were shot down. We stayed at our battle stations from 4 A.M. in the morning until 8 P.M. They do not need us anymore. Our planes from Leyte can take over tomorrow morning. We are going to return to our base for supplies. We will return the same way we came. We received word that we are heading right into a typhoon with winds better than 80 miles an hour. We had to tie everything down so it would not be blown away. We had our chow at battle stations today, it consisted of sandwiches and cake. The mess cooks brought the food to each battle station.

Saturday, December 16, 1944: All hands got up at 5:45 A.M.

this morning. The Capt. spoke and told us that we had to return to Mindoro because the rain and wind from the typhoon at Leyte kept the planes grounded. The carrier planes from our task force will protect the troops and ships at Mindoro and also the empty returning transports. This morning a destroyer came alongside to get fuel, but it did not stay long because Jap planes were close by. We stayed at our battle stations all morning and afternoon until 7:30 P.M., this evening. Jap planes attacked us again, two suicide planes barely missed the carrier U.S.S. *Marcus Island*. It looked like she was hit at first because of the heavy smoke that covered about half the carrier, it rose high into the sky when the bombs and planes exploded. We secured from General Quarters but had to go right back again. More suicide planes came in but the 5 inch guns from our ship shot them down. We had sandwiches, cakes and coffee at battle stations again today. I got the 8 to midnight watch, it looks like you can't get away from those 40 mm. mounts.

December 17, 1944: All hands got up at 5:30 A.M. this morning. About 1 P.M. this afternoon we should be out of the Philippines and out into the open sea again. We stayed at General Quarters until 2 P.M. this afternoon, because we had to go through Surigao Strait, it is very narrow there. The land is very close to you on both sides and you can expect attacks from planes, torpedo boats etc. The light cruiser *Nashville* was attacked by Jap suicide planes, about 140 men were killed. The Capt. was also killed when the suicide planes crashed into them, bombs and all. When they were returning through here at night they were also attacked by torpedo boats. We cannot afford to take any chances after that. Maybe that is why we are going through the Strait in the daytime. Our planes can spot anything hiding behind one of the islands. I never saw so many islands. They are all around us. If you ever came in here without a compass you would be lost for a long time, trying to find your way out. These islands are very green with plenty of jungle. There must be plenty of Japs still on them watching us as we pass by. The islands are all sizes, shapes and forms. If you got lost in here you would never get out and if you landed on one of the islands you don't know if the Japs would be waiting to kill you or one of the cannibals to eat you. I would not want to get stranded here. I suppose the Japs have shore batteries on quite a few of these islands. The Japs have 20 to 24 airfields around here and a lot of them are hidden in the jungle. Our trip through the Philippines was like going into a hornets' nest, we were right in the Japs' backyard. You would say that it could not be done before we started, with all their land-based suicide planes to throw at us, and warships and subs and torpedo boats to use anytime they wanted to try. This was about the most ticklish campaign of the war because we were in sight of Jap-held islands and airfields all the time. I don't blame them for not sending our latest warships in here. The Japs would have loved to knock off one of our big carriers in here. The old battleships we had with us were damaged by the Japs at Pearl Harbor, Dec. 7, 1941. The Press News said that by taking Mindoro, one of the main islands in the Philippines, we now have a sea and air route to China. Mindoro is only about 500 miles from the coast of China. Mindoro was called the boldest amphibious stroke of the Pacific War, it unlocked the sea approaches to embattled China by crossing to the western side of the Philippine Archipelago from Leyte. We covered a few hundred miles when we traveled the width of the Philippines.

It was the 6th army that we landed on Mindoro. When we secured from General Quarters at 2 P.M. this afternoon I had to stay on watch, I got the 12 to 4 P.M. watch. There I go again, I just can't get away from these battle stations. I should get time and a half. I slept topside tonight until 11:15 P.M., then I went on the midnight to 4 A.M. watch.

Monday, December 18, 1944: I hit the steel at 4 A.M. this morning and all hands got up at 6 A.M. I could stand some sleep. I forget when I last got some.

Well, we are out in the open sea again, and on our way to Palau. Two destroyers pulled alongside this morning and got fuel from us. We were kept busy handling the lines. There was a dog on one of the destroyers, he was right at home, he is a real veteran now. I wonder where they picked him up. It was the first time

I ever saw an animal on a warship. Capt. Hoffman spoke this morning and said we will go to Palau for fuel, because we are low on it, and from there we would go to Manus Island in the Admiralty group for ammunition and stores. Manus is just below the equator about 1500 miles from Leyte. It is between New Guinea and New Ireland. It will take us about 3 days to go from Palau to Manus. The Capt. also congratulated us for the fine work we did in this very important campaign. He hopes we can get some rest now after getting very little sleep for the past 5 days. We were at battle stations nearly all the time and had sandwiches for chow. Everyone could stand a good night's sleep. He also said that this task force also destroyed many Jap planes in those 5 days. Over 100 planes were destroyed by our force and most of them were suicide planes. On the way back from the Mindoro invasion the planes from our carriers attacked the Jap airfields, all around us, and destroyed a lot of planes on the ground and in the air. If all those planes that were destroyed by our carrier planes had a chance to attack us it would have been much tougher for us and many of our ships and men would not have returned, plus thousands of wounded. We owe a lot to the men from our carriers, we are very grateful to them. It's too bad Billy Mitchell is not alive to see the great work the planes are doing on the enemy. The country without air supremacy is lost. It is the No. 1 weapon. The Admiral in charge of our task force also sent a message to all the ships and praised us for the great work we did. He also said the escort carriers proved themselves for future operations, and their planes did a fine job. This was the first time old ships and escort carriers were ever called on to do such a ticklish and important job. They buried one of the carrier pilots at sunset last night. Now that we have Mindoro, the rich islands of Borneo, Celebes, Java, Sumatra etc. will be cut off from the Japs. Eighty per cent of the world's supply of tin comes from this territory, plus other important supplies. One of the destroyers in our task force has been holding our mail, but it did not get a chance to give it to us because it would be too dangerous but now it is safe to try, and this evening about 5 P.M. it pulled alongside and transferred 13 bags of mail to our ship. We had mail call at 7 P.M. This was our first mail in almost a month. All the mail was about a month old. I got 2 letters from my sister Mary. I slept topside on some 5 inch ammunition cases. It was a beautiful night to sleep under the stars. It was not as dark as the nights in the Philippines. It was so dark there at night that you could not see your fingers in front of you. I slept with my clothes on as usual, just took off shoes and sox. I read an article today about all the poison snakes in the Philippines. The boa constrictors are 25 ft. long and the cobras 17 ft. long. There is also some very rugged country in the Philippines, and the jungles are real tough, there are also plenty of wild animals and savages in the jungle.

Tuesday, December 19, 1944: I got up at 3:15 A.M., got the 4 to 8 watch. We got paid this morning. I will send the rent money home and also send Mary some money for Xmas. We pulled into Palau at noon today. It was a warm, sunny day. I slept on some empty 40 mm. cases. I put some cardboard on them and lay on top of it. It rained about 1.30 A.M. so I had to get up and wait for it to stop. When it stopped raining there were some swabs close by, so I used one to dry off a place on deck. I then continued my sleep. I had to laugh at one of the fellows, he was running around in the rain, jumping over empty shell cases, trying to pick up his shoes before he got soaked. I'll bet he stubbed his toes a few times. The rain pours down on you before you know it and then it is a big scramble as everyone runs in all directions to get under cover. When the rain stops everyone steps out and goes back to his spot again. There is never a dull moment out here.

Wednesday, December 20, 1944: We pulled next to a tanker this morning at 5:30 A.M. They had a big cat on the tanker, he looked well fed and was purring away, very contented. The Press News said about 200 B–29s hit Japan. They came from bases in China and Saipan. They hit Japan 4 times in 1 week, very heavy damage was done. As we get close to Japan the fighting will get tougher. In the European War the Germans counterattacked and advanced 25 miles, the weather there is cold and the fighting is rugged. At noon today we left Palau for Manus. The mail was passed out this afternoon, it was dated Dec. 3, 1944. The Marines had a catch with a softball this afternoon on the stern. They do this nearly every chance they get.

December 21, 1944: It is really rugged sleeping on those 40 mm. tanks, its like trying to sleep on a lot of pails turned upside down. The edges really dig into you. The Press News this morning said that our forces on Leyte are running into stiff fighting and the weather is very rainy and muddy. When our forces landed there Oct. 17, 1944, 150,000 troops landed. They said over 600 transports and cargo ships were in on the invasion. Bull Halsey's 3rd Fleet has been doing quite a job on the Japs on Luzon. Old Bull would rather do that than eat. The Japs lost hundreds of planes, many ships, trains, trucks, etc., around Manila where the 3rd Fleet hit. They are softening up Luzon for the invasion. Tomorrow we cross the equator. We have crossed it quite a few times.

Friday, December 22, 1944: After getting off watch this morning at 4 A.M. I washed a working shirt and hat and then tied them on the blower on the 2nd level to dry. Then I went below and took a shower. When I finished I went to the crew's lounge and fell asleep on one of the benches. I got about 1 hour's sleep. The fellows usually wash their clothes in their under shorts or shirts off because you sweat so much. You need a special soap when you wash the clothes in salt water. The regular soap is no good, you do not get any suds. I went to Mass in the crew's lounge at 6:45 A.M. It lasted about 15 minutes. We crossed the equator today and the men did not waste any time on the men who were crossing it for the first time. It's an old custom that every time a ship crosses the equator the new men are initated by the men who have crossed it before. The men who have crossed before are called shellbacks and the new men polliwogs. When the ceremony is over the new men are shellbacks. They will then be able to take it out on the new men just like us shellbacks are going to take it out on them today. We had to go through the same thing ourselves in 1942 when we crossed the equator. Even the officers have to take orders from the lowly seamen. The shellbacks have a great time for themselves at the expense of the polliwogs.

I will try to explain some of the things that happen during the initiation. All the shellbacks are on the prowl for polliwogs and when they see one everyone goes after him. It is quite a scramble to see who gets there first. They cut the poor polliwogs hair off in big chunks and when they get through with it you would think the moths were at it. Boy what a mess, he might just as well have all his hair cut off. After the haircut his head is covered with machine grease. Some of the officers had to walk around in a pair of winter drawers put on backwards. Their hair was also full of grease. A special group of shellbacks were dressed like pirates, they were called the royal policemen. They carried long clubs the size of a baseball bat, made of canvas and full of rags and cotton soaked in salt water. When you got hit with one of these you felt it. The officers had to eat the crew's food and shine the lowly seamen's shoes. They also had the big salt water hose turned on them. They looked like a bunch of drowned rats. Everyone was really enjoying the show. The polliwogs also had to kiss the big fat belly of a shellback that was covered with thick grease. When they got their face close to his belly a shellback would push his face into the greased belly. The shellback who had the grease on his stomach only wore a diaper and bonnet. He was something to see with his big roly-poly stomach. Then the lowly polliwogs were brought before King Neptune and his Court. When they bent over to greet his Honor, someone with a rod of electricity would touch him on the rear end and he would jump in the air. He was then put on an operating table with his eyes covered. An electric knife that gave a shock and also shot red stuff that looked like blood was run across his stomach. Every time the knife would touch his stomach he would jump, by now he must have thought they were operating on him. When they took the cloth off his eyes and he saw his stomach covered with red liquid he was positive they had cut him open. By this time everyone was in stitches laughing. There was plenty of room for all to see because it was held topside on the fantail. Then he went on to another shellback who shot some salt water down his throat. The royal barber was next to work on the polliwog. They really chopped his hair, it will take months for it to grow back right. When they finished chopping his hair, they covered his head with catsup, mustard, broke eggs over it. The stuff was dripping all over his face and down his back. He really looked like a sad sack. They did many other funny things to the poor polliwogs before it was over. The last thing the polliwog had to do was to get on their hands and knees and go between a long line of men on both sides of them about 50 altogether. They really warmed the rear ends of the poor polliwogs with their wet canvas clubs. At the end of the line the polliwogs ran into a big fireman's hose that drowned them with salt water. One kid only about 18 yrs. old felt very funny because he only had a pair of girl's pink panties on, and his face was made up with lipstick. He really looked like a girl. If his parents could have seen him they would have died laughing. The ones who had their rear ends paddled will not be able to sit down for a week. When the ceremony was finally finished the polliwogs could call themselves shellbacks. Later on they would receive a big certificate with their name on it stating that they were no longer a lowly polliwog but a shellback. King Neptune's picture would be on it and it would also be signed by one of the officers. If you were watching these ceremonies you would never know there was a war on. Everyone had a great time but the poor polliwogs and they really had a rough time, it was a tough initiation. All the other ships in our task force did the same thing. Some of the fellows ended up in sick bay.

The carrier pilots put on a show this morning, they did every stunt in the books. They also played follow the leader. One pilot came down straight in a roll, we thought he was going to crash into the water but he came out of it on time. Last night one of our TBF planes crashed just as it was getting dark. The pilot was saved, but they could not find the other 2 men. This plane is a torpedo bomber. It was pretty dark to see them even if they were near you. It got dark about 6 P.M. tonight. I slept under the stars but the rain woke me up at 10:30 P.M. After it stopped I went back to sleep.

Saturday, December 23, 1944: I had to get up again because of the rain. It rained about 1:30 A.M. I went below and sweat it out for a while and then got up at 3:15 to go on watch. Went to Mass this morning. We pulled into Manus Island in the Admiraltys at 8:30 A.M. It was very hot here today. This is a very big harbor. There must be over 100 ships in here. There are 14 escort carriers here. We have many steel Quonset buildings here. There are also repair ships here. We have many troops and ships here. This morning we got 88 bags of mail. It was the mail that has been following us for a long time and it finally caught up with us. We had recreation on the beach but there is not much over there. It is just like the rest of the other recreation places we hit. They gave us a couple of bottles of beer and we walked around for a couple of hours. Some of the men had bats and balls with them so they had a game of baseball. You could go swimming also. Only a few men from each division are allowed to go to the beach. I rate recreation tomorrow. We got fuel and supplies today. Capt. Hoffman said we will be here for 5 days. We are ready to leave anytime. There is nothing here, the weather is also much warmer. They can give this place back to the natives. A tugboat pulled in with an escort carrier. It was in bad shape, 3 of the after mounts were blown away. It must have taken an awful licking. Their casualties must have also been high. Someone said it was the *Reno*. We had movies topside tonight.

Sunday, December 24, 1944: All hands got up at 6 A.M. Our section went to the beach for recreation this morning. Everyone got a couple of bottles of beer, we also went in for a swim.

I did not go over on the beach, it is not worth going over there. Mass was held on the fantail this morning at 10 A.M. The Priest said Midnight Mass will be held in the mess hall tonight. Today is the day before Xmas. I had a working party on the fantail this afternoon carrying supplies. We are going to get 4 months' supply of food while we are here, plus ammunition. We will not get much rest while here. The Press News said the Germans have finally been stopped after going through our lines 40 miles. Our super forts from Saipan hit Japan 5 times in 4 days. It gets dark about 6 P.M. It was not so hot today, the rains cooled it off. I was very dirty from the working party so I took a shower. Before going to sleep on the ammunition tanks I told Witt who has the 8 to midnight watch to wake me up at 11:45 P.M. so I could go to the Xmas Midnight Mass. We had a very big turnout, about 150 were there. We sang Xmas carols and I went to Communion. It was all over about 12:30 A.M.

Merry Christmas, Monday, December 25, 1944: We had a mail call while I was asleep last night. When I came from Midnight Mass to the compartment there was a big box of cookies in a wooden box waiting for me. They were good and fresh. I was surprised to get them, I did not expect anything. I passed them out to the fellows. When ever anyone gets food from home he shares it with the rest of the fellows in his division. After I had a good feed of cookies I went up to my nest topside and fell asleep. It rained a little but I did not move. Back home the weather was near zero and the snow had fallen. Out here you can sleep under the stars with nothing over you. The only thing I took off while I was sleeping was my shoes and sox. We sleep that way all the time. All hands got up at 6 A.M. I had an early breakfast because I was on a working party. They let us eat first, that is the only time they let us eat before anyone else. How thoughtful. They can't put us on the working party quick enough. We worked all morning carrying stores. It was a very hot day today. This will be my 3rd Xmas away from the States. This morning one of the pilots from our ship was presented with a medal for rescuing a fighter pilot near Guam. It was right under the Japs' nose, they were also attacked by Jap fighter planes while in the water. This was before our troops landed on Guam. They were very lucky to come out of it alive, because the water all around them was sprayed with machine gun fire from the attacking Jap planes. The Jap guns from the beach also fired at them. Tonight we had a big turkey dinner for Xmas. It was a very good meal. Everyone left the mess hall with a full stomach. We took on a lot of supplies today, we will continue to get them while we are here.

Tuesday, December 26, 1944: About 500 of us got in an LCT for recreation on the beach. We brought sandwiches, cookies and beer with us. Our troops drove the Japs off this island about 10 months ago. Some natives went by in their boats while we were on the beach, one of them had a big, red shirt around him. Some of the others wore American and Australian hats and pants. You could play ball if you wanted to, they had swimming on the other side of the island. Today was a very hot day. The sun was not out but the humidity was tough and there was no breeze. You could sweat just standing around. This is not much of a recreation center but it gives the fellows a chance to get off the ship and walk on land for a change. It also gives you a chance to get out of some working parties.

We have been working very hard, day and night, since we got here. We will handle hundreds of tons of supplies while we are here. Down at the beach the breakers are very high and the undertow is very strong and dangerous. The coral is also very sharp on your feet. One of the men from our ship went swimming today and the undertow sucked him under and out to sea before anyone knew it, he was seen no more, he just disappeared. He tried to grab one of the men next to him but his hands slipped off. This place is a regular trap. The undertow will suck you out and under before you know it. The fellow who drowned must have hit his head on some coral under the water. Everyone looked all over the water but we could not see him. He was a very nice fellow and everyone liked him. An LCT picked us up at 3:30 P.M. to bring us back to the ship. We had movies topside tonight.

Wednesday, December 28, 1944: I got some mail today. I was on a working party today, it was very hot and humid. The men really sweat today while on the working party. The battleship *Iowa* came in this morning, about 10 of our escort carriers left today. Many ships and landing craft of ours have been leaving every day. The invasion of Luzon will take place soon. They call the suicide divers the Happy divers. Mass was said at 6:45 P.M. this evening in the mess hall. The fellow who drowned yesterday while on recreation was well prepared to die. He went to the Midnight Mass Christmas Eve, he also went to Communion. This was the day before he drowned. His name was Henry Mostiller. It rained very hard on the 8 to midnight watch tonight.

Thursday, December 28, 1944: We were supposed to have recreation today but no one went. We might pull out tomorrow, I hope so. All we do here is carry supplies. Yesterday the Press News said the Leyte campaign is over. The Japs' casualties on land and sea were 115,000, they also lost about 3000 planes in the Philippines campaign so far. It rained all day. Mass was held in the crew's lounge at 4:15 P.M. The movie tonight is "Coney Island."

Friday, December 29, 1944: Eighteen big transports came in but they will leave tomorrow. Warships and supply ships have been going out every day. They must be on their way to the Luzon invasion, no one knows when it will come off. Tokyo Rose said it will be invaded Jan. 9, 1945. I will see how close she comes. A big general in Japan said the war now depends on the suicide divers. When we went to the invasion of Mindoro we took the same route Gen. MacArthur took in a torpedo boat when he escaped from Bataan. Tonight we took aboard some men from the torpedo boat outfit. Officers and seamen, they are very rugged looking and earn their money the hard way. They came aboard this evening. They will get off at Leyte, on our way to Luzon. We also took on a lot of mail for other ships, it will go off at Leyte.

Saturday, December 30, 1944: We left Manus Island at 7 A.M. It will take 4 or 5 days before we reach Leyte, we are in no hurry, it is about 1500 miles north of Manus.

Sunday, December 31, 1944: Last night was a good night to sleep topside. Before we fall asleep we usually talk for a while. Last night Stevenson, Modock, and myself talked about our liberty in Calif. and Sydney, Australia, and that Sydney was the best liberty port.

We hit the sack about 7 P.M. It gets dark early here. Some of the other men were playing cards and shooting dice where no one will see them. Some fellows will make enough money gambling to retire, if they invest it right. You could see the moon in the distance as the ships cut through the calm water. Mass was held in the mess hall today. We got very little fresh meat on at Manus. Most of the food we got was canned. The meat we eat for the next 2 months will consist of Spam and baloney and canned hot dogs. Tonight is New Year's Eve, my third one out here.

Monday, January 1, 1945: Happy New Year, today is the first day of 1945. New Year's Day. It is just another day out here. I think the war will be over this year. We are too strong and power-ful now, nothing can stop us. We expect plenty of trouble from the enemy, but we have too much on the ball for him to win. Our supply lines get longer as we advance closer to Japan. It is only about 3000 miles from the east coast of the U.S.A. to Europe but it is better than 11,000 from the east coast to the Philippines. It is a long tiresome trip for the transports to get here and it takes many weeks under the hot sun of the Pacific. The troops are glad to get off and put their feet on land again, after sweating in the holds of the ships for so many weeks, and never knowing when a sub will put a torpedo into them, to drown like rats. Over a month to get out of here is a long time to wait. We passed a big convoy today, it consisted of 116 ships. It was quite a sight. It means another big headache for the Japs. We got a big pan of cake from the bakers today. We had a party for ourselves, nothing is wasted out here, especially if it's sweet. Tennessee and Southern Calif. play in the Rose Bowl today. The sea was very calm and the sunset was beautiful, what a sight.

Tuesday, January 2, 1945: All hands got up at 5:30 A.M. Not much news, still at sea on way to Leyte. We passed a hospital ship today, it was coming from Leyte. The Dr. was around inspecting the ship. We also held field day through the ship today.

Wednesday, January 3, 1945: The U.S.S. *Montpelier* pulled into Leyte at 10 A.M. It is a very big island. They had over 600 ships here when they invaded Leyte. The first thing we did when we got here was to get fuel. A lot of natives in boats pulled close to the ship. There were men, women and children in them. Guess they had the whole family. We threw cigarettes, food, and cloth-ing to them. Their boats held about 4 people. It had a big piece of bamboo on each side so it would not tip over. One of the girls in the boat was 20 years old and she was very good-looking, her teeth were like pearls, she gave us a big smile and was very friendly. Some spoke a little English. One of the boats had the words "American Victory" and a little American flag. On the side it had LST 964. One of the Filipino stewards from our ship spoke to them in their language, he also gave them cigarettes. They wore many different kinds of clothing, mostly Army clothes. Some of the girls wore sailor's dungarees. Leave it to the Navy to take care of the women. The Japs were very cruel to them, they also killed many of the civilian population. They used some of them for bayonet practice. I had to laugh at one of the natives, when the cook gave him a pair of sox he said "No use, me have no shoes." He ended up getting a pair of shoes. Our PT boat passengers left today. We have a lot of planes here, all types. We have planes in the air at all times just in case the Japs should attack us.

I hope the rainy season is over, it was warm and sunny today. A lot of flying fortresses and other bombers left on a bombing mission. They must be going to hit Luzon.

Thursday, January 4, 1945: We had an alert at 5:15 A.M. Jap planes hit Leyte. Our troops on land opened up on them, they did not come close enough for us to fire at them. I watched some of our P–51 mustang fighters put on a show. This is the best fighter plane in the world and it is also the fastest. This plane is terrific. All hands went to quarters this morning. They told us that we will leave Leyte this afternoon at 4 P.M. for the invasion of Luzon. A destroyer came alongside for supplies. There is a lot of talk about the fleet hitting Japan about the same time we invade Luzon. They said the Luzon invasion will be the biggest invasion in the Pacific so far. I was talking to the Filipino steward today and asked him what the natives in the small boats had to say the other day. He said one of the girls was a teacher and the good-looking one was in the third year of high school. When the Japanese invaded the Philippines they wanted the teachers to teach the pupils Japanese and she refused. She had to flee for her life, they lived in the hills all these years. The Japs burned their homes, and attacked the women. The steward asked one of the Filipinos where his knife was and he said that he left it in a Jap's stomach. They wanted to know if we had taken Bataan yet, he told them that we would take it this year. The Press News said the Germans have lost most of the ground they gained in their big drive a few weeks ago. Our Air Force and Army is doing a job on them now.

We cleaned the ship extra good today, because we will be at
General Quarters most of the time. The bakers are baking a lot
of extra bread, rolls and cookies. Our diet will consist of sandwiches for quite some time, we will be at our battle stations nearly
all the time. It is 3:30 P.M. as I write. Someone said that General
MacArthur is going to be in our task force and he will be on the
cruiser *Boise*. I will stop for now and write later.

I am back again writing. At 4:30 P.M. the U.S.S. *Montpelier*
left Leyte for the Luzon invasion. Capt. Hoffman spoke and said
the troops will land on the west coast of Luzon at Lingayen Gulf,
it is above Manila, the capital of the Philippines. A task force is
ahead of us with the old battleships, the ones that were at Pearl
Harbor Dec. 7th. They and the other warships will bombard
Luzon for 3 days, then the troops will land. In the meantime
Bull Halsey's powerful 3rd Fleet will send hundreds of its carrier
planes against Hong Kong, the rest of the China coast, Formosa,
and Japan itself on a daring raid to knock out anything it comes
across. We will take the same route as we took when we invaded
Mindoro. We will go *right* through the Philippines and then
turn north at the China Sea and pass Bataan and Corregidor and
Manila. We will be about 400 miles from Hong Kong. We will
cover the transports against Jap planes and warships. Gen. Mac-
Arthur is on the light cruiser *Boise* No. 47. It is on our starboard
side not too far away. If the Japs only knew he was here in their
midst they would throw everything at us. It must bring back
memories as he sails along through the Philippines. It is over 3
years since he came through these same waters that we are passing
through. The last time he came through here he received orders
to leave Bataan & Corregidor on a PT boat for Australia. Now
his orders are to return and capture all that territory from the
Japs. He has something to fight with now and he will put it to
good use. The last time he fought the Japs here it was on a weak
shoestring, but not this time. You can't beat the enemy with your
bare hands. His men put up a courageous fight but they did not
have enough men or equipment and were badly outnumbered in
every department. This time he is riding in a big cruiser. The last

time he was on a small PT boat with his wife and son and a great man at the wheel by the name of Bulkeley. I'll bet MacArthur would like to have Bulkeley and his crew with him on this trip.

While on the 6 to 8 watch you could see a lot of fires on shore. When you go through Surigao Strait, land is very close on both sides. Four of our transports were sunk in this same place not too long ago. Surigao separates Leyte from the big island of Mindanao.

Friday, January 5, 1945: Had a good sleep topside last night. All hands got up at 5:30 A.M. for General Quarters. Went to Mass and Communion in crew's lounge at 7 A.M. It was the first Friday. I got my hair cut today, took shower, shined my shoes and sewed a patch on my dungarees. There are 18 transports behind us, we are only going about 8 knots. At 3 P.M. this afternoon they sounded torpedo defense. A midget sub about 16 ft. long got into our formation and fired two torpedoes. It was a close call but no damage was done. The sub surfaced and fired its torpedoes. It was a close call for the light cruiser U.S.S. *Boise*. This is the ship Gen. MacArthur is on. He is very close to us on our starboard quarter. All eyes were on MacArthur's ship, they said he enjoyed every minute of the excitement. The fellows liked to put the spyglasses on the cruiser *Boise* and watch General MacArthur. One of our planes dove at the sub and dropped some bombs, after that one of our destroyers rammed it, then they dropped depth charges on it. The depth charges sent an awful lot of water high into the air. This is a good place for subs because there are many islands here to hide behind. The Japs know we have to come this way also. Today was a warm sunny day, the sea is very calm around here because we are surrounded by islands. Capt. Hoffman said that one of our escort carriers was sunk last night by the Japs. The Capt. also said that there will be 850 ships in the Luzon invasion. This does not count small craft or warships. This will be the largest invasion of the Pacific War. The task force ahead of us is the first group, we are the 2nd group, there are about 70 warships in the first group. This includes 12 escort carriers and 6 battleships. Tomorrow morning they will start bombarding and they will continue for 3 days. The troops will land on the morning of Jan. 9. The escort carrier we lost in the force ahead of us was hit by a suicide plane, it was a mass of flames and out of control, it couldn't be saved. It happened off Mindoro. This evening we are in the Sulu Sea heading northward toward Luzon. On Dec. 29, 1944, while we were at Manus I wrote in my diary that Tokyo Rose said we would invade Luzon Jan. 9, 1945. She hit it right on the nose.

Saturday, January 6, 1945: The weather is just like the summer time back home, the sun is out all day, the sea is calm and the sky is blue. At night it is cool. They started Condition 2 watches this morning, we are back to 4 hours on watch and 4 hrs off again but it usually ends up with us being at our battle stations most of the time. We passed a big island by the name of Panay, it is below Mindoro. Our bombarding task force started bombarding at dawn. This morning, while they were bombarding, 70 mine-sweepers started to clear the harbor of mines. At sunset this evening we were in the same place the escort carrier *Ommaney Bay* was sunk. Our task force leads the parade of the 850 ship convoy as we pass Mindoro at midnight tonight. Mindoro is across from China. Tomorrow night we enter the south China Sea and no longer surrounded by the Jap-held islands of the Philippines. We had sunset General Quarters tonight.

Sunday, January 7, 1945: I got off watch at 4 A.M. We were close to Mindoro, you could see it very good. We are not going very fast because of the convoy. Our speed is about 9 knots day and night. We make a good target for Jap subs. It was bright on the midnight to 4 A.M. watch. The moon came out at 1:05 A.M. I hit the steel at 4 A.M. All hands got up at 5:30 A.M. There was a big fire on Mindoro. I do not know what caused it, maybe a Jap plane did it. Mindoro is a very big island. At dawn a Jap bomber attacked us and dropped some bombs very close to one of the destroyers next to us. We didn't fire at it because we did not know if it was one of ours or not, it was not very bright. One of the fighter planes from our carriers caught up with it and shot it down. Some of our destroyers got fuel from the tankers this morning off the coast of Mindoro. The ships do not stop but continue on course with the tankers alongside getting fuel at the same time. About 10 A.M. 130 B–24 Liberator Bombers flew over us on their way to hit Luzon. There is some talk of our warships being hit by Jap bombs, suicide planes and shore batteries at Luzon. Someone said 17 of them were hit so far from our force of 70 warships. This is the bombarding group that was ahead of us. They said the Japs attacked with dive bombers, torpedo planes and fighters. The Admiral in charge was also wounded. We shall get more news later. We should pass Corregidor, and Bataan this evening. We will also enter the South China Sea. The ships in this invasion force will be the first Allied ships to enter these waters since the Japs took over at the beginning of the war in 1942. We are a long way from home and right in old Tojo's kitchen now. Halsey's 3rd Fleet sent his carrier planes against Formosa, they destroyed 100 Jap planes on the ground, plus over 200 more damaged and shot down. Sunday Mass was held in the crew's lounge tonight. At sunset Jap planes attacked us. One of them almost hit the *Boise*, the ship MacArthur is on, but the *Phoenix* shot it down. He had quite a few close calls so far, you would think that the Japs knew what ship he was on.

Monday, January 8, 1945: About 2 A.M. this morning 2 Jap destroyers got close to our warships, they were going to sneak in and knock off some of the big transports. They would have done a lot of damage if they ever got near them, but one of our destroyers sank one of them and the other one got away. At 1 A.M. this morning Jap planes were overhead. They came in on us and we greeted them with heavy gunfire. We stayed at battle stations all day until 8 P.M. For breakfast we had some hash and 1 bun, for dinner baloney sandwich, and for supper we had coffee, baloney sandwich, 1 cookie and 1 candy bar. This morning our ship shot down its lucky #13 Jap plane and one probable. The sun was out all day and the sea was calm. We had rest periods during the day while at battle stations. Some of the fellows read, others played cards and others got some rest. A few men at a time would be allowed to do this while the others manned the guns. This evening our ship and

MacArthur's ship left the front of the convoy with some other war-ships and went to the middle of another group of transports that are supposed to be the first to land tomorrow morning. We stayed with them for a while, but returned to the front of the convoy as Jap planes, suicide planes, attacked the warships up ahead. When we got close to one of our escort carriers a Jap suicide plane flew through all kinds of exploding shells and crashed into it. There was a great explosion and the stern of the carrier looked like a big red furnace, black smoke was also coming from it. It was an awful sight. It looked like it would be impossible to save it, everything was exploding on it and with all that high octane gas and bombs on it you never knew when it would be blown sky high. The cas-ualties must be very high. They finally got it under control and the smoke and flames were not so great. Someone said it was dead in the water and a skeleton crew was left on it. It got dark and we could not see anymore. This happened on our starboard side and not too far from MacArthur's ship. By now I'll bet MacArthur has his fingers crossed. He must be wondering if he will make this in-vasion before his ship is hit by Jap suicide planes. The Japs have been hitting all around him with subs, suicide planes and war-ships. Maybe Tokyo Rose also knows what ship he is on. The 3rd Fleet and our warships are hitting Lingayen Gulf on Luzon. Our troops will land tomorrow morning. Our warships will finish their work today. They have been pounding away at the Japs for the past 3 days. The Press News said that a report from Japan said that a large task force was bombarding Luzon, just above Manila, and that a large convoy of transports were passing Mindoro. At 8 P.M. we left General Quarters, we were there since early this morning. I slept on some ammunition cans under the stars tonight. I'll have to get up at 11:30 P.M.

Tuesday, January 9, 1945: Got up at 11:30 P.M. for watch, off at 4 A.M. then took shower, shaved and wrote in diary. It is 5 A.M. as I stand under a red light and write. It is very quiet, everyone is asleep, the rest of the men are on watch. When I finish I will open a can of peaches that I put away for a time like this. The chow lately has not been good. It was warmer sleeping topside this morning. We must be close to Lingayen Gulf. Our troops did not sleep very good last night. This will be the last day on earth for a lot of them. They are so young and healthy now and in a few hours many of them will be dead or wounded or crippled for life. Some will not even reach the beach. The Japs must have about 200,000 troops on Luzon. I will stop now and write later. I will go to town on the can of peaches now.

I am back again writing, it is 8 P.M. same day. I will try to cover what happened today. All hands got up at 6 A.M. The troops were supposed to land at 8:30 A.M. but they landed at 9:30 A.M. instead. We did not go into Lingayen Gulf for the invasion. Our job was to stay outside the Gulf and cover the transports in case Jap warships should try to get into the Gulf. This is what the Jap warships tried to do at Leyte Gulf. But they missed their chance, they could have gone in and destroyed about 600 transports and cargo ships. It would have set the war back for a long time. We stayed at battle stations all day until 8 P.M. Our food was brought to us as usual and it was no good as usual. You have to expect it under these conditions. For breakfast we had a bun with peanut butter and beans, dinner was a beef sandwich and 1 cookie and for supper baloney sandwiches, cake and cocoa. Things were pretty quiet for us. The carrier planes from our force hit the enemy all day. Our planes were landing and taking off all day. Before the troops landed the warships bombarded. Our planes also attacked and hit the Japs. Our troops did not have too much opposition on the beach but a lot of gunfire greeted them from the hills. About 5 hours after the landing our troops were using the airfields. The Filipino guerrillas gave our troops a lot of help. Jap planes attacked us but no damage was done, just a lot of close calls. I don't think the Japs have many planes left around here. It was a good, clear sunny day. It will take a few days before we get much information on the invasion. Some of the ships that are in on this invasion are battleships *West Virginia, California, Pennsylvania, Colorado,* escort carriers *Makin Island, Lunga Point, Shamrock Bay.* Cruisers *Denver, Columbia,* and *Phoenix.* Destroyers *Newcomb, Leary, Bryant, Smith, Frazier, Fletcher.* Destroyer escorts

Butler and *O'Flaherty,* also the seaplane tender *Currituck.* Last but not least a couple of Australian warships from our friends down under, the *Arunta* and *Warramunga.*

Wednesday, January 10, 1945: I went on watch at 4 A.M. this morning. Today we escorted some empty transports from Lingayen Gulf, almost to Mindoro, and then we picked up some full transports and escorted them back to Lingayen Gulf. It will be our job to protect these ships back and forth just in case Jap warships should try to attack them, because the territory around here is held by the Japs. You never know when they might sneak out and attack them. On the other side is the coast of China only about 500 miles away.

They did not have anything in the Press News about the invasion yet. The escort carrier that was hit by a suicide plane the other night passed us this afternoon. It is on its way back to Pearl Harbor or the States. It will be out of action for a long time. The sea had big swells this afternoon. A big storm or typhoon many miles away was causing it. The carrier planes landed early because of the pitching and tossing in the rough seas. As usual the Jap planes attacked us at sunset but no damage was done to our ships. The Japs like to attack us when our planes are landing on the carriers. One of our planes was shot down when one of our ships opened up on it. A 40 mm. shell from one of our ships hit our galley and went right through but no one was hit. It must have been a green crew that did the firing, we knew it was one of our own planes so we did not fire.

Thursday, January 11, 1945: I got off watch at 4 A.M. All hands got up at 5:45 A.M. The Press News said our convoy of over 800 ships landed troops on Luzon in Lingayen Gulf, 125 miles above Manila, with light opposition, but hard battles would be fought as time goes on. The landing has closed the Japs' back door. They cannot bring in any supplies, they will have to do with what they got on hand. General MacArthur also landed with the troops. He fooled the Japs on invasion day. The invasion force passed Lingayen Gulf and the Japs thought we were going to land some place else but later on we turned around and went into

Lingayen Gulf. This really threw the Japs off. That is why our troops landed at 9:30 A.M. instead of 8:30 A.M.

Last Dec. while we were at Manus we heard Tokyo Rose on the Radio Tokyo program, from Japan, say the landing would come off on exactly the day it came off. It is too bad she did not mention the time, she might have been right about that also. Gen. MacArthur could have chosen an easier way for himself to get to Lingayen Gulf. He could have landed on the day after the invasion by plane. He did not have to spend 5 days sailing through Jap-held islands. When our troops landed in Lingayen Gulf they landed in the same place the Japs landed at the start of the war. We are going to have condition 2 watch. The Capt. spoke and said the Japs had over 200 airstrips on Luzon and the planes were camouflaged under big palm trees. The planes from the 3 carriers in our force hit Luzon all day. The chow was no good as usual. I slept topside tonight.

Friday, January 12, 1945: We are still escorting ships back and forth from Lingayen Gulf to Mindoro. We pulled alongside a tanker and got fuel. A few Jap reconnaissance bombers flew over today. Jap planes attacked today and one of our empty transports was hit by a torpedo from a Jap torpedo plane. Tonight one of our land-based Corsair fighters had to land on one of our carriers because it was in trouble. It was returning from a strike against the Japs. Our carrier planes were also landing at the same time, after returning from a strike against Luzon, they let the Corsair land. We always like to watch the planes take off and land. It is quite a job to land on a small escort carrier in the daytime, but when it starts to get dark it is really tough.

Tonight one of our TBFs (torpedo bomber-fighter) was returning after a strike against the Japs, its landing gear was shot away by Jap gunfire. All eyes were on it as it kept circling the carrier. This went on for a long time and it kept getting darker by the minute. Every time he got near the carrier we thought he was going to land but he would fly over the carrier, he must have been burning up his fuel. You wondered how he could see the moving carrier in the dark. As the ships cut through the water, we figured his goose was cooked. It was after 8 P.M. as he kept circling in the dark. All the ships had their red running lights in the mast on, and the only light on his carrier was some red lights. He finally came in low to land and as he did everyone held their breath and prayed. He made a perfect landing and when the plane stopped everyone on our ship gave a big cheer that could be heard miles away. Every ship in our group must have done the same thing. The torpedo bomber is a good size and it carries six 300 lb. bombs or one 2000 lb. torpedo, plus machine guns. The pilot not only saved the plane but also the 2 crewmen with him. If he landed in the water they might have been lost in the darkness or drowned because the water was pretty rough and the plane would have tipped over and sunk before they could get out. The pilot on that plane deserves plenty of praise and a citation, he really knew his stuff, he also had it in the clutch. The pressure on him was terrific, I can just imagine how his two crewmen felt. None of us will ever forget that ordeal.

Saturday, January 13, 1945: Not much to write about. Chow was pretty good today, first time in a week. The Press News reported Halsey's Third Fleet hit Indochina. This is the first raid by our forces in the China Sea. It also said the Pacific War is ahead of schedule. In the European War, the Germans lost all of the ground that they had gained a few weeks ago. The only thing that is saving the Germans, is the snow and bad weather. The Air Force because of it, is prevented from delivering its punch.

Sunday, January 14, 1945: We are still off Luzon, covering the arrival and departure of ships. The carrier planes hit Luzon all day again.

The Press News reported Halsey's Third Fleet struck a 25-ship Japanese convoy, near Indochina. Every ship in the convoy was sunk including troopships, destroyers and cruisers. Shore installations and enemy planes were also destroyed.

Sunday Mass was held in the crew's lounge today.

Monday, January 15, 1945: No news today. Routine continued the same. Supper consisted of bread, butter and two cookies.

Friday, January 19, 1945: No news is the reason for not writing for the last few days. Condition 2 watches (4 on and 4 off) were not in effect as we reverted to Condition 3 (4 on and 8 off). We have been at battle stations a majority of the time during the past few days. The other morning at 2 A.M., radar picked up an object a few miles away. A destroyer was dispatched to investigate. Turning on their searchlight nearing the unidentified object, they saw a light flashing on and off. It was a distress signal from a patrol bomber that was forced down at sea. The destroyer took everyone on the bomber aboard ship and proceeded to sink the bomber lest it fall in enemy hands. Our radar was the only one in the whole force that detected the plane. The pilots were very thankful to us for saving their lives. It must have been quite an experience for the crew of the bomber. The sea was very rough and darkness prevented easy recognition by friendly ships. The lookout on the *Montpelier* also helped save three men from a TBF that crashed in the daytime, by a good job of spotting. The sea was very rough that day and visibility was very low. Upon spotting the crew, a destroyer was sent to investigate. Among the three that were rescued, one had a broken leg. They had been returning from a bombing and strafing mission against Luzon. These men were also very lucky to be alive. The Good Lord was watching over them. It's a great feeling to know that someone's life has been saved even if you don't even know or see him.

Our troops on Luzon have advanced thirty-five miles already. Stiffer opposition awaits them as they near Manila.

In the European War, Allied troops have recovered completely the territory lost to the Germans previously. On the Russian Front, the Russians have started their winter drive. They have captured Warsaw and are 260 miles from Berlin, advancing 110 miles in six days.

We are still patrolling the Luzon coast in the South China Sea. Six escort carriers are now with us. Their planes are still hitting Luzon. The pilots and crews are really getting quite a workout. Some of the planes have run into heavy gunfire, some never to return. Other planes come back badly damaged, while still others are forced to crash in the open sea. After finishing one mission, they return to the carriers, reload and return again to plaster Luzon, facing Japanese guns and planes. United States bombers destroyed 70 Jap planes on Clark Field, Manila, alone. The death of one of our air aces, Major McGuire, was a great blow to the men of the fleet. He was shot down over Luzon. After damaging his plane, Japanese planes attacked and delivered the finale to a great American flier. Thirty-eight enemy kills were accredited to him. The only flier surpassing Major McGuire was Major Bong, who is now in the States. Major Bong has accounted for forty enemy planes.

I am sitting in the sun on board the *Montpelier* off the island of Mindoro as I write. I had finished a working party in the hangar deck this morning. We carried food to the issue room. Among the goods that were stored were corn, beets, sugar, flour, beans, etc. This breakout occurs twice a week. Since leaving the States in 1942, I have been outside on deck most of the time. The only time I have occasion to be in the interior, on the most part, is to eat and be detailed on working parties in various sections of the ship. Working in the radio shack continuously would not suit me as it is confined to a limited space and is very hot. The only break is that the operators are excused from working parties. Working parties usually fall to the deck divisions. The engine room is another rough job as the heat from the boilers is unbearable.

Three destroyers were swallowed up by a typhoon last December. We were in the general direction and headed for the typhoon when orders were received to return to Mindoro because our planes were grounded at Leyte.

Saturday, January 20, 1945: We arrived at Mindoro for fuel and ammunition this morning. A destroyer with its smokestack blown away was there. It probably was the one that was with us the night we saw the Jap planes come out of the clouds and drop a bomb squarely down its smokestack. We were on our way to the Mindoro Campaign in December of last year.

There is a large airfield here. It has hundreds of planes and bombers in its runways. Manila is only a short run from here.

China, Borneo and other Jap bases are also within range. A native village is quartered nearby.

We left Mindoro about 4 P.M. and continued patrolling off Luzon. A convoy of empty transports passed us. They were returning from Lingayen Gulf. Schools of numerous sharks were predominant in the waters today.

Captain Hoffman issued a statement tonight, saying that he had something of interest to release to us in a few days. I think it may be another landing on Luzon. Paratroopers may be involved. Tonight's chow was spaghetti, bread, jam and one cookie. Sleeping under the stars will follow directly.

Sunday, January 21, 1945: Mass was held in the crew's lounge this morning and again at 4 P.M. I went to Mass in the afternoon as I had the watch in the morning. Nothing new.

Monday, January 22, 1945: All hands were up at 6 A.M. Sunrise General Quarters were followed. We are still patrolling off Luzon. The water is calm and the sun is hot but there is a little breeze.

Our force consists of six escort carriers, four light cruisers and twenty destroyers. Condition 3 watches were again followed (4 on and 8 off). For breakfast we were served canned grapefruit, a bun, butter and a few other choice items I consider not worth mentioning. Dinner consisted of Spam, green beans, bread, butter and pie. For supper we had stew, bread, jelly and one cookie. Sunset General Quarters was staged at 6:45 P.M. Battle stations were maintained until 7:45 P.M. Cap. spoke and said all ships in our force will shut off all air radar tonight so the Japs would be unable to detect the fleet. Two destroyers will be decoys and leave the force with their radar beaming. Jap warships are believed to be in the immediate area. The trap has been baited with these destroyers acting as guinea pigs. If the destroyers are attacked, the fleet will destroy the attackers. I slept topside again.

Tuesday, January 23, 1945: Field day was held throughout the ship. The Doctor inspected the compartments, etc. Ground forces on Luzon are 50 miles from Manila. In Europe the Russians are 180 miles from Berlin. Premier Stalin predicts Berlin will be occupied by his troops in one month. Action failed to materialize last night.

We were disappointed that the Jap warships did not put in a performance.

Wednesday, January 24, 1945: Mail today or the following day is expected to arrive. Two destroyers are under way from Leyte with mail for the task force.

At 4 P.M. a small boat was spotted by one of our planes. A destroyer was sent to investigate. Word from the destroyer reported that four Japs were alive in the boat. The light cruiser *Phoenix* rushed to the area to retrieve them. The boat turned out to be a motorboat type. The men aboard had been drifting for twenty-one days. The only food they had in all that time was two raw fish. As they were Army personnel and quite a distance from the shore when their motor went dead, they were defenseless against the ocean and drifted out to sea. They will be taken ashore when we dock at one of our islands. They may be still on board when our next invasion is launched which is believed to be Bataan. Food was quickly made ready for them. Being picked up by us, four Japs will not have to die for their emperor.

The planes from Bull Halsey's Third Fleet shot down from the air and destroyed on the ground 250 Japanese planes on Formosa. These planes, coming from Japan, were intended to be flown against our navy and the troops on land at Luzon. Formosa is 200 miles from Luzon.

The Press News stated that General MacArthur has four and a half months of fine weather in which to reconquer Luzon. Our first truck convoy to China commenced a short while ago. The Ledo and Burma Road had been completed by the United States.

Thursday, January 25, 1945: The weather is excellent. The sun shone all day. It's a good thing we are stationed in a hot climate as the appetite is not as sharp, for the food doled out is very limited. Appetites in this climate are lazy from the heat. Even so, the men complain of being hungry most of the time. For breakfast we had two slices of bread, butter, coffee and a few prunes. The Priest conducts Mass twice a day when the opportunity is afforded him. Tonight at 5 P.M., while we were under way a destroyer pulled alongside and transferred 40 bags of mail. The letters were almost two months old. Thirty-five bags containing packages were also received. The goods inside were for the most part spoiled because of the heat.

Friday, January 26, 1945: We are still on patrol in the China Sea. Our troops on Luzon captured Clark Field. This is the largest airfield in the Philippines. It boasts of 15 airstrips with room to spare for the care and maintenance of hundreds of fighter planes and bombers.

Three oil tankers were used to refuel our force today. They started at 8 A.M. and completed refueling operations at 4 P.M. Condition 2 was adhered to during the day's activity in the event that Jap planes should attack.

Tonight we headed south for Mindoro, expecting to arrive there tomorrow morning. At 7 P.M. we left the carriers with their escorts and proceeded south. Our force now consists of cruisers and destroyers as the remaining ships will patrol off Luzon. At 7:45 a Jap submarine was directly in our path but warning from a nearby destroyer averted tragedy. Two destroyers from the fleet covered the area with depth charges in the familiar pattern. Our ship shook with the concussions from the charges. Sinking the submarine was only a matter of time as one of the depth charges took its toll. Japanese submarines are numerous in these waters. A troop transport was sunk by one, just the other day.

100,000 troops were landed in two locations this week. One was made above Bataan, the other below, both on the west coast of Luzon and below Lingayen Gulf. We were scheduled to bombard for the second landing but it was called off because as our troops were rushed ashore, friendly natives were waiting on the shore, waving and carrying American flags. Subic Bay, one of our formidable naval bases, was captured without much opposition. It was our task to supply cover for these landings. Lt. Gen. Robert L. Eichelberger's Eighth Army was the group that took part in the invasion. They landed on the Zambales Coast. It's above the Bataan Peninsula near Subic Bay. General Kreuger's Sixth Army landed at Lingayen Gulf, Luzon, January 9. Other Army officers who played a large role in the Luzon Campaign besides Mac-Arthur, Eichelberger, and Kreuger were: Swift — First Corps;

Griswold — 14th Corps; Patrick — 6th Division; Mullins — 25th Division; Wing — 43 Division; MacNider — 158th Regiment Combat Team; Beightler — 37th Division; Bush — 40th Division.

Saturday, January 27, 1945: At 8 A.M. we arrived at Mindoro. The harbor is shaped like a horseshoe, a natural harbor. Airfields are plentiful here. Planes can be seen landing and in flight from the *Montpelier*. The weather is sunny and hot. It's much cooler at sea for a breeze is always blowing. Manila is only a half hour ride by plane. Our troops are about 24 miles from Manila this morning. A few of us left the ship in a whaleboat this afternoon to get some sand from the beach and take some mail to the post office there. We were the first from the *Montpelier* to touch land in the Philippines. We had to take off our shoes and sox while we carried the sand from the beach to the boat because it was some distance away. One of the airfields is not very far from the beach. Many liberators, 4 engine B-24 bombers, were landing. They had just come back from a bombing mission at Luzon. We did not remain on the beach very long. We thought there would be some mail here at the beach for us but they had none. A Black Widow, a night fighter, crashed with its bombs aboard. Clouds of black smoke rolled into the sky. The pilot in that plane did not stand a chance of escaping the inferno. It was similar to a fuel dump exploding. The light cruiser *Cleveland* is here after just returning from the States. It spent two months there. It had a few bags of mail for us. The mail was a little over three weeks old. Movies were held topside at 8 P.M. It was an old Bing Crosby picture.

The Press News reported the Russians 63 miles from Berlin.

Tonight I had quite a treat for myself. I brought my mattress topside and slept in it. It was the first time I slept with all my clothes off since we left Pearl Harbor three months ago and it sure felt good. In the South Pacific we always slept on the steel deck with our clothes on.

Friday, February 2, 1945: All hands arose at 6 A.M. I had the 8 to 12 watch in the morning. Payday was yesterday. A seaman first class receives $79 a month including overseas' pay which is $10 more than if stationed in the States. It's equivalent to a petty officer's pay stateside. I had a working party in the hangar deck all afternoon. Pigg was in charge. It was like a furnace down there, boy did we sweat. We were filthy when we finished the detail. Some torpedo boats and an LCS pulled alongside today. We transferred supplies and water to them. The PT boats carry 50 cal., 20 mm. and 40 mm. guns, 4 torpedoes plus depth charges. They seemed better armed now than at the beginning of the war. A complement of 15 men makes up the crew. One of the fellows aboard was cleaning a Jap rifle he picked up on the beach. Many ships are at Mindoro. We are staying here for five days. The Captain left the ship today to seek our mail. We have a stack of it somewhere but no one knows where. Word will be sent to all places we stopped at and have them send it to us as soon as possible. Rumor has it that Subic Bay will be our home base. The Bataan Peninsula and Corregidor are easily accessible to us from here. About 100 men had recreation on Mindoro this afternoon.

Sunday, February 4, 1945: I was relieved of watch at 4 A.M. Recreation parties left the ship this morning and again in the afternoon. An LCI pulls alongside the ship to transport the men to Mindoro for recreation. I left the ship at 8:30 A.M. and returned at 11:30 A.M. When the LCI stopped to let us off, we were forced to walk quite a distance to the beach. The LCI, if venturing further, would have been stuck in the sand near the shore. As the water was deep, we shed our shoes and sox, also our pants. The short men had to go in nude. The water was almost to my hips. I'm 6'2" tall. The landing craft opened in the front and there was a high drop to the bottom of the water. It was quite a sight to see everyone wading through the water holding their shoes and clothing over their heads. When recreation is held in the Pacific, one can expect anything. The beach finally being reached, clothing was again put on. On our return trip the procedure was reversed. We really have to work for our recreation here. The beach was very sandy. There was not much activity taking place on recreation but putting my feet on land and walking around really felt good. Swimming was optional. There are Army troops stationed on the island. Jap souvenirs can be had for a price. We took a walk into the jungle and came across a Jap bomber. It was a Betty and pretty well banged up. We also spotted a torpedo on the beach and it was the biggest one I had ever seen. For size the Japanese must possess the largest torpedoes in the world. I imagine it was shot from one of their cruisers or a super sub. The Japanese submarines are also of extreme size. Using the size of my shoe as a foot measuring ruler, I measured the torpedo to be 32 feet long, and as round as a large flour barrel. I walked from one end to the other. It compared to the length of two fighter planes. As my shoes are almost 13 inches long, the more exact measurement would be 35 feet long. If this torpedo hit a battleship, there wouldn't be anything left of the ship to identify. It was too big for a destroyer to handle, a real monster. It made the other torpedoes look like a toy. This must be the same type torpedo that hit our ship in sea battle at Bougainville Nov. 2, 1943 but it did not explode. The men in area of hit were knocked down from impact of it hitting ship. This happened below deck. Must be a 3 ton torpedo largest in the world.

As we walked further down the beach, a Filipino family passed by. They had four children with them. They said, "Hello" to us in English. Filipinos in a small boat pulled up on the beach and we purchased a bunch of bananas from them. The fresh fruit hit the spot. Everyone had a good feed of bananas that day. There is a little town about six miles from the beach but only the officers are permitted to visit it. When I arrived back to the ship, I took a shower and had dinner. It's very hot here during the day but at night the weather is nice and cool. Our compartment is so hot from the sun hitting it all day that I cannot put my hands on the steel inside without getting burned.

An officer from the paratroops came aboard the *Montpelier* this afternoon. He said our paratroops landed near Manila this morning and that a larger force will land on Manila tomorrow morning. Our main Army forces are only a few miles from Manila.

The Russians, reported by the Press News, are only 30 miles from Berlin.

This Sunday, while at Mindoro, we will not have any work to

do, except sweep down the decks and ladders. This is the first time that this has happened since leaving the States. It will be nice to loaf for a change. Modified watches were put into effect today. Movies are held topside tonight. I have yet to see one. Our B-29 Super Fortresses made the longest round trip raid of the war, over 3800 miles were traveled from India to Singapore. It's 3 P.M. Sunday as I sit on a 40 mm. machine gun mount and write. The shade from one of the four barrels is keeping the sun from hitting my face as we experience another hot sunny day.

Tuesday, February 6, 1945: I will try to cover what has happened in the last few days. We are still at Mindoro. Yesterday, when the men went over for recreation, they exchanged their jewelry and some rice for corn on the cob. The ears were not very large but they tasted good. We are so low on food and what we have is so bad, we have to barter for it. The men are hungry all of the time. The cruiser *Boise* is eating only two meals a day and small ones at that. The food we are served does not stand by you. We are also exchanging rice for bananas. Two meals a day on the *Montpelier* is inevitable if a supply ship doesn't put in an appearance soon. The work yesterday and today was very hard. After supper we usually retire to the crew's lounge and listen to the radio for recent news details. Tonight we heard that our troops had entered Manila, the capital of the Philippines.

Our troops traveled 125 miles in five weeks. They freed thousands of Americans and other nationalities from prison camps. The prisoners were so happy after being in prison all of these years that most of them cried. They put their arms around our troops.

A group of bombers flew overhead this morning on their way to hit the Japs. It was quite a sight to see. The sky was full of them. The Navy's PBM bombers also leave every day for patrol duty off the coast of China. Anyone can accompany them if authorized. When I was on the beach the other day for recreation, one of the crewmen asked if I wanted to come along on one of their trips. Since we have but a few hours for recreation, the offer was refused. Those bombers are flying boats and take off from the water. I would not want to be in one of them when attacked by

Jap fighters, which happens frequently on their flights off the Chinese mainland.

I looked through the spyglasses today and viewed some of our transports and a tanker near the beach. They were almost under water. Jap suicide planes were responsible for this.

Tonight the ship looked like a barnyard. One would never believe that the *Montpelier* was a flagship with an Admiral aboard. Our trading for food had brought aboard one live pig, 4 hens and a bunch of bananas thrown in for good measure. It looked as if the circus had come to town. The Filipinos must think that we have a zoo on the ship. Pretty soon everyone on board will be singing, "Oh where, Oh where, can that supply ship be." I wonder who's going to eat the chickens. Some of the ships are on two meals a day. We will start Sunday if no supply ships arrive. The PT boats and LCDs get their smokes, soap, writing paper, etc. from the cruisers while they are stationed here. I had a catch with Keiser tonight topside with a tennis ball.

Wednesday, February 7, 1945: Recreation was held on the beach for some of the men this morning. The Captain inspected all the living spaces this morning. I painted all afternoon. The men were allowed to swim over the side of the ship from 4 to 4:45 this afternoon.

The Press News reported Manila is ours although there are snipers in some of the buildings. The Japs destroyed and burnt many of the buildings in Manila. The Chief Steward told me today that some of the people on Mindoro told him that the Japs were going to start killing the civilians there by the end of 1944. Our troops landed here around December 15, 1944, and prevented the Japs from carrying out their plans. The guerrillas had given the Japs a bad time. There was an old Filipino civilian near the Army base the other day and he said that he loves Americans and hates the Japanese. The news tonight reported house to house fighting in Manila. Many fires were burning in the business district. They were put to the torch by the Japs. Before the war Manila was named the "Pearl of the Orient." We had movies topside tonight.

Thursday, February 8, 1945: I received recreation on the beach today. Everyone was given two cans of beer. Each ship carries its own supply of beer. Some of the men played football. The fellows from my division, using a tennis ball in place of a football, went through the motions. A group of Filipinos passed by, a few of them were girls about 20 years old. They had three water buffaloes with them. They must have been traveling to their village six miles distant. About a half hour before leaving for the ship, we lay in the shade under the palm trees and let the breeze blow on us. Away off in the distance I could see the high green hills and mountains. It felt good to lay and look at that beautiful scenery. There are still many Japs up in those hills hiding out. A fellow from the *Denver* was left ashore last night because he walked to the native village and failed to return on time before his ship pulled out. Last night on his way back to the beach from the village, he was forced to walk through the jungle to reach the shore. The Japs opened up on him but failed to hit the target. He remained at the Army base the rest of the night. Going beyond the base, you are taking a chance of running into the Japs. This is the same Army base next to the beach where the LCI stops to let us off for recreation.

A supply ship arrived today. We received a few supplies. Tonight at 6 P.M. we left Mindoro for Subic Bay on Luzon. It's not too far from Corregidor. This is where the cruiser *Phoenix* went the other night to receive supplies. It had only supplies left for one day. Subic Bay will be our new home base. The Seventh Fleet is stationed there. We will take on supplies upon arriving.

The Press News stated that a cold wave hit the east coast of the U.S.A. Out here, we are burning up from the heat and everyone is brown from the sun. I still like the hot weather better than the cold weather.

Friday, February 9, 1945: This morning at 8 A.M. we arrived at Subic Bay with the cruisers *Denver* and *Boise* and some destroyers. It's a natural harbor for ships. It is almost surrounded by land. A group of high hills command the island. Bataan touches Subic Bay. This is where the Bataan death march was held by the Japs against our troops at the beginning of the war. As we entered Subic Bay, I saw that we had to pass a small island in the center of the bay. This island guards the entrance and is heavily fortified. I could see the 8 inch guns entrenched there. Underground chambers for supplies and troops are housed there. Numerous holes made by bomb hits dotted the island. We were scheduled to bombard here but the Japs pulled out before we arrived. The island is a regular fortress and could stand up under a withering barrage. The Japanese held the island up to two weeks ago. The cruisers are the largest ships in the Bay. There is a small town located at the other end of the Bay. On entering Subic Bay, Bataan is on the right side, the hills that surround Bataan are very high with dense jungle. Many American troops died there at the beginning of the war and many more were tortured by the Japs. It's a different story now. Our troops are slaughtering the Japs. I can hear our big guns firing at the enemy day and night. Planes are strafing and dropping bombs on the Japs. As I look at one corner of Bataan, I can see our planes spotting and directing our artillery. About 8:30 this evening I saw a red glow in the sky in the direction of Manila. It was the capital burning, approximately 50 miles away. When leaving the Bay, the South China Sea greets our warships.

We had an idea that there might be supply ships here awaiting us but no such luck. I carried my sack up topside tonight and as I lie here I can hear the guns firing in the jungle. We are not very far from land. It becomes dark around 7 P.M. I hit the sack at 8:30 P.M.

Saturday, February 10, 1945: All hands arose at 5:30 A.M. I had no work this afternoon for we received Saturday afternoon and all day Sunday to ourselves unless working parties were on the docket. The weather on this side of the Philippines is very good. It rained only once in over a month and that only turned out to be a shower. The Japs have come up with something new in the way of boats. It's called a "Q" boat. It's a suicide motorboat. They carry depth charges, bombs, guns, etc. They sneak into the harbor and attempt to sink or damage the ships anchored there. The Japs also try to climb up the anchor chains of the ships and plant their bombs. Depth charges are placed under the ships if they are successful. They think nothing of crashing head on into one of our ships. One of our patrol boats at Lingayen Gulf was sunk in this way three weeks ago. They always use the darkness for cover as they sneak up on us.

The Captain said that we will be busy in about a week. The plan of the day stated that we could write home and tell our folks that we participated in the Philippine campaigns. Thirty days after each campaign we participate in, we have permission to tell of them. This is something new. Mass was held in the crew's lounge at 5 P.M.

Sunday, February 11, 1945: All hands were up at 6 A.M. Quarters were at 8:15 A.M. Lt. Hutchins, our division officer, informed us that we were going to leave here Tuesday and bombard for 3 days. He did not disclose where. That was music to the crew's ears. Catholic and Protestant church services were held this morning. I went to Mass at 9:30 A.M. President Roosevelt, Prime Minister Churchill and Premier Stalin are having another conference. It is being held somewhere in the Black Sea. The Captain's cook, a Filipino, has a wife and children living in one of the towns that our troops liberated. It's only 35 miles away from the Bay. The cook and a couple of other officers left at 7 A.M. yesterday morning in a jeep for the town. When the wife of the Filipino saw him, she almost fainted. She could hardly believe her eyes. They had been separated for a long time. A joyous reunion took place. The Filipino had with him food and clothing for his family. It was very thoughtful on Captain Hoffman's part to arrange this sort of a thing. On the way to the town, they rode through the jungle that was infested with Japs. They returned to the ship the same day around 5 P.M.

This morning Mass was held topside and during the service, I could see our planes dive onto the Japs strafing and dropping their bomb loads. I could also see numerous explosions followed by a large mass of smoke near Bataan. C–47 cargo planes also dropped supplies to our troops below. The Japs have encircled one of our regiments and up to now they have not been able to break through the entrapment. The ground troops had advanced so far into enemy lines that this was made possible. They are cut off from the rest of the army. The division is attempting to free them. This action is taking place just over the hills at the end of Subic Bay in the direction of town. Firing from both sides can be heard quite plainly in the Bay. The fighting is confined to the thick jungles and high hills. Our troops have some savage fighting to do in there as the jungle is so thick that they never know when a fanatic Jap is close by.

This afternoon all the tankers refueled the warships. I had a catch with a tennis ball topside after supper. It fell in the water twice but I retrieved it by using a bucket with a line attached to the handle.

Monday, February 12, 1945: I was relieved of watch at 4 A.M. I spent the morning painting. A terrific artillery barrage took place this morning. The ground shook like an earthquake and we on board ship could even feel it. The barrage lasted a long time. One shell came close to the beach. Our troops are still attempting to free the encircled regiment. It would not take very long to reach the scene of action if we were on shore. There is nothing in the Press News this morning concerning the trapped troops. They should let us fire our guns from here on the Japs. Rapid fire would take care of them. Tomorrow morning, we leave to bombard all day. We will return the same night. We will go back and forth for the next three or four days. There is a point at the tip of Bataan Peninsula before entering Manila Bay that is well guarded with Jap shore guns. If we try to enter Manila Bay to bombard Corregidor, the Japs will open up on us. The only way to enter Manila Bay is to capture Corregidor, the stone fortress that protects the entrance to Manila. Corregidor is a large island in the center of Manila Bay. It is another Gibraltar of solid stone with underground tunnels and compartments. It is a little city under a mountain. We sent a destroyer to the Bataan Peninsula one day to look the ground work over. Enemy guns drove them away. Next PT boats tried but the results were the same. Tomorrow morning we will be sent to bombard the island. These Jap guns will have to be knocked out before Corregidor and the Bataan Peninsula can be taken. Once Manila Bay is open, supply ships will be rushed in to supply our troops and the civilians of Manila. Manila Bay is one of the largest in the world. When we wipe the Japs off this point, we will start to bombard Corregidor, the key to Manila Bay and Manila itself.

This evening we received 10 bags of mail. A PBY, a flying boat, arrived with it in the afternoon. I had two letters waiting. One was dated December 25, the other January 25. It was my first mail in almost three months. They had a movie topside tonight. Red Skelton in "Whistling in Dixie" was the name of it. This is the first time movies were shown in Subic Bay since the war started.

Tuesday, February 13, 1945: All hands got up at 5 A.M. Breakfast was at 6:15 A.M. The U.S.S. *Montpelier* left Subic Bay at 7:30 A.M. Our force consists of 5 light cruisers, 10 destroyers and 18 minesweepers. We will be the initial warships to hit Bataan since the Japs took over control in 1942. These are the same waters that the American survivors of Bataan used when they fled to doomed Corregidor in 1942.

At 9 A.M. we started the bombardment of Bataan and Corregidor. It was a hot sunny day. We are going to make it hotter for the Japs. Our ships were divided as we will take turns hitting Bataan and Corregidor. Minesweepers will clear the Bay of mines. The Bay contains thousands of them. We will bombard Bataan today and change over and bombard Corregidor tomorrow. From where we are situated, we have a good view of both objectives. At noon a large force of B–24 Liberators, A–20 Bostons (bombers) and assorted fighter planes hit Corregidor. They dropped hundreds of tons of bombs on their destinations. Everything must have been shaken up over there. It seemed as if a powder factory had exploded. Corregidor was blacked out for some time. It was covered with smoke and dust. Bombs were exploding everywhere like big balls of fire. It was quite a sight to see, when the planes finished.

Our ships continued to bombard Corregidor. Corregidor is very high at one end. It is one mass of solid rock and cliffs. It tapers off and at the other end it is not very high. The higher part of the "rock" is where the bombers and ships concentrated on. It must be loaded with guns and troops. Corregidor would be next to impossible to capture if we landed below and worked our way to the top. The Japs could easily concentrate their fire below and slaughter anyone attempting to scale the cliffs. A group of buildings were on top of the "rock." Many explosions took place as our ships scored direct hits on ammunition dumps and gun emplacements. Our troops may land on Bataan Thursday and Corregidor Friday. The Japs took a powerful pounding from the planes and ships. Jap troops, supplies, ammunition, etc. were blown sky high. The big guns on Bataan were also knocked out. At 4 P.M. we stopped firing and headed back to Subic Bay. We will return tomorrow morning.

We had movies topside tonight. "Sherlock Holmes' Secret Weapon" was the show.

Wednesday, February 14, 1945: All hands arose at 5 A.M. It was still dark as we had breakfast. Today is Ash Wednesday. The Priest distributed ashes. We left Subic Bay, headed for the Bataan Peninsula. The *Montpelier* was scheduled to fire today at noon but around 9:20 A.M. while the other ships were bombarding and the minesweepers were clearing the bay of mines, Jap shore guns opened up on them. One of our destroyers was hit. We commenced firing and silenced the Japs with plenty of hot steel. Our minesweepers continued their work. We will bombard Corregidor today but we will hold our firing until the planes and bombers complete their noon bombing attack. Some of the light bombers (A–20 Bostons) came in low with their machine guns blazing away and then dropped their load of bombs. Bombs were attached to parachutes for delayed bombing runs. The purpose of this is to allow the bomber plenty of time to escape the explosions of hazardous low bombing runs. We had to give the minesweepers a smoke screen. Some of our planes flew close to shore and covered it with smoke so that the Jap shore guns will be ineffective against the minesweepers. The Japs are well entrenched. The firing from our ship was effective this afternoon. Ammunition dumps on Corregidor were hit as the *Montpelier* guns were brought into range.

The ships on the Bataan side did not fare so well. A minesweeper was sunk when a Jap mine became stuck in its gear. It exploded before they could free it. One of the destroyers that was firing at one of the mines in the bay was hit by another mine which was hidden from view. What an explosion. A large geyser of water went high into the air, covering a very large section of the Bay. When everything had cleared, I could see that part of the bow had been blown off. A destroyer close by, firing at mines in the same way as the stricken ship, rushed to its aid. Before reaching the ship, a mine struck the onrushing destroyer. As with the first destroyer, the second suffered a similar fate. Its bow had been blown off. The water surrounding the two ill-fated destroyers was cluttered with toilet paper, supplies and life rafts. Both ships were dead in the water. We will receive the casualty list later. The men stationed on the bows of the destroyers didn't stand a chance. The bow of the second destroyer was almost completely blown off. What little was left, was submerged. Casualties will be heavy. Torpedoes of the destroyers had to be fired in the beach of the Bataan Peninsula, to make the ships lighter. Some time later at a slow pace, under their own power, they got under way. Darkness was falling when the destroyers left with the other ships for Subic Bay. The U.S.S. *Montpelier* stayed behind while a minesweeper finished sweeping the place. It was dark when we left for Subic Bay. We pulled into port at 11:45 P.M.

Everyone was hungry because we had breakfast at 6:15 A.M. Dinner was served at 11 A.M. For dinner we had a bun with a little peanut butter. Supper at 9 P.M. was little better. We were at battle stations all day commencing at 6:30 A.M. to late in the night. It was midnight for me as I had the 8 to midnight watch. The Japs on Bataan must have enjoyed the trouble that our ships experienced this afternoon.

On one occasion this afternoon, we hit a large ammunition dump, point-blank. The explosion was so intense that much of Corregidor could not be seen, so high and thick was the smoke. It covered hundreds of feet in all directions. This was a once in a lifetime shot. The concussion was intense for those on land.

After being relieved of the midnight watch, I took a shower and slept topside. Today we lost one minesweeper and had two damaged destroyers. The Japs lost a large quantity of troops.

Thursday, February 15, 1945: We received little sleep as we arose at 4 A.M. Breakfast was served at 5:15 A.M. and we left Subic Bay at 5:30 A.M. Troops will land this morning on the Bataan Peninsula. We arrived at our destination early so as to be ahead of the invasion force. The Japs landed here in 1942, now it's our turn. Our force will continue to bombard Corregidor this morning and then again in the afternoon. Others will hit Bataan. About 8:30 A.M., I could see the invasion ships appearing on the horizon. I stopped counting them after 70. They consist of transports, LSTs and LCIs. As our transports neared Bataan they were fired upon by the Jap 6 inch guns. Our ship opened up at once, and silenced the Jap batteries. The transports escaped without mishap. Planes and bombers hit the beach before landing procedures were followed. Our troops landed not too far from the stricken destroyers of yesterday, and met little opposition. A landing craft was hit by the Jap shore guns as it was nearing the beach. There was an explosion but it did not sink. Another craft of the same type came alongside, to help put out the fire that resulted. After failing to do so, the craft was beached. We are very close to the landing and have an excellent view of the beach. Landing craft maintain a steady stream as they go back and forth to the beach with troops, tanks, guns, supplies, etc. From the *Montpelier,* firing on the beach can be heard quite plainly. The weather for the landing is perfect. The sun is very bright and most important, the water calm.

The bombing and bombardments of Corregidor continue as our troops are taking care of the Japs on Bataan. Our big B–24 Liberator bombers dropped a lot of blockbusters on it again today as usual. I do not know how anything can live after they finish. The concussion alone is enough to kill them. The explosions were terrific. That island just shook. Our ship about 2 miles away shook plenty.

Our minesweepers continued to clear Corregidor of Jap mines, to make it possible for a landing tomorrow. From this morning until 2 P.M. this afternoon they swept up 115 mines and they are still sweeping. If any of our submarines had attempted to sneak in here before clearing operations began, it would have been blown to pieces. From where I am sitting I can see the buildings in Mariveles on Bataan where our troops landed this morning. We have a group of PT boats here. They must be going to use them on the Japs for something special. They can take care of themselves and pack a terrific punch. It's rugged duty to be stationed on one of them. They stay close to land, never knowing when the Japs will fire on them. When our Boston Havocs or A–20 bombers hit Corregidor, I could see their bombs float down through the air and then a great explosion could be heard. The two destroyers that had their bows blown off yesterday have not reached Subic Bay. They will be forced to leave for the States. They could only crawl so it will take a long time for them to reach their final destination. New bows will replace what is left of the old ones. Engine rooms may also have to be replaced. We will remain at battle stations all day. We had our meals at battle stations. For dinner, we had hamburg sandwiches, 1 piece of cake and a cup of cocoa. Bombers, fighters and warships hit Corregidor all day. We were very close to the shore today. We could see the heavy cruisers in the distance. We have not used our machine guns yet. We fired only the five and six inch guns. One of our minesweepers came across 78 mines yesterday afternoon. The *Montpelier* ceases fire when the planes arrive and everyone on board watches the show. Yesterday a giant sea turtle came close to the ship as the bombardment was under way. In the bombardment one side of the ship's guns are in operation, while on the return trip, the other side has a go at it. We left at 7 P.M. as darkness was approaching. We will not return to Subic Bay, but will patrol off Corregidor and Bataan until daylight. All hands left battle stations at 8:45 P.M. We had supper at 8:45 P.M. Everyone was starved. Our last meal was at noon and we received very little then.

Friday, February 16, 1945: I was relieved of watch at 4 A.M.

I received very little sleep as all hands were awoken at 5 A.M. We had breakfast at 5:15 A.M. and went to General Quarters at 6:30 A.M. We will stay here until late tonight. Last night three Jap "Q" boats, or suicide boats, sneaked into the bay where our troops landed and attempted to sink our transports. Two of the "Q" boats were sunk. One of our ships was hit and damaged.

More tons of bombs hit Corregidor yesterday than any other spot in the Pacific in one day. The warships added to the total. Our troops will land in the same part of the shore as the Japs did in 1942. But before they land, the Japs are going to be in for a big surprise when we invade Corregidor this morning. We will land paratroopers on the highest points of Corregidor. Later in the day our troops will land on the beaches at the other end of the "rock." The contour is not so high and in that way we will have the Japs in the middle. They believe the landing will be confined to the beach. I would like to see the looks on their faces when they see our paratroopers landing on the high plateau of Corregidor, looking down at them.

It is 8 A.M. as I write this. I can see B–24 bombers dropping tons of bombs on Corregidor. We are near shore and will be able to see everything. Our guns are not firing at this moment. We do not want to hit the planes. Our ship shakes from the terrific explosions. Corregidor is covered with smoke. I cannot see the high cliffs of Corregidor on account of it. It's a good day for an invasion as it is a warm sunny day. Our invasion ships that will land the troops at the other end of the "rock," are not in sight as yet. The troops will land at 10 A.M. and the paratroops at an even earlier time, 8:30 A.M. The "rock" is experiencing its last bombing before the paratroops land. Our heavy cruisers have accompanied us for the mission. Their 8 inch shells will come in handy. One of the heavy cruisers is of Australian origin. One of our light cruisers is on the other side of Corregidor and is surrounded by mines. It is shooting itself clear of them with their machine guns. Mines are exploding all around them. Many Jap mines are still covering these waters. Other warships will cover the troops when they land on the beach at the other end of Corregidor. They have the low end of Corregidor and we the high where the paratroops will land.

Back again — It is 1:15 P.M. in the afternoon: At 8:30 A.M. the 1st wave of paratroops jumped from the C–47 transport bombers. The bombers carrying the paratroops came in from the lowest part of Corregidor and passed over the highest point of Corregidor and then the paratroopers came down. The landings continued until 9:45 A.M. lasting an hour and fifteen minutes. They landed on the highest part of Corregidor. Coloring of the parachutes were green, yellow, white, etc. Not all the parachutes contained men. They were used to land supplies, armament, etc. The planes were about 300 feet above land. It took approximately 15 seconds for the parachutists to hit land. A few of the chutes failed to open. While the paratroops were in the air, A–20 bombers and fighters bored in on the "rock," strafing in waves. Anything that moved below was cut to ribbons. Some of the troops landed on top of the concrete barracks. Many of the buildings contained only the frames, attesting to the accuracy of our bombers. Other paratroops landed in trees and bushes on the side of the hills. A few missed the island completely and landed in the water below. PT boats were standing close to the shore in such an eventuality to rescue them. It was quite a sight to see. The sky was full of parachutes with all their different colors and to see the men jump from the planes was something. The weather was perfect for this operation. There was a B–17 Flying Fortress viewing the action below. At 12:45 P.M. hundreds of more chutes were landed. Many contained supplies. Again some of the chutes failed to open. The last parachute landed at 2 P.M., making both time periods exactly the same. An hour and fifteen minutes covered the morning and afternoon landings. The ground was covered with parachutes. It looked like washday.

At 10 A.M. ground troops landed on the beach at the other end of Corregidor. The warships gave it a good going over before the landings started. This one-two punch was too much for the defenders. They never experienced anything like this before. The Japs really had a rugged time for themselves. The troops who were on Corregidor when it fell to the Japanese in 1942 would have enjoyed the script. Most of the warships departed tonight but a few warships remained to fire star shells at the Japs. This will continue all during the night. We left with the other ships for Subic Bay at 4:30 P.M. We arrived at Subic Bay at 6 P.M. We refueled from a tanker and movies were shown.

The news over the radio reported that Bull Halsey's Third Fleet had struck at Tokyo with 1500 carrier planes.

The Jap "Q" boats that attacked our transports at Bataan last night, did more damage than I first said. Four of our LCIs were sunk.

Saturday, February 17, 1945: The Press News was devoted to the invasion of the Bataan Peninsula. It mentioned that our troops found U.S. officers and enlisted men still hiding out in the hills with the Filipinos. These men were here when the Japs captured Bataan in 1942. They were still fighting the Japs. General MacArthur said that the minesweepers did a daring and spectacular job in clearing the mines. The waters were full of them. Even the warships were exploding them with their anti-aircraft guns. This afternoon, we pulled alongside of an ammunition ship for restocking of ammo. We received a little mail tonight. I had a letter arrive that was almost two months old from my sister Mary. I slept topside.

Sunday, February 18, 1945: We took it easy today. A hospital ship arrived a few days ago. Olongapo, the town at the other end of the harbor, is a mess. As usual, the Japs burnt and destroyed everything usable before leaving. The same thing happened to Manila. The invasion of Corregidor was reported over radio today. It said that it's possible to send ships with supplies to supplement the needs of the people of Manila. By capturing the Bataan Peninsula and Corregidor, Manila Bay was opened to Allied shipping.

Yesterday, a few young Filipino girls came close to the ship. They were very cute. This morning, a tug brought a damaged landing craft into the Bay. It happened at Bataan.

Protestant and Catholic services were held topside. A large group of men from the other ships in the bay came aboard for church services. Last Sunday some English sailors and officers came on here for church. The weather is excellent. The sky is blue and the sun is shining all the time. Moderate cool weather greets us in the morning until 10 A.M. After that it becomes very hot. There is always a strong breeze blowing. At night it becomes cool enough for me to use a blanket but most of the crew sleep in just their shorts. I am listed for the 8 to midnight watch. We started standing modified watches for the first time yesterday. It is 9:30 A.M. as I sit on one of the highest parts of the ship, next to the searchlights. The American flag is behind me flickering in the breeze. As I look below, I can see some of the men standing and sitting on deck, writing letters. Others are playing cards. A few are reading the Press News or some other reading material. Today, being Sunday, we can take it easy unless something comes up. As I look around, I can see men busy, fixing one of the 40 mm. mounts. Yost is in charge of Mount 45.

Tuesday, February 20, 1945: All hands up at 6 A.M. We received our first recreation since we came to Subic Bay. We had recreation on Grande Island. It is the island we passed upon entering the bay. It is situated in the center of the entrance. The LCI that transported us to Grande Island had a little monkey aboard. He was the funniest thing I had seen in a long while. He was on our ship for a while before we left. The island is a regular fort. Ten inch guns are entrenched there. A large underground room houses the ammunition and stores. Ammunition is everywhere. This was one of the islands we were to bombard not too long ago. The Japs pulled out before we had the chance. Grande Island guards the entrance to the Bay. It's similar to Corregidor but on a smaller scale. Underground chambers are also numerous here. Bombs would be useless against it, as the solid cement would only at the worst be dented. The Japs had set booby traps before evacuating the island. When the crew arrived for recreation, a group of fellows started exploring the island. One of our crewmen came across a wire and pulled it. A mine exploded. One of our party was killed while three others were badly wounded. I was near the quarterdeck when they were brought aboard on stretchers. The one that was killed had a large hole in his chest. He lived a few minutes after the explosion. One of the fellows who was there said that when he exhaled, the blood would spray out in large bursts. His face was also blown away. He was a terrible sight. No one could ask for a better person. Everyone liked him. He was handsome and his wife was beautiful. He was only 22 years old. Of the other three men that were badly wounded, one had his hand blown off, another his stomach almost blown out, and the last an eye. The one with the lost eye had his face damaged severely. He will have to have part of a new face made. Blood covered the whole area. The men on ship donated blood for them. After the movies tonight, I walked by the carpenter's shop. They were busy making a casket for the one who had died on the beach. They used ordinary lumber, as a rough box took shape. They are not very wide. Some family back in the States lost a good man.

Wednesday, February 21, 1945: At last we are going to have food. We worked a little harder today, taking on food and supplies. All hands had to assist. We had a picnic for ourselves on the working party. We ate so many oranges and pears that we thought they would come out of our ears. The men did not mind the hard work because we had plenty to eat.

Funeral services were held in the afternoon on the fantail. All hands were assembled aft.

The supply ship had a group of various servicemen aboard who were captured by the Japanese in 1942, and have been prisoners for all of these years. Many of them were wounded and all had white hair. They were nothing but "bags of bones." Their arms were like toothpicks. Some were very young but looked much older than their years. All were very weak. Now, they can have all the food they want. One of the fellows gained 50 pounds in two weeks. Most of them have a faraway look in their eyes. They must have gone through hell under the Jap treatment. They can hardly believe their eyes as they see all of our warships in the harbor. If the Third Fleet was here in force, they would believe it a dream. One of the men who had spent 36 months under the Japs on Corregidor said that all of the work was done by pick and shovel, no machinery. The only food given them was a bag of rice and a little warm water. Whenever they took sick, no help was given to them by the Japs. They either became better or they died. At least 60% of the prisoners died in captivity. Torture was used by the Japs without provocation.

The Press News reported that the Fourth and Fifth Marines landed on Iwo Jima. It is about 700 miles from Japan. Over 800 ships took part in the operation. The Third Fleet carrier planes hit Tokyo with 1500 planes. The Japanese lost 700 planes in two days — 150 B–29 super forts also hit Japan.

Sunday, February 25, 1945: Not much to write about today. The food is the best we had in a long time. We received butter, fresh fruit and potatoes. Fresh meat was also served. Usually our meat is served out of a can. There are so many men in this area that it is difficult to procure supplies. We did not draw any flour but the light cruiser *Cleveland* came to our aid in giving us some as we had only one day's supply left.

The Press News reported that the fighting on Iwo Jima is the roughest in Marine Corps history. The Third, Fourth and Fifth Marine Divisions are doing the brunt of the fighting there. Iwo Jima is the most strongly fortified island in the world — 6000 casualties in the first four days was reported by the United States. The beach is covered with wrecked landing craft.

In Europe, the American Armies started a drive and the end is in sight for the Germans.

Much painting on board was completed in the last three days. We painted the whole outside of the ship. It is painted like it used to be, dark blue and light blue on the superstructure. Classes are conducted in the mess hall, identifying planes. I had recreation on Grande Island. All the buildings there were destroyed by the Japs before they pulled out. Everyone received two cans of beer. I had a look around the island and then played football. A pier juts out on the island and the fellows dove off it for swimming. Last night, we took on board much mail. I received four letters.

Yesterday afternoon, Saturday, our new Captain came aboard. He will replace Captain Harry Hoffman, who was promoted to Admiral. Captain Hoffman was a fine Captain and everyone liked him. He always gave us the latest news. I liked to hear him speak over the loudspeaker because he could relate some interesting stories. Yesterday evening at 6 P.M. we left Subic Bay. We arrived at Mindoro this morning at 8 A.M. There is another operation coming up in a few days and we will be in on it. We will receive instructions later. This is the season of Lent and church services were held in the mess hall last night. We took on fuel today. We had a good dinner, the best since Christmas. There are many invasion craft anchored here, LSTs and LSIs. The fellow who had his arm blown off the other day was transferred to the beach. He will return to the States. Not having to wear our shirts during the day, everyone on board is tanned from the sun. An LCT passed nearby loaded with troops and trucks. I washed some of my clothing today.

Monday, February 26, 1945: I had recreation on the beach this afternoon. Each man on shore received two cans of beer. I took a walk to the airfield and had a look at all of the planes and bombers stationed there. The B–24 bombers had pictures of girls in various poses painted on them. The bombers had many bombing missions to their credit. We were allowed to enter the insides of the bombers and look around. The ground crews lived in tents, close to the airfield. One of the crewmen was sitting on his cot in one of the tents and was reading a letter from home. It said that he had inherited a million dollars. I hope that he gets through the war in one piece to enjoy it. He looked like a nice guy. One would never take him for a millionaire. He was very friendly. I forgot to ask him his name. They have their clothes washed by the Filipinos.

Tuesday, February 27, 1945: At 6:15 we had breakfast after arising at 5:30 A.M. We left Mindoro at 7 A.M. We will invade Palawan. It is a long island, north of Borneo and south of Mindoro. Our troops will land tomorrow morning. The Captain will give us the details tonight. This afternoon, the sea started off rough but calmed down after a while. We ate supper at 4:30 P.M. All hands went to sunset General Quarters. The Captain informed us that part of the Eighth Army, about 3500 men, would land at 8:45 A.M. on the island of Palawan. The island is 225 miles long and 25 miles wide. Airfields are the primary objective for taking the island. Our troops will attempt to capture the town, the only one on the island. At 3:30 A.M. tomorrow morning, our minesweepers will start clearing the harbor of Jap mines. At 7:15, the three light cruisers in the task force will commence bombarding. The task force consists of three light cruisers and eight destroyers. The Japs have at least 2000 troops stationed on the island. The Japs have a prison battalion on the island, consisting mostly of American sailors. When our invasion forces were on their way to land on Mindoro, the Japs thought that we were going to make the landing here. The prisoners were forced to dig long trenches and then gasoline was poured on them. A match was then set to the gasoline. The prisoners were human torches. As they tried to escape this horrible death, they were shot down by the Jap machine guns. A few made it to the water but were mowed down by the Jap guns. Others that had not been burnt to death were buried alive. These men were Japanese prisoners since 1942 and spent all that time under the cruel treatment of the Japs until the end. Some of the prisoners escaped and were picked up by our subs. It is going to be a pleasure to bombard this island and blow its defenders to bits. It's too bad the poor prisoners cannot be here to see it happen. This will be the end for another Jap prison camp.

The surrender of Palawan will put our bombers closer to Borneo, Saigon, China, and Mindanao, the large Philippine island in the South. I slept on deck tonight.

Wednesday, February 28, 1945: I was relieved of watch at 4 A.M. All hands arose at 4:30 A.M. Breakfast was at 5 A.M. At 7 A.M. we catapulted our two spotting planes. At 7:15 A.M. we started our bombardment of Palawan. The landing craft are behind us as we commence firing. At 8:45 A.M., they will come in with the troops.

We gave the Japs quite a blasting and at 8:45 A.M. our troops were on schedule, landing with very little opposition. We stayed offshore all day. At supper, we left for Subic Bay. This was only a minor operation. They will not need us.

Thursday, March 1, 1945: The U.S.S. *Montpelier* pulled into Subic Bay at 6 P.M. We had movies topside.

Friday, March 2, 1945: No news. Had recreation today. I saw 10 nurses on the beach. It was the first time we ever saw anything like that since leaving the States.

Saturday, March 3, 1945: Captain Hoffman showed our new Captain around the ship. Everyone was kept busy getting everything in order. All hands went to quarters and both Captains inspected us. We wore dungarees and blue hats. After inspection, all hands assembled aft on the fantail. Captain Hoffman gave a farewell speech and introduced the new Captain. His name is William A. Gorry. He looks very young, about 45 years old. He looks like a pretty good scout. We hated to see Harry "The Horse" leave. His nickname is what everyone calls him. He was a regular guy. If he ever leaves the Navy, he can always have a job as a radio announcer. He always captivated his audience with his voice and on board kept us up to date with the news. He insured the comfort of his crew whenever possible. His experiences and anecdotes were always pleasurable to listen to. Captain Hoffman will be Admiral when all the paperwork is completed. Everyone wishes him the best of luck. He left the ship for the States about 3:30 P.M. I was awoken at 11 P.M. for a working detail on the supply ship. I will be there until daylight. We are going to take on 150 tons of food.

Sunday, March 4, 1945: I worked on the supply ship from 11 last night until 8 A.M. this morning.

Monday, March 5, 1945: General Quarters sounded at 2:30 this morning. We did not fire our guns on ship but on the beach guns could be heard firing at Jap planes. I replaced Stoyka in the mess hall as he went to the beach for recreation. Typhoid shots were distributed to the crew today. We receive them once a year.

Tuesday, March 6, 1945: A group of the men who missed the ship in the States returned today. They had just returned from the States. A destroyer arrived today with a lot of mail. We received 50 bags with packages and 20 bags of air mail.

Wednesday, March 7, 1945: I left the ship at 7:15 A.M. on a working party. We will load 800 bags of flour and one hundred bags of coffee. We were transported to a place called Olongapo. We are anchored near the entrance of Subic Bay, some distance from the town. It was a treat to visit the town. It gave us a chance to walk around and talk to the Filipinos and to our troops. We left the ship for the town in an LCI. The LCI looked like a little zoo. The crew had aboard a large hen, two little pups and a little monkey. It was like a circus to see the monkey and dogs play with each other. They had everyone in stitches. One of the fellows put a paper cup on the monkey's head for a hat and then gave him a cigarette. He looked very funny. The crews on these landing craft can just about do what they want and wear whatever they please. It took us about 20 minutes to reach the beach. We walked around the town to look the place over. The people have very little clothing to wear because the Japs took about everything away from them. The clothing that they had was Army and Navy issue. I came across a Filipino who said that he would trade Jap invasion money for the undershirt I was wearing. I traded the shirt for the money. The money was worthless but I wanted it for a souvenir and to help him at the same time. Both of us were happy at the exchange. While we were loading the LCI, I talked to a Filipino who appeared to be around 35 years old. He was married and spoke good English as most of the Filipinos do. He said that he spent three years with the guerrillas up in the hills. They had to eat leaves, roots or anything else that could be scavenged from the earth, and it was very hard to scrape up enough to eat. He further related that the people of this town went into the jungle and the hills to live because of Jap cruelty. Before the Jap occupation, the population totaled 5000 people. Today only 1000 are alive and many of them have malaria and other diseases. The Japs killed and tortured at their slightest whim. Many died from lack of food and medical supplies. If a Jap soldier wanted anything, he just took it. One day the Japs approached him and seized all the clothing that he was wearing except his sox. He figured the sox were the wrong size or they would have taken them. After this episode, he took for the hills with only a pair of sox to his name. He made a pair of shorts from the sox. He also told how he killed many Japs who held his wife prisoner. He freed his wife and both escaped to the hills. The Japs attacked girls from 10 years old and upwards. After finishing with some of the girls, the Japs would then cut off their heads. A rope would then be tied around their feet and they would be left hanging from a tree. A favorite sport of the Japs would be to take little children and toss them up into the air, then catch them with their bayonets. The only food the Filipinos received was a handful of rice daily. The Filipino then told me how he and his friends would come down from the hills after midnight and kill many Japs in the town. At first guns were scarce, but they got more little by little by killing Japs and taking their guns and food and clothing. When they were through with the Japs, they would bury them. Bows and arrows were used as a silent means of extermination. The Japs were never aware of the noiseless deaths that awaited them. The Filipino had a large scar near his ear that he received when he was captured by the Japs. During his capture, the only thing he was given was water. His hands were tied behind his back and his feet were also bound securely. When thirst became overwhelming, the Japs stuck an ordinary garden hose into his mouth and turned on the water full force. The Japs would not take the hose from his mouth until no more water could be forced into him. They would then throw him on the ground and jump on his stomach. Water would gush out of his mouth, as he was blown up with it. When he escaped from the Japs, nothing was left of him but the frame. He was skin and bones. He said that he looked like a skeleton. I talked to others there, and similar stories were related to me. These Filipinos still go to the hills at night but this time it's to kill Japs hiding there. I had to laugh when he told me that he worked two shifts. In the daytime he worked at his regular job on the pier. At night he would go into the hills with the rest of the guerrillas and kill Japs. The Filipinos are very

honest and a friendly people. This was a beautiful town before
the war started. Now everything is destroyed. There is real com-
panionship between the Filipinos and Americans.

At noon we knocked off for lunch. We had our dinner at the
Sea Bees' mess hall. The Filipinos received the same food as us.
We had meat balls, corn, potatoes, bread and jam. Cold lemonade
quenched the thirst. Everyone enjoyed the food, American and
Filipino. There were two good-looking Filipino girls eating in
the mess hall. They had nice outfits on and looked like any American girl in the States. They looked very refined.

In the afternoon we boarded a truck and rode through the
town. It was a very interesting trip. We passed a brick church
with a cement walk around it. The roof of the church was blown
in by the Japs. Filipinos were working everywhere in town. They
are being paid by the United States. When passing through town,
we approached a large clearing out in the wilderness at the foot
of an enormous mountain. All I could see was the jungle. The
Japs could very easily be there, looking at us, and we would not
know it. Supplies were piled sky high. We stayed there all afternoon, loading trucks with coffee. It was a beautiful sunny day and
we worked with our shirts off. We were given all the pineapple
juice we wanted to drink. The Sea Bees are still constructing this
area. It will be a large supply depot when finished. Supplies are
coming in here steadily and large buildings will be constructed
to house the goods and to keep them dry. The Sea Bees had a
shower hooked up under a tree and some of them were taking a
shower. It's not too far from the area where our troops were
trapped last month. The casualty list was very high. While we
were talking to the Sea Bees, the Japs must have been in the
nearby hills, watching our every movement. They kill Japs up
there every day. When the Sea Bees have nothing to do, they go
into the jungles for Japs and souvenirs. While we were there, one
of the fellows had returned from killing two Japs. He also had
many souvenirs with him. He said that it took nine bullets to kill
one of the big Japs. The dead Jap was an Imperial Marine, a
Mongolian, they grow very large. One of the Sea Bees had found

a book and some letters belonging to the Japs. At night the Japs try to sneak in to steal food which is covered by canvas. About a week ago, while everyone was watching the movies in town, some Japs came down from the hills and wounded four men.

At the completion of the working party, we boarded the truck and headed for town. We met the LCT and arrived back at the ship at 4:30 P.M. I took a shower and had supper. I then went up to the third level and started to write. Everyone received a deeper tan today on top of the one they already had.

Friday, March 9, 1945: Not much to write about in the last few days. Yesterday I had a tooth filled. I received mail from home. The Press News reported that the American Army in Europe crossed the Rhine River. The Armies are making big advances against the Germans, gaining thirty miles in twelve hours. Berlin was hit for the 21st straight day and the 17th straight night by our planes and bombers. The British Air Force also took part in the bombing. The Marines on Iwo Jima are still finding the going rough against the Japanese. Over 300 B–29 Super Fortresses hit Tokyo. It was the largest raid so far. At 7 P.M. we left Subic Bay for Mindoro.

Saturday, March 10, 1945: We arrived at Mindoro at 8 A.M. We transferred a group of men from the ship this morning. Our division officer, Lt. Hutchins, was among them. They will leave for the States today. Our new Executive Officer came aboard yesterday, Commander Roy A. Mitchell.

Friday, March 16, 1945: Nothing to write about in the past week. We left Subic Bay, traveled to Mindoro, then cruised to the Lingayen Gulf. We remained at the Gulf for a few days. This morning at 8 we anchored at Mindoro. At first we were ordered to Mindanao, the second largest island in the Philippines, but other warships were used in the invasion instead. Our troops landed on the southwest side of the island. We may be ordered to land troops on the other side of Mindanao. I had recreation on the beach at Lingayen Gulf. Here, recreation leaves much to be desired. Our time there was spent on the beach. The Filipinos arrived to do a little trading. We gave them clothing for Jap

money and goods that they made. Whole families were present.
Nearly all of the old women in the group smoked cigars they received from the sailors. It seemed as if they were all Catholics,
according to holy medals and rosaries that they wore. They all
spoke excellent English, and wrote exceptionally clear English.
Nearly all of the clothing that they wore was Army or Navy issue.

While the *Montpelier* was at sea, gunnery practice was conducted. We shot down a lot of sleeves that were towed by planes.
Plane recognition every day as usual. We have movies of our
planes and the enemy's so we can tell the difference between theirs
and ours. Tonight many B–24 bombers returned after a raid on
China. One of the planes came in on three motors.

The Press News reported the Japs lost approximately 4000 airplanes in the Philippine Campaign. British Lancaster Bomber
loads were increased to carry 11-ton bombs for the first time yesterday. They are capable of destroying five city blocks each, being
the largest bombs in the world. The Marines on Iwo Jima have
the island close to being secured.

Tuesday, March 20, 1945: No news. We would rather be in
some campaign than just hang around at Mindoro. The weather
is still holding excellent. There is always a good breeze. There
is talk about men being sent to the States the 1st of April. They
will be the men who left the States with the ship in 1942 and who
have clean records. I have a good chance of being one, if I miss
this draft I will get the next one, about June. I would rather go
back in June when the weather is good. I have 27 months of sea
duty now.

In Boston and New York, they experienced the hottest St.
Patrick's Day on record. It was 70 degrees in Boston and 80 degrees in New York.

B–29s dropped leaflets on Japan telling the inhabitants that the
bombing would cease when they stopped fighting. They also
warned the people to stay away from military areas. Bombers from
Iwo Jima will bomb Japan soon. It's only 700 miles away.

I left the ship today for recreation on the beach at Mindoro.
We received a ride from an Army truck and went to the town

about 10 miles away. We stayed there about an hour and left because we did not have much time left. There was not much to see or do there. An Army camp is situated near the town. Headquarters for the Fifth Air Force is also accommodated on the island. I saw a couple of Red Cross girls there. The people of the town had many chickens, cows and water buffalo.

Some of the men of my division bought corn whiskey from the soldiers. They paid $17 for one pint. That must be some kind of a record. It was very strong but that's the way the southern boys like it. The soldiers on the beach were busy loading landing craft for an invasion planned in the near future. The roads are very dusty on the island. After arriving on board ship at 11:30 A.M., I took a shower.

Sunday, March 25, 1945: Today is Palm Sunday, our third in the Pacific. Church services were held topside. There was a large group of men from the other ships to attend the services. Everyone received some palm. It was picked on the island yesterday. I did not write lately because there was not much to write about. We left Mindoro and now are at Subic Bay.

The Australian cruiser *Hobart* was here but left yesterday with the two light cruisers *Phoenix* and *Boise*. The *Cleveland, Denver* and *Montpelier* are the only cruisers here now. The men would like to join Bull Halsey's Third Fleet and hit Japan. I wish we would leave here and go up around Japan with the Third Fleet. There is nothing to do here in the Philippines. Some ships have to stay here and just because we have been out here so long, they are letting newer ships go with the 3rd Fleet. We were ordered to battle stations the other night. Around midnight Jap bombers struck at Manila. They did not attack the ships in the bay. Manila is about 50 miles from here.

The Press News reported that 274 tons of bombs have been falling on Germany every hour for the past three weeks. This is more than England received during the entire war. The Japs lost 10,000 aircraft in the past seven months.

Beer on recreation has been stopped as the supply of it has been exhausted.

Sunday, April 1, 1945: Today is Easter Sunday. It is another fine day. Protestant sunrise services were held on nearby Grande Island. The shore is only 300 yards from the *Montpelier*. The Protestants aboard ship arose at 5 A.M. and were transported to the beach in an LCD. Hundreds attended the services as it was a very large turnout. At 9 A.M. Catholic Mass was held topside. Many of the churchgoers received Communion. Captain Gorry was present. He never misses Mass on Sunday. Every one of our Captains, both Protestant and Catholic, were devoted church members. They set an example for the rest of the crew. Approximately 500 men attended Catholic services, among the group was a Filipino. Palm freely decorated the altar. It was acquired on the beach yesterday. The chaplains of both faiths get along together famously. One would think that they belonged to the same faith. This is the type of "team play" everyone on the *Montpelier* appreciates. We are proud of all of them.

I will try to cover what has taken place in the past week. I received a letter from my sister. We will be paid $10 a month for now. On paydays we are allowed to draw only $10. If more money is needed, a very good reason has to be provided. Many on board are gambling and this curtails it somewhat. During the first of the week, three men from each division were selected for a sightseeing trip to Manila. Other cruisers followed the same procedure. Sixty men from our ship were chosen. They left aboard a couple of destroyers at 6:30 A.M. It takes two hours to arrive at Manila as the destroyers travel at a speed of 25 knots for the short journey. Whites with no tie was the uniform of the day for them. They will remain in Manila until 3 P.M. This will be the first time that sailors in whites have been in Manila. The idea behind the wearing of whites is to build up the morale of the civilians. It must have brought back fond memories to the people of Manila to see them. It must have made them feel a little better, bringing back old times before the war, even if their city is almost in ruins. The "Pearl of the Orient" will be rebuilt. The people of Manila were very happy to see the sailors. They said that we were the first ones in whites since the war began. I was not one of the fortunate fellows to go. The sailors returning said that Manila was in a terrible condition. The Japs destroyed every major building in the city, before evacuating. The place stunk, etc. Manila Bay was loaded with sunken Jap ships. Water had to be brought along in their canteens and their own food was provided for. There is talk aboard ship that we will pull into Manila Bay in a few days. If that is so, the remaining crew will have an opportunity to view the city. There is also rumor that the *Montpelier* will leave for Borneo around the 15th of this month to land troops.

A British task force is now operating with the American Fleet off Japan. The Pacific War has been strictly an American effort up to now. Today at noon approximately 100 LCIs arrived. Some action must be in store.

Monday, April 2, 1945: We left Subic Bay at 7 A.M. and dropped anchor in Manila Bay at 9 A.M. the same morning. Three destroyers and the light cruiser *Denver* accompanied us. As we entered Manila Bay, we passed Corregidor in the center of the bay. Traveling further into the bay, we passed a cement casing in the water, shaped like a battleship. It had a couple of 16-inch turrets on it. It was built by the United States in peacetime and was used as a fort. Bombs could be dropped on it all day without doing extensive damage to it. It has been very difficult to recapture it from the Japanese. In approaching Manila, sunken cargo ships cluttered the bay. Manila Bay is 40 miles long and 40 miles wide. We were the largest warships to enter the Bay after the surrender of Manila. It is only two months since Manila has been recovered by our troops. Jap ships were on both sides of us as we neared Manila. Japs are believed to be hiding in some of the ships. We dropped anchor about one mile from shore. Closer to shore, the water was full of Jap ships. There must have been over a hundred ships sunk in Manila Bay. Warships, transports, cargo, etc. dotted the waters. Some were turned on their sides; some had a large part of the ship showing above water, while others only the smoke stacks or masts were visible. I counted twenty-five sunken ships in one small area. Those were above water. The ones underneath were impossible to number. The major part of this victory belongs to the pilots. The Japanese Navy had taken a disastrous defeat here. Docks and piers were extensively damaged. I could see Manila from the *Montpelier*. It seemed like any large city in the United States. Before the war the population of Manila was over half a million. This morning the 1st section was permitted to enter Manila. The 3rd section will be allowed to go there in the afternoon. The second section will round it out tomorrow. The uniform of the day was whites. I will leave tomorrow afternoon with the 2nd section. We had movies tonight on board ship.

Tuesday, April 3, 1945: All hands were up at 6 A.M. This afternoon I went to Manila. We left the ship at 11:45 A.M. aboard an LCT. As we got closer to the shore, I could almost touch the sunken Jap ships on both sides of me. I could see Filipinos on one of the ships taking what they could use. The water was only one foot above the main deck. Many of the ships had their anchors in the mud and this seemed to be the only means of keeping the ships from turning over. The merchant ships carried little in the way of guns. When we reached the shore, we met the men from the morning excursion. They were waiting to return to the ship. They all had bundles of Jap invasion money in their possession. The post office was distributing it free. While in Manila we could travel by truck or walk. In most of Manila all the buildings were destroyed. Japanese demolition crews did a complete job before evacuating. The city was a mess. The buildings were constructed of steel, brick and cement. Destroying such as these was an enormous task. Japanese and English words were written on most of the buildings. It was just two months ago today that our troops entered Manila. It was a shame to see such beautiful buildings destroyed. Street after street was nothing but ruins. The Japs did a thorough job. Machine gun and artillery entrenchments were numerous. Manila will take years to rebuild. The sections of the city that had been destroyed were deserted. They looked like ghost towns. Japs are still hiding in the ruins and are hard to get at. I came upon the section where the trolley cars were housed. Every one of them was destroyed. A dead horse lay across the street. The odor from it was very strong. Not too far away, a crushed tank barred the middle of the road. We passed the walled city where the Japs held out for such a long time. The walled city is a very old stone fort, its walls very thick. Only the other day, a couple of Jap snipers were killed there. We arrived at the compound for the Jap prisoners of war but were not permitted to see them. We went to St. Thomas where the Americans were imprisoned by the Japs. We could not enter because the repatriated prisoners were being readied for the return trip to the United States. The area was surrounded by a steel fence. Before leaving for the ship we saw the American civilians, who were held prisoners for three years. They looked very sickly. The girls among them looked very pale and run down. Their skin had the color of bleach, it was so white. A faraway look, as in all of the prisoners' eyes that I have seen so far, was there. It will require a long while to restore the health that they lost. Some of the girls were very attractive. They wore no makeup and sunglasses were prevalent. The poor diet that they had received under Jap treatment made their eyes very sensitive to the sun. In one instance the Japs furnished the prisoners with one pig to feed 2000 people. Very little was given them to eat and many were tortured. When the sailors arrived last week, decked out in their whites, the girl prisoners said that they were a sight for sore eyes. After looking at the Japs for three years, this was really a treat.

When we left the ship at noon, we were told not to buy any whiskey. Sailors before us went blind and others died from it. It was made out of the alcohol left behind by the Japs. Each man carried a canteen of water with him. While in Manila, I went by the residential section of the city. The destruction to the beautiful homes there was overwhelming. The area was in such a state that in clearing the wreckage, one would not know where to start. I saw a little Filipino boy and he had the appearance of a skeleton. In the city some of the stores were opened for business. They were the lucky ones whose stores were not destroyed. Many goodlooking Filipino women were on the streets as we passed by. American WACs were also there. As we neared the Chinatown district, a large truck of wounded soldiers passed by. A large building was in view and the clock on it stopped at 2 o'clock. The weather was hot and the streets dusty from the destroyed buildings. While in Manila, I purchased a few goods from the civilians. They were of Japanese make that they had left behind them. I had to pay $1.00 for a large paper bag to put them in. A paper bag of this kind would sell for three cents in the States. There is much more to relate but I cannot remember it all for the present. We arrived on board ship at 3:45 P.M. We then left Manila Bay for Subic Bay at 4 P.M. We pulled into Subic Bay at 6 P.M. Movies were held topside as usual. Our troops are still fighting the Japs on Luzon.

Wednesday, April 4, 1945: I spent the day on Grande Island, digging trenches for water pipes. We had sandwiches and cold grape juice for dinner. We left the island at 5 P.M. for the ship.

Thursday, April 5, 1945: We got paid today. There is not much to write about. The Press News reported that our troops invaded Okinawa this week. It is about 250 miles from Japan. The Americans are 130 miles from Berlin. Russia discontinued relations with Japan. It's about time. The war will be over this year.

Friday, April 6, 1945: Admiral Riggs arrived on board ship today. We will be the flagship for the task force again. When we left for the States in August, we gave the flag to the *Denver*. The Admiral transferred to the *Denver* at that time and took his staff with him.

Tuesday, April 10, 1945: All hands on deck at 5:45 A.M. I left the ship this afternoon at 3 for a working party aboard a supply ship. I stayed there until 10 P.M. We handled many cases of beer — 2000 cases were placed on an LCT, our own ship and a few of the other ships. Some of the men broke into the beer and were feeling pretty good. After the completion of the work, everyone was given two bottles of beer. Our supper was brought over from the ship. It consisted of sandwiches and orange juice. Cookies were provided for dessert.

At 2 A.M. Sunday morning all hands were at stations as we left Subic Bay in a hurry. Four cruisers and the destroyers left with us. We headed north towards Formosa at full speed. We went at

30 knots all the time but at 9 A.M. we turned back. The Japanese warships that were headed in our direction retreated to their own shores. I've come down with a cold. It's very bothersome. First cold since last Oct.

Wednesday, April 11, 1945: We departed Subic Bay for Mindoro today. We will stay there a few days and then leave for Mindanao where we will land troops. Near the end of this month, we will invade Borneo.

Thursday, April 12, 1945: We anchored at Mindoro this morning. The first thing on the docket was to refuel. Most of the crew on the tanker were from India. They wore funny clothing. Their wearing apparel consisted of a pair of pants with a blue skirt and red belt. Some of them were pretty mean looking. We took on many supplies and will receive them every day that we are here. We expect to leave Saturday.

Friday, April 13, 1945: It came over the radio this morning that President Roosevelt died Thursday at Hot Springs, Georgia. He was sitting for a portrait before severe pains in his head overtook him. A few hours later he was dead. The people all over the world were shocked by the news of his death. On board ship we could not believe it at first. The flags on all of the ships will be at half mast for a month in honor of a truly great American. We lowered ours this morning.

In the European War the Americans crossed the Elbe River, west of Berlin and only 50 miles from the capital city. The Russians are 30 miles from the gates of Berlin. Fighting on Okinawa is fierce.

At 11:45 this morning, a three star General and his staff came on board. He will be in command of the Mindanao Invasion. They will remain on board until we reach Mindanao. A war correspondent was with them. The General's name is Lt. General Robert L. Eichelberger. He is in command of the Eighth Army. His army took an active part in the Luzon and Palawan Invasions. When the General arrived, everyone wanted a look at him. His outfit has made quite a name for itself. The Japs will see plenty of him and his troops before the war is over with. Admiral Riggs,

Captain Gorry and some of the flag officers greeted the General when he boarded. At 4:30 P.M. the General, Admiral, Captain and a few other officers left the ship in a skimmer for a picnic. They wore their bathing trunks. Food and drinks were carried with them. It was a beautiful day for a picnic and a swim.

More supplies were taken aboard this afternoon. Swimming was allowed over the sides of the ship.

Saturday, April 14, 1945: We were kept busy carrying stores this morning. The General and the war correspondent passed me as they were strolling around the ship. We are now on our way to the invasion of Mindanao, the second largest island in the Philippine group. It is located south near Borneo. It feels good to be on our way to an invasion again. It puts new life into the crew. We have not received any information of the oncoming invasion but some of the men seem to think that we will take our time arriving at the island. Our speed is 10 knots. At this rate we will arrive there in two and a half days.

When we arrive, more bombarding will be assigned to us. The light cruisers are the largest warships in the group. The cruisers *Cleveland* and *Denver* have accompanied us, plus many destroyers. A communications ship is also with us. The invasion fleet is over a hundred in number, not including the warships. Other ships may join us later. The day was beautiful as the warships were the first to leave Mindoro harbor. We waited outside the harbor until the convoy formed. Everyone believed our troops would land on Mindanao last October during the early weeks of the Philippine invasion, because it was situated in the south, but we landed on Leyte instead. The Japs have their most notorious prison camps on Mindanao.

The sea is calm and the sky blue. From my vantage point on the highest part of the ship, next to the searchlights, I can view the transports spread out for many miles as they position themselves in the convoy. There is nothing in front of the warships but open seas.

At 7 P.M. all hands were ordered to sunset General Quarters. Captain Gorry spoke to the crew informing us that we will land

50,000 Army troops near Davao, Mindanao, Tuesday, April 17. Our speed will be held to seven knots at all times. He also mentioned the three star General and his staff, also the war correspondent from the Associated Press.

Memorial services for the late President Roosevelt will be conducted tomorrow morning topside. Everyone will be present. At 8:15 I slept topside. The sky above was full of beaming stars. The waters below were calm and peaceful. The *Montpelier* will lead the convoy with a few destroyers paving the way in front of us. As the ships behind us cut through the blue Pacific, it's quite a thing to behold.

Sunday, April 15, 1945: Arising at 5:30 A.M., breakfast was served at 6:45 A.M. Had church services this morning on forecastle, memorial services for the late President. At 4 P.M. Mass was again conducted in the crew's lounge. The sun is very warm. I notice it more because of the reduced speed. Today we passed the islands of Panay and Negros. We expect little opposition from the Japanese air force on our way.

Monday, April 16, 1945: All hands were up at 5:30 A.M. Today we passed the city of Zamboanga. It's the second largest city in the Philippines. Our troops landed there March 25. More ships joined the convoy. As we passed, natives in canoes waved to us on board. Today is another sunny day with calm seas. The invasion time tomorrow is 9 A.M. The name of the town we will attempt to capture is Parang. It has a highway that leads to the main objective, Davao, which is further to the south.

Tuesday, April 17, 1945: I was relieved of watch at 4 A.M. All hands arose at 4:30 A.M. for breakfast. Battle stations were manned at 5:30 A.M. At 6:15 A.M. both of our sea planes were catapulted. They will spot for the bombardment. At 6:30 A.M. we commenced firing. Our five and six inch guns blazed away as the minesweepers were clearing the Gulf of mines. The town is located at the other end of the Gulf. Our troops will land there. In the early morning hours, the air was damp and cool. Sunlight is an hour away.

At 7:30 A.M. the convoy neared the landing area. At 8 A.M. we ceased firing. The LCIs, close to the shore, opened up with their rockets. As the barrage was under way, I could see the air teeming with missiles. A trail of smoke followed the rockets to the beach. The beach shook with terrific explosions. At 9 A.M. the invasion barges headed for shore. The invasion was on. A short while later, a two star General came aboard the *Montpelier*. Fifteen minutes passed and he and General Eichelberger left the ship with the remainder of his staff and the reporter. They waved goodbye as they headed for the beach. We will remain here all day, then pull out to sea at night to protect the transports in case the Japs attempt to send warships into the harbor. This afternoon a PT boat pulled alongside for some cigarettes. The crew had just returned from the beach and had Jap souvenirs with them. The day turned hot as we left the Gulf at 5:30 P.M. We stayed at General Quarters all day.

Wednesday, April 18, 1945: All hands awoke at 5:15 A.M. We returned to Moro Gulf this morning after patrolling all night. We will stand by in case we are needed. Everything is progressing smoothly. When our troops reach Davao, opposition will be heavier. Before the invasion took place yesterday, a B–17 circled the fleet. A similar occurrence happened at Corregidor. Everyone believes that the plane is carrying General MacArthur. It is warmer in the Gulf because of being surrounded by dense jungle. The natives on the beach are large and rugged looking. They specialize in cutting heads off. A few Japs are probably missing something, like their heads.

My whole body ached all over, and I felt very sick. I turned hot and then cold with all my body shaking at times. I wanted to lay down because I felt terrible. Every chance I got I would lay down on the deck even if it was for a short time. I reported to sick bay and they told me that I had a fever and was running a temperature of 103. I was told to get things from my locker that I needed during a convalescence and to report back there at once. I did not return for I thought that I would feel better tomorrow. We left the Gulf again tonight. An officer came aboard tonight who was in command of the guerrillas on the island.

Thursday, April 19, 1945: We returned to Moro Gulf this

morning. Yesterday, when the PT boat arrived to pick up the General, an American soldier was in the boat. He had one of his arms missing up to his shoulder. He was probably a prisoner of the Japs at one time. I believe he knows where the Jap strong-points are on the island. His information will be invaluable. In the States he would be rejected. Out here his handicap is ignored. He is still fighting the Japs with only one arm. While he was standing in the PT boat, waiting for the General, he kept staring in the distance with a faraway look in his eyes.

I will turn myself in to sick bay as I feel as bad as I did yester-day. I had no sleep at all last night. This is the first time I have come down with a sickness since joining the Navy.

Saturday, April 21, 1945: At 4 P.M. I was released from sick bay. I had been there since April 19. I lost a little weight but I will regain it soon. It was cool in the sick bay. I had the top bunk. They fed me pills and juices all the time I was there. I had no appetite. It felt great, sleeping on something soft and not waking early in the morning when General Quarters sounded. We are out at sea now and headed back to Moro Bay with another convoy. We will arrive there tomorrow.

The Press News reported that Ernie Pyle, the famous war corre-spondent, had been killed in the Okinawa Campaign. It hap-pened on the small island of Ie Shima. This was to be the last invasion that he would cover. A Jap sniper's bullet struck him between the eyes. He reported mostly from the European cam-paigns. This was his first campaign in the Pacific. The Russians are four miles from Berlin.

Sunday, April 22, 1945: We arrived with the convoy at Moro Bay at 8:30 A.M. Mass was held at 9 A.M. topside. The Japs are using suicide planes against our fleet at Okinawa. Many warships were damaged.

Monday, April 23, 1945: We left Mindanao for Subic Bay to-night at 6 P.M.

Wednesday, April 25, 1945: We returned to Subic Bay at 4 P.M. We refueled and had mail call.

Sunday, April 29, 1945: No news for the past few days. Church services were conducted topside. We took aboard ammunition and supplies yesterday. We expect to remain here until the middle of May, then hit Borneo. It was announced over the radio that Hitler has asked the United States and England for an unconditional surrender. It was turned down, because he had not included Russia. It is reported that Hitler is very sick and may die in a few days. A German war correspondent gave the war a few days at the most to last. The Russians have captured three quarters of Berlin where they met the American troops.

The Japs have in operation a 19 foot bomb that is guided by a live Jap inside. It is then aimed at one of our ships. When exploded it kills the Jap operator and inflicts heavy damage on the vessel.

Life Magazine ran an article concerning the *Montpelier*. It said that the sea battle that we participated in at Empress Augusta Bay off Bougainville in the Solomons in November 1943 was the most skillfully fought battle of the war. Not only being the longest sea battle of the war, it was one of the longest in Naval History. Admiral "Tip" Merrill was our commander at that time.

We took on supplies tonight. Admiral Kinkaid, commander of the Seventh Fleet, and General Eichelberger, commander of the Eighth Army, sent congratulations for our part in the Mindanao Campaign.

Monday, April 30, 1945: All hands were at stations at 5:45 A.M. I had recreation today. I had a catch with a baseball and bought some bananas from the Filipinos.

Tuesday, May 1, 1945: Target practice was held this morning. We shot down several sleeves. The crew was supplemented by 250 new men. These men in turn will be transferred to other cruisers and destroyers based here. They were all dirty looking from the bouncing around they received aboard the transports, and from one island to the next until reaching us. They will be happy to settle down to an assignment on ship. Sleeping on the ground at Samar in the Philippines and other islands, they were almost eaten alive by the insects there. They were all marked up. They had also encountered snakes and scorpions on their travels. They had a rugged time of it. They got water from an old well and had to put pills in it to kill the germs. Liberal doses of quinine had to be administered for offsetting malaria. Some of the areas that they were taken to had no water to drink. They had to do with no water in the steaming jungles. K rations were their only food and washing was out of the question. After leaving the States with the best of everything, they were in for quite a disappointment, but they have become used to Pacific life.

Food has been running low, we are fed nothing but hash and canned figs.

Wednesday, May 2, 1945: All hands arose at 5:45 A.M. We received a new Junior Division Officer. We had physical drills at quarters this morning. The new men were on the main deck scrubbing their clothes this morning. They had taken a shower and had their long hair cut. They resembled tramps when first aboard but now one would never know them. They were given assignments to various ships in the harbor. They are all very happy to be stationed on a ship after their ordeal.

The radio announced that Hitler had died in Berlin.

The plan of the day said that we could write home and tell them that we were in the Palawan Campaign and that we had visited Manila.

Thursday, May 3, 1945: Things here are pretty quiet. Every three months our working stations are changed. No one likes to work in the compartments below because of the heat. Working down there, only the shorts are worn. I was on top level, now on main deck. We have the sun shining on us all day but at least we get some air. The steel deck is like a hot stove. Exercises are conducted every morning, push-ups, etc. Exercise is not looked forward to in this heat by anyone. The compartments are like an oven. If anyone puts a match on the steel bulkheads, it will light, because of the heat. Discipline is becoming very strict. No one likes it. Everyone is fed up with it. We have Captain's inspection on Saturdays when not at sea. Water cannot be used before inspection after being dirtied from cleaning our working stations. This ship follows the regulations closer than any ship in the U.S.

Navy. If we didn't know that a war was going on, we'd think that we were in the States during peacetime. After 4 P.M. if they catch you on deck with your sleeves rolled up or without a hat, they will give you extra duty. When you go down to the hot mess hall, you have to have your sleeves rolled down at all times. It becomes so hot there that the sweat pours off us in rivulets. You throw the garbage down in a hurry to get to topside as fast as possible where it is not so uncomfortable. Some people are so intelligent and yet when it comes to everyday common sense, they are complete failures. You see much of this in the Navy. When will some people grow up?

For breakfast we had hash that no one ate, a piece of bread and jam, a big sour apple that had to be thrown away with the hash. The food, we expect, but the regulations are the reason for our gripes. The war prisoners back in the United States are treated better than us. It was never like this before. Everyone is disgusted the way things are run. All these regulations should be saved and put in use after the war and not in these steaming hot Pacific holes. No wonder one of the chiefs received a beating when the ship reached the States last October. On board he doled out extra duty for the slightest excuse. His shipmates waited for him to enter a barroom in Frisco, and then one of the crew there closed the door behind him, barring the entrance and exit. Another of the crew then went to town on him. After returning to the ship, the chief had to lock himself in his cabin, because the men were going to beat him up again. He was one master of arms that learned his lesson the hard way. After all, we are not a pack of animals. It looks like the same plan will be put in effect the next time we anchor in the States. If you take off your hat to brush your hair back, there is always some ignorant master at arms waiting with the extra-duty roster. The extra duty is worked out in the hot, steaming scullery from 6 to 8 P.M. There is always someone watching. We would rather be out to sea fighting the war than to put up with this senseless routine.

This afternoon our section rated recreation. There is nothing on the beach but it excuses us from work on board and everyone goes. Two bottles of beer were distributed to the men. We bought bananas from the Filipinos and ate them as we were hungry. The Australians landed on an island just off the northeast coast of Borneo. Borneo has yet to be invaded. We may be in on the first landing of troops there. It has been officially announced by President Truman that Hitler is dead. Names of the men who have 18 months or more duty overseas are being taken. They also want to know the type of duty they want in the States. They must be sending all the men from the States that have no overseas duty to their credit over here.

Sunday, May 6, 1945: The cruisers *Boise* and *Phoenix* returned yesterday. The *Denver* arrived this morning. Do not know where they were, guess they bombarded Mindanao. We received some mail and twenty-five new men for the *Denver*. The weather is becoming hotter. We have only had a few sprinkles of rain in the past four months. The sun is shining all of the time. I bought some clothing at the small stores. Clothing is scarce on board. Some have only one shirt to wear and that is pretty well used.

Sunday, May 13, 1945: Today is Mother's Day. Because of rain, church services were held in the mess hall. I have not written because everything is quiet.

On May 7 we received the best news since the war started. The war in Europe ended. Germany surrendered unconditionally. Some Germans are still fighting the Russians in Austria. We received word at 10 P.M. that the war was over. Everyone gave a big cheer. It was great to hear the good tidings. Now the Pacific War will rate the men and supplies. The Press News reported that our troops are on their way here from Europe. Over 300,000 troops per month will be transferred to the Pacific. Discharges are being awarded by the point system. It takes 85 points to qualify. One point is credited for every month in the service and one extra point for overseas duty, plus 5 points for each campaign that rates a battle star and for each battle ribbon. This is the system the Army initiated. When the right time comes, the Navy will put this system in effect. Using this system everyone on the *Montpelier* would have an easy time for a discharge. We will not get out until the war is over in the Pacific. I have over 100 points already but they will do me no good. A lot of men are becoming sick and are coming down with the runs. We cannot swim in the bay now, because it is polluted. Our work continues until 11:30 A.M. and we eat at 11:45 A.M. The other ships in the harbor knock off at 11 A.M. and eat at 11:15 A.M. They have more time after chow to take it easy and less time to work in the morning than us. Everyone is burnt up and would like to see the kids who give these orders go back to the States and send some pros out here again. We have taken aboard many stores. Everyone is getting a good workout. Entering the holds where the supplies are stored is like entering an oven. I was soaked from head to toe with sweat.

In Washington a record is kept of each ship in each class. In the light cruiser class, the *Montpelier* heads the list. We must also be first when it comes to hard work and strict enforcement of regulations. As I sit next to the searchlights, the sky is still bright with the sun shining. A few submarines arrived from inflicting heavy damage on Jap shipping. They anchored here a few days ago. They patrol the whole Pacific and keep us informed of the movements of the Jap navy.

I attended colors as the flag was lowered at 7:10 P.M. The flag is always taken down at sunset when in port. At sea it is kept flying twenty-four hours a day. We will leave tomorrow for gunnery practice. Tuesday we will have damage control problems under simulated battle conditions.

Tuesday, May 15, 1945: It has been raining hard for the past few days. The rainy season is about to set in. There are two seasons in the Philippines, an eight month dry weather period with four months of wet weather following. With the rain pouring down in buckets, we were ordered to wash and scrub down the deck. This included the outside of the ship. The rain felt cold as we worked only in our under shorts. Battle stations were called for at 10:30 A.M., for damage control problems. It rained all the while we were there. The clouds are so low it seems that I could touch them with little effort. We cannot sleep topside on account of the rain.

Wednesday, May 16, 1945: I left the ship this morning for a stores working party on the cruiser *Nashville*. It had just returned from the States. It had procured supplies at Manus for the *Montpelier* and the other ships in the harbor. It was raining as we left the ship in an LCT. We worked all day until 6 P.M. on stores. We loaded landing craft that transported them to the other ships. It was good to be able to eat chow in the mess hall on the *Nashville* with our sleeves rolled up. Our ship could learn some things from the *Nashville*. We would have been tagged with extra duty aboard the *Montpelier*.

I was talking to the crew of the *Nashville*. They told me that 168 men had been killed when a Jap suicide plane crashed into them with its bomb load. This had occurred on their way to Mindoro to take part in the invasion there. Seventy men had been wounded in the same action. The Executive Officer had his head blown off. Only four men in the Marine division had escaped death. The remainder had all been killed. A light cruiser carries 50 Marines in its complement. Her decks were covered with the dead and wounded. Nearly all of the machine gun mounts were knocked out of action by the explosion. A 5 inch mount and 95 of its live shells blew up, sending chunks of hot steel raining down upon the crew. They spent three months in the States for repairs. Each man on board was allowed a 28 day leave while there. They also told me that the carrier U.S.S. *Franklin* was docked stateside. It was a mess of tangled steel. They don't know how it ever reached there, it was in such bad condition. The *Franklin* was hit by Jap planes last Feb. about fifty miles off Japan. A Jap airplane had flown out of the clouds and crashed into the parked planes on the flight deck. Everything exploded, bombs, high octane gas, shells, etc. Over 1600 casualties were reported. It was a miracle that it did not sink. We have a lot more ships damaged than they say.

Thursday, May 17, 1945: All hands on deck at 5 A.M. We left Subic Bay at 6:30 A.M. for Manila. We will stay there for four days. It was raining this morning when we arose. We dropped anchor in Manila Bay at 8:30 A.M. Our section rated liberty. We left the *Montpelier* at 12:15 P.M. in a landing craft. We can stay in Manila until 6 P.M.

Prices are very expensive in the city. A bottle of Coca-Cola costs $1.00 to $1.50 each, compared to five cents in the States. A small spoon of ice cream costs $1.00 also. In the center of the city, an Army truck loaded with Jap prisoners went by. The young Filipino children yelled and threw stones at them. American soldiers with machine guns were the guards. The Japs I saw on the truck were short and very husky. I talked to one of the nearby Filipino men. He seemed to be well educated. He had spent much of his time under Japanese rule, in the hills. While hiding out from the Japs, they were kept informed of the latest news by short wave radio. He had seen the infamous Death March. He said that an abhorable amount of cruelty had been shown our troops by the Japs. He had watched the American prisoners work on the docks, loading and unloading ships in the bay. The only clothes they wore were a pair of short pants and worn-out shoes. They were very weak and pale and thin. They only got a little rice to eat each day. Anytime a Jap soldier felt like sticking a bayonet into one of them, he would do so. The Jap army troops were a very poor lot, ignorant and uneducated. They had been recruited from the farms and rural areas of Japan. Whenever drunk, they committed obscenities unheard of before. They were like animals. The men in the Japanese Navy were of a better caliber, being educated, and their outrageous actions more limited. When they went in a place to drink they stayed by themselves and kept quiet. The Japs stripped Manila bare and sent all the good stuff to Japan. The Filipinos were left with nothing except their faith that the United States would liberate them from the oppressors. He told me that the city was left in rubble, but freedom again was enough to satisfy him. Everyone is overjoyed at being liberated.

The people in the States do not know how lucky they are. They have come out of this war very easy. The country is all in one piece, and they have clean homes to go to. Over here the people have nothing, the Japs took everything away from them, and the Japs brought bad habits upon the girls. It's a shame the way the girls make money. It's the same way all over the city. I never saw anything like it. Most of the girls are from 15 to 20. Little kids about nine years old are out drumming up business. They say about 70% of the females are diseased.

The whiskey that the fellows buy here is mostly homemade and it is very bad stuff to drink. I never saw so many fellows knocked out by it. Of course, being away from whiskey for eight months might explain that. It's very potent and smells like alcohol that is put in car radiators in the wintertime. A few have gone blind from drinking it, the last time we were here. Others had to be strapped in stretchers when brought aboard the *Montpelier*. They acted like crazy people.

Saturday, May 19, 1945: I got up at 5:45 A.M. and took a shower. At 6:15 all hands turned to. We broke out the fire hose and scrubbed the deck with brushes. After finishing, we ate breakfast. Our division does the same routine every morning. The rest of the crew have other jobs to perform before breakfast. I always work up an appetite before eating but am the last in the chow line because of the late finish every morning. Today is a beautiful sunny day to tour Manila. The other section rates liberty today. They left at 9 A.M. We have little to do in the way of work while at Manila Bay. I am again up by the searchlights writing and can see the city of Manila very clear from here. Manila is called "Little New York" in peacetime. Some of the men did not return to the ship until early this morning from the city. They were handed 20 hours extra duty for this. The news on the radio said that the fighting on Okinawa is still fierce. In one section our troops gained only one mile in a week. The Navy has fired 25,000 tons of shells on Okinawa in the past month. The Japs there are fighting from underground caverns. Hand to hand fighting is now developing. 50,000 Japs have been killed and only 1000 have been taken prisoners. It was also on the radio about the carrier *Franklin* that took such a licking off the coast of Japan. Of course the Navy cut the casualties down and tried to make it look not as bad as it was. They should let the people know what's really going on. We are powerful now and can afford to tell them all. B–29s dropped

3400 tons of fire bombs on Japan. The scuttlebutt now has it we will invade Borneo June 10, 1945.

Saturday, May 26, 1945: We left Manila Bay on Monday and arrived at Subic Bay the same day. The weather for the past week has been sunny and dry. It is very hot in Subic Bay. The light cruisers *Phoenix, Boise* and *Nashville* left for Manila for four days. They returned this morning. Thursday evening 15 Australian soldiers came aboard. They carried all of their belongings with them. They are the fire control party that will direct our gunnery on Borneo. Someone said we will leave for Borneo June 5. Nearly all of the Australians are big fellows. We had recreation on Grande Island yesterday and the Australians accompanied us. Two bottles of beer were given each man. Hopkins, Myers, Fields, Stevenson and myself sat under a tree on the island and chewed the fat. It was too hot to have a catch. The Australian cruiser *Hobart* arrived yesterday. Its commander came aboard the *Montpelier.* Admiral's inspection was held.

We now have seven cruisers in the bay.

Sunday, June 3, 1945: I have not written because of no news. Sunday Mass was held on the fantail. Men from the other ships and the Australian sailors from the *Hobart* attended Mass and received Communion. This week all hands were given cholera shots. Cholera is very common in China. It kills thousands every year there. One of the Marines on board was stationed in China for a long period of time, before the war. He had seen what cholera could do to a person. He said a big healthy looking person would be walking down the street and all of a sudden he would fall down, shake, shudder and twist and inside 20 minutes he would be dead. We received two shots in two weeks, both in the left arm. We will have another in six months.

It looks like that we will take part in the invasion of China, when it comes. Wood has finally received his record player from home. He has on board many records. After working hours, the men sit around and listen to them. This afternoon while the records were playing, a large group of men was present. Some of the men present were: Sam, Goon, Tomato, Chick, Tweedie, Mike, Steve, Hank, Brink, Hop, etc.

Saturday Admiral Berkey from the cruiser *Nashville* came aboard and presented medals to the crew. Tuesday we went over to Grande Island and viewed a stage show. Comedian Joe E. Brown was the main attraction. It was very good. This was his 693rd show for servicemen, more than anyone else has attempted. His son was killed in action in the Pacific at the beginning of the war. There were no girls in his act or in the whole show.

Subic Bay will be an enormous base in a few months. At least 25,000 sailors will be stationed here. Many have arrived in the last few days alone. We went to sea a few times last week for gunnery practice. Ships are leaving every day. This morning the commander of the Seventh Fleet, Submarines, came aboard. A large submarine base is at Subic Bay. They leave here for strikes against China, Japan, and the hostile waters. A PBY has just landed in the water. We should receive mail this evening. P–51 fighter planes are always overhead. It is the best fighter plane in the world, fast as lightning.

Jim Donovan is next to me as I write. He is kidding me about my worn-out shoes. We had a happy hour Thursday night, boxing, music, etc. It was enjoyed by all. Chick Bartholow broke his elbow on recreation Friday.

Tuesday, June 5, 1945: Back home, my brother John and Alice Sweeney will be married today. They will go to Canada for their honeymoon. Four of our cruisers left today for the invasion of Borneo. We will leave in a couple of days.

Thursday, June 7, 1945: We left Subic Bay at 8:30 A.M. We had gunnery practice in the morning. The sea was very rough. It rained all afternoon. Some of the fellows were seasick. We scraped paint off the deck in all the cold rain.

BORNEO

June 1945–July 1945

Friday, June 8, 1945: I was relieved of watch at 4 A.M. this morning. It rained very hard while I was on watch and the wind was very strong, it was also very dark and the ship pitched and tossed, we could not get under cover from the rain. It was like standing under a shower, you could hear the sound of the waves beating against the sides of the ship and the wind whistling in the air. The typhoon season should start pretty soon. All hands got up at 5:30 A.M. this morning. The sea was not so rough but it was cloudy. The sun came out in the afternoon and the weather was very good.

Our task force consists of 3 light cruisers and 6 destroyers. The cruisers are the *Montpelier, Cleveland,* and *Denver.* The destroyers are the *Cony, Metcalf, Easton, Conway, Hart* and *Stevens.* Tonight before we had sunset General Quarters the record player was brought topside and we listened to some music. It was like a summer night back home, the sea was calm and the fellows gathered around and everyone was doing something different as the music played and the "Mighty Monty" made her way to Borneo. At 7:25 P.M. all hands went to General Quarters. Capt. Gorry spoke a few words, he said we are going to land Australian troops on the northwest coast of Borneo at a place called Brunei Bay. It is about 70 miles above the big, rich oil fields. He said the oil is so pure that you can run it into the tankers. It does not have to be refined. The other task force of warships, 4 cruisers and 8 destroyers, will bombard Borneo this morning and cover the minesweepers while they clear the Bay of Jap mines. Our job will be to patrol 75 miles from the landing between Singapore and Borneo. The Japs still have warships in these waters. It will be our job to stop them if they should try to attack our convoy or beachhead.

The Japs are supposed to have some big warships down here such as battleships and heavy cruisers. A heavy cruiser can fire a 320 lb. shell 20 miles, a light cruiser can fire a 135 lb. armor-piercing shell about 15 miles. He said the waters around here are very dangerous because there are so many small islands with Japs still in control and we might also run aground because the waters in some areas have never been charted. We must be the first warships to enter these waters since the Japs took over in 1942. The Australians will land Sunday morning, June 10. Our force will not do any bombarding in this landing but when we land troops on the southeast coast of Borneo next week, we will do the bombarding, and the other task force of warships will do the patrolling. There will be two landings on Borneo. I do not know what kind of troops will land in the 2nd invasion. Our ships and landing craft will land the Australians in the first landing Sunday. This will be the richest prize of the war, Borneo is the second largest island in the world. It is about 850 miles long and 600 miles wide. It is rich in oil, gold, etc. It is the only place in the world where you can get black diamonds. It is close to Java, Bali, Sumatra, Celebes and not too far from China. The islands down here are the richest in the world. Java has a population of 40,000,000, about the same as Italy, and 90% of the rubber, tin etc. comes from these islands. I suppose we will land on them later. We secured from General Quarters at 8:30 P.M. It was a beautiful warm night so I slept topside under the stars, it was too hot to sleep below.

Saturday, June 9, 1945: I got up at 3:15 A.M. for the 4 to 8 watch. Tomorrow morning the Australian troops invade Borneo. Our warships in the other task force bombarded Borneo again today and the minesweepers continued sweeping the Bay. Someone said the Jap shore guns opened up on them. The weather is good down here. The sun was out all day, the sky is blue and the water is so calm that it looks like a mirror. We continued scraping the deck today. The radio said that light naval units bombarded Borneo. It happened yesterday and was on the radio today. It is 3 P.M. in the afternoon as I sit on a bucket in the 40 mm. mount with my shirt off getting the sun. There are many flying fish in the water, they come out of the water and fly quite a distance before they hit the water. We are not going very fast, about 12 knots. I will stop writing and return later.

I am back again. It is 8:30 P.M. This afternoon a piece of wood floated by with a bird sitting on it, we must be close to land. You could see big clouds of smoke coming over the horizon. It was coming from the big oil fields of Borneo, 90 miles away. Our warships must have hit the jackpot. We had sunset General Quarters at 7:30 P.M. I hit the steel at 9 P.M. It was another beautiful, warm night. As I lay on the deck and looked up in the sky I could see the Southern Cross. It is always something to see, the stars are in the form of a cross. You can only see it in the southern waters.

Sunday, June 10, 1945: All hands up at 5:45 A.M. for sunrise General Quarters. At 10 A.M. the Australian troops landed at Brunei Bay on the northwest coast of Borneo. The Australian troops are the famous Rats of Tobruk division that made history in the North Africa campaign against the Germans. Brunei Bay is in Sarawak, it is British territory. I wonder how the wild men of Borneo felt when they saw the Australians landing to drive the Japs out.

When the troops land they will head for Miri, a big oil production site about 90 miles south of Brunei Bay. We are still patrolling between Borneo and Singapore. All hands went to battle stations this morning because a Jap bomber was overhead at a great distance, 25,000 ft. We did not fire. It was out scouting around. We had a good dinner today. It was very hot on watch, another hot, sunny day. The sea was calm, there is not even a ripple on the water. It is 3 P.M. in the afternoon as I write. The Dutch also own some of Borneo along with the British, a lot of it is unexplored. They have some fabulous islands down here, but I suppose we will not get a chance to go on them. I will stop writing and come back later.

A British sub sank a Jap heavy cruiser off Singapore. It was coming up this way. The Jap bomber that was overhead this morning was a Francis. They said the Australian troops landed this morning with light opposition, they will run into tough opposition as they go inland. On the 8 to midnight watch the sky was lit up by the burning oil wells, and storage tanks on Borneo 90 miles away.

Monday, June 11, 1945: All hands got up at 5:45 A.M. and at 8:15 we had physical drills. They said that we will leave Borneo and will pull into Tawi Tawi. It is about 45 miles off the northeast coast of Borneo. Our troops took this island in April. The Cruiser *Cleveland* left us today, it will join Cruiser Force 74.01. We are 74.02. It will take the *Boise*'s place because it is going back to the States. General MacArthur is on one of the cruisers. It is cooler today as we head north. We passed some islands this afternoon. On the 8 to midnight watch we had the record player with us. We passed the time listening to music.

Capt. spoke tonight and said we left our patrolling area at 8:30 P.M. We will pull into Tawi Tawi tomorrow morning. Only one casualty in the landing. Gen. MacArthur landed with the troops on Borneo. This evening we went through Balabac Strait, land was on both sides of us, it is on the northern tip of Borneo. We passed a Jap tanker as we went through. The water is so shallow here that the ship is only 5 ft. from the bottom. There are Japs on these islands, we have no troops on them.

Tuesday, June 12, 1945: All hands got up at 5:45 A.M. It rained very hard on the midnight to 4 A.M. watch. The weather here is cooler, cloudy and rainy. Maybe it's because we are close to the Philippines, where they have the rainy season. We pulled into Tawi Tawi this morning. This must have been a big island at one time, but a volcano came up through the center. Now it is a big circle of water with land all around it. We are only 45 miles from Borneo. Only a few ships are here, they said the Jap fleet left here last Oct. when it went up to the Philippines to take on the American Navy at Leyte Gulf. This is where they planned their attack on our Navy and when the battle was over the Japs pulled into Brunei Bay, Borneo, with their crippled warships. There are many natives in boats here, they look like a mixture of Jap, Javanese, Spanish, Filipino and Chinese. They have quite a mixture in them, they are copper colored, and are the meanest looking people I ever saw. They have funny looking knives, they look like a half moon. They speak English and we traded our cigarettes for their fruit and knives when they pulled alongside the ship. It rained part of the morning. We were supposed to get fuel this morning but the tanker did not get here. It came in this afternoon at 4:30 P.M. The native huts we saw were built on high stilts, above the water. The land here is very green with jungle. We are supposed to leave here tomorrow and head south to invade the southeast coast of Borneo. We will go through Macassar Strait. We should not be too far from the Java Sea, only a few hundred miles. We will go between Borneo and the big island of Celebes. There are supposed to be a lot of sunken American ships in Macassar Strait. We will take a tugboat along with us in case some of the warships get damaged. Our minesweepers will clear the harbor at Balik-papan Bay and we will do the bombarding. Someone said the Japs have 50 shore batteries and the guns are 3 inch, 6 inch and up. The waters there are supposed to be full of the most powerful mines in the world. Over 200 ships were in on the invasion of Borneo at Brunei Bay last week.

Wednesday, June 13, 1945: I went on a supply ship this morn-ing at Tawi Tawi before we pulled out for the invasion of Balik-papan, Borneo. It was 2:30 P.M. in the afternoon when our force of 2 light cruisers and 4 destroyers left. I will write a few lines about Tawi Tawi while we are here. It is part of the Philippines in the Sulu Archipelago it consists of 88 islands, for many years the hiding places of pirates. The islands are sparsely populated. The chief industry is fishing and pearl diving.

At quarters this morning our division officer, Lt. Westfall, said the Japs have over 200 shore guns from 3 inch and up and we might get a hot reception. He said there will be plenty of mines in the water. Capt. Gorry spoke tonight at sunset General Quarters and said that we would join the minesweepers tomorrow morning near Macassar Strait.

He also said we were the first ships to go through these waters since the war started. The Japs knocked off a lot of our ships and our Allies in these waters at the beginning of the war. It was cloudy all day and night.

Thursday, June 14, 1945: All hands got up at 5:30 A.M. this

morning for sunrise General Quarters. We ate at 7 A.M. and also
joined the minesweepers about 7 A.M. There were 15 of them with
some destroyers. Some destroyers also joined us. As we went
through Macassar Strait you could see land on both sides of us.
Macassar is on our port side and Borneo is on our starboard as we
head south. This is about the closest part of the Strait, land is not
too far away. Our poor war prisoners are not too far away, but we
cannot help them. Maybe some of them can see us pass. I know
the Japs must be watching us from both islands. We have the
honor of being the first ships to go through here since the Japs
took over in 1942. Celebes is Dutch controlled. It is one of the
largest islands of the Indian Archipelago. It is a most picturesque
spot. The most beautiful and magnificent tropical vegetation can
be seen here. It is a very healthful place, the natives and outsiders
who live here enjoy a long life.

Gold is found in all the villages of the north peninsula. Diamonds are sometimes found almost at the surface of the ground
and precious stones are carried down in the sand of the torrents.
This article about Celebes was printed in the Press News so everyone would learn something about the rich, fabulous island down
here. They also gave us some history about the others. The islands
in this section cover a large area, you could fit Europe in here very
easily.

The Pacific Ocean is so vast that you could put the rest of the
world in it and still have plenty of room left over. Europe would
only make a small dot out here. Someday many of these islands
will be up to date with the latest of everything. It was cloudy all
day and it rained off and on. A couple of destroyers pulled alongside and we took on some official mail, it was about 11 A.M. A PBY
landed close to our ship and we sent a skimmer to pick up an Army
Air Force Capt. He must be going to work with us in this operation. He must have photos of where we will bombard. Our minesweepers stay in front of us at all times, we can't take a chance of
running into Jap mines. Our speed is about 9 knots. At 11:30
A.M. this morning we were 200 miles from our destination. A big
swarm of porpoises passed us this afternoon. The sea is calm. We
scraped the deck today.

Friday, June 15, 1945: All hands got up at 5:45 A.M. We are going to stand Condition 2 watches during the daytime. That means 4 on and 4 off. This morning we are outside the entrance to Balikpapan Bay, Borneo. We are about 25 miles from the beach where our troops will land. It will take some time to clear this place of mines. Our minesweepers cleared Macassar Strait on the way down here.* I can see land on my starboard side. The waters around here are supposed to be the most heavily mined waters because the Dutch, English, Australians and Americans and Japs put mines here. Our 15 minesweepers will be kept very busy. We have a small tanker with us that will refuel the minesweepers. They use a high grade fuel, not the same as we use.

This morning we got our paravanes in operation just in case we come across mines that the sweepers miss or that get loose. In the evening we took them off. The ship stopped when we put them on. The minesweepers are ahead of us and when they clear a spot we follow right behind them. We are not moving very fast, sometimes the ship stops while the sweepers continue to clear the mines. The weather was warm and sunny. At the end of the day we left here and will return the next day to continue the same operation. I do not know how long it will take to clear this place. When we get control of Borneo we will have control of the whole southwestern Pacific, because it is the key island down here and our planes will have a short trip to Java, Sumatra, Celebes, Singapore, etc. The Jap troops will be up against it when they are driven into the jungle to the unexplored interior. The place is full of poison snakes, wild animals, and the wild head hunters. They say you can find gold in the streams of Borneo. It is a very rich island, also a wild country. I would not want to get lost there. They say that Borneo was a part of Asia many centuries ago. I would like to own some real estate on Borneo. We did not sight any enemy planes

---

* We were the first Allied ships to pass over the grave of the Jap destroyer *Amagiri*. It destroyed President Kennedy's PT Boat 109 Aug. 2, 1943, and was sunk by mines in Macassar Strait about 8 months later. On July 6, 1943, the *Amagiri* and other Jap warships met a U.S. task force in Kula Gulf. The *Helena* was sunk and the *Amagiri* was damaged but escaped in the dark. If it had not been for radio silence, we might have got there in time to help them out and the *Amagiri* might never have sunk PT 109.

today. Our B–24 bombers passed over us all day on bombing missions against Borneo. The Capt. spoke tonight and said that out of
a force of 25 B–24 bombers that hit Balikpapan the other day, 12
were hit by ground fire. The Japs have over 200 big guns that can
be used for air and surface action. They are supposed to have big
6 inch guns at entrance to the Bay.

Saturday, June 16, 1945: Today is a hot, sunny day, we are
about 20 miles from the beach where the troops will land. We
are still outside the Bay with the minesweepers as they continue
to clear the place of mines. Our B–24 bombers hit Borneo again.
This morning a PBM Mariner landed in the water near our ship.
It had mail for all the ships. Our motor mailboat picked it up
for the rest of the ships. We did not move much today, while they
were clearing the mines. About 6 P.M. in the evening the sweepers
left the sweeping area. All the ships then got into formation and
left, we will return tomorrow morning. They passed the mail out
and some of it was only 16 days old. This time last year we were
bombarding Saipan, time sure flies. I slept under the stars tonight.
I never thought that some day I would be sleeping in the area of
Borneo, Java, Bali, etc.

Sunday, June 17, 1945: All hands got up at 5:45 A.M. After
breakfast we scrubbed the deck, then we continued scraping the
deck. As usual we were the only division working on Sunday. We
will keep scraping paint right up to the time we start bombarding
Borneo, then we will be at battle stations all the time. We stopped
working at 9 A.M. because of church services. It was held in the
mess hall, I went. After Mass all hands went to General Quarters,
we are closer to the beach today. We opened up with our 6 inch
guns and bombarded the rest of the morning, and all afternoon.
This is our first day to bombard Borneo and our 39th bombardment against the Japs. It will be our 21st invasion and 36th operation against the Japs and more to come. Can any ship top that
record? Our B–24 Liberators also continued to drop their bombs
today. We could see some big fires raging all day. They must be
big storage tanks. We have to knock out some of the pipelines
because when our troops land the Japs could turn the oil on them,
then set it off, burning them in a sea of fuel and flame. The sea

is calm and the weather is hot and sunny. We stayed at General Quarters until after sunset. We picked up a message from the island today sent out by the Japs, they asked for an air strike against us tonight and sure enough at 8:30 P.M. on a bright moonlight night Jap bombers attacked us. Several bombs fell in our wake, if we were going a little slower they would have hit us. It is a good thing for us that the Japs don't know we broke their code years ago.

Bombs also fell close to the other ships. There were some close calls but none of our ships were hit. We could not go too fast because the screws or propellers would leave a big, white wake and they would not have any trouble spotting us. If we were going just a little slower the bombs would have landed right near the smokestacks amidships. They had us lined up beautiful but we were going just a little too fast. The phosphorescence in the water out here lights up the place like a big, white light. When the Jap bombs exploded in the water they left a big, red glow for a while. The planes were twin engine bombers. We gave the Japs a hot reception, all of their planes did not return to their base, and for a change they did not try any suicide dives. Maybe the pilots down here do not want to die for the Emperor.

Monday, June 18, 1945: I washed some clothes early this morning. The Press News said that our military men believe Japan will give up in 90 days. Some time ago I bet Chick that Japan would give up in Sept. 1945. [P.S. they did.] Things were quiet this morning in the Bay. You can see a lot of buildings on Borneo where our troops will land. When they hit the beach they will have high land and hills in front of them. The Japs will be looking down at them if we do not knock them off. You can see some high towers, maybe they are radar towers. Our ship cannot get too close to shore because the water is shallow. Someone said our ship hit the bottom today. We got a good view of the B–24s dropping their bombs, they came in very low and what a job they did. There were some terrific explosions, the place was full of smoke and explosions. One big fuel dump has been burning for days, you can see big black clouds of smoke rising high into the sky. This used to be the Dutch Refining Co. before the war. The sweepers are very close to shore and the Japs could open up on them at any time. They have a very ticklish job, it would not take much to sink a minesweeper. Everything was going along very smoothly until one of the sweepers had its bow blown off with a magnetic mine. It was dead in the water only 200 yards from shore and right under the Jap guns. The Japs did not waste any time firing at it. We opened up on the Jap guns at once and silenced them. The Japs still have plenty of guns hidden here. They want to hold off until our troops land. Two LCVP landing craft had the ticklish job of going close to shore to rescue the crew from the minesweeper, one shell could sink these small craft. They finally made it and rescued the men right under the Jap guns. They brought some of the wounded to our ship and the only clothes most of them had on was a pair of pants. They were soaking wet from being in the water. Someone said that a couple of them swam to shore, if they did that the Japs will kill them. Before we left the *Denver* was given the job of sinking the minesweeper. It opened up with its 6 inch shells and sunk it. About 5 P.M. a PBM Mariner landed with some mail for the ships, it also took our mail. I got a letter from Mary, my brother Joe finally came back from the Pacific after being out there 5 years. He got a 30 day leave. The Capt. spoke tonight and said that our firing this afternoon uncovered 3 camouflaged shore batteries. Tomorrow we will open up on them. A Jap plane came close to our force tonight, but got away because our P–61 Black Widow night fighter ran low on gas, it had to return to its base.

Tuesday, June 19, 1945: This morning we had something for breakfast that we never had before. When they gave us fried eggs we almost passed out. This was the first time we ever had fried eggs while in the Navy. Someone must be cracking up. Everyone hit the chow line twice. Our B–24 bombers put on another show, it's quite a thing to see those big bombs explode one after another. We bombarded all day. The Japs opened up with their 6 and 8 inch guns. You could see the big flashes from their guns. After they opened up on the minesweepers, they really threw the shells at them, it was a miracle that none of them were hit. They were only about 300 yards from the shore. The Japs shells were falling all around them, the water was full of big splashes as the shells exploded. Sometimes you could not see the sweepers, they were covered with big sprays of water. The men on those sweepers must have been scared stiff. I'll bet they thought they would never come out of it alive. The cruisers and destroyers opened up on the shore guns to take the pressure off the sweepers, and no more firing was seen from the beach, but I bet we did not knock them out. The Japs are dug in very deep and are well camouflaged. The place is also alive with hidden guns. I would not want to be one of the troops in the first wave when they hit the beach. There is some talk of us going to Okinawa when we leave here. This evening a Dutch light cruiser joined us.

Wednesday, June 20, 1945: The Press News said that General Buckner in command of the Tenth Army on Okinawa was killed instantly by Jap artillery. They had a big parade for General Eisenhower, he just returned from Europe. Two destroyers came alongside and got fuel from us. We continued bombarding today, and the sweepers continued to sweep mines. We knocked out a lot of Jap shore batteries but the Japs still fired back. The minesweepers had another bad day, from the Jap shore guns, the Japs really laid it on, they could not get any closer without getting hit. It is an awful strain to get close to shore and have the Jap guns open up on you. The continuous fire from our ships makes it hard for the Jap guns to hit our minesweepers. Our B-24s dropped bombs all day on the Japs. The oil storage tanks have been burning day and night since we got here. Enormous flames rise high into the sky when the bombs explode on the fuel tanks. The place looks like a battlefield. When the bombs explode in the fuel and storage tanks the area is covered with smoke of many different colors. It is quite a sight. You can just imagine what would happen if you dropped a bomb on one of the big fuel tanks in a city, only this place is full of huge tanks. It is fantastic to see the terrific explosions. You must be able to see the smoke a hundred miles away. Everything is exploding on the beach, big oil storage tanks, bombs and the shells from our guns. What a display of explosions. The ground must be shaking like an earthquake around the Japs. There is a huge haze over the area at all times.

The trees on the hills are blown to bits and the few that are left have no leaves on them. The place is full of big holes from exploding bombs and shells, I don't know how anything can live over there. We left again tonight as usual. Some Jap planes got near our force tonight but they did not attack. It was warm and sunny today.

Thursday, June 21, 1945: I got up at 3:15 A.M. to go on the 4 to 8 A.M. watch. While on watch we could see a big red glow many miles away, the oil wells and storage tanks were blazing away. It could be seen for miles around. The fires have been burning for over a week. All hands got up at 5:45 A.M. for sunrise General Quarters. We scraped paint on the main deck until guns opened up on beach. Then we started bombarding when we returned to the Bay. This morning we really gave the Japs an awful blasting, we knocked out several Jap shore batteries and killed many. The shore batteries opened up again today as usual and the poor minesweepers had another nerve-racking day, if this keeps up their nerves will be shot. None of the sweepers were hit but many times they were showered with big sprays of water. It looked like they had it. The Jap guns were 6 inch. You could not ask for worse duty than what the minesweepers have, day in and day out, they go through the same thing, it's a good thing the sweepers are not very big. Our B–24s came over again as usual. Sometimes you cannot see them as they come in very low to drop their bombs and go right through the big thick clouds of smoke. They go down behind the hills and you think that they have been hit but then they come up again, they get a hot reception from the Jap guns. The place is a regular hornet's nest. The Japs were really going to defend this rich prize. The concussion from our big guns is terrific on the ears.

After this operation is over Slim Chrisner will get out of the Navy, his eardrums are broken. His hearing is shot from the concussion of the big guns. It is torture to have to stay near those guns when they go off. Some time ago a few of the men were near the

6 inch guns when they went off, and the concussion ripped their rain gear completely off from head to toes, jacket and pants. You can just imagine what it does to your eardrums and head. You can even feel it inside your chest, like something was being ripped loose. I have trouble with my ears also. Several of the men have trouble with their ears.

The troops will land July 1, "Fox Day." We are supposed to leave after that and join the good old 3rd Fleet up around Japan. We are supposed to pick up 2 battle cruisers on the way. They are the *Guam* and *Alaska,* we will get more dope on it later. This afternoon the Jap shore batteries opened up again with their 3 inch and 6 inch guns. One of our minesweepers was damaged and some of the crew were killed and wounded. All the dead and wounded were brought aboard our ship about 4:30 P.M. Four of the men were wounded very badly, two were nerve and shock cases, and 4 were dead. One of the men had to be given many transfusions from loss of blood. His face was as white as snow. An LCVP brought them from the sweeper to our ship. They took the chance of getting killed to rescue the men from the sweeper. When the men were brought aboard our guns were still blazing away and the fellow with bad nerves was shaking like a leaf when the guns went off. He could not control himself, he shook all over and he was crying. His nerves were completely shot, he was in bad shape. They could not find a quiet place for him because all the ships were bombarding and one ship was as bad as another. When the convoy gets here they will be transferred to a quieter place. But they will not get here for over a week. The crews on the minesweeper had another rugged day from the Jap guns. We left here about 6 P.M. for the open sea as usual. The PBY that landed here this morning has engine trouble, it was secured to the stern of one of our minesweepers and will be towed around all night with us.

Friday, June 22, 1945: All hands got up at 6 A.M. We returned as usual and started bombarding at 8:15 A.M. We fired over 500 rounds of 6 inch yesterday plus hundreds of 5 inch. The shore batteries opened up again this morning. One of the sweepers was hit with shrapnel but no one was hurt. Some of the Jap guns are in such a position that you cannot hit them. I'll bet some of the shore batteries cannot be knocked out because the bunkers are too thick. Many of the ones on Saipan were 8 ft. thick. The only way to knock them out is by assaulting them with troops, the hard way. When we open up on the shore batteries they stop firing. We have not had any fighter protection since we came down here because our bases are too far away. We bombarded all day and the sweepers swept all day. Our B–24s hit them all day as usual. Something new was added this afternoon and it was quite a show. About 100 P–38 and B–25 twin engine bombers came in strafing and dropping bombs on the Japs. They looked like a swarm of bees. They were all over the place, flying very low. There were explosions everywhere. When they left the place was a mass of flames and smoke. They have a good sized city here with good streets and sidewalks and plenty of buildings. There will not be much left to it when our troops land. The Japs are gluttons for punishment. I suppose they think the bombings and bombardments will never end.

It came over the radio that Okinawa fell, more than 90,000 Japs were killed in the 82 days of bloody fighting. We had 10,000 killed and 25,000 wounded, there will be some fighting on it for some time because a lot of the Japs are still hiding out in the hills and caves. Gen. Stillwell of Burma-China fame has taken Gen. Buckner's place as commander of the Tenth Army. This morning about 7 A.M. we buried the 4 men from the minesweeper at sea, each man was put in a dark canvas bag with a 5 inch shell in it. The reason for the 5 inch shell was to make sure they sank to the bottom. All hands assembled for the ceremony. The Chaplain said prayers, taps were sounded, and the Marines fired their rifles with a 21 gun salute. One body at a time was put on the chute with the American flag draped over it. Then the dark canvas bag with the sailor's body in it would slide into the sea. This took place off the southeast coast of Borneo near Balikpapan. These watery graves are over 9000 miles from the west coast of the United States. Those 4 American sailors were the first to be killed in the recapture of

Dutch Borneo. About 5 P.M. the Jap shore guns opened up again on the minesweepers and we returned the fire silencing their guns. Our minesweepers used smoke screens today to hide themselves from the Jap shore guns. This afternoon our B–25 Bill Mitchell Bombers dropped all kinds of bombs on the Japs, they even used skip bombs, and still the Japs came out firing. We have knocked out a lot of Jap guns but they still have plenty more. There is enough black smoke over the area and out at sea to cover any big city in the world. The huge fires can be seen many miles away. They are having a war bond drive on the ship for the 8th war bond drive. Most of the men bought bonds. We have the crew from the PBY on board. They are Australians. Their PBY was sunk. We left again tonight.

Saturday, June 23, 1945: We returned to Balikpapan this morning. A big tanker pulled in this morning with quite a few Australian soldiers. While we were getting fuel the Jap guns opened up on us and one of our destroyers not too far away. We fired back at once and continued firing as we refueled from the tanker. This was the first time that we ever got fuel and bombarded the Japs at the same time. It must be the first time it ever happened. I suppose the men on the tanker did not know what to expect. They were glad to get away from us and out of the range of the Jap shore guns. We have to drop anchor when we bombard, because the water is very shallow and we might run aground. There is supposed to be a big air strike this afternoon, about 200 medium bombers, A–20, B–25, P–38. They are all 2 motor jobs. The B–25 is the most heavily armed plane in the world. It carries 3 inch gun, 20 mm., 40 mm., 20 cal. and 50 cal. plus rockets and bombs. You need something like this against the Japs because of their Navy and land forces. It comes in strafing like a fighter plane. When the B–25s finished their bombing and strafing attack they stayed very close to the water until they were some distance from the Japs. They did not want the Japs to hit them from behind as they climbed. The Jap guns used to wait until they finished their run and when they started to climb they would open up on them with little chance of their doing much firing back. When the tanker was alongside we transferred the wounded, and some of the Australian soldiers came aboard with all their gear, they had phones etc. with them. They must be the fire control party that will direct our fire when the troops land. Yesterday we fired over 1000 rounds of 5 and 6 inch shells. I think we will bombard for 14 straight days. When we are bombarding and all the big guns are blazing away the ship rolls back and forth and kicks up the mud from the bottom of the water. This is a very funny bay, it is very shallow and dangerous. The hills here are not too high here, near the beach. There are more storage tanks on the other side of them. The pilots from our ship said the place is loaded with oil and that it is rolling down the hills like water. If you dropped a bomb on it the place would look like a river of fire. You could even drown in some places, it is so deep. It was another clear, hot day. The heat on the beach must be terrific with all that fuel burning and the hot sun beating down at the same time. Our air strike hit the Japs this afternoon and what fireworks, it was better than a movie. Our P–38s came in like streaks of lightning, strafing and dropping bombs. They were followed by the B–25s, they did the same, and when they finished our big 4 engine B–24s dropped tons of big bombs from a high altitude. When it was all over big fires and explosions could be seen everywhere. I don't know how anything could live after that, but about 2 hours later the Japs opened up with their big guns. They must be in underground bunkers that are 15 ft. thick and bombproof. Our sweepers were only about 300 yards from the shore when the Japs opened up on them. The ships returned the fire with rapid fire to silence them. It was quite a thing to see the light cruiser *Denver* firing her big 5 and 6 inch guns, they were firing like machine guns. This afternoon the light cruiser *Columbia* joined us. It just came from the States. It was badly damaged by Jap suicide planes in the invasion of Lingayen Gulf on Luzon. Another minesweeper got hit this afternoon but it was only slightly damaged. One of the shells landed in the skipper's quarters on the sweeper but it did not explode, it was thrown over the side at once. The past ten days are something the crews of the minesweepers will never forget, they have been working under the noses of the Japs all this time. The Japs fire on them every morning and afternoon, any minute could be their last on this earth, and every day they get closer to shore. We cannot go in any closer because we would get grounded. This afternoon at about 5 P.M. one of the sweepers pulled alongside with 5 shell shock cases. We were bombarding when it came alongside and every time the guns fired the poor fellows almost went insane, their nerves were completely shot. If they stayed aboard our ship they could have gone mad so we had to send them to the tanker where it was out of range of the noise — 4 of the men had to be held and the 5th one had to have two men hold on to him. He was shaking so much that he could not control himself, he was crying at the same time. His teeth were chattering like a machine gun. Every time our guns went off he doubled up and brought the two men down to the deck with him and at the same time he was holding on to a package with one hand. He wanted to get away from here as quickly as possible and you could not blame him. He might have jumped over the side. Everyone felt sorry for him. When I told the marine officer from our ship who was standing next to me that they never should have been brought to our ship because of all the noise from our guns, he looked at me very funny as if to say they would be all right. He did not agree with me and we had a few words. He was a good scout because he could have given me a bad time if he wanted to use his rate. He fought at Guadalcanal in 1942 and came from the South. They say shock is worse than getting wounded. These fellows shook all over, it was just like you put them on a big vibrating machine. The Japs must be in big caves where they push the big guns out to fire and then pull them back into the cave again. This place is also full of mines and obstructions in the water.

Sunday, June 24, 1945: We returned again this morning as usual. Sunday Mass was held in the mess hall at 9 A.M. One of the Australian soldiers attended. We still have the Australian soldiers and officers with us. We had a good dinner today. The chicken was good, we get one good meal a week. An LST came in this morning with ammunition for the ships. Our B–24s dropped a lot of bombs very close to shore in order to explode the Jap mines. One of our B–24s accidentally dropped a bomb very close to the ammunition ship. The *Denver* and a destroyer were alongside at the time getting ammunition. The *Denver* took about 6 hours to get ammunition, they must have fired almost all their ammunition. The Japs opened up again today but they did not do any damage. We pulled alongside the LST for ammunition at 6:30 P.M. and stopped at 8 P.M., we will get the rest of it tomorrow. All hands had to carry ammunition. When it got dark we put the big lights on. We have fired thousands of 5 and 6 inch shells in almost 10 days of bombarding.

Monday, June 25, 1945: This morning the demolition crew landed, quite a distance from where we are bombarding. They went ashore in rubber boats. They have a very rugged job. They carry about 90 lbs. of equipment with them. They also stay in the water for quite a few hours and do not wear very much. The minesweepers cannot get any closer to land without getting grounded. We pulled alongside the LST and got the rest of our ammunition. All hands carried ammunition, even some of the officers helped. We took on about 3000 rounds of 5 and 6 inch today. We bombarded as usual and the sweepers continued to sweep and the bombers gave the Japs another plastering. The Japs opened up again today and our minesweepers had another day of shells falling all around them. Tonight about 9 P.M. after securing from sunset General Quarters we had to return to our battle stations because our radar picked up Jap planes. It was a very bright night, you could read a book without any trouble, and a good night for the Japs to attack us. They would not have any trouble spotting us. It was not long before the Jap planes came in on our ships. We gave them a hot reception, it looked like the 4th of July as all the guns opened up. They were mostly torpedo planes. The ships had many close calls but none of them were hit. Some of the Jap planes came down in flames blowing up when they hit the water. One of them came so close to us that we thought it was all over but we managed to escape without any damage. I slept under the stars as usual. The decks are covered with men sleeping, you have to watch where you walk or you will trip over someone. It is too hot to sleep below.

Tuesday, June 26, 1945: We got a little rain this morning. The Japs had several big storage tanks with fuel in them but you could not see them because they were camouflaged, but after all the bombings and shelling they are beginning to show up. We got our first look at them today. They are huge and hold thousands of gallons of fuel. The Japs did a terrific job at camouflaging them. If the Japs turned this fuel on our troops when they landed and then set it afire it would be all over for them. The demolition crew that landed the other day were not too far away from one of the Jap airfields. One of our P–38 Lightnings was shot down by Jap guns today, he crashed into Jap territory, he will never return alive. Late this afternoon 2 more of our minesweepers were lost by Jap mines, one went down in 90 seconds. That makes it 3 sunk and 2 damaged so far. The Japs must put mines in the water at night while we are out at sea. Anyone who says the minesweepers have an easy job is crazy. I would not want their job for all the money in the world. They are sitting ducks out there only about a couple of hundred yards from the beach, and the Jap guns pointed right at them. They have no place to hide and they never know when they will be blown to bits by mines. On land you can at least dig a hole and get some protection but those fellows are out there for everyone to see. After a while you think all the guns are pointed at you and expect them to start firing any minute. These men are all heroes and the dangerous work that they are doing will save thousands of lives.

Wednesday, June 27, 1945: It was cloudy this morning it rained hard but it did not stop our bombers from hitting the Japs or prevent us from bombarding. The bombers started early this morning, it was 7 A.M. The men on the 5 and 6 inch guns will be glad when we leave here. The past ten days they have been in those hot steel mounts and turrets passing big shells and powder cases. They sweat all day, and the men down below in the powder and shell rooms also have a very hot spot. They start passing the ammunition at 7:30 A.M. and don't stop until 6 P.M. Then they stay up all night standing their regular watches. It is pretty rugged when you get off watch at 4 A.M. in the morning and in a few hours you start firing at the Japs and continue firing all day. It is also a long, hot day down in the hot engine room.

The Japs opened up again today and the fireworks started all over again. There were some close calls for the sweepers but none of them were hit. We continued to knock out Jap shore guns. One of the sweepers pulled alongside today and the skipper was talking about the two sweepers that were sunk yesterday. He said it could have been magnetic or electric mines that sunk them. The Japs could attach a wire to the electric mines and have it run on to the beach, then they could set them off. They lost a lot of lives on both sweepers. One sweeper was blown in half. Some of the men fell in between the two sections when it blew in half. A little dog who was on the sweeper that was sunk a couple of days ago was also on this one and he was saved again. The Australian cruiser *Hobart,* one heavy cruiser and some destroyers came in today, many PT boats and gunboats also came in. A destroyer pulled alongside tonight with 60 bags of mail. It had packages and letters. The air mail was only 16 days old. I got a letter from my sister Mary, she told me all about John's wedding. The demolition squad returned to our ship this morning, they were soaking wet. They have a very dangerous job clearing the place of mines and underwater obstacles put there by the Japs, they must have worked all night. One of our B–25 medium bombers came in so low on a strafing run that it hit some trees and landed in the water. One of our small boats was sent to pick up the crew, lucky for them no one was hurt.

The Australian soldiers that we have with us are always studying their maps, charts and photos. These men are special troops and have important jobs to do when they land. It was cloudy and cool today, it rained most of the time. When we left the bay tonight we left some destroyers behind to fire star shells on the Japs all night, this will keep them awake and it will also be something new to them. Our PT boats will also patrol all night in the harbor. It was a good night to sleep topside. As you lay on the deck you could see the huge fires burning many miles away. They have been burning for over 2 weeks. The bright light that the huge fires throw could light up any big city. Millions of gallons of fuel have gone up in flames since we first got here almost two weeks ago. I had to get up at 11:15 P.M. to go on watch.

Thursday, June 28, 1945: I got off watch at 4 A.M. All hands got up at 6 A.M. We returned to Balikpapan at 7 A.M. We really opened up on the Japs today and so did the bombers. When it was all over you could see nothing for miles around but thick black smoke, it rose high into the sky for miles, it went so high that it was out of sight. I never saw anything like it before. There was enough black smoke here to cover many big cities, at the same time it was enough to choke you. I don't know how the Japs can stand it. There were many huge storage tanks exploding and so many miles of Borneo were blacked out that it looked like the end of the world. It looked like a big storm was coming the way everything was blacked out. Millions of dollars worth of fuel must have gone up in smoke and flames since we first hit this place. Borneo is one of the biggest producers of fuel in the world.

The troops are supposed to land Sunday July 1, 1945. We must have most of the big guns knocked out by now. The gunboats went in and opened up on the shore with all their guns blazing away. They really got rid of a lot of ammunition. A Jap plane came in here today but our P–38 shot it down. There is a lot of talk about the *Montpelier* joining Halsey's 3rd Fleet, and then hitting Japan, after we leave here, everyone hopes so. We would rather be at sea getting the war over so we could go home for good, instead of sitting in the same place. They said Gen. MacArthur will be down here for the invasion. He will come down on the light cruiser *Cleveland*. Today while we were covering the demolition crew, the Jap machine guns opened up on them, they had some casualties. They had a very rugged job to do, they were in the water near shore and the Japs were looking at them not too far away. They must have ice water in their veins, no wonder it is such a tough outfit to join. I can see why they have such heavy casualties. The Japs gave them a hot time with their machine guns

and mortars. The demolition crew set off long chains of explosions. They have to clear a path in the water for our landing craft
when they hit the beaches with our invasion forces. There is a big
wall and many steel posts plus mines to prevent our troops from
landing and it is up to them to clear a big path. The demolition
men can stay under water for a long time but when they come up
the Japs opened up on them. We also fired back at the Japs and
knocked out their guns and crews. Whenever the minesweepers
or landing craft run low on water and supplies it is the cruisers' job
to supply them. We also give fuel to the destroyers. We received
a message for the Australian ships today, they sent one of their
destroyers alongside to receive the message. It was a very large
destroyer.

Friday, June 29, 1945: It was cloudy and rained most of the
morning. We continued bombarding as usual and the minesweepers continued sweeping.

We gave some 40 mm. ammunition to the gunboats this morning. They can get close to the shore and spray it with machine
gun fire. We also gave water away this morning. Our bombers
gave the Japs another plastering this morning. While a destroyer
was alongside getting fuel the Priest from our ship went aboard the
destroyer and said Mass. It came over the radio that we are down
here. The communiqué from Gen. MacArthur said the 7th Fleet
was operating in Macassar Strait between Celebes and Borneo.
This was the first time in almost 3½ years that Allied ships have
operated here. It also said that we were under air attacks and are
bombarding Balikpapan, the big Dutch refinery on the southeast
coast of Borneo. This afternoon our medium and heavy bombers
hit the Japs very hard. One of our B–25s after a strafing and bombing run tried to climb but it crashed into the water as it headed
for the open water. It was between us and the beach but not too
far from the beach. It broke in two and only two men from a crew
of 6 were saved, the other 4 went down with the bomber. The
sea plane from our ship landed close to the two men in the water,
and saved them. One of the men was just going under but he
was picked up just in time. Both men were injured, they were

brought aboard our ship and put in sick bay. We expected the Japs to open up on them while they were being rescued but they did not. The weather for the past few days has been cloudy and raining most of the time. At sunset General Quarters Capt. Gorry said the troops will land Sunday July 1, 1945 and "Fox Day" is the code name for the day. He also said the light cruiser *Cleveland* and 3 escort carriers with some destroyers will be here for "Fox Day." The fighter planes from our carriers will be the first fighters to be used here because our land bases are too far away for the fighters to make the round trip down here. I slept topside and chewed the fat with Stevenson and Hays before going to sleep. There were plenty of stars in the sky. There was a big red glow in the sky as the big fires continued to burn on Borneo. They have been burning for over 2 weeks, I don't know how they are going to put them out when our troops land, they could burn for months. It's quite a sight to see at night. Our ship knocked out many different targets but one of the prize ones was a big natural gas plant, it looked like the huge fiery pits of hell with its huge balls of fire that covered a great area. The thick black smoke that shot up from it blacked out everything for miles, it was worse than thick black soot. You would get lost in it and die from suffocation. The people must have been in a panic.

Saturday, June 30, 1945: Our sleep was interrupted at 3:30 A.M. this morning because it started to rain. It was funny to see the fellows running in all directions as the rain came down. It was quite a scramble to get under cover. We started bombarding about 7 A.M. The gunboats got close to shore again and opened up with their 40 mm. machine guns and the bombers continued their bombing. The place was covered with thick, black smoke. It was also quite a sight to see the phosphorus shells explode with their big white sprays. The black smoke and the white colored phosphorus streaks made quite a picture, it looked like a painting. We are still knocking out Jap guns and Japs. They should be running out of shore guns by now. I saw some Corsairs today. They are the first fighters to come down here since we got here, they must be from our carriers. It is nice to have them around. It was cloudy

all day. There is talk about this being the last operation for the
7th Fleet. It will dissolve and join the 3rd and 5th Fleets. They
are going to let the British, Australian, and Dutch warships take
over the other islands down here. A small ammunition ship
pulled alongside today and we took ammunition on. We are going
to bombard tomorrow morning before the troops land. We gave
water to a landing craft today. The light cruiser *Cleveland* pulled
in late this afternoon. It just came from Manila with Gen. Mac-
Arthur. It has mail for us. The Capt. said that after this operation
we will go to Leyte and then join the 3rd Fleet. We are supposed
to land troops somewhere July 20, on "George Day." It will be
like old times working with Bull Halsey's 3rd Fleet. Everyone
wants to operate with him. I guess we will hit Japan. Everyone
hopes so.

   Sunday, July 1, 1945: Today is "Fox Day." Balikpapan, Borneo
will be invaded at 9 A.M. this morning, by the veteran Australian
7th Division. These troops have fought all kinds of warfare, they
also fought the Germans in North Africa. Many of them fought
the Japs in Burma and other islands in the Pacific. All hands got
up at 5 A.M., we had breakfast at 5:15 A.M., and at 6:15 A.M. all
hands went to their battle stations. Today will be the 53rd time
for the *Montpelier* to bombard Jap-held territory since it left the
States in 1942. This must be a world record for all wars. At 7 A.M.
we started bombarding. All the ships opened up on the Japs, this
included heavy and light cruisers and destroyers. While we were
bombarding, our 4 engine B–24 bombers dropped tons of bombs.
It was quite a sight, bombs and shells were exploding everywhere.
The place was covered with many colors of smoke. Huge explosions could be seen everywhere. Just before the troops landed the
LCI rocket ships opened up with rockets. It was really quite a
sight. After about 2 hours of bombarding the troops landed.
While the troops were hitting the beaches we continued to fire over
their heads to prevent the Japs from firing on them and the landing craft. You could see a lot of big splashes in the water very close
to the landing craft as the Japs opened up on the landing craft with
guns and mortars. Some of the men were sprayed with water from

the exploding shells as they hit the water close by. It was really
quite a sight. There were so many different things to see. We
never had an invasion like this before. The long beach where the
troops landed was covered with our landing craft as they put our
troops and supplies ashore. The noise from the guns on our ship
was deafening and the concussion was really bad, it hurt you all
over. The guns just blazed away for two continuous hours without
stopping. The ship kept rolling back and forth as the guns blazed
away. The men who were on topside took an awful licking from
the big guns exploding close by. When the guns fired they would
almost lift you off your feet. The boys will have plenty of trouble
with their eardrums after this. Everything close to the guns was
ripped up and loosened. Sometimes the concussion would knock
the cotton out of your ears. Today was our 15th straight day to bombard Borneo. In that time we fired thousands of 5 and 6 inch shells
and our bombers dropped thousands of tons of bombs. It was a
beautiful sunny day for the invasion. I do not know how many
troops are going to land. But the place is full of large troopships,
cargo ships and other large landing craft. The sweepers did a great
job of clearing the place of mines, none of the landing craft came
across any mines. Our troops were held up when the Japs blew up
all the bridges. Gen. MacArthur went ashore with his troops this
morning. He also had a very close call when the Japs opened up on
him. They said it did not bother him in the least. He did not
bother to get under cover.

This afternoon one of our B–24 bombers had to crash, so the
crew bailed out. They landed very close to the beach. One of our
seaplanes rescued them. We will stay here tonight for a change.
Sunday Mass was held at 6:30 P.M. in the crew's lounge.

Gen. MacArthur left here late this evening on the light cruiser
Cleveland for Manila. Before he left he sent a message to our ship
congratulating us for our part in the campaign. I slept topside in
Balikpapan Harbor tonight and as you looked towards the beach
you could see plenty of gunfire. It was a very dark night but the
place was lit up for miles around like daytime. The *Montpelier*
was about 400 yards from shore but it looked like a bright, clear

day. The huge storage tanks are blazing away just as they were over two weeks ago. The troops on the beach must be roasting from the terrific heat. I don't know how the Japs stood it so long. This campaign was different from all the others. We never came across a place like this before. The rivers of oil and huge fuel tanks never stop burning. I'll bet an awful lot of Japs were roasted to death and drowned in oil. I have to go on watch at midnight. I will not get much sleep.

Monday, July 2, 1945: While I was on the midnight to 4 A.M. watch my friend Donovan told me that two Jap heavy cruisers and some destroyers were going past Java and heading up Macassar Strait to knock off our transports and supply ships and bombard our troops on Balikpapan. Our subs must have spotted the Jap ships. We did not waste any time getting under way. About 2:15 A.M. the light cruisers *Montpelier, Denver* and *Columbia* and some destroyers left Balikpapan Harbor to intercept the Jap warships. The other warships were left behind to cover the transports and troops. The hours passed as we sailed south through Macassar Strait in the direction of Java and Bali. It was very dark and it reminded us of the old days in the Solomons when we used to go up the Slot after midnight to take on the Japs. Admiral Merrill and 31-knot Burke would be right at home if they were with us. The hours passed and it finally got daylight but still no Jap warships. They must have returned to their base. We continued sailing south but it began to look like we would never catch up with the Japs so we turned around and headed back to Balikpapan. We were disappointed but we at least had the satisfaction of being the first ships to sail this far south since the Japs took over 3½ years ago. Everyone was hoping that we would go to Java and Bali. It was about noon when we returned to Balikpapan and the two light cruisers *Nashville* and *Phoenix* were waiting there to relieve us. The Australian soldiers and the pilots we rescued were transferred to the *Nashville* and about 2:30 in the afternoon we left Balikpapan and headed north for Leyte. Balikpapan was our 21st invasion and our 36th operation against the Japs. When we reach Leyte in the Philippines about one thousand miles away we will get food supplies and ammunition and then leave and join Bull Halsey's 3rd Fleet. His 3rd Fleet was very small when we first joined it when we left the States in 1942. Now Halsey's 3rd Fleet is the largest and most powerful the world has ever seen. We will be in task force 33 or 38. The *Columbia* and 3 destroyers left with us today. The *Denver* will leave later today. The Press News said that when our bombers started bombing Balikpapan June 15, 1945, the antiaircraft fire was the heaviest you could run into, it was terrific, the place was covered with all kinds of guns. It got lighter as the days passed and as our ships and bombers continued to knock them out. The city of Balikpapan is in ruins from the planes and warships. The Australians have about a 2 mile beachhead so far.

CHINA
AND JAPAN

July 1945–December 1945

Tuesday, July 3, 1945: We got paid today, the men can only draw $10 plus money for war bonds. We are still going through Macassar Strait this morning. Borneo is on our port side and Celebes on our starboard. Our trip to Leyte is over one thousand miles. I had a working party in the hangar this afternoon. We had sunrise and sunset General Quarters. Capt. Gorry spoke today and as we were passing Tawi Tawi he said the big Jap fleets used to stay there. In the darkness you could see a light. He said we would not stay in Leyte very long and that we would be in Task Force 33. It is a part of the 3rd Fleet. He said tomorrow was the 4th of July and we could have a holiday routine. Everyone gave a big yell when he said holiday routine. It will give us a chance to get some rest and write some letters. It rained a little at 11:15 P.M. while I was sleeping topside tonight. I got under cover and when it stopped we went back to sleep again.

We received the following message from the Supreme Commander, General MacArthur:

As the Seventh Fleet leaves the Southwest Pacific Area I desire to express my admiration and grateful acknowledgment for the magnificent manner in which all of its fleet elements have performed their assigned tasks in the campaigns of this theatre. To you and your officers and men who have with great gallantry, resourcefulness and devotion so fully upheld the highest traditions of our naval service send God Speed.

Wednesday, July 4, 1945: Today is the 4th of July. Last July 4th we were in the Saipan Campaign and the July 4th before that we were in the South Pacific in the Solomons for New Georgia campaign.

We had a good dinner today, it was a good celebration. They served turkey. We will pull into Leyte tomorrow morning. They said we will be busy for a long time up around Japan. That's the way we like it. I wrote a letter to my sister Mary, it was the first in about a month. We were too busy to write. Someone said we chased the Jap warships to the Java Sea the other morning. This afternoon we fired our 20 and 40 mm. machine guns. The cruiser *Cleveland* joined us about 6 P.M. tonight.

Thursday, July 5, 1945: We did not have sunset General Quarters last night or sunrise General Quarters this morning because it is safe here. We pulled into Leyte at 11 A.M. this morning. It took almost 3 days to get here from Balikpapan. The last time we were here was the first of Jan. It is very hot here. There must be hundreds of ships of all types here in Leyte Gulf. I saw 4 hospital ships here. We got fuel as soon as we got here. We got a good burn from the sun while on watch. I hope we don't stay here very long. This afternoon the two new battle cruisers came in, the *Guam* and the *Alaska*. They are the only 2 battle cruisers in the Navy. They are like a pocket battleship. Their largest guns are 12 inch but they can fire farther than a 16 inch gun. These ships are very slick looking and pack quite a wallop. They are covered with all kinds of guns. They can really maneuver and can sink a battleship. They also carry the latest equipment in the world, and are almost the same length as a battleship. They are going to operate with us. This evening we took on supplies. We also got some mail, some of it was only 10 days old. My sister said that my friend Arthur Shaughnessy was killed June 17 on Okinawa. He was only 24 years old. I could hardly believe it. He was sergeant in the Marines. Arthur Shaughnessy was one of the best all around athletes to come out of our city. We played many a football, baseball and hockey game together. Gen. MacArthur said all the Philippines are free, and the Philippine Campaign is over. Our troops first landed on Leyte Oct. 1944. It took almost 9 months. A lot of Japs are still hiding in the hills and jungle and it will take some time to get them all. The Japs had almost four hundred thousand troops there and almost all of them were killed.

Friday, July 6, 1945: All hands up at 6 A.M. We will take on over 100 tons of food. We started getting it last night. We brought a lot of apples and oranges on and everyone was eating fruit while they carried stores. This is the first time we got so much fruit in about ten months. The ammunition ship pulled alongside and we got thousands of 5 and 6 inch shells plus machine gun ammunition. We worked all day until 6 P.M. It was a very hot day. All hands went to battle stations while we were sleeping tonight but the Jap planes did not attack us. We secured and went back to sleep. I had to get up at 11:15 P.M. to handle small stores. I might get a night's sleep tomorrow.

Saturday, July 7, 1945: This morning something happened that never happened before since we joined the Navy. All hands were able to sleep until 7 A.M. Boy were we surprised. It must be because we worked very hard carrying ammunition and stores. We did not get much sleep during that time. We had breakfast at 7:30 A.M. We painted this morning and the fellows in the 3rd section went to Samar. It takes about 2½ hours to get there. We expect to see Japan this month. We are going to give it a bombardment. This should be a very interesting operation.

The storekeepers are getting the cold weather clothing ready, just in case we need it. I have not had any winter weather since 1942. The ship fitters are rigging the ship so we will be able to take on ammunition and supplies while we are at sea. About 15 men left for the States today. Hall, one of our old shipmates, is on the heavy cruiser *New Orleans,* he came aboard to see us. He said a huge force of warships left here before we pulled in. There are so many ships in here now that you could not count them all, and I do not mean any landing craft.

Sunday, July 8, 1945: We are still in Leyte Gulf. There are still plenty of bugs in our bread. The flour is loaded with small hard bugs. When you carry a big bag of flour on your shoulder you are covered with bugs. It would be impossible to separate them from the flour, so they just leave them there when they bake the bread. When you pick up a slice of bread it is covered with bugs. It does not bother us because we have been eating them for a long time. It is so hot out here that everything turns bad very quickly. We still have water hours, we had them off and on since we came out here in 1942. The water is off from 8 to 11:30 A.M. and from 1 P.M. until 4 P.M. and then goes off at 8:30 P.M. The showers are turned on at 4 P.M. The drinking water is always on. Yesterday our ship made 42,000 gallons of water and we used 40,000 gallons. Mass was held in the mess hall. Some ships do not stand gun watches during the day, only at night.

Tuesday, July 10, 1945: The radio said Halsey's 3rd Fleet was hitting Japan with its carrier planes. Over 1000 planes were in on the strike. Everyone is mad because we missed the 3rd Fleet when it was here. We got here too late to join it. They pulled out of here for Japan before we got here. We were supposed to leave with them. We don't know what we will do now.

We went out for gunnery today.

Wednesday, July 11, 1945: At quarters this morning our division officer Lt. Westfall said Admiral Lowe of the *Guam* left for Guam a couple of days ago for orders and that he will be back tomorrow at midnight. We are supposed to have everything secured and ready for sea tomorrow night just in case we pull out at once. The radio said that Japan is talking Peace but Ambassador Grew said the U.S.A. has not been informed about it. The B.M. 1/c in charge of our division might go to the hospital soon. Everyone hopes he makes it. The Filipinos from the beach put on a show for us tonight. It was held on the fantail, they had girls with them. It was very good.

Thursday, July 12, 1945: I went over to the beach for recreation this afternoon. It was very hot there. I never saw so many fights. Every time you looked around two sailors were slugging away at each other, there was never a dull moment. The boys put on some good bouts. There is not much to do here, just play basketball and softball, but it was too hot to play today. It was not too hot for the boys to fight though. Everyone got two cans of beer. The band from the *Dixie* came on tonight and put on a show for us, everyone enjoyed it. It looks like we got our orders. We will be in the 9th Fleet instead of the 3rd. We will be in the Task Force 95.02. If we got here a couple of days sooner we would be operating with Bull Halsey's 3rd Fleet. We have operated with about every fleet out here. They said the 9th Fleet operates out of the Aleutians. We might operate with the 9th for this operation and then work out of Okinawa. We will get more dope later.

Friday, July 13, 1945: All hands got up at 5:30 A.M. and we left Leyte Gulf at 7 A.M. Our force consists of two battle cruisers, the *Guam* and the *Alaska*, 4 light cruisers and 8 destroyers. We are on our way to the China coast, guess we will be very close to Shanghai. It is about 1500 miles from here. It will be our job to sink any Jap ships that try to transport troops from China to Japan. We will stop at Okinawa on the way and get fuel and ammunition. We might get there Monday. We did a lot of firing this morning and afternoon at sleeves and drones. They are changing the men around on the machine guns. I am now on Mt. 47 as a 3rd loader, every man is able to take over any position on the mount. Our mount is very high, it is also past midship aft. We had night firing, we fired star shells and also fired our big guns at a sled that was towed by a small boat. It was just like firing at a Jap ship. It was a very dark night. We also had a busy day, we fired all day. All hands secured from gunnery at 9:30 P.M. I hit the steel at 10 P.M. and got up at 11:15 P.M. for midnight to 4 A.M. watch.

Saturday, July 14, 1945: It was not worth hitting the deck after getting off watch at 4 A.M. because all hands had to get up at 4:55 A.M. for sunrise General Quarters. Boy, was I tired. I slept on the 40 mm. ammunition tanks topside when I got off watch. We had a first aid lecture early this morning while at General Quarters. We secured from General Quarters at 6 A.M. Then we took our shoes and sox off and scrubbed the deck before breakfast. After breakfast we spent the morning painting the main deck. After dinner we went to General Quarters and had drills and maneuvers. We did this all afternoon. It is a little cooler here than at Leyte. We are off the northeast coast of Luzon, our speed is about 20 knots. The radio said that planes from Halsey's 3rd Fleet were hitting Japan and the warships were bombarding the home island, about 200 miles from Tokyo. We would miss out on that operation. Everyone is talking to himself. We had sunset General Quarters tonight.

Sunday, July 15, 1945: I had to get up at 2:30 A.M. because it began to rain. I waited under a shelter until it stopped raining and then went back to sleep again. It is too hot to sleep below. I got a little sleep before getting up at 3:15 A.M. to go on watch. I got the 4 A.M. to 8 A.M. watch. All hands got up at 4:45 A.M. for sunrise General Quarters. We had a first aid lecture again this morning while at General Quarters. Two destroyers came alongside for fuel today, the other destroyers got their fuel from the other cruisers. It took about one hour to fuel each ship. Mass was held in the mess hall. Church services have been held in about every place in this vast Pacific. We are now between Luzon and Okinawa. It is a little cooler here. Our speed is still about 20 knots. It rained a little today. They gave a blow by blow description over the radio of our warships bombarding Japan, and also the names of the ships. The *Massachusetts* and *Quincy* are two of them. We would be there now bombarding if we returned from the Borneo Campaign sooner. The cruiser *Pittsburgh* had its bow ripped off when the 3rd Fleet ran into a typhoon some time ago. Some ships were sunk by the storm, 21 other warships were also damaged. The wind from these typhoons gets as high as 150 miles per hour.

Monday, July 16, 1945: All hands got up at 4:45 A.M. for sunrise General Quarters. We pulled into Okinawa at 9:30 A.M. It took us 3 days to get here from Leyte Gulf about 1500 miles away. We are now only 325 miles from Japan. The place we pulled into is Naha, it is the capital and also the last place the Japs were driven from, there are still plenty of Japs hiding out. Our troops are still killing them. We can see the high cliffs where the Japs jumped to their death. We have many ships in the harbor. We got fuel today. This place looks like any country section in the States. There are not many trees but it is covered with plenty of green grass. Our fighters and bombers are coming and going all the time, a lot of B–29 super forts also flew over, they must be on their way to hit Japan. Our planes are hitting Japan 24 hours a day now. I thought it would be cooler here than in the Philippines but it isn't. I think it is hotter. There is a good breeze and if you are in the shade it is nice, but if you get in the sun the heat is terrific. The sun is really hot here. It is so hot in the compartments that you cannot stay there. The sky is blue and there is not a cloud in the sky. They said it was cold enough here to wear heavy underwear a few months ago. The light cruiser *Columbia* came close to us, you could see the Jap flags painted on its bridge, for bombardments, planes and ships. It shot down 24 Jap planes. It shot down quite a few in Lingayen Gulf before 3 Jap suicide planes crashed into them. They had 167 casualties. These four light cruisers *Columbia, Cleveland, Denver* and *Montpelier* have been operating together from the first of 1943 and they have made quite a record for themselves even if I do say so. We have been in every kind of naval action in the books. These 4 light cruisers have set an all round record that no other 4 light cruisers in the world can match. This statement is not to brag but just to keep the record straight.

The Capt. spoke and said that we were part of the 9th Fleet. We are to carry out a special mission for Fleet Admiral Chester W. Nimitz. We will be his special task force. We are going to patrol from the Yellow Sea between China and Japan and go south to Foochow. We will also be in sight of land, and will be able to see Shanghai. Our job is to sink all Jap ships, barges, small craft we come across. The Japs move a lot of troops around here from China to Japan, and from Formosa to China etc. At 4 P.M. tomorrow we will be in our operating area. This will be the first time American warships have gone here since the war started. We will stay up there for a couple of days.

Tuesday, July 17, 1945: All hands got up at 4:30 A.M. for sunrise General Quarters. We are at sea heading for the China coast. We spent the morning scraping the towing cable. We might use paravanes when we get to the patrol area, because of Jap mines. The sun is very hot, you feel it more when you don't get much sleep. We worked in the hot sun all morning. At 11:30 A.M. we had to turn back because a typhoon was coming down this way along the China coast. Everything happens to us. This afternoon while we were heading for Okinawa, the radio said that over 1500 planes from Halsey's 3rd Fleet hit Japan. Capt. Gorry spoke tonight and said Admiral Nimitz called off our mission against the China coast because of a typhoon heading our way. I slept topside as usual.

Wednesday, July 18, 1945: I got off watch at 4 A.M. and had a few minutes of sleep before getting up at 4:30 A.M. for sunrise General Quarters. We are still at sea near Okinawa. The cruisers fueled the destroyers this morning.

We worked all morning but they let us get some rest in the afternoon. The radio said that our forces are doing an awful job on Japan and Fleet Admiral Nimitz said that invasion is near. Pres. Truman crossed the Atlantic in a cruiser for a big conference in Europe with Churchill, Stalin and the German Pres. At 1 P.M. this afternoon we turned around and headed for the China coast again. We should get there tomorrow morning at 5:30 A.M. They passed the word to secure everything for bad weather because a storm is coming up behind us from the Philippines. We had sunset General Quarters at 7:25 P.M. The Capt. said the typhoon is heading our way, so we will not be able to hit the China coast until the weather clears.

Thursday, July 19, 1945: We fueled two destroyers about 11 A.M. The sea got very rough. We are about 230 miles south of Okinawa. The storm is getting close to us, but I guess we will keep moving out of its path. They said all the ships had to leave Okinawa because of the typhoon. The winds were blowing around 140 miles per hour. It is taking everything in its wake. We are on the outskirts of the typhoon but the winds are very strong and the sea is very rough. The ships are pitching and tossing around like little balls. It is very cloudy and dark. The destroyers are being swamped with huge waves as they go out of sight. No one is allowed on the forecastle because the big waves sweep the deck. It is a good thing the main decks were secured. The ship rides up a big wave and then it comes down bow first and out of sight into the water, it was like riding a wild horse. The Capt. said a typhoon stayed at Okinawa for 9 days once. He also said we will start our sweep of the China coast Sat. July 21, 1945. I hope so. This is getting to be a nuisance, trying to miss typhoons.

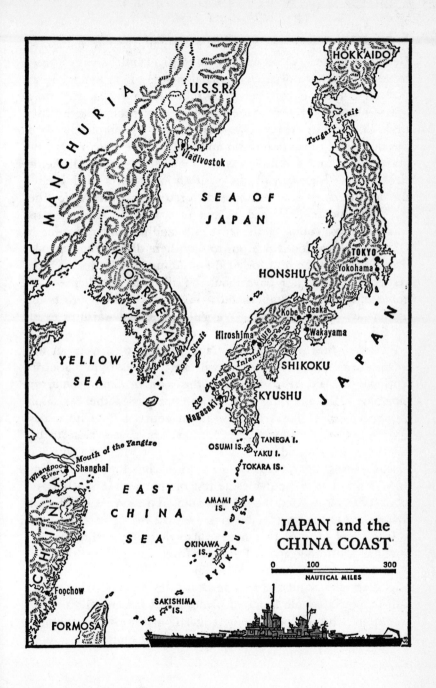

HOKKAIDO

U.S.S.R.

MANCHURIA

Vladivostok

SEA OF
JAPAN

Tsugaru Strait

KOREA

HONSHU

TOKYO
Yokohama

Kobe Osaka
Hiroshima   Wakayama
Inland Sea
SHIKOKU

YELLOW
SEA

Korea Strait

Sasebo
Nagasaki   KYUSHU

JAPAN

TANEGA I.
OSUMI IS.   YAKU I.
TOKARA IS.

Mouth of the Yangtze

Whangpoo River   Shanghai

EAST
CHINA
SEA

CHINA

AMAMI
IS.

RYUKYU IS.

OKINAWA
IS.

JAPAN and the
CHINA COAST

0   100   300
NAUTICAL MILES

Foochow

SAKISHIMA
IS.

FORMOSA

Friday, July 20, 1945: All hands got up at 4:30 A.M. for sunrise General Quarters, we secured at 5:45 A.M. While I was on the 8 to 12 noon watch a destroyer came alongside to get fuel. The sea was rough and the destroyer really rolled and pitched. Big sprays of water soaked the men on the destroyer, they looked like drowned rats. The bow of the destroyer would come up completely out of the water and then crash down and under. The spray even came up to the 40 mm. mount I was on, about 70 ft. high. All the destroyers were fueled by 9:15 A.M. It's a lot of extra work fueling the destroyers. We were supposed to return to Okinawa for fuel but the plans were changed. About 10 A.M. this morning the sea was calm. We could see the ships and landing craft returning to Okinawa, it was too dangerous to stay there during the typhoon. The storm must be over for good now. Our intelligence reported yesterday that the Japs have about 100 suicide boats where we are going and over 200 bombers and 100 fighters. These bombers and fighters are all suicide stuff. We will be the first warships to hit the China coast.

Saturday, July 21, 1945: The Capt. said that we are on our way to the China coast. I guess we will start at the Yellow Sea and work south. We will come down the coast of China tomorrow morning. This morning at 5:30 A.M. we passed the Sakishima group of islands, they are below Japan between the China coast and Japan. The past few days we have come very close to big mines floating around in the water. We blow them up with our machine guns. It was cloudy this morning but the sun came out at 11 A.M. It stayed out for the rest of the day. It was hot and sunny with clear skies, the sea was calm. There are a lot of birds flying close to the water, land must be close by.

In control forward they have a map that shows where we are going and also the reports from our Intelligence about the Japs. It said that 16 Jap destroyers, a couple of battleships, and some aircraft carriers, and 200 suicide boats are in the area where we will be plus a couple hundred planes and bombers. This report was up to July 19th, only two days ago. Our force is Fleet Admiral Nimitz' special task force. This is a special mission, we are to act as guinea pigs and to feel the Japs out. Our information will pay off when the invasion of China and Japan comes off. Japan is the No. 1 prize of the war. It is an honor to work for the boss himself, Fleet Admiral Nimitz. We are the first Allied ships to get this close to China, and also the first to get this close to Korea, since the war started. The radio said 200 planes and bombers from Okinawa hit Shanghai for the second straight day. This is the first time it was hit like that. It will make things that much easier for us. All hands went to sunset General Quarters at 7:15 P.M. It rained very hard a half hour before, but then it cleared up. Capt. Gorry spoke tonight and said we are now 70 miles above Formosa, and heading west towards the China coast. He said that we are the first ships to go here. Our speed is about 25 knots or about 28 miles per hour. We are 12,000 miles from the east coast of the U.S.A. Our job is to sink anything we come across. We secured from General Quarters at 8:30 P.M. Condition 2 watches were set. I slept under the stars until 10:30 P.M. All hands went to battle stations because Jap torpedo planes attacked us. The ships opened up but no damage was done, we secured about 11:15 P.M. I got the midnight to 4 A.M. watch.

Sunday, July 22, 1945: I got off watch at 4 A.M. All hands got up at 5 A.M. for sunrise General Quarters.

We are now heading north on our way up the coast of China. We passed a small group of islands off the coast, they are called the Seven Stars. We came across a good size Jap schooner and sunk it. Our speed is about 25 knots. We will fire at anything as we speed up the China coast, our orders are to sink everything and pick up no survivors. We can't take the chance of getting knocked off by Jap subs and land-based planes. This territory is in the Japs' back yard. When we come across any small stuff we let the destroyers do most of the firing. The big ships will take care of the big stuff. The schooner we sunk tried to make a run for it but it did not do them any good. The chances are all these coastal craft have radio sets and report to the coast anything they come across. About an hour later we came across six more coastal boats and they also went to the bottom. Some of the cruisers fired a few rounds just for practice. We kept on the same straight course as we kept firing. We did not slow down while firing. Our fighter cover in the morning was 8 Corsair fighters and in the afternoon we had 12 fighters flying overhead. We went to breakfast in sections, that way the guns were always manned. The sea was calm and the sky was clear and blue. There was also a good breeze. The sun is shining brightly as we go up the China coast. We are between Foochow and Shanghai. I never dreamed that I would get this close to China. We are not close enough to see the coast of China yet. Some of our destroyers left us and went out of sight. They were supposed to get about 5 miles from the coast. We must be about 25 miles from the coast. The destroyers should come across some Jap shipping where they are going. All the radio programs today are from China and Japan. The only men who had to stay at General Quarters all day were the men on the 5 and 6 inch guns plus the lookouts.

We are still doing 25 knots. This is a good way to spend the day before your birthday. I sit topside as I write this, 2:30 P.M. in the afternoon. No work was done today and wherever you turn, you see someone crapped out, getting a little rest. I will stop writing for now.

The closest we got to Shanghai was 60 miles south of it and about thirty miles from the coast of China. This is the first time Allied ships got that far into the East China Sea. Late this afternoon we started on our way back to Okinawa.

Sunday Mass was held in the mess hall. I went.

Monday, July 23, 1945: Today is my birthday. We are on our way back to Okinawa. We expect to get there at 3 P.M. in the afternoon.

We changed our plans and did not return to Okinawa but patrolled many miles from it. We will go in tomorrow morning instead because our Intelligence said that Jap planes will attack Okinawa tonight. I worked all morning in the hangar, carrying stores. The hangar is loaded with bugs. No wonder there are so many in the bread that we eat.

The Press News reported that the entrance to Tokyo Bay was

bombarded by our light cruisers, about 35 miles from Tokyo proper. We were scheduled for that task but returned from Borneo too late. Jap planes have been hitting Okinawa for the past four nights and have caused some damage. The fellows were talking about the time in 1942 before the *Montpelier* left the States for the Pacific War, when we rammed an ammunition schooner, carrying 100 tons of dynamite and caps. The *Montpelier* cut a large hole into the schooner and broke open the ammunition and concussion caps but there was no explosion. The ammunition ship sunk from the result of the huge damage inflicted upon it by us. Only a miracle saved the *Montpelier* from being blown to bits and severe damage to Norfolk, Virginia.

Tuesday, July 24, 1945: All hands arose at 4:30 A.M. We pulled into Okinawa at 7 A.M. A tanker was there to refuel us. Being very low of fuel, we stayed alongside the tanker for five and a half hours. We worked all day until 7:30 P.M. carrying supplies and ammunition. It was cool and cloudy most of the day. The *Montpelier* is anchored not too far from Okinawa. I can see from the ship the large caves in the sides of the nearby hills, where the Jap gun emplacements were entrenched. The hill is of solid rock. Our shells and bombs gave it quite a pounding. It's similar to Saipan, only not as high. The area is covered with green grass and hills and dales. There are large tombs on the island where the natives bury their dead. It looks like any peaceful countryside in the States. There are still 10,000 Japs holding out on Okinawa. Spasmodic gunfire can be heard on the *Montpelier* from the island. Okinawa is covered with poisonous snakes. On the opposite side of the island is the capital city of Naha. The bay that we are in has been renamed Buckner Bay, in honor of the general in command of the Tenth Army, who was killed in action on Okinawa. The Bay is large in size. We were going to pull out tonight but did not. General Quarters were sounded tonight. Jap planes were detected on radar. All the ships put on their fog screen machines plus plenty of small craft whose only job is to cover the place with this white smoke. In a short while visibility was only a few feet. It would put the thick London fog to shame. The ships in the Bay were ordered not to fire their guns as the suicide planes could follow the tracers and crash into the ships. We would also hit our own ships with our gunfire. When the Japs do attack into the blanket of fog, they crash dive in the hopes of hitting a well concealed vessel. At night a Jap favorite is to follow the red tracers from our guns to our ships. It is almost impossible to stop them in their dives. When an attack is expected, the men on the 20 and 40 mm. machine guns wear flash-proof gloves. It covers their arms up to the elbows. We also apply grease and cover our faces with a cloth cover. When a bomb explodes there is a big flash and you do not have to be very close to get a flash burn which is very dangerous. No one likes to wear the extra apparel but it is a necessity. When the light cruiser *Columbia* was struck by Jap suicide planes in Lingayen, over 100 men received severe flash burns. The Jap planes failed to attack tonight. A movie was held in the mess hall at 9:30 P.M.

Wednesday, July 25, 1945: The weather was cloudy and cool today as the battleships *Tennessee* and *Virginia* steamed into the Bay. We may go out to sea tomorrow for gunnery practice.

Thursday, July 26, 1945: We left Okinawa at 4 P.M. A storm was on its way as we were leaving. Our force consists of two battle cruisers, 4 light cruisers and 9 destroyers. We passed about 20 LSTs as we were leaving. The Captain informed us that we were on our way to the China coast. We will enter the Yellow Sea above Shanghai and up to the mouth of the Whangpoo River and Yangtze River. We will be the first ships to travel this far. It will put us about 1200 miles south of Vladivostok, Russia.

Friday, July 27, 1945: All hands were on deck at 4:40 A.M. I bought a pair of shoes this morning. We had locker inspection, the only division of the entire ship to stand by, this morning. I put my diary under my shirt when my locker was inspected. Now we are only allowed to send a certain amount of clothing to the laundry, and if we are caught washing the rest of them, we are put on report. This afternoon we were ordered to knock off work and told to get some rest. We will stay at General Quarters all night. The weather is clear and sunny. Our speed is 20 knots. All hands went to General Quarters at 7:15 P.M. Four engine privateers are flying overhead, headed for their home base. They left the fleet at 9 P.M. Our speed tonight is 27 knots. We are approximately 120 miles from Shanghai, about 1 A.M. we should be above Shanghai in the Yellow Sea. We have little worry concerning Jap airplanes. The only planes traveling the skylanes would be transports flying between China and Japan. If we keep traveling up the Yellow Sea, it would take no time at all to reach Port Arthur near Manchuria. I wonder what our main reason is for going up here. It is for more than knocking off Jap ships. Maybe to keep the Japs guessing. We will remain at General Quarters until 6 A.M. tomorrow morning. It was cool tonight at battle stations. Coffee and sandwiches were given to us at midnight. No Jap ships were sighted.

Saturday, July 28, 1945: Early this morning our mission was completed. No action was encountered as we felt the Japs out. They are saving everything for the homeland. A few months ago, traveling the same route, the Japs would have been swarming around us day and night with bombers and warships. Today we could land on the coast of China with little opposition. The Japanese still have thousands of planes in Japan awaiting the invasion that is sure to take place in the near future. We secured from General Quarters at 6 A.M. this morning. The Japs have seemed to have conceded China. Their last stand will be made on home grounds. They must see the handwriting on the wall. Their empire is gone. They are worse off now than at the outbreak of the war. Nothing is left but ruins.

We joined another task force this morning. It consists of two old battleships, three small carriers and destroyers. They will return to Okinawa with us. We will arrive there tomorrow. We were traveling at 31 knots this morning. Someone said the planes from the three baby flattops had hit Shanghai.

Suicide planes are still raiding Okinawa. A few ships were sunk the other night.

Sunday, July 29, 1945: We entered Buckner Bay this morning at 10 A.M. This evening at 9 P.M. we went to General Quarters.

Jap suicide planes were reported in the vicinity. We secured from quarters 20 minutes later. We were again called back later and remained there until 11:15 P.M. Suicide planes crashed into two of our ships in the bay. The superstructure was blown off the destroyer *Young*. The two damaged ships were anchored just outside the bay. They had opened up on the enemy planes. The Japs could not see the ships in the bay because of the smoke screen, but the planes came in too close for comfort. A little closer and our guns would have commenced firing. It's better to hit them at a distance than in one of their dives. Our radar tracking devices would with little trouble line up their bearings for us. The battle cruisers *Guam* and *Alaska* were stationed not too far from the *Montpelier*. If the Jap planes maneuvered between us, and we attempted to knock them out of the skies, our shells would land among the cruisers and theirs among us. We could have done more damage to ourselves than the Japs would do.

Monday, July 30, 1945: Suicide planes afford little in the way of sleep. They attacked again this morning. I was on duty on the midnight to 4 A.M. watch. At 2:30 A.M. the alarm was sounded. No damage was reported during the raid. We always seemed to be stationed at some spot in the Pacific during the hot season. The weather today is likewise. I lay down tonight for some sleep around 7 o'clock but General Quarters were ordered 20 minutes later. Jap planes were 25 miles away. Fog generators were put into action as everyone manned General Quarters. All warships will hold their fire unless absolutely necessary. No damage to the ships was reported during the raid. At 10:30 P.M. another alarm sounded. We stayed at battle stations until midnight. The Japs were on the receiving end once more as no damage to the ships was inflicted.

Tuesday, July 31, 1945: I fell asleep topside after midnight. At 2:45 A.M. I was awoken by the rain. Before I knew it, I was on the 4 A.M. to 8 A.M. watch. We were pretty discouraged this morning. We had secured the gear for the boom and were working on the other when they passed the word to rig the first boom back again. We were scheduled to leave the bay today but plans had been changed. Rigging a boom entails quite a bit of manual labor. The change of orders left the crew talking to themselves. The task force with the three small carriers arrived at the Bay this morning. They spent the remainder of the day refueling. We will go out with them tomorrow, I guess.

About 7 P.M. the gunboats took their position in the bay with their fog making machines. When an alert is sounded, they are assigned a specific area of the bay to cover with the white fog. Our positions are covered immediately as they go into action. The harbor is completely fog-bound. It has saved many lives and ships from destruction by the suicide planes. The past few nights have been very bright. Get all night in if Japs fail to strike.

Wednesday, August 1, 1945: All hands arose at 6 A.M. We received a good night's sleep for a change. The Japs must have been tired too. For the past three months my cleaning station has been on the main deck topside. We change stations every three months, I was assigned the passageway and fan room near the bake shop. I'll have an opportunity to obtain some sweets now and will remain dry inside when it rains. I am now the pointer on the Mount 46 on the 40 mm. machine guns.

We left Buckner Bay at 10 A.M. The other task force containing three small carriers, three battleships, heavy cruisers, light cruisers and destroyers accompanied us. My friend Donovan R.M. 2/c was transferred to the States yesterday.

Thursday, August 2, 1945: All hands arose at 4:30 A.M. Because of storm warnings, the ships turned back 110 miles from Shanghai. A typhoon is heading north towards our position. We will then travel south and patrol around until the danger passes. The sea was full of enormous swells today.

Friday, August 3, 1945: It was very chilly on the midnight to 4 A.M. watch. The sea was very rough. All hands were up for sunrise General Quarters at 4:30 A.M. We were to refuel the destroyers today but could not because of the condition of the ocean. All hands were kept off the forecastle because the waves would sweep you overboard.

The radio reported that 820 B–29 super forts hit Japan — 819 planes returned to their home bases. It was the largest raid in history. They dropped 6600 tons of bombs.

Clement Attlee defeated Churchill in the election for Prime

Minister of England. The Detroit Tigers are in first place by three games in the American League. A B-25 medium bomber crashed into the Empire State Building in New York City. Fourteen were killed and many suffered injuries.

The weather cleared this afternoon and we headed up the China coast again. Captain Gorry spoke over the loudspeaker at 7:30 P.M. informing us that we were 140 miles from Shanghai. We will advance north of the mouth of the Yangtze River and then proceed to the one fathom curve. The battle cruisers *Guam* and *Alaska* will not go up as far as us. We will return and join the cruisers at approximately 2:30 A.M. It will be a very dangerous mission because of the many reefs we could be grounded upon. I wonder what Fleet Admiral Nimitz has in mind when he made plans to send us up here. This is a very bold undertaking.

Saturday, August 4, 1945: We cruised up the Yangtze River in the heart of Jap-held territory. The only ship we came across was a Chinese fishing schooner with five aboard at 1 A.M. The Chinese aboard the schooner told an interpreter on one of the destroyers that they were coming from Shanghai.

It was very chilly on watch again. During the day we patrolled about 150 miles from Shanghai. We refueled a destroyer in the morning. In the afternoon we fired at sleeves that were towed by our carrier planes. The carrier force is close behind us. Captain Gorry said that we will again proceed on the same course tonight.

Sunday, August 5, 1945: We left the Yangtze River and the Shanghai area about 3 A.M. We did not come across anything. Last night about 7 P.M. our ship came close to ramming a 1000 pound mine. We were heading towards the mine but detected it in time. A destroyer blew it up with machine gun fire. The explosion was terrific.

We had machine gun practice against the sleeves today. It was interrupted because of Jap airplanes. Our CAP combat air patrol planes from our carriers went after them. The Japs dropped their bombs in the water and ran for home, but our fighters caught up to one and shot it down. Our fighters shot down a couple more about 4:30. It must have burned the Japs up to see us having practice in their own back yard. We were 150 miles from their large base in Shanghai at that time. Sunday Mass was held in the crew's lounge. We will go up to Shanghai again tonight.

Monday, August 6, 1945: We finished our scouting missions at Shanghai and the Yellow Sea early this morning. The weather was very clear and sunny as we went to General Quarters. Jap bombers were overhead at 30,000 feet. We held our fire. They looked like little white spots in the sky. It took some time to locate the planes in the sky. They were directly overhead and remained there for some time. As they positioned themselves in formation, they headed away from the fleet.

In the afternoon we took a course to Okinawa. Captain Gorry mentioned that we should not be disappointed because we did not run into anything around Shanghai and the Yangtze River. The next time we are up that way, the Japs might come out of hiding and we will have a chance to knock them off. If the Yangtze River is opened to Allied shipping, we will be able to supply the interior of China. The Yangtze River cuts through the heart of China making this possible. The Yangtze is a strategically centered river used as a lifeline through China. It is the sixth largest river in the world. The big brass learned a lot from our sweeps around Shanghai and the Yangtze River. They have all the information for an invasion if needed.

Tuesday, August 7, 1945: We arrived at Buckner Bay, Okinawa at 7:30 A.M. We refueled and then worked all day taking aboard supplies. We will receive plenty of food. We have more ships in the bay than ever before. They are mostly warships. Japan reported that we are building a supply depot at Okinawa to ready us for the invasion of the Japanese Isles.

All hands went to battle stations at 10:30 P.M. because of Jap planes. No resulting damage was reported.

Wednesday, August 8, 1945: All hands reported to stations at 1:30 A.M. We did not secure battle stations until 4 A.M. Jap planes were spotted in the immediate vicinity. No damage to the ships in the Bay was received. I stayed on watch as I had the 4 A.M. to 8 A.M. detail. A night's sleep is something I rarely receive out here. Jap planes raid the Bay nearly every night. I almost forgot to mention that the greatest invention of the twentieth century has been achieved. It's an atomic bomb. It was dropped on Hiroshima, Japan, a couple of days ago, August 6. The bomb has the power equivalent to 20,000 tons of dynamite. It wiped out everything for miles around. President Truman conveyed a warning to Japan to stop hostile actions but the Japanese refused. The Jap Premier ordered a special cabinet meeting right after news of the bomb was relayed to him. The atomic bomb has the heat of the sun at its core. The pilots ten miles away could sense the concussion from it. Debris flew 40,000 feet into the air. Everyone is discussing the topic on board the *Montpelier*. The war may end soon now. The weather was hot and sunny today. I received a letter from my sister Mary.

Thursday, August 9, 1945: The Japs failed to attack last night. It was announced over the loudspeaker that Russia declared war on Japan at 2 A.M. I won $5 from Hays. Some time ago I bet him that Russia would go to war against Japan. The only thing I hear on the radio now is the atomic bomb and Russia declaring war on Japan. Russian troops crossed the Manchurian border and are in Manchuria. B-29s flew overhead yesterday. I guess we will leave here August 12 for a fast bombardment of the China coast.

Friday, August 10, 1945: Field day today. Everyone was very busy cleaning up ship for inspection, scrubbed decks, paintwork, shined up everything, etc. We are still at Okinawa. I hit the sack at 8:30 P.M. At 8:50 P.M. Captain Gorry spoke to the crew. He said that Japan would agree to our terms but wanted to keep the Emperor. They do not want anything to happen to him. When the Captain finished speaking, everyone gave a big cheer. Some of the men were whistling and yelling. There was plenty of rejoicing. Everyone went wild. Right after the men on Okinawa were informed of this news, we could hear guns firing, flares of all colors and star shells lit the sky. The searchlights were turning in all directions. They went wild over there. Some of the ships here fired their guns and others blew their foghorns. It was quite a celebration. This was the happiest day of our lives. Everyone on the *Montpelier* was having a great time. We did not have much sleep but we did not care.

Saturday, August 11, 1945: It was announced over the radio this morning that the United States, Russia, China and England are now in conference. Their answer to Japan will be given tonight. A few of the crew say we should not accept their terms but most of the crew say we should accept. Our B–29s are being grounded to-day until word is passed whether we accepted the terms or not. Everyone hopes we convoy the occupation troops to Japan. We would like to see Japan before going home.

Sunday, August 12, 1945: The Allies did send their answer to Japan. They were informed that they could keep their Emperor Hirohito but he would have to take orders from us. We now await their answer. In Japan the Emperor is considered a god. Everyone here wants the war to end as soon as possible. The ones back in the States who send telegrams to continue the war have no one out here. They should let those people swap places with our prisoners in concentration camps. They would change their tune. I guess they like to earn blood money.

Today was a hot, sunny day. Mass was held, it being Sunday. Everyone is anxious to hear Japan's reply. The Jap radio is now telling its people that it is foolish to commit suicide and that the Army and Navy no longer rules Japan. It said the cabinet now is the ruling power in the Japanese Isles, and to do whatever the Emperor instructs them to do.

Tonight I hit the sack at 8 P.M. and slept topside as usual. At 9:30 P.M. all hands went to battle stations because Jap planes were attacking us again. At 10:10 P.M. when we secured from General Quarters, there was bad news. The battleship *Pennsylvania* was hit by a torpedo near its stern, leaving a huge hole. The Jap plane then crashed into a nearby hillside. If we had not changed places with the *Pennsylvania*, we would have been the ship to be hit, in-stead of the *Pennsylvania*. We were anchored in their position in the Bay but moved out relinquishing it to them. The area that was reserved for us, was very close to them when they were hit. If the torpedo had struck the *Montpelier* the same place that it did the

Pennsylvania, we would have been sunk. It would have set off
the ship's ammunition directly under my battle station. The Good
Lord was watching over us again tonight. All the close calls we had
since 1942 were more than just luck. Any one of them could have
put us out of action. The Hand of the Good Lord prevented them
from happening. As I said before, there is someone on this ship
that He likes extra special. Tonight could have been the last night
on earth for many of us. I went back to my position topside and
fell asleep after securing from General Quarters. I was very thankful for God's protection. The Japanese are talking peace and they
pull something like this. The war might be over but you would
never know it. At Okinawa the Jap suicide planes are still attacking.

   Monday, August 13, 1945: Jap planes came in again at 3:30 A.M.
and all hands went to their battle stations. The latest dope on the
Pennsylvania is one dead and 19 missing in action. That means the
ones who are missing are dead. It did not say how many were
wounded. It was a miracle that it did not explode. The torpedo
hit near its magazines. Tugboats moved it closer to us. It could
not move under its own power. There is a huge hole on the port
side of the stern near the fantail. The fantail is almost under water.
They have large pumps attached to barrels and water is being
pumped out. The Japs really did a great deal of damage to the
Pennsylvania last night. A big battlewagon like that and so helpless. Vice Admiral Jesse B. Oldendorf was aboard when it was hit.
He was the commander of our warships when they defeated the Jap
fleet at Leyte Gulf in the greatest sea battle in naval history. He
accomplished the impossible there when he crossed the T against
the Jap Navy. The *Pennsylvania* was also hit at Pearl Harbor
when the Japs attacked December 7, 1941. It took part in many
campaigns in the Pacific. It was just their luck to have it happen
when the war is over. They won't see Japan now. It was considered
one of the luckiest ships in the Navy until this happened. It was
called the luckiest battleship in the fleet. They may move it out of
the bay by tug to Guam and repair it enough so that it may reach
the States.

All the warships pulled out of the harbor at 5 P.M. We will return tomorrow morning. We don't want to chance any more of our ships getting hit in the last days of the war. The Japs might return again tonight. The radio at 6 P.M. said there was no news from Japan and we are to continue to hit Japan with everything until we get an answer. The Japs should have given an answer before now. Maybe they have a trick up their sleeve. It was announced over the radio concerning the celebration the troops had on the beach the other night, when it was announced that the war was near completion. Many on Okinawa were wounded because of the wild gunfire. An air alert was sounded to stop it before any more were killed or wounded. Captain Gorry spoke tonight and he said that the Jap plane that hit the *Pennsylvania* came in with its lights on in the darkness. It wanted the ships to think that it was one of our own planes. What those Japs won't do for the Emperor. I should receive a letter from Mary soon.

Tuesday, August 14, 1945: We returned to Buckner Bay this morning. It's a good thing we did not stay here last night because one of our cargo ships was hit. Some say it was hit by a Baka Bomb, a torpedo with a Jap inside. It crashed head on into it like a plane. The weather today was hot and sunny.

Wednesday, August 15, 1945: I washed some clothes in a bucket at 1 A.M. while on the midnight to 4 A.M. watch. When I was relieved of watch, I rinsed them out. We are too busy to wash our clothes in the daytime. I caught a few minutes sleep before sunrise General Quarters sounded at 4:45 A.M. I attended Mass in the crew's lounge. We returned this morning at 8:15 to Okinawa. We refueled this morning from a tanker. It came over the radio that President Truman officially declared the war over. All that remains is for the Japs to sign the peace treaty. Some day this week will be set aside as V–J Day. When word was passed the whistles on every ship in the harbor sounded, and everyone on the ship was making plenty of noise. We were alongside the tanker and the light cruiser *Denver* was on the other side of us at the time.

The weather was again hot and sunny. We left the Bay again tonight at 5 P.M. We do not want to take any chances. It was a good night to sleep under the stars. Myers and Renteria enjoyed the candy bars I gave them before we fell asleep. My sister Mary knows every place we go because I have a code name for each spot we are stationed at. It is right under the censor's nose and he does not know what it means.

Thursday, August 16, 1945: We returned to Buckner Bay this morning. Word was sent to Japan for them to send their peace envoys to a small island called Ie Shima. It is not too distant from Okinawa. Ie Shima is where the famous war correspondent, Ernie Pyle, was killed. The password will be Bataan. The Jap officials will leave Ie Shima in one of our bombers for General MacArthur's Headquarters in Manila. The Japs were told to leave Japan in a white bomber with colored stripes on it. The island of Ie Shima is not too far from where we are stationed. We might be able to see the Jap plane as it passes. We left the harbor as usual at 5 P.M. We conducted sunset General Quarters. We are leaving nothing to chance.

Friday, August 17, 1945: We returned to Okinawa at 7 A.M. this morning. Today was the first time we ever had Condition 4 watches. That means we do not have to stand as many watches. It will afford the fellows an opportunity to catch up on some sleep.

I received a letter from my sister Mary. It only took seven days for it to reach here. That's a record. Our band practiced on the fantail today. At last we are going to have a band. All the large ships have their own bands.

The Jap envoys said that they would not arrive today because they were not allowed enough time. They will arrive tomorrow to sign the peace papers. Nearly everyone sleeps under the stars. The climate here is dry, not damp like the South Pacific.

Saturday, August 18, 1945: It came over the radio that the Jap officials will leave Japan Sunday to sign the surrender terms. I saw a dispatch in the Officer of the Deck's shack. It said Jap peace plane will arrive and to hold our fire.

We had mail call today. Ohrt received a package from home with a can of meat and candy in it. We acquired bread from the bakery and made some sandwiches from the meat. We ate the sandwiches this afternoon. It was another hot day. Some of the men were permitted to go over to the beach on Okinawa for recreation. There is not much to do over there but tombs and skeletons are always of interest. It is also very hot there and smells. The fellows are not allowed to enter the tombs but they do. Not too long ago, one of the sailors on recreation stuck his head into one of the tombs to see what it was like inside and at the same time a Jap soldier stuck his head outside. When the Jap saw the sailor, he surrendered to him. There are still plenty of Japs loose around there. One thing about the Navy, they can pick some great places for recreation. Half of the time it would pay to go armed on recreation. The radio announced the Japs in China are surrendering by the thousands. The heavy cruiser *Indianapolis* was sunk, 100% casualties were reported. The *Indianapolis* carries a complement of 1300 men. It was returning from delivering a part for the atomic bomb that was in turn dropped on Hiroshima.

Sunday, August 19, 1945: All the ships here have been refueling for the past few days. We will pull out as soon as Japan signs the surrender. Some of our bombers were attacked over Japan yesterday, while they were taking pictures. The scuttlebutt here is that we will leave for the States September 18 with the cruiser *Denver*. That we will tow the *Pennsylvania* back with us. The other talk is that we will escort a convoy to Japan. Sunday church services were held topside. Protestants and Catholics thanked God that the war is over. At church services I could see the battleship *Pennsylvania*, it must be the last warship to be knocked out of action in World War II. It was not too far away. Water was being pumped from it. The repair crews are working on it. The hole was so big where the torpedo exploded that you could drive a truck into it with plenty of room to spare. The *Pennsylvania* will not be in on the peace celebration. Vice Admiral Oldendorf, commander of battleships in the Pacific, and its Captain, Captain William Moses, were both knocked down when it was hit. At church services I could also see the green hills of Okinawa on this hot, sunny day. Captain Gorry was also at Mass this morning. A large crowd attended church services. We had fellows from about every state in the Union present. There were officers, seamen and Marines. We closed the services by singing "God Bless America." It was very nice.

All the crew talk about now is when we will go back home. The *Montpelier* has fired over 100,000 rounds of five and six inch shells. By the time we reach the States, we will have traveled almost 200,-000 miles. Of that total approximately 95% was spent in enemy-infested waters. The Jap peace delegation arrived today. They landed on Ie Shima. The radio broadcast originated from there for the whole world to listen to. It gave a graphic description of everything that took place. Two twin engine bombers with green crosses and carrying 13 Jap officials landed about 1 P.M. After leaving their planes, they stepped into a C–54 skymaster. At 1:30 P.M. they left for General MacArthur's Headquarters in the Philippines for the signing of the surrender terms. The Japanese pilots were left behind as they did not want to make the trip. Air time will take five or six hours to reach Nichols Field in Manila. Ie Shima was full with military officials who were on hand to witness the history-making event.

The fellows returned from recreation at 5:30 P.M. They said that one sailor was killed and another had his arm blown off when they came across Jap booby traps. This afternoon Joe Renteria dove into the water after a softball that fell from the *Montpelier*. He had quite a rough time swimming back to the ship because of the strong undertow. When he neared the ship Chick Bartholow grabbed him from the Jacob's Ladder. He was exhausted and about ready to go under. It's next to impossible to swim against the strong undertow. It tends to push back anyone that bucks it. The swells look very innocent but are very powerful. It does not take long to be carried out to sea. Sam and Frazer plus Stevo and Olson put on a wrestling bout before they hit the steel for a night's sleep.

Monday, August 20, 1945: Sunrise watch was held at 5 A.M. We secured at 6 A.M. At quarters this morning about 8:15 A.M. we were informed that 10% of the crew will be transferred. A month later another 10% will return to the States. We were paid today. The men can still only draw $10 each.

The radio announced that the peace conference was still going on at 2 A.M. this morning. General MacArthur has not yet appeared at the meeting. American paratroops landed in Manchuria and rescued General Wainwright and other Americans. Another battleship arrived yesterday in the bay.

Tuesday, August 21, 1945: Not much news to report. The radio said that Jap officials left Manila and have returned to Japan. The meeting was held in Manila City Hall. Sixteen Japs participated. General MacAuthur did not appear at the conference. He will leave for Tokyo in ten days and sign the peace terms. Everyone was under the impression that the peace terms would be signed in Manila. The Japs relayed all information concerning their airfields and the areas where our troops will land. The Jap government told its people to cooperate with our troops when they land.

Well, it looks like they are going to start transferring the men now. About 20 men were called to the Ex office, they say 10% of the crew will go this month and 20% next month. I will be satisfied if I get home for Christmas.

Friday, August 24, 1945: Hundreds of ships are anchored at Buckner Bay, Okinawa. They consist of all types of warships. Among them are 10 battleships and two hospital ships. Some of the crew of the *Montpelier* were transferred to the States tonight.

Five battleships left for Tokyo Bay and the peace ceremonies. The battleship *Pennsylvania* would have been one of them if it was not hit by a Jap torpedo while they were talking peace. At noon the dope was that our Admiral Riggs would have charge of Task Group 95.02 that will land troops on Japan. I hope this is true. The paratroops are scheduled to land Sunday and the ground troops Tuesday.

Admiral Riggs and Captain Gorry left the ship for the beach this afternoon. The Captains and Admirals from the other ships also went. They had a picnic over there. I guess it is a going away party. They will never have a chance like this to get together again.

Saturday, August 25, 1945: We had Captain's Inspection in blues this morning. Only one division wore blues. It's too warm to wear any clothes at all. Some had heavy blues on, others wore whites and the remainder wore dungarees. The officer asked the crew what uniforms we would like to have our picture taken in. We favored dungarees. This morning at 7 A.M. the temperature was 107 degrees. The bulkheads were so hot that I could not lean my hand against them. This is the hottest time of the year and it seldom rains. The sun beats down all day.

The radio announced the invasion of Japan was called off for 48 hours because of typhoons near Japan. The surrender papers will be signed on the battleship *Missouri* in Tokyo Bay.

Sunday, August 26, 1945: 40 minesweepers arrived at the bay yesterday plus more warships, cargo, supply and one hospital ship. The Captain and a few officers came aboard with huge flowerpots. They acquired them on the beach. Stevenson went over to one of the small islands where the officers had recreation on a clean-up detail. He said that there was a deserted village there. He brought back some things with him that he had found on the island. The island is situated near Okinawa.

The fellows who were transferred a couple of days ago are still on the beach and will not get transportation to the States for at least 6 weeks. They are working pretty hard over there building up the place. I think I will take my chances on going back with the ship.

Tuesday, August 28, 1945: The battleship *Pennsylvania* left Buckner Bay, Okinawa with 5 tugs escorting it, this morning at 7 A.M. It was traveling at approximately five knots. It was sixteen days ago that a Jap torpedo plane put a fish into it. It would have been at Tokyo Bay for the celebration only for this. The crew must be very disappointed.

One of the fellows flooded a big magazine and we were forced to carry all the powder and shells up three decks and dry each one of them. Then they were again stored in the hold. There were thousands of shells and powder cases to be lugged by the crew. It will go tough on the individual who let this occur.

Sunday, September 2, 1945: The Japs signed the peace papers on the battleship *Missouri* in Tokyo Bay. It was about 8 P.M. Sat. night on east coast.

Monday, September 3, 1945: This afternoon at 5:30 P.M. the word was passed that no more gun watches would be stood. Watches will be stood on guns only at sea. In port all guns will be secured. This is the first time the guns have not been manned. I sometimes thought that I would never see this day. After gunnery tomorrow most of the ammo will be removed from the shields. It looked good to see them lock the five inch mounts. I never saw them like that before.

Wednesday, September 5, 1945: The peace signing in Tokyo Bay is history and the *Montpelier* is still anchored at Buckner Bay, Okinawa. We expect to leave for Japan in a day or so. For a while we thought that we would not make it.

About noon today 30 transports left. They were loaded with troops. Their next stop is Korea. All the ships are lit aglow at night now. The hatches are open to allow the air to enter the compartments. It seems strange after having it so dark and everything aboard ship was secured. The movie started late tonight because Admiral Riggs boarded Admiral Spruance's flagship, the *New Jersey,* for special orders. We are supposed to pull out of the Bay tomorrow. Two destroyers and a couple of hospital ships will accompany us. Our mission will be to bring back the prisoners of war. We will be about 200 miles south of Tokyo. Everyone was happy to hear the good news. We could hardly believe it. I gave the fellows some food that I had put away in the afternoon. The boys always get hungry about sack time. The U.S.S. *Montpelier* did not go to Tokyo for the celebration but we will at least have a chance to see Japan before heading home.

Thursday, September 6, 1945: We were scheduled to leave Okinawa at 2:30 P.M. for Japan. Two destroyers left for the States at 7 A.M. with their homeward bound pennants waving. A large transport loaded with troops also left with them. At 1:30 P.M. everyone was disappointed because the operation was canceled until some later date. Planes were taken off two of the carriers to make room for the prisoners of war under the Japs. There are believed to be 9000 Americans and 11,000 British, Australian, Dutch and other nationalities there.

Saturday, September 8, 1945: After inspection today the Div.

officer asked each man if he wished to sign over into regular Navy. I don't think anyone signed over. They may get a lot of fellows who spent most of their time in the States, but not us. Almost three years out here is all the Navy we want.

Sunday, September 9, 1945: At 1 P.M. we finally left Buckner Bay, Okinawa, for Japan. Admiral Riggs will be in command of the group. Our ship is the flagship. The group consists of the three light cruisers, *Montpelier, Denver* and *Cleveland*. Two small carriers and two hopsital ships, five transports loaded with Marines, one LSD, destroyers and destroyer escorts, rounds out the force. The cruiser *Columbia* did not come with us. It was going to Guam. The two carriers had all their planes taken off except for a few. The hangar decks are full of Army cots for the prisoners of war. Our speed will be about 12 knots. We expect to reach Japan in two days, on a Tuesday.

It was a clear, sunny day as we left Okinawa behind us, never to see it again. We held a large celebration aboard ship to commemorate the U.S.S. *Montpelier's* commission. It was commissioned in Philadelphia, September 9, 1942, three years ago today. We were served a turkey dinner and everyone was given a carton of cigarettes.

We did not have to man the ship's guns. This was the first time it's happened since I was in the Navy that we did not have to man guns at sea. It felt as though something was missing. We have an American officer aboard who speaks Japanese. He will be our interpreter when we reach Japan.

Monday, September 10, 1945: All hands arose at 6 A.M. Last night the ocean was well lit up by other ships as we made our way to Japan. It felt strange to be so close to Japan and have all the ships silhouetted by their own lights. The two hospital ships were aglow like a Christmas tree. It was quite a sight. This is the first time we ever had hospital ships with the force. Now that the war is over, they do not have to travel by themselves. The sea is calm and it was a warm, sunny day.

The fellows were all over topside. It was like back home in the neighborhood. Some of the fellows were shooting the breeze, others were around the record player listening to music, while still others drank coffee. Our photographer Tripp was taking pictures in the dark. He was on one of the turrets.

We are off the coast of Japan as I sit in the mess hall and write. The time is 6:30 P.M. Sunset was at 6:20 P.M. The Captain has not given us any information yet but some say we will arrive at our destination at 6 A.M. tomorrow. The part of Japan that we are going to is about 15 miles from Osaka, Japan's number one industrial city. I have no idea how far inland we will sail.

This morning pistol and machine gun firing was held for the men who are going to carry firearms when we arrive at Japan. These men will patrol the area near the ship. They are to insure the safety of the crew at dock side.

I washed one of my blankets this afternoon. We have not been standing any gun watches but might man the guns when we pull into Japan tomorrow. Tomorrow will be the big day, Japan at last. We participated in the first Allied offensive in the Pacific at Guadalcanal and we will be in on the last invasion of the Pacific War. This has been the longest retreat in history, almost 4000 miles.

Tuesday, September 11, 1945: All hands were up at 5 A.M. I slept under the stars as usual. It was like a warm summer's night back home in Massachusetts. This morning at 7 A.M. it was hot and sunny but the humidity was high. We reached Japan early this morning.

The *Montpelier* began its trip into the Inland Sea of Japan. Condition 3 watches were set at 5 A.M. The *Montpelier*'s guns were manned. A Jap boat about the size of a tug pulled alongside. The Jap pilot who will show us the way to Wakanoura Bay entered a whaleboat and headed for our ship. A Jap officer approached our ship with the pilot and then returned to his boat. The Jap officer stood very straight in the whaleboat and rendered us a salute in approaching. The crew in the boat were of medium height and were well built. They wore khaki clothing and army caps. They all took a long look at the Jap flags we had painted on the bridge denoting the Jap ships sunk, planes shot down and islands bombarded. The Jap flags really caught their eyes.

The Jap pilot wore a tweed civilian suit and carried a large map and a bag. He was about 55 years old. When he came aboard, he took off his hat and bowed his head. He then went to the bridge of the ship where the ship's steering devices are manned. It did not take long before we were on our way. Captain Gorry spoke over the loudspeaker. He said that the Jap navigator has been doing this type of work for thirty years. That the pilot was served bacon and eggs, bread, butter and orange juice for his breakfast and he was very pleased with it. I'll bet this was the best breakfast he's had in many a year. The Captain also stated that as far as he knows, about 10,000 prisoners are here. The majority being civilians. We may be stationed here from one to three weeks. The army has not arrived yet. We are the first to get here. The army will follow later.

The cruisers *Denver* and *Cleveland* plus the carriers remained outside the channel. Our planes will fly overhead all day long. A few of the Japs might want to continue the war. We cannot leave anything to chance. The other ships will enter the harbor later. 50 minesweepers were ahead of us as they cleared the waters of mines. The further inland we travel, the more overcast the skies become. In time we will advance far into the interior of Japan and be almost surrounded by Japan's largest island, the island of Honshu. I wonder if all of the Japs know the war is terminated. We passed many small islands as we made our way to our destination, Wakanoura Bay. We were completely surrounded by these islands. It would be impossible to enter these waters in wartime. The higher elevations of the islands have enormous guns entrenched there. We would have made ideal targets.

The hours passed and after twelve hours of traveling, we finally reached Wakanoura Bay near the city of Wakayama. It was 6:30 P.M. when we dropped anchor. The *Montpelier* was to the forefront leading the other ships. All the ships in the harbor were glowing and the watches were secured. That means we will have a night's sleep. At 4:30 P.M. Mass was observed in the crew's lounge. It must have been the first Mass ever celebrated here. Only four of us attended church services.

The weather was calm during our trip in here. I can see the

lights of Wakanoura, not too far away. It is a little fishing village. The city of Wakayama is on the largest island of Japan, Honshu, not too distant from the *Montpelier*. I could not see much because it was dark and a little drizzle was falling.

Tomorrow will be a big day for the prisoners. Our ship was assigned the duty of flagship for naval forces entering this area. It will be our mission to evacuate the liberated prisoners of war. Rear Admiral Ralph S. Riggs will be in command of the operation. It is a lot cooler here so I will sleep below.

Wednesday, September 12, 1945: All hands were on deck at 6 A.M. I slept below in a sack last night. It was the first time in about a year that the opportunity presented itself. It was chilly this morning as we are anchored close to shore. Early this morning a train passed, it had many coaches attached to it.

At quarters this morning Ens. R. L. Katz reported that Admiral Riggs has supreme charge of the area from here to Osaka and Kobe, two of Japan's largest cities. Osaka is Japan's second largest city and the number one industrial city. It has a population of over a million. Kobe is the location of a naval base that is considered second in importance in all of Japan. All the conferences will take place on our ship the U.S.S. *Montpelier*. This will be a very important operation.

The army will arrive in about 15 days. The *Montpelier* and the carriers will supply the prisoners with food. The bake shop will bake bread 24 hours a day. The R. Division constructed 27 showers and then took them to the hotel where our prisoners will be brought when they arrive. The prisoners are many miles inland. They will be transported here by train. We commandeered the hotel and will use it as our headquarters. Everything will be ready when the prisoners enter the town. Arrival time is expected to be 1 A.M. tomorrow morning. Awaiting the prisoners will be medical supplies, clothing, blankets and also a large tank for washing clothing. The prisoners will take a shower, receive haircuts and be deloused. The barbers from our ship will assist in the cutting of the hair. At first we expected to receive 20,000 prisoners but now it is learned that only three thousand survived. The rest of them must have died. The prison compounds are located 20 miles from here.

The Marines from our ship will be stationed on the beach until the army arrives. The officers from the other ships came aboard the *Montpelier* today to receive their orders. We spent the day preparing everything for tomorrow. It should be a pretty busy day. This is a very beautiful place. It's similar to a summer resort in the country back home. The weather is not as hot as Okinawa. It is perfect. The sun is shining all day and the nights are cool. The contour of the island is very hilly and they are covered with greenery. All the valleys are little towns. They are crowded with houses. I can see the Japanese walking around town from the *Montpelier*. I saw two girls crossing a bridge this morning. One of them had a sun umbrella bearing fancy colors. Down near the beach is a high wall. The purpose of it is to combat the waters when the weather becomes rough. The villages are next to the water and many small fishing boats are on the beach. I saw a Jap catch a fish on his line earlier. The beach seems to be ideal. The houses in the village are all of wood and are very close to each other. In another section there are new cement and brick buildings. These are located near the hotel and train depot.

This morning the LSD shed all of its landing craft, about 40 LCVPs. The LSD is like a floating dry dock. It submerges and the LCVPs sail out of its interior when the ramp is opened.

We observed the nurses in their bathing suits, taking a sun bath this afternoon. We were watching the nurses on the hospital ship through the field glasses and they were looking at us through theirs and waving at us. A movie will be held on the fantail tonight.

Thursday, September 13, 1945: The prisoners did not arrive today but are expected tomorrow. This afternoon I placed my feet on the main island of Japan, Honshu. I was the first one from my division to set foot on Japan. We went over in the afternoon with a large supply of canned meat for the prisoners and two hundred loaves of bread. We were ferried in a LCVT. We carried the food up three stories in the hotel. The hotel is ready for the prisoners. After the prisoners are washed up, deloused, receive medical care and chow, they will be sent to the hospital ship. We expect to process 300 to 500 a day. When we finished carrying the supplies, the officer in charge allowed us to look around. A couple of us took a walk through the town. We were the only Americans in town. The Japs kept staring at us. We were not supposed to be here. The only ones who are allowed here are the Marines and our top officials. We were the first Allies to enter the harbor since the war ended. It was like we were explorers as we walked through the streets. We were very curious of the Japanese and they of us. Some of the Japanese were looking out windows and standing in doorways to catch a glimpse of us as we passed by. A few of the girls smiled at us and we returned their smiles. The girls were very good-looking. There is another hotel not too far away from the hotel we were working. Everyone who enters is compelled to take off his shoes and place sandals on their feet. There were many girls working in the hotel. All the young men must be in the army. Most of the men were wearing army uniforms. The girls wear something similar to pajamas. A man passed me with a child on his back just like the Indians carry them. The people looked healthy and some spoke English. The Marines from our ship are the only troops here and the Japs speak to them. This is strictly a Navy show and our ship is the headquarters. The hotels here are used by the people from the big cities during their vacations. The city of Wakayama with a population of over one hundred thousand is not too far away. As we strolled down the street without a care in the world and really enjoying the sights, who should pass us only a few feet away in the opposite direction but Admiral Riggs, Captain Gorry, a New Zealand naval officer from a heavy cruiser that came in today, and the Chief of Staff. You could have knocked Stevenson and me over with a feather when we saw them. They were riding in a big, black Packard. If they did not look like the rulers of Japan, no one did. I had to chuckle to myself when I first saw them. They were right at home as they passed us by.

It was not very long after, that Stevo and I were being led down the street like a couple of prisoners with the Marine in charge blasting us out. I imagine the Japs did not know what the armed Marines were doing as we marched down the street. We were brought to the Marine Captain at the hotel. He took our names from instructions issued by the Chief of Staff. We told him that the supply officer told us that we could look around. He said that he would forget it if the Chief of Staff overlooked it this time.

We arrived back at the ship at 5:30 P.M. after spending a very enjoyable day around the town. After chow I went down to the mess hall again, this time to write. The only ships here besides the cruiser *Montpelier* are the New Zealand heavy cruiser and destroyer that arrived today, two hospital ships, one LSD, one small carrier and a couple of fast marine transports, they resemble a destroyer. The name of the movie tonight is "Halfway to Shanghai." I'll bet that the Japs never had movies on their ships in here.

Friday, September 14, 1945: At 11 A.M. the trains bearing the Allied prisoners of war pulled into the railway station at Wakanoura. The bands from the New Zealand cruiser *Gambia* and our cruiser were there to greet them. Stretcher cases were handled first and the men were given cigarettes and magazines. The prisoners were all smiles. This was the happiest day of their lives. They could hardly believe it after being tortured in Jap prison camps for three and a half years.

The bandmaster from our ship met an old friend of his while he was leading the band. When they saw each other, they both broke down and cried. His friend was captured in 1942 when Guam fell to the Japs. The bandmaster from the *Montpelier* let his friend take over the stick to lead the band. Everyone in the crowd shook with emotion. All the prisoners were military personnel. They were Americans, Australians, British and Dutch among them.

It did not take long before the men were at the hotel taking their clothes off which were then decontaminated. Their valuables were placed in paper bags and tagged. They then took a shower, installed by the shipfitters from the *Montpelier*. They were sprayed with D.D.T. after the showers. After filling out identification cards, they were given a medical examination by doctors from our ships in the harbor. The barbers and dentists were also there. Last but by no means least came the food. They were served beef stew with vegetables, bread, jam, coffee and a candy bar. Following the meal they were interviewed and atrocities against them were recorded. Afterwards, they were transferred to the hospital ships. Many of the fellows from the *Montpelier* had a chance to talk to the prisoners. Their job was to get the prisoners ready and assist them in transferring to the hospital ships. We will work around the clock until everyone is aboard the hospital ships. Late this evening another crew will relieve the ones on shore. They will return tomorrow morning.

Many of the prisoners were in bad shape. Some were completely lost mentally. They were talking very foolish. You felt sorry for them. Others said that they would have died in a month if the war lasted that long. Some had scars where the Japs beat them. Some of the prisoners were forced to work in a mine from three in the morning until five at night. They had very little to eat under Japanese rule. The prisoners went through hell under the Japs and most of them died under cruel hands.

This afternoon 3 star Vice Admiral Oldendorf in command of squadron battleships and his staff landed in a four engine sea plane. They came aboard the *Montpelier* baggage and all.

Saturday, September 15, 1945: The 45,000 ton battleship *New Jersey* arrived today. Admiral Raymond Spruance, commander of the Fifth Fleet, was aboard. The light cruisers *Cleveland* and *Denver,* one carrier and a few destroyers also arrived in the harbor.

One of the men from our division by the name of Gemza brought his cousin aboard for a while this morning before he left with the rest of the prisoners for the States. He looked very bad. When I touched his bones, they were as soft as a sponge. He was 16 miles away when the atomic bomb was dropped. He thought that it was an earthquake as the land shook so.

After working all day yesterday and this morning, the last prisoner was taken care of. They were a very happy group of men as the two hospital ships left for the States about noon. There were approximately 2500 prisoners aboard.

The American prisoners who fought at Bataan and Corregidor in 1942 told some of the men from my division that they never gave up hope. They knew General MacArthur would return with ships, planes, tanks, troops etc. and free them. They never lost faith in him. They think he is a great man and would fight under his command tomorrow. When they get better, they would like to be under his command again. They think there is no one like MacArthur.

A Japanese Catholic priest was allowed to visit the prisoners on two occasions during their three and a half years of Jap slavery.

The carriers that we were going to use for the prisoners left today. Someone said that they were leaving to pick up more prisoners elsewhere. The LSD also left today.

Sunday, September 16, 1945: All hands got up at 6 A.M. Sunday Mass was held topside at 9 A.M. New Zealand sailors also attended services.

About 40 Jap fishing boats left early this morning. Some of the men aboard the vessels wore only a small piece of cloth in place of trunks. Admiral Oldendorf left this morning by sea plane. The *New Jersey* pulled out also today.

Monday, September 17, 1945: This morning the ship was really rolling although the sea was calm. There must be a strong undertow. It started again while I was in the hangar on a working party. It rolled so much that I could not walk in a straight line. The Pacific is a strange place. The sea is calm and serene but the ship pitches from side to side. The water almost touched the main deck. All I had to do was reach out to touch the water. Conditions are like this before a typhoon. We had no movie tonight because of the ocean.

Tuesday, September 18, 1945: We really had a rugged time starting late last night and lasting until 5 A.M. this morning. A typhoon hit the harbor with winds registered as high as 125 miles per hour. We had no sleep as the ship pitched, tossed and rolled. It seemed at times that we were about to tip over. We took 38 degree rolls. The ship is constructed to take a 45 degree roll. We are very top-heavy with all the additions that have been made. It really looked bad. I had to hold on to the bunk or would have been thrown out. We had both anchors dragging and the screws turning. The wind was so strong, we had to keep the screws turning or we would have been tossed into the cliffs on the beach. We were tossing around like a little ball. The water came through the ventilating system, sending water all through the ship. Some of the big lockers in the compartments were ripped loose, crashing onto the deck. Things were ripped and torn from stationary objects. Debris was scattered everywhere. Topside all the life rafts were scattered over the ship. Thick steel plates were bent like paper. The steel plates in the water ways were tossed around and bent. Large cables were broken. It was like riding a wild horse as I lay in my bunk. When the ship rolled, I thought that it would keep on rolling and tip over. There was even sand on the deck. It must have been turned up by the mountainous waves.

Three LSTs, each 327 feet long, and a minesweeper were tossed up on the beach and against the stone cliff. They were smashed like toys. The minesweeper was split in two upside down on the beach. It must have crashed into the cliff. Its crew must have gone through hell during the storm. I don't see how any of the crew could survive the storm. The tanker had some men blown off, never to be seen again. A crew in a sea plane also went down.

This morning the Japs were down on the beach, looking at the wrecked ships. Their homes were also destroyed. The sea was dirty. It looked like the bottom was turned upside down. The air even smelled like the bottom of the ocean. I suppose the Japs thought that we would be sunk or smashed against the cliff, this morning when they awoke. When the 327 foot steel LST crashed against the cliff, the Japs must have thought that it was the end of the world. The *Montpelier* stopped rolling about 11 A.M. and the waves subsided. The storm left the weather cool. I had to wear a winter P coat at the movies at 7 P.M.

Wednesday, September 19, 1945: The weather is still cool. Many bodies were recovered from the beach today as a result of the typhoon yesterday. Church services will be held for them tomorrow. The unlucky men went through the war and they would have been going home soon. This would happen to them. This was the worst typhoon to strike here in fifteen years. It's a good thing there were not a lot of ships in here. Typhoons usually cover an area of hundreds of miles. We were very lucky to come out of it as well as we did.

I worked in the incinerator topside today with Champ Renteria. It was a very hot and dirty job. Supper was over when we returned from taking a shower so we got some cookies and a big can of peaches from the bakery. We went up to the top level and put them away. We had to chuckle as we enjoyed them. When we finished we went to the movie topside. The name of it was "Fighting Lady." Renteria is a very friendly person and a very good all round athlete. He is either Mexican or Indian.

Since arriving at Japan, we sleep below. The lights are out at 9 P.M. but before the fellows go to sleep, there is never a dull moment. In the compartment someone is usually playing the record player, others will be fooling around or maybe Rusty will be telling how a big alligator got away from him, back home in the swamps of Florida. Rusty is better than a movie. Nothing seems to bother him and he is never in a hurry. Then if you want a boxing lesson, Champ Renteria will always oblige. Every so often there is a good fight between a couple of the fellows which takes place in the compartment or topside while the ship rolls and pitches in the rough seas. I saw a good one when we were in the South Pacific. Two fellows fought to the finish under a boiling sun. They were hardly able to raise their hands. One of them finally fell from exhaustion and as he lay there, the salt water hose was turned on him.

Thursday, September 20, 1945: The carpenters from our ship made some white crosses for the graves of the men who lost their lives in the typhoon. They were buried on the beach. A Protestant Chaplain from one of the other ships and the Catholic Chaplain from our ship, Father Wilson, said prayers at the funeral. The Marines from the *Montpelier* rendered them a 21 gun salute with their rifles.

Tuesday, September 25, 1945: Not much to write about in the past five days. The army finally arrived today. For the past eleven days we were the only ones here. The troops started to land at

8 A.M. The convoy consisted of 50 transports and 50 large LSTs. The 1st place they took over was the city of Wakayama. All the factories were destroyed by our B–29s (Super Fortresses). They did not hit the homes. The population is over one hundred thousand. During the landings, all guns on the warships were manned but nothing happened. The *Montpelier* was the first American ship to enter the harbor but now there must be close to 200 ships here. The Navy was the first outfit to take this area over. At night the harbor looks like a large city. All the ships are lit up. It is quite a sight. Now that the Army has taken over, we will leave for another area and more troop landings. These troops will occupy Wakayama, Kobe and Osaka areas on Honshu.

Thursday, October 4, 1945: We left Wakayama, Japan, at 10 A.M. for Hiro. It is situated next to Kure which boasts of Japan's largest naval base and a good size city. We have a long voyage ahead of us as we travel further into Japan. Some of the ships that will go with us are the *Biloxi, Frankford* (CDS 16), *Champlin, Gainard, Compton, Rowan, Ellyson* (DMS 19), and *Pierce*. The army will land about Saturday. The convoy will follow behind us. Captain Gorry spoke to the crew. He said that we expect to reach Hiro tomorrow. He also said that the waters in the Inland Sea are full of mines and there is a chance that the sweepers will not recover all of them. A couple of our damaged ships with a volunteer crew will be in the forefront. If there are any mines in our path, they will be the first to get hit. They really picked themselves a dangerous job. The *Montpelier, Biloxi* and four destroyers will be the first American warships to enter the Inland Sea of Japan. We will enter the Inland Sea about 1 A.M. tomorrow morning. We will rig our paravanes for mines at midnight. It rained all day and the sea was rough. It was very cold, dark and cloudy all day.

Our force consists of two light cruisers and four destroyers. We will have sunrise General Quarters and all guns will be manned.

As I lay on my sack and write, it is 7 P.M. I will give a bird's eye view of what is going on in the compartment. Some of the fellows are laying in their sacks, reading and writing. Some have all their clothes on, others just have their shorts on. Dixon is cutting the fellow's hair on the P coat locker. In one corner of the compartment, a crap game is in progress and in another corner, the fellows are playing cards. Some of the fellows just came back from taking a shower. All they have around them is a towel. Others are fooling around and talking. Some of the men had to go topside in the rain and close the hatches because the rain was coming in. It gets dark at 6 P.M. now. The sea is very rough and the ship is rolling.

Friday, October 5, 1945: All hands got up at 4:50 A.M. We also had General Quarters. It seems funny to be going to battle stations and the war ended over two months ago. It was very cold this morning. The temperature is about 40 degrees.

We had quite a job laying in our bunks last night. The sea was rough. It is 240 miles from Wakayama to Hiro. All day long we sailed through the Inland Sea. Land could be seen on both sides of us at all times. The Inland Sea is about 35 miles wide. I never saw so many islands. One right after the other are on both sides of us. I imagine the Japs have guns on most of the islands. These islands are all very high. It would have been suicide if we ever had to come in here and fight for them, island by island. We never would have gotten in. There must be hundreds of islands in the Inland Sea. It is like a fortress guarding the main island of Japan. Almost all the hundreds of miles of land I have seen in Japan have been hilly. There seems to be a lot of pine trees in Japan. Every now and then, we pass a village almost on the banks of the water.

At 4:40 this evening the *Montpelier* anchored and the ships behind us did the same thing. We are about 25 miles from our destination, Hiro. We will remain here for the night. There is a little town on the beach close by. We will leave here early tomorrow morning. We had movies tonight.

This evening a Jap officer came aboard and stayed for the movies. The movie was held topside. The Jap will show us how to reach Hiro and also guide us away from the mines and shallow water. It was chilly again tonight.

Saturday, October 6, 1945: All hands arose at 5 A.M. At 6 A.M. we were on our way again. All the warships and transports pulled up their anchors and followed the *Montpelier*. It reminded me of a wagon train out west in the last century. We were one long line of ships, as we continued on our way to Hiro. We passed many farms this morning. The scenery was very pretty. We also passed some little sailing boats. I saw a horse on the side of a hill. The Japs do not waste any land. All the hills are large farms. I wonder how they could grow anything on the steep hills that are hundreds of feet high. They have it fixed so the rain will not run down the hill and wash everything away. The Japs are famous for farming. We had loading drills while on watch this morning. We also had General Quarters this morning.

We reached Hiro this morning about 8:30 A.M. after a 240 mile trip from Wakayama. Hiroshima, where the first atomic bomb was dropped, is not too far from here. It did not take long before our army troops were hitting the beaches. About 40 ships were in the convoy. No LSTs were used. They were all large transports in the operation that carried the thousands of troops and their equipment.

The *Montpelier* served as flagship for the gunfire support unit. Admiral Riggs is in command. These troops will occupy the Hiro and Kure area of Honshu. They will take over this area for miles around. Their first stop will be at Kure, Japan's large naval base. The troops we transported here were the 41st Division of the Sixth Army, about 15,000 troops landed. They were the first Allied troops to land here. The warships were ready to commence firing if there were any trouble from the beach. Everything went smoothly. These landings are a snap.

Tuesday, October 9, 1945: Well this morning I had a good walk. We walked up one hill and then up and down another. Japan seems to be one hill after the other. Some violets were still in bloom and also black berries, they are almost like blueberries. We got back to the ship at 11:30 A.M.

The third section went on the beach in the afternoon, and some fellows came back with sticks of stuff they picked up on the beach. The sticks were about six inches long and about as round as a quarter. They were wrapped in paper with Jap writing and soft sticky stuff was around it. The fellows thought it was Jap candy.

Some of the fellows used it to put out cigarette butts, others tossed it around. Some threw it in the trash cans and others put it in their lockers to take home. We had a Jap interpreter, Lt. Owen, on board, so some of the fellows asked him what it was. It was dynamite. The interpreter told the Exec. to have the word passed over the loudspeaker for every man to bring what they thought was Jap candy but which is Jap dynamite to his cabin at once. I took a look into the Ex.'s cabin when it was all picked up and the table was full of dynamite. There were over 100 sticks of it. Tomorrow no trash will be burned in the incinerator because there might be some dynamite still in the trash cans. It's a good thing we have a Jap interpreter or the old "Monty" would have been blown up by its own men.

Monday, October 22, 1945: We covered another landing today. The convoy consisted of about 15 transports. The Army troops wore their heavy clothing. The *Montpelier* again served as flagship for the gunfire support unit. All guns were manned but nothing happened. These troops will take over the Matsuyama-Shikokku area of Japan. This will be the last landing for the U.S.S. *Montpelier* to cover.

I saw a monster of a Jap submarine. It was much longer than one of our destroyers. It must be the largest in the world. It had a catapult on the bow for launching planes. It also carried two planes.

During the rest of our two months stay in Japan, we visited many places and met many Japanese. The most famous place we visited was Hiroshima. We were one of the first to see the extensive damage caused by the atomic bomb. Hiroshima was the first city in history to be hit with an atomic bomb.

When we saw Hiroshima, a city of approximately half a million, it was deserted except for a few people walking through with white cloths over their nose and mouths. I will never forget what I saw there. You have to see it. I cannot explain it. A few frames of buildings were the only thing that was left standing. Everything was ground into dust. The city of Hiroshima was a city of large buildings. They were made of stone, cement and steel. I bought some pictures in the next town and could see how well constructed the buildings were. We passed a mother nursing her baby in the cellar of a destroyed house. She did not pay any attention to us as she sat there in the dust. Her whole family might have been wiped out and the both of them might die later from the effects of the bomb. We felt very sorry for them. The only thing they owned was the clothes on their backs, and that was not much. We saw a few stumps of trees that were barren. They were completely black from burning. The trolley cars were blown off the tracks. Only they did not look like trolley cars anymore. They were completely destroyed. I could just see pieces of them. The fire engines were still in the building. Everything was reduced to a lot of rubble, building and trucks. The enormous buildings with walls over a foot thick were all in small chunks. Even if you were in the basement of strongly built buildings of steel and cement, you would still suffer the effects of the bomb. No place was safe to hide. As far as the eye could see, there was nothing but destruction. The force from one of these bombs is fantastic. There is only one defense against the bomb, prevent it from falling.

When we left Hiroshima, we stopped at a town not too far away. I spent some time talking to a Jap who lived in the States for 32 years. He finally returned to Japan in 1940. He said that it was a warm, sunny day when the bomb was dropped, about 8 A.M. He was thrown to the ground but thought that it was an earthquake. Then a huge red flame rose high into the sky. He said that Hiroshima burnt for two days. Out of a population of half a million, two hundred thousand were killed and another two hundred thousand were injured. People were still dying. He treated many of the bomb victims. He said that there must have been poison in the bomb because it affected the victims' heads. It made them very sleepy and the next thing, they were dead. He was very angry and said the bomb never should have been dropped on Hiroshima because it did not help the war effort. He spoke very good English. While we were talking to him, some girls about 20 years old were cooking their meal over a little stove out on the sidewalk. It was a warm, sunny day but on the way back to our ship, the day became cool.

On our way back to the ship, we took a look at the damaged warships in the Kure Naval Base. It was quite a sight. Every Jap warship was severely damaged from the planes of Halsey's Third Fleet. They were hit with bombs and torpedoes. Every type of a warship was in the harbor. They even had a battleship with a flight deck on it. One of the Jap carriers we passed had some Jap sailors on it. They waved and we waved back. We also pulled alongside the *Haruna*. This is the ship Colin Kelley crashed into. He told his crew to bail out before he crippled the Jap battleship and lost his life for his country in the following action. The *Haruna* suffered extensive damage.

While I was in Japan, I was invited to the home of a student from Nippon University. He lived near Kure. The city of Kure was destroyed by our planes. We had to pass through it on our way to his house. The neighborhood where he lived was not touched by the bombs. I met his mother and sister. Before we entered the house, my friend from the ship and I took off our shoes. The house was very clean inside. They had a very nice place. I could see that they came from a good class of people. In one room there was a large fancy table and a radio in the corner. They also had a picture of Emperor Hirohito, hanging on the wall. To them he is their God. Before we left we shook hands and waved goodbye.

On our way back to where we would board the landing craft for our ship, we passed a long line of women who were buying sweet potatoes. When they saw our tall American sailors, they began to laugh. They got a kick out of them. We laughed along with them. Everyone had a good time. They were very friendly.

The Japanese people are honest, hard working people who were bluffed along by their cruel leaders. They were helpless to do anything about it. It was the Military Men. Their greed for power brought destruction down upon Japan. If they let the people run the government, it will be in good hands. The Japanese people are no different from the people in any other part of the world. The people all over the world are good. It's the leaders who are to blame.

While we were in Japan, Admiral Riggs had the honor of re-commissioning the old destroyer *Stewart* # 224. The Japs captured it at the beginning of the war in dry dock at Surabaya, Java. It was later brought to Japan by the Japs. Our band was also aboard for the ceremonies. It was not very far from our ship. I went aboard it one day and they told me that there were many rats on it at one time. It will return to the States soon. The men from our ship did a lot of work on it, getting it seaworthy. Some of the men from our ship will be part of the crew that will bring it back to the States soon.

When the men went to the beach for liberty in Japan some would take sugar, cigarettes, soap, flour, etc. with them to trade with the Japanese. The Japanese were waiting for us in the cities and towns with plenty of things to trade and sell. It was funny to see the men returning to the ship with musical instruments, women's kimonos, household goods, etc. Both sides were satisfied with their exchange.

On November 8, 1945, we received our sailing orders and on November 15, 1945, we left Japan for the United States. It was a cold, dark morning when all hands arose at 5 A.M. to get the U.S.S. *Montpelier* ready for sea. The gangways were taken in and the boats and booms were secured. At 6 A.M. the *Montpelier* left Japan's naval base at Kure and began its long voyage of 13,000 miles to the east coast at New York. The ship's band was on the quarterdeck. They played many songs and finished by playing "Anchors Aweigh." The homeward bound pennant with its white stars and red and white stripes waved in the breeze. This long, large piece of cloth reached from midship to the fantail.

The light cruiser *Oklahoma City* # 91 relieved # 57. It will take over command.

We had passengers aboard. They will go back to the States with us. They included 419 enlisted men, 28 officers, 3 Army men and a Major General from the Tenth Infantry.

We sailed south through the Inland Sea of Japan. After travel-ing about 200 miles, we finally reached the open sea at 5 P.M. Everyone took their last look at Japan as it passed out of sight.

At last the war was over for the *Montpelier*. The war ended almost three months ago but we have been on the go ever since.

The U.S.S. *Montpelier* was in the first Allied offensive of the Pacific War at Guadalcanal and was in on the last landing when the curtain was brought down for the last time in Japan.

The U.S.S. *Montpelier* set a record that will be hard to touch. It bombarded Jap-held strongholds 53 times. It participated in 26 invasions, 42 operations and 30 campaigns against the Japanese. Over 100,000 rounds of five and six inch shells were fired at the enemy not to mention the thousands of rounds of ammunition of the machine guns and the warships sunk and damaged and planes shot down. The hundreds of dead Japs left in its wake can testify to the prowess of the fighting cruiser and its crew. The *Montpelier* traveled almost 200,000 miles most of it in enemy waters.

Back in 1942 if someone told me that the U.S.S. *Montpelier* would come through all this, I would not have believed him. I am not saying this because I want to brag. I am saying it to show how the Good Lord always watched over us at all times. The U.S.S. *Montpelier* was also His flagship.

On our way to the United States sixty men reported to sick bay every day for a physical examination.

On our way to the U.S.A. the food was not too good because of the extra passengers. Before going to bed or hitting the sack as the boys would say we would chip in and buy a five gallon can of ice cream from our friend in the soda fountain. The can of ice cream was put in the center of the deck and everyone would help himself with his own spoon. A bull session would be in progress and some of the fellows could really tell some great stories. Just a bunch of gee dunk sailors. That's a Navy word for ice cream, just like Joe is coffee, poggy bait is candy, etc.

We stopped at Pearl Harbor for one day. Admiral Riggs left us there. Everyone liked the Admiral.

After we left Pearl Harbor we had to go off our course and search for a large transport plane loaded with passengers. Everyone was topside that night when our searchlights covered the area where the plane crashed but no survivors were found.

We arrived at San Diego, December 1, 1945. The United States was a sight for sore eyes.

They had a band and five girls at the bandstand to greet the ship as it pulled alongside the pier. Some of the crews' families were there to greet them. There was a large sign that said, "Welcome Home Veterans," "Well Done." The men who live in this part of the country will leave the ship here.

We remained at San Diego for three days and then left for New York. We passed through the Panama Canal on our way to New York. Captain Gorry had the ship at full speed when we went through the Panama Canal. Must have been 25 knots. The pilot who guides the ships through the Canal said he never saw a ship go through the Canal that fast before. The Executive Officer brought his dog aboard at San Diego. On our way through the Panama Canal the crew broke out the hose and washed down the ship with fresh water. The Executive Officer's dog was also given a good washing as the hose was also turned on him too. After traveling for twelve days we reached Sandy Hook, New York. We stayed there two days unloading all of our ammunition. Tuesday morning at 7 A.M., December 18, 1945, we docked at the Brooklyn Navy Yard. It took us 33 days to travel from Japan to New York. Our journey covered 14,000 miles. I never thought that my last stop on the *Montpelier* would be the city where I was born.

Most of the crew left the ship here for their home towns and in a few days they would be civilians again. Before we departed, there were plenty of hand shakes and goodbyes. We would not see the old gang any more. We would be carrying memories of the many friends we met and the places visited for the rest of our lives. When I look back over the years I spent in the Pacific, it seems like it was a dream.

I left New York for Boston where I was discharged from the Navy. A few days before Christmas I was a civilian once again. It was a very cold winter's night when I was discharged from the Naval Separation Center in Boston. When I walked in on my sister and her mother-in-law, Mrs. Sweeney, you could have knocked them over with a feather. They did not know I was in the States. Both of them put their arms around me and gave me a big kiss.

It felt great to be a civilian again but it did not seem like the war was over. For some time after, I would catch myself trying to conserve water. I would not let the water run, only when using it. After having water hours in the Pacific, it took some time before I got away from it. There were other habits I caught myself doing. It was quite a treat to sleep in a bed for a change with a roof over my head instead of a steel deck with your clothes on and never knowing when the rain would send you running for cover.

This will be my first Christmas in the States in four years and the best Christmas gift I ever received.

No harm came to me during my years in the Pacific and I am very grateful to the Good Lord.